BEYOND a REASONABLE DOUBT

Edited & Introduced by Larry King

PHOENIX
BOOKS

BEYOND a
REASONABLE
DOUBT

Edited & Introduced by Larry King

ISBN: 1-59777-503-7
Library of Congress Cataloging-In-Publication Data Available

Edited by: Larry King and Henrietta Tiefenthaler
Book Design by: Sonia Fiore

Printed in the United States of America

Phoenix Books
9465 Wilshire Boulevard, Suite 315
Beverly Hills, CA 90212

10 9 8 7 6 5 4 3 2 1

Of the more than two thousand books and audiobooks I have published, "Beyond A Reasonable Doubt" is the one that I am most proud of. Every writer who contributed to the collection did so because he or she believes in the dialogue that the book will further stimulate. I am proud of the opportunity to be in such stellar company.

No single phrase in the English language is so well know or so little understood as "beyond a reasonable doubt," so I thank you, dear reader, for coming with us on this journey to understanding.

A very special bouquet of Thank You's:

First, to every participant, I am grateful for your time, energy and valuable contribution. To Larry King, I am thankful beyond measure; this project only exists because of his intellect, generosity and friendship. I admire his unceasing ability to talk to everyone with equal interest and dine with kings, presidents and all who are famous or infamous and return happily to his roots on a daily basis.

To Henrietta Tiefenthaler, my special thanks for making this book become a reality, only because she didn't know that the task I had set for her was within the shadow of impossible.

To Chief Judge Sol Wachtler and David Gould, whose wisdom served as a beacon and who were always ready to lend guidance, I am also most appreciative.

To all the others at Phoenix Books I sincerely thank you for your hard work and friendship: Julie McCarron for her editorial guidance and Sonia Fiore for her visual ability and design contributions. I am most appreciative.

Michael Viner, Publisher

For more information and a discussion of *Beyond a Reasonable Doubt* please visit www.reasonabledoubtblog.com

TABLE of CONTENTS

MEDIA and the JUSTICE SYSTEM

PROTECT VICTIMS

INTRODUCTION by LARRY KING

Do Juries See
Beyond a Reasonable Doubt?
A Historical View

By Larry King

There are countless articles that emphasize the heavy burden that the "beyond a reasonable doubt" standard for conviction in criminal cases places on the prosecution. Far less noted is the even heavier burden that the "beyond a reasonable doubt" standard places on jurors.

In a country that is so divided that even the most innocuous issue causes opposing sides to gird their loins for battle, there is virtual unanimity that the heavy burden of making the Government prove a defendant's guilt beyond a reasonable doubt should remain inviolate. There are respectable mainstream people who advocate keeping certain people convicted of sex crimes incarcerated after their prison term has ended. There is presently a respectable mainstream Administration that alleges that certain people accused of being linked to terrorism should be denied the right to have either lawyers or a trial. Yet even the proponents of those radical proposals have never advocated changing the burden of proof for the Government in a criminal trial.

There is no reason why the "beyond a reasonable doubt" standard should be so sacrosanct. A person's life is usually far more impacted by the financial havoc that can be wrought by the Internal Revenue Service or other Government agencies than it would be by spending one day in a jail. Yet, various government agencies have the power to pound a life's work to smithereens by meeting the low bar civil standard of proving that the Government was "more likely than not" correct. Yet, if the Government wants to prove that you disturbed the peace by urinating on your neighbor's lawn or on your neighbor, the Government must meet the heavy burden of proving its case beyond a reasonable doubt. In many jurisdictions, if the potential penalty is less than six months in prison, the Government need not even afford the defendant a jury trial; but even in trial before a judge without a jury the "beyond a reasonable doubt" standard remains inviolate.

A perceived sense of something being part of the American heritage provides a free pass through hostile territory for certain traditions of ours. Three quarters of the provisions of the Bill of Rights are designed to protect persons accused of crimes. In a time of terror where one cannot find much sympathy for protecting individual rights from a Government with both a real and perceived need to protect the greater community from sinister outside forces, there would be little support for those provisions of the Bill of Rights today if it were not a part of our Constitutional heritage.

The strange thing about the "beyond a reasonable doubt" standard is that it is thought of as being an anchor of our freedoms, but those words never appear in our Constitution or the Bill of Rights. It, like the "presumption of innocence," benefits from a perceived belief in the public that attacking either the Government burden of proof or the presumption of innocence is somehow un-American. Most of the public and probably most attorneys think that both of those provisions are found in our Constitution. They are not.

It was not until 1970 that the United State Supreme Court determined that the "beyond a reasonable doubt" standard was required by the Due Process Clause of the United States Constitution. With predictable regularity, each Supreme Court case, which finds a right not explicitly found in the Constitution, is met with a cacophony of denunciation and a stack full of proposed constitutional amendments to undo the Court decision. What was the reaction to the Supreme Court decision, which read into the Constitution a right to make the Government prove a defendant guilty beyond a reasonable doubt by those who adamantly oppose "coddling" criminals? Silence. Nor did we hear a word from the strict constructionists who viciously attacked every other Supreme Court decision that read into the Constitution mandates that were not clearly and explicitly spelled out in the document.

Nor have we ever heard anyone complain about the presumption of innocence, a concept twined with the concept of the Government burden of proving guilty beyond a reasonable doubt. Like the "beyond a reasonable doubt" standard, the presumption of innocence is always treated as an unassailable hallmark of our freedom and heritage. We never stop to ask why. Why shouldn't we have the same standard for a criminal case as we have in a civil case—both sides starting from a level playing field? Instead of tilting the field against the Government why don't we just make certain that every potential juror has a totally unbiased mind before the trial starts...neither thinking the person guilty nor innocent but rather awaiting the evidence to determine the outcome.

How realistic is it to demand that jurors presume everyone innocent? When asked during questioning, every potential juror will tell a defense counsel or judge, that he has no problem presuming that the defendant is innocent. Yet, how many jurors really glance over at that man sitting at the defense table and say to themselves, "Ah, there sits an innocent man?" Shouldn't it be enough and more consistent with human nature and logic, merely to instruct the jurors to keep an open mind and to always remember that it is the government that has the burden of proving the defendant's guilt beyond a reasonable doubt?

Why has no one ever argued that the burden on the Government of proving a case beyond a reasonable doubt makes the presumption of innocence supernumerary? If the Government has any burden in the case, then if it fails to meet that burden, the defendant will be acquitted even if he does nothing at trial. The burden of proof on the Government in a criminal case is a presumption of innocence. Why give the defendant a second bite at an apple already chewed to the core with a heavy burden of proof?

How did these two aspects of our criminal law become so exalted as to render them immune from even questioning their viability when apparently equally important "rights," some even anchored in the Constitution, such as the right to an attorney, have always been open to discussion and, now, even assault? Even the right against self-incrimination, firmly anchored in the Constitution, has been chipped away over the years allowing, for example, the Government to extract incriminating blood or hair samples from a target of an investigation. And there are very cogent and reasoned advocates who claim that the right against self incrimination can be further circumscribed without doing damage to the original intent of the framers of the Constitution. But these same people do not advocate taking even a flake of brick off the wall of separation between presumption of innocence and the State, or between the "beyond a reasonable doubt" burden and the State. Why are we willing to discard the requirement of unanimous juries in some criminal cases but unwilling to even discuss eliminating the presumption of innocence or the "beyond a reasonable doubt" standard in the same type of cases?

Even the legal tsunami known as the Patriot Act and its yearly accretions has left the presumption and the burden of proof untouched even as it overflows countless other rights that had been thought of as being inviolate. Why have the presumption and the burden always been ceded the high ground by even the "criminal rights" harshest critics? It is certainly a beneficial thing for any democracy when any individual right can weather the harshest storms created by a sometimes understandably and sometimes baselessly frightened public. But it is still a mystery why some "rights" are immunized from the flood waters of public rage and others get submerged in a mere high tide. It can't all be because the presumption and the Government burden of proof had better PR agents than countless other rights which are always under attack.

The presumption of innocence is nowhere to be found in the Constitution. It is merely an evidentiary rule that says that a criminal defendant is presumed to be innocent. Hence, if the Government puts on insufficient evidence to overcome that presumption, the presumption stands and the person is acquitted without having to put on any evidence. It is one of a countless number of presumptions embedded in our laws. Yet, even the most far right commentator prefaces his attack on an accused person by saying, "I know we have to presume him innocent at this point, but..." Why? The presumption of innocence is merely a garden-variety rule of evidence to be applied in a courtroom. There is no reason why a person sitting in the comfort of his home has to presume anyone innocent. A juror has to presume the defendant innocent, but that is no more remarkable than a juror having to follow a myriad of other laws that apply to a particular case. If we really had a presumption of innocence like the public thinks we have, no one would ever be held in prison or jail before his or her trial commenced. After all, in the United States we do not knowingly keep innocent people in prison. Yet, not even the ACLU has ever claimed that no one can be held in prison before trial. So much for the presumption of innocence. It makes us a better country that every talking head or news person commenting on legal matters feels the obligation to preface every remark about a suspect or arrested person with "of course we must presume he is innocent until he is proven guilty," but there really is no legal basis for such a caveat. And many times, what we are all really thinking is that the guy definitely did it.

Somehow, the "presumption of innocence" has been changed from a simple rule of evidence into a hallmark of the American way, to the extent that commentators get their hands slapped for talking as if a person is guilty when he has not yet been tried. The same transformation of the "beyond a reasonable doubt" standard has also occurred in our society. It began as a courtroom rule of law that was transformed into a public rule of etiquette and later, much later, elevated by the Supreme Court to the level of a due process right.

The beatification of the "beyond a reasonable doubt" standard and the presumption of innocence are certainly beneficial occurrences. They are just strange occurrences in that the American public has ended up embracing substantive protections for people accused of crimes because it mistakenly mistook them for being part and parcel of American scripture. They were not part of the original canon, but they are part of it now. And so, people feel free to advocate for the elimination of the right of certain accused to have lawyers or even to have a trial, but they dare not tamper with that heavy burden of proof in criminal cases.

When a jury is being selected for a criminal trial, each potential juror is asked if there is any reason why he or she cannot be fair and impartial as a juror in the trial. If you gather together a group of prosecutors and defense attorneys with thousands of cases under their belts, they will tell you that they have heard just about every reason imaginable why a juror could not be fair and impartial and even some reasons that were theretofore unimaginable. But we have never once heard from any seasoned criminal trial attorney from either the prosecution or defense side, of a potential juror who said he could not be fair and impartial in the case because he could not accept the heavy burden placed on the Government by the "beyond a reasonable doubt" standard. However it is that we have arrived at this juncture, America is now all about mother, apple pie and beyond a reasonable doubt.

This now brings us back to the original assertion that the "beyond a reasonable doubt" standard places a greater burden on the jury than it does on the Government. Why should that be? The jurors, after all, are being asked to follow a standard that, for all appearances, they and all of their neighbors accept. So what's the problem?

The reason that the "beyond a reasonable doubt" standard is so emotionally and practically difficult to apply is because it forces a person to act in a manner contrary to logic and human nature. The civil standard of proof of "more likely than not" tells a juror to decide the case for the side that you think has the better of the argument. The "beyond a reasonable doubt" standard tells a juror that if you think the Government is probably right, or even most likely right, you still must cast your vote for the side that you think has the weaker argument on the issue. And by acting against the normal instincts of a logical mind, you realize you are likely releasing a toxin into the societal bloodstream.

We are asking our fellow citizens in their capacity as jurors to be able to say to themselves, "Yeah, well I think he probably raped those little girls, but I am not convinced beyond a reasonable doubt, so I will let him go." The instinct of most people, even liberals, is to give the benefit of the doubt to keeping someone who might be a rapist in prison.

So, how do jurors cope with their heavy burden? Consciously, jurors almost always try to do the right thing even if their verdicts are not always rational. There is some incredible transformation that comes over even the most opinionated citizen once he or she becomes a juror. People make decisions as jurors that they never in a million years would have made watching the trial tracked by their favorite cable television station. By and large, one of the greatest successes of the American legal system is the seriousness with which jurors take their responsibilities to be fair and follow the law as the judge gives it to them. But I used the word "consciously" for a purpose. Jurors do their best to be fair, but the truth is that jurors often deal with the almost impossible demands that the "beyond a reasonable doubt standard" puts on them by subconsciously, adjusting the rigor with which they follow that standard according to the case before them.

Any prosecutor, defense counsel or judge will tell you that different types of cases require a different weight of evidence. For instance, jurors will be looking for reasons to convict someone accused of being a big time drug dealer while the Government better have an extremely strong case if it intends to obtain a perjury conviction. In reality, the drug dealer is less of a threat to our way of life than the perjurer because the drug dealer is a fungible passing menace while perjury is a dagger aimed at the heart of our legal system. Yet, juries feel threatened by the former and not by the latter. If a juror is thinking of acquitting an accused major drug dealer, he will probably think to himself, "If I let this guy go, he's liable to involve a whole bunch of young kids in drugs and destroy countless neighborhoods." On the other hand, a juror about to acquit an accused perjurer is unlikely to be thinking to himself, "Oh my gosh, if I let this guy go, there is going to be a liar walking the streets of my community."

Truth be told, while the Government's burden never changes legally, as a practical matter, it changes dramatically according to the

type of case it is and where it is being tried. It would take a very courageous juror to vote to acquit someone accused of having a direct
involvement in the 9/11 massacres. And one thing you could take to the
bank...no jury will hold the Government as rigorously to its burden in
such a case as they would in a case involving a person accused of
shooting a drug dealer.

So is the heavy burden of proof on the Government in a criminal case a mere buncombe that has no real effect at all? There is a
kind of jury nullification that lessens that burden in cases that either
greatly repulse or greatly threaten the community at large. But even
in those cases, it is important that the Government be given the
burden even if it does not actually have to shoulder it. The principle
that the Government must prove a defendant's guilt and that it must
do so beyond a reasonable doubt has beneficial reverberations beyond
the confines of the legal system. The fact that the public at large feels
it is un-American to presume someone guilty, even someone being
accused only in the media, is a healthy development in an age where
the Internet every day proves the aphorism that a lie can travel half
way around the world before the truth can lace up its shoes.

The beyond a reasonable doubt burden on the Government
also has an unintended benefit for the most ardent purveyors of law
and order at all costs. The burden serves as a perfect beard for the
words in the legal system that dare not speak their name...the
nullification verdict. The nullification verdict is relevant to a discussion about the "beyond a reasonable doubt" burden because the latter
is an enabler of the former.

A nullification verdict is a verdict delivered by a jury, which
acquits the defendant even though the jury knows that the defendant
is guilty of the charges leveled against him. The nullification verdict is
historically based, legally binding, and can result in no legal retaliation
against the jurors who rendered it. Every jury has the right to render
a nullification verdict and no defense lawyer or judge is allowed to
inform the jury that it has that right. Ham handed defense lawyers
attempt unsuccessfully to directly inform juries that they may acquit
the defendant even if the Government has proved its case beyond a

reasonable doubt. More skilled practitioners will try to sneak the message in through the back door by reminding the jurors that "your verdict is final and cannot be second guessed by anybody, and nothing can happen to you for rendering your verdict."

There are several ingredients that are often found in the mix of a nullification verdict. Often, the defendant is someone who is greatly admired by or greatly charms the jury. Often, the victim is someone who the jury finds to be unpleasant or even vile. In Texas, this type of case is called the "he needed killin'" defense. The most explosive ingredient in a nullification verdict is the desire of a jury to send a message by their verdict. The message can be that the jury did not like how the Government conducted itself with regard to this particular case, or it can be a more overarching message involving disfavored laws or Government conduct in general.

The reason juries are not to be told of their right to nullify a verdict is that the nullification verdict is a slippery slope that ends up in anarchy and a country ruled by jurors and not laws. Hence, jurors are told that they must follow the law as it is given. What is left out of that charge is the following, "but if you don't, it is perfectly legal."

One of the best kept secrets in our legal system is how many nullification verdicts do occur. We don't usually read about them because they are called by a different name...reasonable doubt. The strongest criminal case imaginable has many "doubts" in it. Juries are told it is wrong not to adhere strictly to the law, and those running the legal system do not want the word to get out that juries sometimes do otherwise. Hence, jurors rarely explain their acquittal in terms of a nullification verdict. They usually claim they had a reasonable doubt because this or that fact was uncertain or that perhaps Mother Teresa's glasses were a bit fogged up when she witnessed the murder.

Some times for better and some times for worse, the nullification verdict is as American as apple pie and the presumption of innocence. Public school students are often taught about the case of John Peter Zenger, prosecuted unsuccessfully for seditious libel during our colonial days in 1735. Ask anyone about the case, and they will respond automatically that the Zenger case established freedom of the press in the colonies, and hence later in the United States. In actuality, the Zenger case only indirectly established freedom of the press in America. A nullification verdict directly brought about the freedom of the press. No law or extra legal protection for the press arose directly out of the Zenger case.

John Peter Zenger was a publisher who published attacks against Governor William Cosby, a corrupt, self serving knave of a politician...in other words, a man ahead of his times. John Zenger was indicted for seditious libel, but it was not certain that the Government could prove he published the materials. The Governor appointed the two judges to sit on the case, the greatest conflict of interest imaginable short of going on a hunting trip with one of the judges sitting on the case. One of those judges appointed by the Governor promptly disbarred both of Mr. Zenger's attorneys. Fortunately, Mr. Zenger was able to obtain a real Philadelphia lawyer, a Mr. Andrew Hamilton.

Mr. Hamilton opened the trial by, in effect, conceding guilt. He admitted that Mr. Zenger published the articles in question. The issue of libel was to be decided by the judges. And, at that time, truth was no defense to a claim of libel. The only defense Peter Zenger had to the jury was that it was not proven that he published the alleged libelous statements. And now his lawyer had conceded that he had published the statements at issue. There was really nothing for the jury to do but return a ministerial verdict of "guilty."

Mr. Hamilton gave an eloquent speech to the jury and judges about the importance of a free press, and the unfairness of not allowing truth as a defense to a libel suit and in the unfairness of not allowing the jury to decide the issue of libel. Well crafted words, beautifully spoken, but as the jury was informed, the law was the law, and they had to abide by the law. The jury retired to deliberate...and, well, the rest is history.

The "not guilty" verdict rendered by the Zenger jury did not establish the right of a free press or even truth as a defense in a libel case. What the verdict did was to scare the authorities into allowing a freer press for fear that they would face an unending series of nullification verdicts which would generate more discontent and weaken respect for authority. Nowhere is the Zenger case taught as a template for the value of nullification verdicts. Too many people have too much to fear if nullification verdicts become too routine. There will never be a verdict sheet in our legal system that gives the jury three choices: Guilty, Not Guilty, Guilty But Who Cares.

When a nullification verdict occurs, we prefer to treat it as a case involving reasonable doubt when often it would be better to call it by its real name. After all, the Southern nullification verdicts endemic to the South in the early and mid 20th century were proudly rendered without any varnish. When those all-white juries acquitted some racist murderer of a black, you didn't hear them trying to justify their verdict by pointing to some reasonable doubt they had. They let 'em go because he was white and the decedent was black. The fact that those verdicts were seen as nullification verdicts and not cases of jurors mistakenly hung up on reasonable doubt proved to be of great benefit to this country. Those verdicts were seen as nullification verdicts throughout the country, and stirred a complacent country to a rage against such blatant racism it never would have felt over a verdict based on even unreasonable reasonable doubt.

The nullification verdicts did send a message to the country, but not the one the jurors intended. The message sent to the country reverberated far beyond the cases themselves. The Southern nullification verdicts awoke the country to the un-American terrifying daily harm being done to African-Americans, harm that had largely occurred beneath the radar of the public sensibility before the nullification cases splashed sunshine onto the dark corners of American life in the South.

Much of the fuel for the great Civil Rights Movement of the 1960s came from Southern nullification verdicts. Nullification verdicts on the eve of our Revolution, when activists of the day were let off for politically based crimes by sympathetic juries, brought attention to the complaints of the colonists. The Civil War was presaged by nullification verdicts in the North, freeing those who "unlawfully" helped runaway slaves. In the Vietnam era, the difficulty of obtaining guilty verdicts in some areas of the country for Draft Evasion cases, sounded the alarm bell that the war was rapidly losing support.

Even one of America's modern heroes, Rudy Giuliani was sent a strong message through a nullification verdict. When Rudy Giuliani was a deservedly much praised United States Attorney, he indicted Bess Myerson and Judge Hortense Gable on the very strained allegations of bribery and conspiracy. A former Chief Judge of New York, named Sol Wachtler, once stated that a prosecutor could get a Grand Jury to indict a ham sandwich. What he failed to add was that sometimes that prosecutor ended up wishing that he had remained kosher.

The Bess Myerson case had all of the ingredients of a nullification verdict. The defendants were very sympathetic people. Bess Myerson, the first Jewish Miss America had spent a lifetime building up good deeds in her bank account...this case would allow her to draw down on that account. Judge Gable was an aged sick woman who had always treated people honorably and fairly in her court. The transgression was not one that would make people feel threatened. The Judge had sat on a divorce case of a person who was Bess Myerson's lover at the time and Bess Myerson was a friend of Judge Gable. The borderline ethical transgression was, at most, deserving of a complaint to the Judicial Oversight Commission against Judge Gable and some nasty publicity for Ms. Myerson. But the only way to criminalize the behavior was to secure the testimony of a very emotionally disturbed, almost pathetic daughter of Judge Gable. The fact that both Judge Gable and Ms. Myerson had always treated the daughter with great kindness and understanding only made the nullification brew more volatile. When the acquittal was delivered, everyone knew that the jury was not finding reasonable doubt so much as sending Mr. Giuliani a message...you don't turn an emotionally unstable daughter on a caring and sympathetic mother in order to gain a high publicity conviction of a famous person whose "crime" was hardly a threat to the commonweal, particularly when there were no pay-offs or evidence of direct interference in the divorce trial itself. Our fiercely independent citizen-jurors have the great sense and courage to know just when to slap the overreaching hand of Government.

This very parochial nullification verdict sent an important message to Mr. Giuliani. Rudy Giuliani had made his bones as a prosecutor by courageously and brilliantly loosening the grip Organized Crime had on the City's economy by being a tougher guy than the mob men he was facing. But the Myerson jury sent a message that what might be acceptable Government hard ball tactics to take down the heads of the Five Mob families would not be acceptable to take down two very sympathetic people who had a lifetime of good deeds to their credit. For all of Mr. Giuliani's many strengths, he had a problem husbanding the awesome power of the prosecutor...and later of the Mayor's office. He attacked hot dog vendors with the same zeal, and unbending intransigence, as he did the heads of Organized Crime. Every once in a while prosecutors with limitless power need to be reminded that certain Government conduct will not be tolerated, even if it is technically legal. Without the heavy burden of the "beyond a reasonable doubt" standard, jurors would be deprived of a safe harbor in which to shelter their nullification verdicts.

Today jurors are far more cautious than those arrogant Southern juries of the early and mid-20th century. They will always feel compelled to claim that it was only reasonable doubt that spurred their verdict. It is in some ways good that jurors feel compelled to at least state they followed the law, but sometimes, it probably would have been better had they just admitted that they were delivering a nullification verdict. No verdict better illustrates that point than the quintessential modern day nullification verdict—the O.J. Simpson case.

Any sentient attorney would know that if the jury decided the O.J. Simpson case on the evidence, there would be no chance of acquittal. Even a mediocre attorney would have realized that the only chance for O.J. Simpson was a nullification verdict. Yet, that same attorney would realize that jurors try to act responsibly, and certainly would not admit they did not follow the law, so an attempt would have to be made to make them feel as comfortable as possible with their verdict by developing as much "reasonable doubt" for them to cling to as possible. Johnnie Cochran was no mediocre attorney. He knew where the prize was, and he kept his eye on the prize. As Johnnie

Cochran knew, O.J.'s only ticket to freedom was race, even though race had absolutely nothing to do with these murders.

It is difficult to discern a case with stronger direct and circumstantial evidence than the O.J. Simpson case. The acquittal had no legal justification. But that being so, it is still difficult to understand the over-the-top furious reaction from white America over the verdict. The families of the deceased were justified in having an over-the-top furious reaction to the verdicts, but why was the country so inflamed? After all, this was not a case of nullification that had broader implications for the country as a whole such as the white nullification verdicts that freed racist lynchers of American blacks. Stripped to its essence, O.J. Simpson was simply an otherwise very nice and caring person who got away with murder. He was no threat to the community at large and there were then, and are today, countless murderers who never even get tried for their offense. So, what caused the uproar?

The furious backlash against the Simpson verdict was based to a great extent on the jurors' feeling they had to justify their verdict in lawful terms. They had to claim that they found reasonable doubt because they knew they were not allowed to acquit if they were convinced beyond a reasonable doubt that O.J. Simpson was guilty. The heavy burden of proof placed on the Government in criminal cases provides ample refuge to any nullifier. The countless and mutually contradictory theories about the assassination of President Kennedy proves that if you put any case under a strong enough microscope, you will find so many flaws that any person looking for doubt will find it.

Midway through the O.J. Simpson case, all of the defense lawyers, black and white, Christian and Jewish, walked in wearing ties made of African Kente cloth. Can you imagine the uproar if the jury had been predominantly Jewish, and Johnnie Cochran and his cohorts had walked in to court wearing yarmulkes? When Johnnie Cochran kept telling the jury in summation to keep their eye on the prize, he was intentionally invoking the iconography of the Civil Rights Movement to a predominantly African-American jury. What he was trying to convey was "keep your eye on the prize and not on the evidence." By using the Civil Rights motto as his rallying cry to the predominately minority jury, he was telling them to decide this as a civil rights case for blacks, not as a murder case.

When supporters of the verdict tried to justify the case on the lines of "reasonable doubt," it infuriated many people who would likely have accepted a nullification explanation. According to the defense in the O.J. Simpson case, The District Attorney's investigators made Jesus' turning water into wine look like a simple parlor trick, since their negligent collection techniques apparently managed to turn some drug dealer's DNA into that of O.J. Simpson.

At the trial and afterwards, O.J. Simpson denied ever owning Bruno Magli shoes, the kind of rare shoes worn by the killer. Later at O.J. Simpson's civil trial, the Plaintiff's attorneys discovered pictures of O.J. Simpson published several months before the murders in which he was wearing Bruno Magli shoes. When one of the criminal case O.J. Simpson jurors was contacted about the newly found evidence, she responded that it's easy to superimpose things on pictures. Well, yes, that's true. But in order to follow her reasoning, one must conclude that someone stated, "Hey, when we publish this newspaper, let's superimpose some Bruno Magli shoes on O.J. Simpson, so if in a few months someone murders his wife and is wearing Bruno Magli shoes, we can frame O.J. Simpson." In short, the attempts to justify the verdict by references to reasonable doubt were an affront to the American intelligence and, to some, infuriating. It is very possible that an honest explication of the verdict would have gone down far better with the majority of the American public.

Let us look at the testimony of Detective Mark Fuhrman. Mark Fuhrman committed perjury at the trial, had constantly made racist comments to people, and had even asked to be let out of the police department because he had developed racist feelings from his interaction with the black community. Yet, any assertion that his testimony was enough for an acquittal based on reasonable doubt defies all logic. Is such a man capable of planting a glove on O.J. Simpson's property to frame a black man...particularly a black man married to a white woman? Of course he is. But did he do it here? Of course not.

At the time Mark Fuhrman "found" the glove, nobody knew where O.J. Simpson was. Everyone from that area knew that O.J. was usually out of town. If Fuhrman was planting the glove, he had to know O.J. was innocent. And if O.J. was innocent, he was not at the murder scene, which meant he likely had an airtight alibi. When they found O.J. in Chicago giving a speech on the night of the murders, Fuhrman would be a dead duck. When police plant evidence, it is usually on the person of the target. There is no way Fuhrman would have planted the glove when O.J., if innocent, likely would have had an airtight alibi to the murder. Moreover, Fuhrman did not make O.J. bleed from the same right side as the murderer, nor did he leave blood in O.J.'s house or code O.J.'s DNA into the recovered blood, etc. Hence, when the jurors and supporters of the verdict stated that the Fuhrman testimony created "reasonable doubt," it infuriated much of the American public. Fuhrman's testimony proved only that he was a perjurer, a racist, and a hot head who found a fairly inconsequential piece of evidence in the case. (Any prosecutor with functioning radar would have kept Fuhrman off the stand even if it meant sacrificing the glove evidence. Johnnie Cochran did what any good attorney would do. He assumed that God sent him Mark Fuhrman for a reason and he took full advantage of the gift from the heavens.)

Now, what if the jurors had talked about Mark Fuhrman in a different way? What if they said they are sick and tired of the L.A. Police Department putting admitted racist and lying cops back into the police department, even when they had reason to know of the man's racist views? If you, the Government wants to make Fuhrman the messenger of your case, we will send you back a message of acquittal. Like in the Peter Zenger case, the nullification message might have had a far greater influence in how the black areas of Los Angeles are policed than to conjure up some transparently strained justification based on reasonable doubt.

There might even have been some value to white America feeling the sting of a nullification verdict so they could better understand that what most of white America views as the distant past—the white nullification verdicts that benefited racist murders and a segregated society—is still such a festering wound in the African-American community. We will never know if white America would have accepted the O.J. Simpson verdict better if it had been an honest verdict. By feeling an obligation to state that they followed the law, the only message the O.J. Simpson jury delivered was that they were either easily duped or not very intelligent. They were very likely neither of those things. They may have even convinced themselves that they found reasonable doubt, but if they scoured their souls, they would know that they were perhaps delivering a much needed message with their verdict, but by justifying the verdict by claiming reasonable doubt, the only message they delivered was that the verdict was an outrage.

Perhaps, then, one reason why even strong advocates of law and order at any cost do not attack the heavy "beyond a reasonable doubt" burden put on the Government is because they know that lowering the standard would not only expose more nullification verdicts, but might actually generate a backlash that generates more nullification verdicts. Once the word got out that nullification verdicts were legal and safe for the practitioner, all hell would break loose with the court system. Nullification verdicts are an essential part of our legal heritage. They have, by and large, served a good purpose even when they have sent a bad message...they have brought problems out into the harsh glare of public scrutiny. Yet, if nullification verdicts became the norm or even a known accepted alternative for a verdict, the legal system would collapse under the weight of free lancing juries. As with many other matters in our society, the American public appears to have gotten it about right—nullification verdicts are rare, but occur often enough to help keep all-powerful prosecutors within the boundaries of acceptable Government behavior. That delicate balance could never have been struck, absent the burden of proving a case beyond a reasonable doubt that has been put on the Government in criminal cases.

It has been a blessing for this country that it stumbled blindly into raising the "beyond a reasonable doubt" burden on the Government in criminal cases and the presumption of innocence into icon status. It is good for our legal system that those concepts are so sacrosanct. They do less damage to law and order than one would think because of the massive below the radar jury nullification that takes place as jurors adjust the application of that standard to the type of crime involved.

The burden and presumption also allow us to preserve our rich and valuable tradition of nullification verdicts without destroying the rule of law by cloaking the verdicts in the rule of law by claiming a nullification verdict was really a reasonable doubt verdict. And perhaps most importantly, our raising the presumption and the burden to icon status has greatly enriched society as a whole because it has made even the floodtide of public rage and opinion give due deference to a presumption that a person is innocent of accusations made against him, and that if the Government wants to take your freedom, they should have to do it with a heavy burden of proof. That does not mean that someone should not feel free to question the continued unaltered use of the presumption and the burden. People should feel free to express their doubts...so long as they don't express beyond reasonable doubts.

BEYOND a REASONABLE DOUBT

Sol Wachtler

David S. Gould

Vincent Bugliosi

Alan M. Dershowitz

Jerry Falwell

Richard M. Strassberg

Vicki Roberts

Richard D. Parsons

Frederick Forsyth

Robert L. Shapiro

William W. Taylor, III

Edgar H. Haug

Commissioner David A. Ziskrout

Adam S. Hoffinger

Carol Elder Bruce

"Beyond a reasonable doubt, one of our most cherished constitutional principles, is not to be found in our Constitution."
—Sol Wachtler

SOL WACHTLER served as a Justice of the New York Supreme Court (1968-1972) and Judge of New York's highest court, The New York Court Of Appeals (1973-1992). In 1985 he was appointed Chief Judge of that court and Chief Judge of the State of New York. He was Chairman of the National State/Federal Judicial Council. An honor graduate of Washington and Lee University and its law school, he has been awarded thirteen honorary Doctor of Law Degrees and has been a scholar in residence at several law schools, as well as lecturer abroad on behalf of the United States Information Service. He authored the book *After the Madness* (Random House) and was a critic at large for *The New Yorker* magazine and recently authored a section in the book, *Serving Mentally Ill Offenders* (Springer). He is a co-author of the recently released novel, *Blood Brothers*. He is currently a Professor of Law at Touro Law School and served as Chairman of the 2002 Wannsee Seminar held in Berlin, Germany.

He has served on the Board of Trustees of the Albany Law School, Long Island University, and the Judicial College of the University of Nevada. He currently serves as a member of the Board of Overseers of The Touro Law School and is a member of the Executive Committee of the North Shore Long Island Jewish Health System. In the 2003-2004 issue of the *Syracuse Law Review* there appeared a compendium of Judge Wachtler's opinions while on the Court of Appeals. The article concluded with the following: "Judge Wachtler's role in shaping new York law puts him in select company in the state's rich judicial history. Wachtler showed imagination when needed, restraint where called for, and a clear sense of expression always."

Do Juries See
Beyond a Reasonable Doubt?
A View from the Bench

By Sol Wachtler

The story is told of the Mayor from the fabled Village of
Chelm, in which dwelled all of the world's fools. The Mayor had set
himself to the task of determining what kind of prison should be built
in Chelm. When he returned he told the Chelmites of his travels and
his conclusion: "After speaking to many persons in many prisons," he
reported, "I have been told by half of those persons in prison that they
are guilty, and the other half say they are innocent, so here in Chelm
we should build two prisons…. One for those who are guilty, and one
for those who are innocent."

Thankfully our jurisprudence was not developed in Chelm. In
the United States we believe that those who commit crimes should be
found guilty, and those who do not commit crimes should not be
charged at all. Unfortunately, given the fact that any prosecutor who
wanted to can use the grand jury to indict innocent people, or even a
ham sandwich, we must see to it that those innocent people who are
charged with the commission of a crime are not convicted. Or, as was
said in the 18th Century by William Blackstone in his *Commentaries on
the Laws of England*: "It is better that ten guilty persons escape, than
that one innocent suffer."

Recognizing that those who are responsible for determining
facts during the course of a trial were not present when some earlier
event occurred, the law has fashioned various bases upon which a

conclusion as to what happened can be drawn. This is called "the burden of proof," and it is imposed on the person who asserts the claim. In civil cases we say the jury must determine the facts "by the preponderance of the evidence," so that in order for a person to win his case, he has only to prove his claim by the modest burden of presenting sufficient evidence to support that claim.

The next level of "burden of proof" was fashioned by the New York Court of Appeals when confronted with several "right to die cases." Writing for the majority of our court I noted that: "Clear and convincing proof should...be required in cases where it is claimed that a person, now incompetent, left instructions to terminate life sustaining procedures when there is no hope of recovery." This standard was later adopted by the United States Supreme Court in the Cruzan case and has been applied by most states, including Florida, in the recent Schiavo case. "Clear and convincing," of course, is a higher evidentiary standard than is typical of civil cases; however, it does not reach the significant burden imposed by the "beyond a reasonable doubt" standard, which has been uniformly adopted for criminal cases. This standard imposes the burden on the prosecutor to prove the guilt of an accused beyond a reasonable doubt.

As has been noted, the words "beyond a reasonable doubt" are not to be found in our Constitution; however, the principle articulated by Blackstone's *Commentaries* about not allowing an innocent person to suffer, even if it means letting a guilty person go free, found fertile soil in our colonial past.

The concept of requiring the prosecutor to meet this high burden had its beginnings in a trial held in 1770. At 9:00 p.m. on a bitterly cold evening during March of that year a lone sentry posted in front of Boston's Custom House was the only visible sign of the British occupying force, but his presence was enough to attract a large crowd, brandishing sticks and clubs. When several hundred of the mob began attacking the lone guard, eight British soldiers came to his rescue with loaded muskets and drawn swords. The hated Redcoats were pelted with rocks, oyster shells, and pieces of ice, but this was no match for the British muskets, which opened fire killing five men.

Paul Revere characterized this as the "slaying of the innocent" and historians were quick to mark this "Boston Massacre" as a symbol of British tyranny.

Because there was no one else to take the case, the task of representing these eight British soldiers fell to the then 34-year-old John Adams. Although reluctant to represent the enemy, Adams felt strongly that if we were to be a free land, no man should be denied a fair trial—and to be certain the trial was a fair one, Adams told the jury that guilt must be proven beyond a reasonable doubt: "because it is of more importance to community, that innocence should be protected than it is, that guilt should be punished." The jury felt, at least in the case of six of the Redcoats, that the prosecutor had not proven their guilt beyond a reasonable doubt.

The burden of proving a defendant's guilt beyond a reasonable doubt has been the prosecutor's burden since that trial in Boston; however, it was not until 1970 that the United States Supreme Court was to embrace this standard as a constitutional imperative. Its development was considered as a fair way to express the belief that only when the jury is very certain of a defendant's guilt should they convict. "In the administration of criminal justice, our society imposes almost the entire risk of error upon itself." Justice Warren Burger wrote: "this is accomplished by requiring under the Due Process Clause (of the United States Constitution) that the state prove the guilt of an accused beyond a reasonable doubt."

Of course, establishing this burden of proof was one thing—but a judge's obligation of instructing a jury how to determine if that burden has been met, is quite another. There has been a fierce debate among academics, lawyers, and judges as to whether "reasonable doubt" should be defined for the jury and, if so, how it should be defined. All are in agreement that a definition given by a New York trial judge in 1974 missed the mark when he said:

> It is not a doubt based upon sympathy
> or a whim or prejudice or bias or a caprice, or
> a sentimentality, or upon a reluctance of

> a weak-kneed, timid, jellyfish of a juror who
> is seeking to avoid the performance of
> a disagreeable duty, namely, to convict
> another human being of the commission of a
> serious crime.

The New York State Court of Appeals ruled that a conviction based on that instruction had to be set aside because it violated the defendant's right to due process.

Although trial judges generally stay away from the "weak-kneed, timid, jellyfish" analogues, there remains a tendency on the part of many of these judges to minimize the prosecutor's burden of proof by rendering the judges' own special definitions of "reasonable doubt." Some of these variations have passed appellate review (i.e., "Reasonable doubt can be defined as something which is substantial and actual rather than doubt based on mere possibility or speculation.") and some of these jury instructions have been ruled improper (i.e., "It must be such a doubt as would lead you to believe that it would be close to impossible for the defendant to have committed the crime charged.").

Many judges refuse to risk defining the phrase "reasonable doubt" on the ground that it is self-defining and that there is no equivalent phrase more easily understood. Reviewing the O.J. Simpson trial, where it would appear that guilt was indeed proven beyond a reasonable doubt, many, including Simpson's own attorney, Alan Dershowitz, have concluded that his acquittal was due in large measure to Judge Ito's charge on reasonable doubt.

In fact a study of the O.J. Simpson trial illustrates, according to some commentators, the need for a unique kind of jury instruction, which would prevent the distortion of exactly what "beyond a reasonable doubt" means. Much of this distortion comes from reading books and watching television where the public—potential jurors—somehow feel that the accused defendant has some sort of an obligation to create reasonable doubt by punching holes in the prosecutor's case. Of course, in a criminal case, the defendant has no burden at all so that it becomes incumbent upon the judge to see to it that this preconception must be dispelled.

Just as the reasonable doubt standard can disadvantage an innocent defendant who can't come up with an alibi or who cannot meet his perceived "burden" of creating doubt, so too it can also aid the wealthy defendant whose canny lawyer can raise remote theories in the case that are entirely unconvincing but are capable of creating some small doubt. If the jury feels that any doubt at all compels acquittal, it has not applied the proper reasonable doubt standard. Just because the glove doesn't fit, there really must not be a need to acquit.

The argument has been made that to avoid the necessity of defining "reasonable" and "doubt" and to prevent the contortion of its meaning and use by judges and lawyers, we should do what England did decades ago: the jury is simply instructed that they should convict only if they are satisfied "that they are sure." The French Code of Criminal Procedure provides that there be posted in the jury room the single standard that they, as jurors, be "thoroughly convinced of the guilt of the accused."

We need not abandon the phrase "beyond a reasonable doubt," but we must be certain that the use of the words do not cause the jury to focus its attention on whether the defense has come up with reasonable alternative explanations to respond to the prosecutor's case. To follow that course would be to place an impermissible burden on the defendant to, in effect, prove his innocence.

One solution would be for our courts to adopt the language of the Federal Judicial Center in its pattern instruction: which is directed toward explaining how strongly the government must prove its case. The words "beyond a reasonable doubt" are used, but the jurors are told that they must be "firmly convinced" by the prosecution that the defendant is indeed guilty.

Governor George Romney of Massachusetts, in his effort to convince that state's legislature to adopt a death penalty statute, has proposed yet another rung on the burden of proof ladder. He has proposed that before a defendant can be sentenced to death in Massachusetts he must be found guilty "beyond any doubt." I would assume this would require more proof than a glove that fits.

DAVID S. GOULD, the son of the Pulitzer prize winning composer Morton Gould, graduated cum laude from both Princeton, where he served as Editor and Principal writer of the *Yearbook*, and Harvard Law School, where he served as an Editor of the *Harvard Civil Rights-Civil Liberties Law Review*. He served as the Staff Director of the Presidentially appointed National Institute for Consumer Justice. He later became an Assistant United States Attorney for the Eastern District of New York. After going into private practice as a top rated criminal and civil litigator and appellate advocate, Mr. Gould served as Special Consultant to the Chief Judge of the New York Court of Appeals, Sol Wachtler. Mr. Gould was named as the sole public representative on the Committee to Establish an Individual Assignment System in the New York State Court System. He also served as Chairman of the Ethics Commission for the Unified Court System.

Do Juries See
Beyond a Reasonable Doubt?
The View of a
Former Prosecutor

By David S. Gould

I was an Assistant United States Attorney for the Eastern District of New York from 1974-1978. I tried more cases than any other Assistant in the office during that time. I put my experience to good use by helping to train new federal prosecutors. One of the points I drilled home to them was not to be defensive about the "heavy" burden of the beyond a reasonable doubt standard that we had to meet to prove our case. Rather than be defensive about the burden, a good prosecutor should turn the burden on its head and emphasize to the jury that the key to that jury charge about the Government burden was the word "reasonable." Too many jurors come into the case thinking the Government has to prove the case beyond all doubt. In fact, commentators every day characterize the burden on the Government in just such a manner. Take the offensive and point out that all the defendant was doing was showing that there is nothing in this life that is free of doubt. What the defendant has not done is demonstrate that there is any reasonable doubt in the case.

There is an old aphorism which states that sometimes you can't see the forest for the trees. What it means is that sometimes we get so involved in the details of an issue that we lose sight of the big picture. The defense in a criminal case always wants the jury to be fixated on the trees while the prosecutor must back them up so they can view the forest. I often told juries that it is like looking at one of those French pointillism paintings. If you stand close, all you see are a lot of dots which seems unrelated and unconnected. But when you back up, an understandable clear picture suddenly comes into focus.

In their summations, good defense counsel find the opportunity to refer to "beyond a reasonable doubt" as often as possible, usually about twice in every sentence. Every case in the history of criminal law is shot through with pieces of evidence that don't seem to make sense or witnesses that have some inconsistencies in their testimony or possible bias in their backgrounds. Good defense counsel will cherry pick the problematic testimony, and after each recitation state to the jury, "There's reasonable doubt right there." Piece of evidence by piece of evidence, the jury hears "there's some more reasonable doubt." By the end of the summation, it will seem like the case is drowning in reasonable doubt.

The prosecutor must make it clear to the jury that the "beyond a reasonable doubt" standard applies to the elements of the crime not to every piece of evidence in the trial. Then the prosecutor must connect all of the dots that the defense counsel had tried to isolate. One of the greatest weapons in the prosecutor's arsenal is an element that is too easily overlooked in the hunt for clues and in the inspection of evidence...common sense. Take the O.J. Simpson case for example. There were countless points of doubt in that case.... Why wasn't there more blood? How can anyone rely on the testimony of Mark Fuhrman to reach a decision beyond a reasonable doubt? The blood samples were negligently collected and even more negligently preserved. The glove didn't fit. There was no eyewitness to the crime. There were countless other people with a possible motive to kill Mr. Simpson's wife. (This assertion is always a favorite of defense counsel. You can take any murdered person on earth, even a Mother Teresa, and you can conjure up a laundry list of other people who could have had a motive to kill the person.) There were numerous contradictory statements and crime scene evidence that didn't always make sense. Picked apart, the case was, as a defense counsel would put it, full of more holes than a piece of Swiss cheese.

Rather than spending most of the Government summation trying to refute or explain each point the defense made about a weakness in the case, the prosecutor should put his principal emphasis on taking the jury out of the trees so they can look at the forest. This is where common sense becomes the prosecutor's greatest ally. As often as the defense counsel mentioned the "heavy" burden of proof on the Government, the prosecutor should keep the jury tethered to the word "reasonable." In the real world things don't happen like the defense wants you to believe happened here. Instead of looking at the evidence in isolation, the jury must be shown it as part of a whole picture. For instance, in the O.J. Simpson case, the sole exhibit I would have used in summation would have been a huge oak tag exhibit showing all of the coincidences that would have had to have happened in order for O.J. Simpson to be innocent. And as the prosecutor ticked them off, instead of following the discussion of each piece of evidence with "that's reasonable doubt," each discussion should be followed by a comment about how long the odds are that each individual coincidence could have taken place. When the odds of the coincidence are low, you are showing the jury that there is no REASONABLE doubt. Without going through the countless list of coincidences that should have been on the O.J. Simpson prosecutor summation chart, let's just run through a few:

1) The evidence that O.J. Simpson was out of town for more days of the year than he was home was not contradicted. By an unfortunate coincidence for him, he was in town at the time of the murders. What were the chances of that?

2) Just think of the numerous perfect alibis he could have had if he was not the murderer. He could have been on the phone with someone all night. He could have spent the day of the murders at his children's sports events. He could have been on the phone long distance with the Pope...now there's a great alibi witness. But, no there was no evidence that O.J. Simpson was doing anything with anyone at

the time of the murders. There's that lousy luck of his again. The odds of his being totally alone without anyone to vouch for him were minimal, but poor O.J., the coincidence got him again. (While the prosecutor cannot comment on the failure of O.J. Simpson to testify, it is perfectly proper for the prosecutor to point out that there was no evidence that he was with anyone else or doing anything else at the time of the murder.)

3) The person who was murdered just happened to be a person whom O.J. attacked and threatened in the past. That darn luck again.

4) The killer was bleeding from his right hand, and poor O.J. just happened to have cut his right finger at the same time as the murders took place. Could a guy have worse luck than that? That must be a million-to-one shot.

5) There was blood in O.J.'s house, not in your house or my house. Think of the number of times O.J. had blood on the carpet of his house. Once a year? Once in two years? So that's once out of every 770 days? Well, poor O.J. had that blood in his house just when the murders occurred. Came up short on a 770-to-1 shot there.

6) And when the so-called incompetent investigators screwed up the collection of the blood samples, did it turn the DNA test into Arnold Schwarzenegger's blood? Nope, you got it, O.J. again.

At the time of the trial, I wrote out 45 different coincidences that had to have taken place for O.J. Simpson to have been innocent of this crime. When I got through detailing them all, I would have noted that the possibility of any one of those coincidences happening was remote, and the chances of all of them happening was virtually impossible. I would have told the jury that either O.J. Simpson was guilty or he was the unluckiest man on the face of the earth. Even Job felt badly for him.

Now, of course, no amount of argument or evidence would have swayed the O.J. Simpson verdict because that jury would not have convicted if there was a videotape of O.J. doing the killing. ("Oh those things can be manipulated.") A nullification verdict might have been justified either as payback for all of the white nullification verdicts against clearly guilty racists in the pre-civil rights era or to send a message to the L.A. police department that the community would not tolerate the department keeping in its employ police officers like Mark Fuhrman who had demonstrated and even admitted in writing to racial bias. But it was not a justifiable verdict based on reasonable doubt. However, for instances when the jury really is in play, the O.J. Simpson case is a good teaching tool for prosecutors. Johnnie Cochran brilliantly steered the jury into the trees and the prosecution never backed them up to look at the forest.

Nullification is not the only fly in the ointment that can derail even a well tried prosecutor's case. Reasonable doubt can arise from forces exogenous to the trial. When I was a federal prosecutor, there were no cable television channels. The number of movies shown on television were finite and there was no internet or video games to suck up peoples' leisure time. So when a movie was shown on television, even late at night, it was likely to be seen by at least a couple of the jurors. The movie that was the prosecutor's kryptonite in the early 1970s was *Twelve Angry Men*. That movie, which took place in the jury deliberation room, was centered on what is reasonable doubt. The jury in that film was all ready for a quick conviction until the "hero" started leading the other jurors back into the trees. We all know how that turned out. Whenever that movie was shown on television, the hung juries spiked through the roof. At our office, we used to assign a different prosecutor each week to what we called the TAM watch. TAM stood for *Twelve Angry Men*. The TAM watcher's duty was to check the TV Guide for the week to see if *Twelve Angry Men* was going to be on television. If it was, we all scrambled for excuses to get our trial adjourned. If a prosecutor found out during questioning that a juror had seen *Twelve Angry Men*, he would use one of his challenges to get that person off the jury even before the prosecutor challenged the social worker.

Truth be told though, the burden of proof of beyond a reasonable doubt was not really that onerous back three decades ago. I had only one acquittal in my four years at the prosecutor's office. Back then as soon as you called to testify an FBI Agent or even a local policeman, you were pretty much on your way to a conviction. That is why I and my colleagues took our screening job extremely seriously. We would only bring cases for which we had no doubt about the guilt of the defendant.

The world is very different today. For better or for worse, the public is far more cynical today than it was back when I was a prosecutor. One jury charge that had to be given when I was prosecuting was the one that stated that just because a witness was an FBI Agent or a police officer, did not mean the jury should give his testimony more credibility than other witnesses. Today, the judges practically have to tell the jurors that just because the witness is a cop or an FBI Agent, that doesn't necessarily mean he's lying.

What all of that underlines is that the Zeitgeist might change, jurors' attitudes and expectations ebb and flow with the decades, but that the one thing that has remained inviolate through all of the upheavals in American society is the Government has always been held to the heavy burden of proving guilt beyond a reasonable doubt. As I once told a very frustrated FBI Agent, there is no harder job than being in law enforcement in a democratic and free society...and that is the way it should be. Law enforcement officers' and prosecutors' only burden, in autocratic and dictatorial societies, is to figure out who they want to be found guilty. What helps make this country so great and unique is that we make it very hard for the Government to deprive a citizen of his freedom. And may it always be so.

VINCENT BUGLIOSI received his law degree in 1964 from UCLA Law School, where he was president of his graduating class. In his career as a prosecutor for the Los Angeles County District Attorney's office, he successfully prosecuted 105 out of 106 felony jury trials, including twenty-one murder convictions without a single loss. His most famous trial was the Charles Manson case, which became the basis of his true crime classic, *Helter Skelter*, the biggest selling true crime book in publishing history. But even before the Manson case, in the television series *The DA*, actor Robert Conrad patterned his starring role after Bugliosi.

Bugliosi has uncommonly attained success in two separate and distinct fields, as a lawyer and an author. Three of his true crime books: *Helter Skelter*, *And the Sea Will Tell*, and *Outrage, The Five Reasons Why O.J. Simpson Got Away With Murder*, reached number 1 on *The New York Times* hardcover bestseller list. No other American true crime author has ever had more than one book that has achieved this ranking.

As a trial lawyer, the judgment of his peers says it all. "Bugliosi is as good a prosecutor as there ever was," Alan Dershowitz says. F. Lee Bailey calls Bugliosi "the quintessential prosecutor." Harry Weiss, a veteran criminal defense attorney who has gone up against Bugliosi in court, says, "I've seen all the great trial lawyers of the past thirty years and none of them are in Vince's class." Robert Tanenbaum, for years the top homicide prosecutor in the Manhattan District Attorney's office, says, "There is only one Vince Bugliosi. He's the best." Perhaps most telling of all is the comment by Gerry Spence, who squared off against Bugliosi in a twenty-one hour televised, scriptless "docutrial" of Lee Harvey Oswald, in which the original key witnesses to the Kennedy assassination testified and were cross-examined. After the Dallas jury returned a guilty verdict in Bugliosi's favor, Spence said, "No other lawyer in America could have done what Vince did in this case."

Bugliosi lives with his wife in Los Angeles and is working on a book about the assassination of President John F. Kennedy.

Beyond a
Reasonable
Doubt

By Vincent Bugliosi

In 1981, I wrote a law review article titled "Not Guilty and Innocent—The Problem Children of Reasonable Doubt." The article dealt with the critical distinction between the terms "not guilty" and "innocent." (At the time, it was remarkable that with legal treatises having been written on virtually every point of law imaginable, apparently none had ever been previously published on the subject in question. At least none were listed in the *Index to Legal Periodicals* or the *Criminal Justice Periodical Index*.) The genesis of the distinction is in the requirement that in the prosecution of a defendant in a criminal trial, his guilt must be proved "beyond a reasonable doubt." But what does that hallowed phrase actually mean?

The doctrine of reasonable doubt is, as Sir Winston Churchill once said of Soviet Russia, "a riddle wrapped in a mystery inside an enigma." "This elusive and indefinable state of mind," said J. Wigmore, the foremost authority on the law of evidence, in reference to reasonable doubt. "It is coming to be recognized that all attempts to define reasonable doubt tend to obfuscate rather than to clarify the concept," said E. Morgan, another authority. However, one all-important principle is implicit in the doctrine of reasonable doubt—namely, that a jury does not have to believe in a defendant's innocence in order to return a verdict of not guilty. Even the jury's belief in his guilt, if only a moderately held one, should result in a not-guilty verdict. To convict, their belief in his guilt must be beyond a reasonable doubt.

In federal courts throughout the country, the judge properly instructs the jury that to convict, guilt must be proved beyond a reasonable doubt. Inconsistently, however, in the very same instruction (No. 11.06 of *Federal Criminal Jury Instructions* by Devitt and Blackmar), the judge tells the jury: "You are here to determine the guilt or innocence of the accused." Under existing law, this added instruction should not be given, since it is not the central purpose of a criminal trial to decide the factual question of the defendant's guilt or innocence. Yet even the U.S. Supreme Court, in case after case (e.g., in Jackson v. Denno, 378 U. S. 368 [1964], the court spoke of the jury's task of "adjudicating guilt or innocence"), uses this language, continuing to define loosely and erroneously the jury's function in a criminal trial. Needless to say, far less insightful state, county, and municipal courts throughout the land, as well as authorities on the criminal law, make the same mistake.

In ordinary lay usage, the term "not guilty" is often considered to be synonymous with "innocent." In American criminal jurisprudence, however, the terms are not synonymous. "Not guilty" is simply a legal finding by the jury that the prosecution has not met its burden of proof, not that the defendant is innocent, although they may also believe this. While a defendant's guilt or innocence obviously is the most important *moral* issue at every criminal trial, and could not possibly be more *legally* relevant (since if a jury believes a defendant is innocent they must find him "Not Guilty"), the ultimate legal issue for the jury to determine is whether or not the prosecution has met its legal burden of proving guilt beyond a reasonable doubt. If the jury does not fully understand this critical distinction, its ability to fulfill its function as the trier of fact will almost necessarily be impaired.

Instead of the correct term "guilty or not guilty," the incorrect "guilty or innocent" has insidiously crept into the American language and consciousness. Although the precise date and locus of its misconceived birth are not known, it has led a very robust life, shows no signs of aging, and, as I have said, has received the imprimatur of the highest court in the land.

When jurors are deliberating, the media report that they are deciding "the guilt or innocence" of the accused. So too, in novels, theater, movies, and television. With this constant bombardment, many jurors start out believing that their principal duty is to determine "Did he do it, or did he not do it?" as opposed to "Did the prosecution meet its burden of proving guilt beyond a reasonable doubt or did it not?"

This is not the forum to debate whether guilt or innocence should be the issue at a criminal trial. Many philosophical and societal considerations are involved. But since it is not the issue, as long as juries are told by the courts (along with the correct instruction) that it is, thousands of defendants throughout the nation will continue to be tried before juries who are misinstructed on the most fundamental issue at a criminal trial. Along with judges not disabusing jurors of this misconception, the great bulk of prosecutors use the phrase "guilt or innocence," and defense lawyers everywhere can be heard arguing to juries that the prosecution has not proved guilt beyond a reasonable doubt, and in the next breath stating, "Now, in determining the guilt or innocence of my client, take into consideration..." In fact, the textbook of the Association of Trial Lawyers of American states that, "the determination of guilt or innocence is the sole province of the jury, and is the essence of our system."

Trial lawyers who use the term "guilt or innocence" (both sides did, for instance, in the O.J. Simpson murder trial) do not have a firm grasp of the doctrine of reasonable doubt. They obviously understand it, but not well, because if they did, it would not be possible for them to utter those words. Their grasp of reasonable doubt exists in what Dutch Protestant theologian Willem Visser't Hooft has described in a different context as "a twilight between knowing and not knowing." You can talk about guilt and you can talk about innocence, but never in the context of "guilt or innocence" being the issue for the jury to resolve.

When I first started out as a prosecutor, I was always troubled by defense counsel's arguing to the jury that the prosecution had the burden of proving guilt "beyond" a reasonable doubt. Their voices emphasized the word "beyond" as if the prosecution had to go beyond the horizon and to the ends of the earth to prove guilt, which is consistent with laypeoples' erroneous impression that guilt has to be proved "beyond a shadow of a doubt." I sensed something was wrong but I didn't know what it was. So I sat down with my yellow pad (my security blanket) one day and started to analyze the word "beyond" as it related to the doctrine of reasonable doubt. Finally, it dawned on me that the word "beyond" was not only a needless appendage, but much more important, in the term "beyond a reasonable doubt," it is misleading to the jury because it is not used in its principal sense of "further" or "more than." If it were, the prosecution would have to prove there is *more* than a reasonable doubt of a defendant's guilt, when obviously, they have to prove just the opposite—that there is *less* than a reasonable doubt. Instead, "beyond" is used in its secondary sense of "to the exclusion of."

In my cases thereafter, after explaining to the jury the true sense in which the word "beyond" is used, I would say this to the jury: "The prosecution, then, has the burden of proving the guilt of this defendant *to the exclusion* of all reasonable doubt. With this in mind, we can completely eliminate the word 'beyond' from the term 'beyond a reasonable doubt' and come up with this (which I'd also write on the blackboard): If you do not have a reasonable doubt of the guilt of this defendant, convict. If you do have a reasonable doubt, acquit. We have eliminated the word 'beyond' from the term 'beyond a reasonable doubt' and we still have a very accurate definition and statement of the doctrine of reasonable doubt."

When I was a prosecutor, I never had any judge or defense counsel object to the verbal surgery I had performed on the term "beyond a reasonable doubt," and as a prosecutor I found this surgery to be an important point.

I would then go on to tell the jury: "As his honor will instruct you, 'a reasonable doubt is not a mere possible doubt, because everything relating to human affairs and depending upon moral evidence is open to some *possible* or *imaginary* doubt.' What is a reasonable doubt? It's a sound, sensible, logical doubt based on the evidence. Based on the evidence in this case, ladies and gentlemen of the jury, there is absolutely no *reasonable* doubt of the guilt of this defendant." If appropriate in a given case, I would add: "In fact, even though the prosecution, under the law, only has the burden of proving this defendant's guilt beyond a *reasonable* doubt, as the evidence in this case clearly shows, we've proven his guilt beyond *all* doubt."

I believe the doctrine of reasonable doubt has been around long enough for a good definition of it to emerge if one were possible. But, as previously indicated, it may not be. The current standard definition in many states that a reasonable doubt is "that state of the case which, after the entire comparison and consideration of all the evidence, leaves the minds of the jurors in that condition that they cannot say they feel an abiding conviction, to a *moral certainty*, of the truth of the charge," only begs the question—what in the world does "moral certainty" mean? We know it doesn't mean *absolute* certainty inasmuch as we know that guilt doesn't have to be proven beyond *all* doubt, just a reasonable doubt. But if moral certainty is something less than absolute certainty, how much less? Are we going to end up trying to measure the immeasurable with a rubber ruler?

The standard definition of reasonable doubt has another inherently disabling defect. For purposes of clarity and understanding, it would obviously be better to tell the jury what reasonable doubt *is*, as opposed to telling them that the proper state of mind for reasonable doubt exists only if they do not have an opposite state of mind. And courts have held that a judge instructing the jury that "reasonable doubt means just what it says, a doubt based upon reason," is an incorrect statement of the law (People v. Garcia, 54 CA 3d 61 [1975]). It should also be noted that virtually all people (including jurors) believe they are reasonable, and therefore any doubt they have must, by definition, also be reasonable. But we all know this isn't true. Indeed, even a genius can say the silliest of things.

The last time I checked a few years ago, at least one federal circuit court (the Seventh Circuit) had thrown up a legal white flag, resigning itself to the fact that reasonable doubt could not be adequately defined and any effort to explain it only causes more confusion and uncertainty. In that circuit, after the judge instructs the jury that to convict it has to be satisfied of the defendant's guilt beyond a reasonable doubt, he makes no effort to go on and define the term reasonable doubt to the jury. Sometimes in life, an acknowledgement of defeat is a wise decision, particularly when to do otherwise only creates more mischief that inures to your detriment.

ALAN M. DERSHOWITZ is a Brooklyn native who has been called "the nation's most peripatetic civil liberties lawyer" and one of its "most distinguished defenders of individual rights," "the best-known criminal lawyer in the world," "the top lawyer of last resort," and "America's most public Jewish defender." He is the Felix Frankfurter Professor of Law at Harvard Law School. Dershowitz, a graduate of Brooklyn College and Yale Law School, joined the Harvard Law School faculty at age 25 after clerking for Judge David Bazelon and Justice Arthur Goldberg. While he is known for defending clients such as Anatoly Sharansky, Claus von Bülow, O.J. Simpson, Michael Milken and Mike Tyson, he continues to represent numerous indigent defendants and takes half of his cases pro bono.

Dershowitz is the author of 20 works of fiction and non-fiction, including 6 bestsellers. His writing has been praised by Truman Capote, Saul Bellow, David Mamet, William Styron, Aharon Appelfeld, A.B. Yehoshua and Elie Wiesel. More than a million of his books have been sold worldwide, in numerous languages, and more than a million people have heard him lecture around the world. His most recent nonfiction titles are *Preemption: A Knife That Cuts Both Ways* (2006, W.W. Norton), *The Case For Peace: How the Arab-Israeli Conflict Can be Resolved* (August 2005, Wiley), *Rights From Wrongs: A Secular Theory of the Origins of Rights* (November 2004, Basic Books), *The Case for Israel* (September 2003, Wiley), *America Declares Independence*, *Why Terrorism Works*, *Shouting Fire*, *Letters to a Young Lawyer*, *Supreme Injustice*, and *The Genesis of Justice*. His novels include *The Advocate's Devil* and *Just Revenge*. Dershowitz is also the author of *The Vanishing American Jew*, *The Abuse Excuse*, *Reasonable Doubts*, *Chutzpah* (a #1 bestseller), *Reversal of Fortune* (which was made into an Academy Award-winning film), *Sexual McCarthyism* and *The Best Defense*.

When are
Doubts Reasonable?

By Alan M. Dershowitz

The dilemma of reasonable doubt is among the most perplexing challenges faced by our legal system. How a society resolves inevitable doubts about fault or innocence tells us a great deal about that society's values.

Under what circumstances is a doubt "reasonable" in the U.S.? The U.S. Supreme Court, in an act of abject intellectual cowardice, has declared that the term "reasonable doubt" is self-explanatory and, essentially, incapable of further definition. "Attempts to explain the term 'reasonable doubt' do not usually result in making it any clearer to the minds of the jury," the Court has declared, which brings to mind Talleyrand's quip that "if we go on explaining, we shall cease to understand one another." Judge Jon Newman of the U.S. Court of Appeals for the Second Circuit recently criticized this approach as follows: "I find it rather unsettling that we are using a formulation that we believe will become less clear the more we explain it." Such a lazy attitude toward the central concept underlying the constitutional presumption of innocence is a bit like the late Justice Potter Stewart's approach to the interpretation of hardcore pornography: I can't define it, but "I know it when I see it."

The problem with "reasonable doubt," however, is that juries do not necessarily know it when they see it because legislatures and the courts have been utterly unwilling to tell them what it is, beyond a few unhelpful clichés. Courts are quite willing to tell juries what reasonable doubt is not. A standard instruction reads as follows:

> Proof beyond a reasonable doubt does *not* mean that the state must prove this case beyond all doubt.... *Nor* [must the state] prove the essential elements in this case beyond the shadow of a doubt; it does *not* mean that at all.... [N]o defendant is ever entitled to the benefit of any or all doubt [italics added].... The oath that you took requires you to return a verdict of guilty if you are convinced beyond a reasonable doubt. And, members of the jury, equally, your oath requires you to return a verdict of not guilty if you are not convinced beyond a reasonable doubt.

Courts further insist that "reasonable doubt is *not* a speculative doubt, a feeling in your bones. [I]t is *more than* a doubt based on guesswork or possibilities [italics added]."

Some courts that do define a reasonable doubt do so in a way that virtually shifts the burden of proof to the defendants. These courts tell the jury that the doubt must be "based on reason," thus excluding a deep feeling of uncertainty, or a generalized unease or skepticism about the prosecutor's case. Other courts instruct the jury that the case must be proved with "the kind of certainty that you act on in making your most important personal decisions." This instruction fails to tell the jurors that they are supposed to err on the side of freeing the guilty rather than convicting the innocent. In personal decisions there is no comparable rule. A rational decision-maker goes with the preponderance of the evidence in most instances.

Judge Newman, who surveyed the social science literature on the traditional reasonable-doubt instruction, came to the following disturbing conclusion: "These studies suggest that the traditional charge might be producing some unwarranted convictions. At the very least, the conclusion one draws from such studies is that the current charge in use is ambiguous and open to widely disparate interpretations by jurors." He proposed a simple definition of "beyond a reasonable doubt" as "proof that leaves you firmly convinced of the defendant's guilt."

It is because the typical instructions given by judges on reasonable doubt are so pro-prosecution that many defense attorneys, citing the Supreme Court's dictum, ask that the term not be defined. They prefer to leave its meaning to the common understanding of jurors and to the analogies they can come up with during closing argument. One common example used by lawyers to illustrate that reasonable doubt can come from the gut as well as the mind involves a hunter who sees a distant object that looks like a deer. He takes aim, but then he experiences a sudden uneasiness in the pit of his stomach. He doesn't know why, but he hesitates. Something tells him not to pull the trigger. As he is deciding what to do, the distant object moves and the hunter sees that it is a little girl.

For me the reasonableness of the doubt required to acquit should depend on the seriousness of the crime and the severity of the punishment. No doubt is reasonable if the punishment is death. Very little doubt should be deemed reasonable if the punishment is life imprisonment. But if the punishment is merely a fine or a suspended sentence, the required degree of doubt might be greater.

We should rethink the concept of reasonable doubt and make it fluid rather than static.

JERRY FALWELL is a fundamentalist Baptist minister who founded the Thomas Road Bible Church in Lynchburg, Virginia, and became its first pastor in 1956. He gained national prominence through television and radio on the *Old-Time Gospel Hour*. In the late 1970s he became active in politics, founding and leading the Moral Majority, a lobbying group made up of conservative Christians. Falwell is also the founder of Liberty University (originally Lynchburg Baptist College) and heads a variety of educational organizations that include a theological seminary and a correspondence school.

A fundamentalist interpreter of the Bible, he is known for publicizing his extreme conservatism. He has issued controversial statements about homosexuality, racism, abortion, the Muslim faith, feminism and, in 1994, he released a documentary about the alleged criminal activities of Bill Clinton.

Falwell has been involved in a list of high-profile court cases. In 1972 he was involved in litigation against the U.S. Securities and Exchange Commission; in 1981 he filed a lawsuit against *Penthouse* magazine and, two years later, he famously sued *Hustler* publisher Larry Flynt, over a 1983 cartoon, depicted in the 1996 feature film *The People vs. Larry Flynt*. Even as recent as this year, Falwell has ignited lawsuits based on recurring accusations of the trademark infringement of his Web site Jerryfalwell.com.

Reasonable Doubt

By Dr. Jerry Falwell

It is sometimes easier to think of what reasonable doubt is not, than it is to assign a precise definition to the concept. For instance, reasonable doubt is not moral certainty. That is, it is not like the certainty people have imprinted on their hearts that it is wrong to take the life of an innocent and helpless human being. That is moral certainty. Neither is it absolute certainty, like one would find in the answer to a mathematical equation.

In very simple terms, reasonable doubt is a doubt to which one can attach a reason. In other words, it is not just a free-floating sense that "something is not right here," or an intuition based on emotional feelings. It is a real and convincing doubt based on common sense or the exercise of rational faculties. "Beyond a reasonable doubt," while a legal standard in criminal cases, is simply proof that we are willing to rely and act upon because there are convincing reasons for so doing.

If I say that I have reasonable doubt to believe that something has occurred, I am asserting that sufficient reasons have been presented to me in the form of evidence to convince me to question the event's occurrence. The converse is also true. If sufficient reasons have been presented in the form of evidence to believe an event has occurred, it would be unreasonable to doubt its occurrence.

Take, for example, the resurrection of Jesus Christ. Throughout His time on earth, Jesus repeatedly predicted that He would be killed and that He would rise from the dead three days later (e.g., Matthew 12:40; 17:22-23; 17-19; 27:63). He was indeed crucified and undeniably dead (See John 19:33-34: Following the crucifixion, He suffered a ruptured heart, based on the eyewitness description of the blood and water that poured from his punctured side). Following entombment and a subsequent empty tomb, Jesus appeared to well over 500 eyewitnesses in many different places and under many different circumstances, giving many convincing proofs that He was alive (See, e.g., Mark 16:9; Matthew 28:1-10; I Corinthians 15:6). On these facts alone, is it thus reasonable to doubt the resurrection of Jesus? Many do, but is their doubt the kind to which a reason can be attached? Or, is it the kind of doubt borne of a predisposition against Jesus, what He taught and stood for, or the tenets of Christianity?

Prior prophesies—undeniable crucifixion and eyewitness accounts of death—eyewitness testimony of an empty tomb—scores of eyewitness statements of live appearances after entombment. The evidence for the resurrection will not convince to a moral certainty, or to an absolute certainty, but is there reasonable doubt in the sense that it lacks evidence of the kind people normally rely and act upon? However one answers that question, it must be candidly admitted that American juries have for centuries sent criminals to their punishment, under a reasonable doubt standard, with less evidence.

RICHARD M. STRASSBERG, chair of the White Collar Crime & Government Investigations Practice at Goodwin Procter, LLP, in New York, is an attorney specializing in white-collar criminal defense and complex financial litigation. Mr. Strassberg represents individuals and entities in almost all the major white-collar cases that have occurred over the last few years including: (i) the KPMG tax fraud case, <u>US v. Stein, et al.</u>, (alleged by the government to be the largest criminal tax case in history) representing a former KPMG partner; (ii) the Martha Stewart case, representing Peter Bacanovic, Ms. Stewart's former Merrill Lynch financial advisor; (iii) the Bristol Myers Squibb case, <u>US v. Schiff, et al.</u>, representing the former President of the Worldwide Medicines division of BMS; and (iv) the Enron investigation, representing a banker from a large international financial institution involved in structuring off balance sheet transactions with Enron.

Mr. Strassberg is actively involved with pro-bono work and has served as a member of the Criminal Justice Act panel, representing indigent defendants in criminal cases. He has published numerous articles on topics such as: parallel criminal and civil proceedings; prosecutions targeting attorneys; obstruction of justice; waiver of the attorney client privilege; honest services fraud; money laundering and the Patriot Act; and the Sentencing Guidelines. He has also been a frequent speaker on white-collar criminal issues, including ethical considerations for lawyers. In 2005 and 2006, Mr. Strassberg was recognized in *Chambers USA: America's Leading Lawyers for Business* as being one of the top white-collar litigators in New York. He was likewise honored in 2005 and 2006 by inclusion in *The Best Lawyers in America* and *New York Super Lawyers*. In June 2004, Mr. Strassberg received the Burton Award for Legal Achievement, which recognizes excellence in legal scholarship. Prior to joining Goodwin Procter, Mr. Strassberg, a graduate of Harvard Law School, served as a federal prosecutor in New York and as Chief of the Major Crimes Unit in the United States Attorney's Office for the Southern District of New York, responsible for supervising approximately 25 Assistant United States Attorneys in the prosecution of white-collar criminal cases.

Redemption...
Beyond a Reasonable Doubt

By Richard M. Strassberg

As a white-collar defense attorney intimately involved in the defense of high-profile cases like the Martha Stewart trial, and as a former senior federal prosecutor, I have heard the words "beyond a reasonable doubt" countless times during the last two decades. I have sat on both sides of the courtroom as judges uttered these words to jurors contemplating the fate of violent drug dealing defendants, doctors accused of stealing tens of millions of dollars from Medicare, a couple who kept little girls from Africa as virtual house slaves, financiers who were accused of complex securities and accounting frauds, and individuals facing almost every type of criminal case in between.

We all know the standard by heart: everyone is presumed innocent until proven guilty "beyond a reasonable doubt." It may be the phrase that best defines our criminal justice system; the beating heart of how we attempt to value and cherish individual liberty.

When I was a prosecutor, it always struck me how exacting the standard "beyond a reasonable doubt" seemed to be—conviction only if twelve jurors agree that the proof has established guilt beyond a single doubt based on reason. Now, as an experienced defense attorney, I'm struck by the irony in these words. Juries often disregard them and convict defendants based on a common sense assessment of whether they believe the person committed the crime. The burden that the law puts on the government—and that we trumpet as the means by which our society protects the individual—is often lost in the process.

And that burden was on the government for a reason. There is little more frightening than staring down the barrel of a government investigation when the prosecutor decides that you are his chosen target. No matter how innocent of the charges you may be, your life, and the lives of your close family and friends, are thrown into turmoil in ways that are so personal and intimate, it can seem as if nothing will ever be right again. It can be paralyzing and horrifying, and the stress compounded by the fact that it is often secret, with few outside the closest circles of your life even aware of what is happening.

But as both a criminal defense attorney and a prosecutor, I have seen the power of redemption, forgiveness and second chances.

In many cases, I have witnessed first-hand the transformative powers of redemption. When a client under siege by the government beats back the threatened charges and secures his freedom, the awareness that "it could have been me" as a defendant in a criminal case is powerfully sobering, and often life-altering. And when charges are filed, there are chances for vindication in court, regardless of the jury's dilution of the beyond a reasonable doubt standard, and second chances for redemption, no matter the outcome.

As lead counsel for Peter Bacanovic, the broker involved in the Martha Stewart trial, I endured the many twists and turns of that truly unique and troubling case. But perhaps the most fascinating twist occurred when Martha Stewart began to serve her jail sentence. The public responded by buying her company's stock and, in the process, reportedly more than doubling her net worth. Surviving the trial of a federal criminal case and putting the consequences behind her was rewarded in real terms—in her case with pubic forgiveness and an unprecedented financial windfall. But this scenario—of forgiveness, redemption, and second chances—plays itself out again and again in cases far away from the spotlight.

"This is the best day of my life," was a funny statement coming from a defendant sitting across a shabby conference room table at the United States Attorney's Office as I told him he was about to be indicted for wire fraud. It was spoken without a hint of sarcasm, but instead with deep relief and gratitude. It wasn't that he was crazy or happy to be caught—but now that he was caught, he had a chance to work for redemption. As a result, he helped me unlock one of the biggest securities fraud scams that had ever been prosecuted, going back more than ten years and involving scores of people and hundreds of millions of dollars of losses to investors. And while he reaped substantial leniency from working with me, he also was able to change the direction of his life and lift the burden that his conscience had saddled him with for years.

The same sentiment was repeated to me by a client the day after his office had been searched by the FBI and he had confessed his involvement in a multi-million dollar bank fraud. "I've been waiting for this day for years. I have been stuck in place; I feel so relieved, I can finally move on with my life." While he violated the first rule I tell all clients—which is never speak to anyone without your attorney present—I worked to secure a sentence that avoided jail time for him, and watched as he underwent an inspiring transformation. He seized the opportunity to change the course of his life, from his profession to his interactions with his family. In a very emotional moment after the criminal case was over, he confided in me that, while the path was not the one he would have wanted to travel, he had arrived at the place he wanted to be with his life. A fairly remarkable statement by someone who had just been convicted of bank fraud.

Both are examples of scenarios that play themselves out day in and day out in connection with the white-collar criminal defense attorney's world—and reaffirm again and again that life provides second chances for redemption.

And for the most tragic of scenarios—those individuals who truly did nothing wrong but who are wrongly convicted by jurors giving too little credence to the need for proof "beyond a reasonable doubt"—the thought that there will be second chances and opportunities for forgiveness and redemption is a powerfully hopeful belief that I hold "beyond a reasonable doubt."

Nationally renowned celebrity attorney and legal commentator **VICKI ROBERTS**, whose clients include Gary Busey, David Carradine, Michael Madsen, Armand Assante, Sally Kirkland, and Jermaine Jackson, has been seen frequently on the syndicated television show *Celebrity Justice*, and has also appeared on *Extra*, on MSNBC's *Dan Abrams Show*, and on VH1's legal music show, *Rock and a Hard Place*. She has been quoted on MSNBC's *Scarborough Country*, on the television show *Inside Edition*, and in newspapers and publications worldwide. She is regularly consulted by high-profile celebrities and executives in the film and television industries and is often sought out for her legal commentary by media outlets around the globe.

Vicki Roberts is also the Executive Producer and co-producer of the film *Passengers*, which was featured in the Montreal Film Festival and was part of a September 2004 exhibition at the Queen Sofia Museum in Madrid, Spain. *Passengers* was also submitted to the Academy of Motion Picture Arts and Sciences for Academy Award consideration in 2004. A 23-year veteran civil and criminal litigator and former Los Angeles Municipal Court Judge Pro Tem, Ms. Roberts supports numerous charities and has often been seen co-hosting live charity auctions in and around the Los Angeles area. She can be reached through her Web site, www.restmycase.com, for any and all event appearance requests and/or speaking engagements.

Reasonable Doubt

By Vicki Roberts

The finding of the commission of an act to be true beyond a reasonable doubt should be a determination that the matter in question is of such a convincing character that one would conclude its commission unhesitatingly and would have an unwavering belief in the truth of its occurrence. Reasonable doubt, therefore, suggests a slight hesitation or lack of certainty, a nagging incertitude in a certain conclusion that is based upon a well-thought-out analysis of the facts presented in a particular case within the confines of the applicable law. Of course, if there are two competing conclusions that could be drawn from a set of circumstances, one presupposing guilt and one supporting lack of guilt, such a conundrum must weigh in favor of establishing reasonable doubt, which would therefore defeat a finding of criminality in such a situation.

The difficulty often arises in cases where the majority of the evidence, or sometimes all of the evidence, is of a circumstantial nature, that is to say, there is no or little direct evidence establishing the elements of a criminal act allegedly committed by the accused. In those cases, if there exists reasonable doubt as to any of the elements of a particular crime, the accused is entitled to a verdict of acquittal.

This does not mean that the individual has been found innocent; indeed, there is no such plea at arraignment. I have often seen in newspapers and other media coverage a statement that the defendant has pled innocent to a charge. This makes no sense, since there exists no such plea. The plea is "not guilty." The defendant does not have to prove his or her innocence; in fact, the defendant does not have to prove anything. It would, however, behoove a defendant to present competing or exculpatory evidence or a reasonable alternative, innocent explanation of the evidence to compete with or challenge the prosecution's evidence so as to create the reasonable doubt to defeat the charge. This is only necessary, however, if it appears that the prosecution's case in chief is so convincing and compelling that there would be virtually no hesitation on the part of the trier of fact in concluding that all of the elements of the charge were met by the facts presented by the prosecutor.

Reasonable doubt does not mean all doubt, or any doubt, or doubt not based on the evidence, or doubt that is not rationally related to the matter in issue. It is rather a vacillation in the mind of an ordinary and reasonable person that there may be a belief, however slight, that the accusatory machinery in a particular case and the evidence presented thereby, while designed to generate a conviction, instead causes one to question the prosecution's conclusion rather than to support it. It is worthy of note that while a prosecutor's duty and obligation under the law is to seek the truth and justice, such an obligation does not by definition necessarily mean to seek a conviction (the concepts are not inherently interchangeable). However, as a practical matter, it is generally presumed that the prosecution, after having exercised its executive discretion to charge an individual, will in fact place all of its efforts toward obtaining a conviction.

The concept of reasonable doubt and the requirement imposed upon the prosecution to prove each and every element of a criminal charge beyond a reasonable doubt is designed to protect against errors, whether intentional or innocent, in matters where an individual's freedom and liberty are at stake. There is perhaps no greater contribution to the wisdom and humanity of our system of jurisprudence than this noble and imposing requirement.

RICHARD D. PARSONS is Chairman of the Board and Chief Executive Officer of Time Warner Inc., whose businesses include filmed entertainment, interactive services, television networks, cable systems and publishing. He became CEO in May 2002 and Chairman of the Board in May 2003.

Since becoming CEO, Mr. Parsons has led Time Warner's turnaround and set the company on a solid path toward achieving sustainable growth. In its January 2005 report on America's Best CEOs, *Institutional Investor* magazine named Mr. Parsons the top CEO in the entertainment industry. Before becoming CEO, Mr. Parsons served as the company's Co-Chief Operating Officer, overseeing its content businesses—Warner Bros., New Line Cinema, Warner Music Group and Time Warner Book Group—as well as two key corporate functions: Legal and People Development.

Mr. Parsons joined Time Warner as its President in February 1995, and has been a member of the company's Board of Directors since January 1991. As President, he oversaw the company's filmed entertainment and music businesses, and all corporate staff functions, including financial activities, legal affairs, public affairs and administration.

Before joining Time Warner, Mr. Parsons was Chairman and Chief Executive Officer of Dime Bancorp, Inc., one of the largest thrift institutions in the United States. Previously, he was the managing partner of the New York law firm Patterson, Belknap, Webb & Tyler. Prior to that, he held various positions in state and federal government, as counsel for Nelson Rockefeller and as a senior White House aide under President Gerald Ford. Mr. Parsons received his undergraduate education at the University of Hawaii and his legal training at Union University's Albany Law School.

The Reasons
We Need the Rule of
Reasonable Doubt

By Richard D. Parsons

A *New York Times* article on the acquittal of actor Robert Blake, who was tried for the murder of his wife, quoted the foreman of the jury as explaining that "the circumstantial evidence presented by the prosecution had left reasonable doubt." The celebrity nature of the Blake trial guaranteed a surfeit of media attention. But every day, in courtrooms across America, whether the trials receive intensive coverage or are barely noticed, the same requirement to establish a defendant's guilt "beyond a reasonable doubt" is used by juries to decide whether to acquit or convict.

Fundamental to our system of criminal law, reasonable doubt is built upon two important principles, which took centuries to evolve. The first is the right of defendants to a trial by jury. Before jury trials came into practice, "trial by ordeal" was widely used amid the disorder that followed the collapse of the Roman Empire. Under this system, defendants were forced to grasp a red-hot iron or plunge their limbs in scalding water. If they emerged unharmed, it was taken right as a sign that God had protected them, thus proving their innocence. Although the records are scant, it seems likely few passed the test, which led to a search for a more reliable system.

The spread of trial by jury was gradual. At first, it was a privilege claimed by the nobility, but over time became a right of "freeborn English men," a legacy enshrined in the U.S. Constitution,

Section 2, Clause 3, which states that "the Trial of all Crimes, except in Cases of Impeachment, shall be by Jury..." Concomitant with the rise of trial by jury was the development of basic rules of evidence—fixed standards to determine what could be admitted or should be excluded—as well as the rule that the burden of proof lay on the prosecution, not the accused. The state had to establish the guilt of the defendant, who was presumed innocent, and it couldn't do so by merely raising a few suspicions. It had to establish guilt beyond a reasonable doubt, a standard that seems to have first been spelled out in American jurisprudence during the Boston massacre trials of 1770.

The crux of the phrase "reasonable doubt" is in the first word—reasonable. Some scholars have recently suggested that it was introduced by prosecutors, not defense lawyers, in an effort to ensure that they didn't have to meet a burden of proof beyond any doubt. Whatever that historical truth, the concept is a mainstay of our criminal justice system, providing defendants with vital protection against arbitrary convictions dictated by the state.

The criterion for establishing a defendant's guilt beyond reasonable doubt isn't a scientific formula, applied in cookie-cutter fashion in every case with uniform results. It depends on subjective judgments about what reasonable doubt is and whether it is present. Sometimes, the standard of reasonable doubt has resulted in acquittals that have generated public scorn or outrage; other times, it hasn't prevented miscarriages of justice that have condemned the innocent to prison and even death.

Imperfect as it may be, reasonable doubt is a central, irreplaceable part of a system of law designed to protect every citizen from verdicts based on nothing more than the whims or prejudices of the powerful. Though, on occasion, it frustrates police and prosecutors whose evidence for conviction falls short of what a jury believes is beyond a reasonable doubt, for ordinary citizens facing prosecution for crimes they didn't commit, it can make all the difference.

Perhaps nowhere has the rationale for reasonable doubt and the rule of law been given more eloquent expression than in Robert Bolt's play *Man for All Seasons*. The protagonist of Bolt's play is Sir

Thomas More, the Lord Chancellor of England, who surrenders his position rather than assent to King Henry VIII's insistence that he give public approval to Henry's divorce and remarriage.

More had spent most of his career in service to the King, as lawyer, ambassador, and judge, and had helped strengthen the jury system as it then existed, insisting that no one be allowed to give evidence to jurors outside the court. Brought to trial for his refusal to swear an oath in support of Henry's actions, More used every legal device possible to avoid the charge of treason.

At the heart of More's defense—and of Bolt's play—is the role of the law in preserving the rights of the individual from the collective power of the state. The intent of the law should be, not to obstruct the apprehension and punishment of the guilty, but to ensure the rights of the innocent, even when the rights slow down the wheels of justice. The trade-off is eloquently expressed by Thomas More when confronted by the zealous orthodoxy of William Roper, his son-in-law, who avers that in the struggle against the Devil he'd "cut down every law in England" to achieve his end. More gives this reply:

> Oh! And when the last law was down, and the Devil turned round on you where would you hide, Roper, the laws all being flat? This country's planted thick with laws from coast to coast—Man's laws, not God's—and if you cut them down— and you're just the man to do it—d'you really think you could stand upright in the winds that would blow then? Yes, I'd give the Devil the benefit of law, for my own safety's sake.

As Americans, we stand as the ultimate beneficiaries of the long evolution that has secured the rule of law. It hasn't always been an easy struggle. Often, there have been setbacks and, unfortunately, egregious violations of the rights of individuals and entire groups. But the system of legal protections and assurances that we enjoy—the thickly planted forest of which reasonable doubt is a crucial part—is what preserves us from the nightmare of religious and political totalitarianism in which indictment equals conviction and all are guilty until and unless they can prove otherwise.

FREDERICK FORSYTH, born in 1938, is a British author and occasional political commentator, best known for his thrillers *The Day of the Jackal*, *The Dogs of War*, and *The Odessa File*. He was born in Ashford, Kent, and attended Granada University in Spain. At 19, he became one of the youngest-ever pilots in the Royal Air Force, where he served until 1958. He then became a reporter and spent three-and-a-half years working on a provincial newspaper before joining Reuter, the international news agency.

As a foreign correspondent he covered Paris, Bonn, East Berlin, Prague, Budapest, Madrid, Brussels and Rome, leaving after four years to join the BBC. Here he became assistant diplomatic correspondent. As such he was sent to cover the Nigeria-Biafra war on the rebel side. He returned, resigned and went back to the jungle for two more years. He stuck it to the end, then came back to London to write his first novel, *The Day of the Jackal*, based on things he had eye-witnessed in Paris seven years earlier. This became an international bestseller and was later made into a movie with the same title.

In this novel, the Organisation de l'Armée Secrète hires an assassin to kill Charles de Gaulle. His second novel, *The Odessa File*, was published in 1972 and depicts a reporter attempting to track down a network of ex-Nazis in modern Germany. *The Odessa File* was also made into a hit movie. In 1974, he wrote *The Dogs of War*, in which a mining tycoon hires a group of mercenaries to overthrow the government of an African country so that he can install a puppet regime that will allow him cheap access to its substantial mineral wealth. Forsyth's latest book, *The Afghan* (2006), is about a Canadian millionaire who hires a Vietnam veteran to bring his grandson's killer to the U.S.

Forsyth eschews psychological complexity in favor of meticulous plotting based on detailed factual research, and his novels read like investigative journalism in the guise of fiction. Forsyth's books are full of information about the technical details of such subjects as money laundering, gun running, and identity theft. His is a harsh moral vision in which the world is made up of predators and prey, and only the strong survive.

Reasonable Doubt—
But Whose?

By Frederick Forsyth

Two hundred and thirty years ago thirteen very small British colonies, strung out from north to south down the eastern seaboard of a huge but almost wholly unexplored continent, entered into a state of rebellion.

It is often overlooked that back then the British homeland belonged to the people, who had their representatives in the world's first imperfect but nevertheless elected Parliament. But colonies belonged to the monarch as personal fiefdoms. The monarch at the time was George the Third.

Americans to this day choose to overlook something odd that happened next. When King George petitioned Parliament for funds to fight what was widely seen as "his" war against "his" rebels, the answer was a flat "No." That was why he had to beg and borrow impressed farmboys—unwilling mercenaries—from his kinsfolk scattered across what is modern Germany. He bankrupted himself trying to pay for them. But impressed farmboys are not good soldiers. Unsurprisingly, they lost.

The inhabitants of the thirteen colonies then faced a choice. They could stay separate from each other, declare a chain of mini-republics and become one day the Nicaraguas and San Salvadors of the Atlantic coast of the New World. Or they could be united by volition into one federal republic. They chose the latter, and it worked. But why did it work?

I am convinced that it was because, and only because, they shared the six pillars of commonalty. They shared the same ethnicity; back then far over ninety-five percent were of the same Anglo-Saxon and Celtic stock that had come over from the British Isles. They shared the same history: for the same reason.

They shared the same culture and faith, an immensely crucial factor in the building of a nation. An educated man in Vermont and another in Georgia would have been educated in the same way, have read the same Classics, have studied the same Shakespeare and Milton. And they would go on Sunday to the same Christian church or chapel.

They shared the same dream of government. It is (again) forgotten that they did not rebel because they loathed and repudiated the parliamentary democracy of the British and all those freedoms granted and guaranteed in the English Bill of Rights of 1689. Just the reverse. They wanted all those things and resented the King for denying them. One day they would incorporate those same freedoms in their own Bill of Rights.

There were two more of the six pillars. They spoke the same language and they were accustomed to the same jurisprudence. In short, they inherited because they wished to inherit the basic principles of English Common Law.

Within two decades of the drawing up of the American Constitution a dictator had conquered almost all Europe; the "almost" means he failed to invade and conquer the British Isles. He would eventually be defeated but he left behind him a quite different legal code to that of the British and the Americans.

The first of the three precepts that tower over Anglo-American law is the idea that the citizen is supreme and the state is his servant. As such, he is free to do whatever he wants unless it is specifically forbidden.

But Bonaparte was a tyrant. He loathed and despised the idea of democracy. The Code Napoleon, still the basis of Euro-law to this day, decrees that the state is supreme and the citizen its servant. All is therefore forbidden unless it is specifically permitted.

Precept Two is that any man, accused of whatever it may be, is presumed innocent until proven guilty beyond a reasonable doubt. Napoleon decreed the reverse. Arraigned before a court, the accused must be able to prove his innocence.

But the Anglo-American insistence on guilt "beyond a reasonable doubt" posed a quandary. Who should adjudicate? Who should decide whether guilt had, or had not, been proved beyond a reasonable doubt? To respond to the quandary Anglo-Saxon law, going back over centuries, insisted that an accused man had the right to be judged by a jury. This concept was utterly alien to the Code Napoleon where judgment is decreed by a professional judge, or a judge and lay assessors qualified in the law.

Long before Napoleon, the English reasoned thus: the judgment cannot be left to defending counsel, for he is bought and paid for. Nor can it be left to prosecuting counsel for the same reason. And even the judge, wise though he may be, is still an employee of the State and thus a paid-up member of the Establishment. So they came up with the idea of "twelve good men and true."

And that is a jury, based on the idea of that deeply marvelous creature, the reasonable man. He may be the short-order cook who serves your eggs over-easy. He may be the janitor of the local school. Or a professor, or a bond trader. But for one small time, enclosed with eleven others in a pen, impassive, a bit over-awed but aware of his solemn duty, he will decide whether your guilt has been proved beyond a reasonable doubt.

Advocates earning huge fees must nevertheless plead with him. On the issue of verdict the judge must defer to him. He must sit mute for days listening and watching as evidence is paraded before him. He must study charts, examine artifacts, tolerate outbursts, and keep his opinion to himself.

But when the captains and the kings have sat down; when the ushers have called for order; when the judge has summed up; then that reasonable man, with his eleven fellow jurors, will retire to privacy to decide one thing. Has the guilt of the frightened man or woman in the dock been proved beyond a reasonable doubt?

The miracle is not so much that the system works but that it works so remarkably well. Juries make mistakes, but so do professionals. Juries are rarely bribed or intimidated; they do not seek preferment or political office. Their careers are not on the line. They will not create learned papers. They will go back to the skillet, the boiler room, and the trading floor. But for one brief hour they will do their duty to judge fairly between a fellow citizen and the power of the state. And whatever the mighty state may think of them and their verdict there is nothing it can do to them, no sanction it can invoke, no punishment it can inflict to express its displeasure.

"Reasonable doubt" is just an idea, just a phrase. The important thing is: whose reason? Whose doubt? To answer that our forefathers created a truly remarkable phenomenon. Twelve good men and true.

Back then in the war two hundred and thirty years ago the New Americans won at Albany, and at Saratoga, and at Yorktown. But the greatest victories of all were those of freedom under law, the presumption of innocence and trial by jury.

ROBERT LESLIE SHAPIRO is a prominent West Coast defense lawyer. After earning his law degree in 1968, he joined the Los Angeles County District Attorney's Office as an assistant district attorney. In 1972 Shapiro left the public sector for private practice. Mr. Shapiro's first well-known case was his defense of Linda Lovelace, an adult film star charged with a cocaine offense in 1975. Shapiro got the charges dismissed. He has worked for famous athletes Darryl Strawberry, José Canseco and New York Mets outfielder Vince Coleman, as well as other celebrities like television comedian Johnny Carson, film producer Robert Evans, and actor Marlon Brando's son, Christian Brando. Shapiro also won an acquittal for his friend, attorney F. (Francis) Lee Bailey, who was charged with drunk driving.

Mr. Shapiro's most prominent case was the trial of former football star O.J. Simpson for the 1994 murders of his ex-wife, Nicole Brown Simpson, and her friend, Ronald Lyle Goldman. The "dream team" defense won the case and Simpson was ultimately acquitted of murder. By the trial's conclusion, Shapiro had gained nationwide fame for his part in one of the most widely followed cases in U.S. history. He continues to practice law in Los Angeles.

The Defense Attorney's
Strongest Weapon

By Robert L. Shapiro

United Supreme Court Justice Potter Steward was asked to define obscenity. His reply was "I can't define it, but I know it when I see it." Such is the case with reasonable doubt. The instruction jurors are given as to what constitutes reasonable doubt it so vague, that it is up to the jurors themselves to define it.

It is easier to define what it is not. It is not proof beyond any possible doubt for if that were the standard, there would never be any convictions. It is also not proof positive. For only a proven scientific theory will reach that standard. We know everything in life can have some possible doubt. It lies somewhere between those two standards.

Reasonable doubt is more a feeling. A belief that a case has been proven to your satisfaction, that when you leave the courthouse you will sleep well that night. It is when you believe your decision is one you can live with for the rest of your live. If you get that pit in your stomach feeling that you are not sure of your decision, that's when you have reasonable doubt.

I don't expect that anyone can define reasonable doubt, but as Potter Stewart said, "You know it when you see it."

WILLIAM W. TAYLOR, III is a partner in the Washington, D.C. office of the national law firm Zuckerman Spaeder LLP. Mr. Taylor's law practice focuses on white-collar crime and regulatory matters, commercial litigation, and Native American rights. With more than 30 years of experience in private practice as a civil and criminal litigator, he has represented individuals and entities involved in defense procurement, antitrust, environmental, health care, securities, and tax investigations. He has tried numerous civil and criminal cases in state and federal courts.

His clients include current and former public officials, lawyers, and law firms. Mr. Taylor represented the Chief of Staff to President Clinton, the Finance Chair of the Democratic National Committee and other public officials in the Whitewater and DNC fundraising investigations. He represented Senator Alan Cranston of California in proceedings before the Senate Ethics Committee, arising from the collapse of the Lincoln Savings & Loan Association. He represented the former president of the Salt Lake City Olympic Committee in his successful defense against federal charges arising from the selection of Salt Lake City as the site for the 2002 Winter Olympic Games. He is counsel to the Oneida Indian Nation of New York in its land claim and other litigation.

Before joining Zuckerman Spaeder, Mr. Taylor was a Staff Attorney and Special Assistant for Training at the Public Defender Service for the District of Columbia. He was a law clerk for the Honorable Caleb M. Wright, Chief Judge, U.S. District Court for the District of Delaware. He has been a Visiting Professor at the University of North Carolina Law School and an adjunct faculty member at Catholic University and George Washington University Law Schools. He is a fellow of the American College of Trial Lawyers.

What is Proof
Beyond a Reasonable Doubt and Why Do We Require It?

By William W. Taylor, III

In this day of a trial-savvy media and nightly trial-centered television series, most everyone has heard about proof "beyond a reasonable doubt." Jurors in criminal cases hear without surprise judges instruct them that to find a defendant guilty, they must conclude that the government proved he committed a crime "beyond a reasonable doubt."

In neither the media's fascination with criminal trials nor in the jury instructions, however, do we find any explanation of why this cumbersome form of words is imbedded in our criminal justice system. Beyond a reasonable doubt literally means something close to absolute certainty.

I can think of no other decision a human being or governmental body makes which requires that persons be convinced beyond a reasonable doubt. We make important—even life and death—decisions in our own affairs with much less certainty about them. People decide to marry, take a job, buy a house, or have a child, always with some lack of certainty about the choice. They have reasonable doubts and decide to proceed anyway. Indeed, people decide to undergo major surgery while maintaining serious and reasonable doubts that it will be safe and effective. People make these decisions as much upon risk analysis as upon certainty about the outcome.

Even people who are the most religious acknowledge at some level a lingering but rational doubt that in fact God exists.

Our government declares war based upon a majority vote. It permits companies to sell food and drugs without absolute certainty that they are safe. We license people to operate automobiles and fly airplanes with full knowledge that some of those licensing decisions will turn out in retrospect to have been ill-advised.

We permit the police to invade our homes on a showing of probability, and we permit plaintiffs in civil cases to win phenomenal sums of money simply by showing that their claims are simply more probable than not.

Why then does our criminal justice system insist upon proof beyond a reasonable doubt in criminal cases? The answer to that question has to do both with a societal choice and an historical experience.

It reflects a preference that the guilty go free rather than innocent be punished. It implements our view that freedom is our most precious commodity and that we will not take freedom away unless we are certain that it is warranted. It represents an acknowledgement that incarceration is the most severe power government exercises and that its very severity requires close to absolute certainty about guilt. It is a tough standard and is meant to be.

In my view, however, the standard derives from more than this. It expresses a distrust of governmental power and of the people who exercise it. Prosecutors and police are, after all, human. They do prosecute and arrest people who are innocent. Our founding fathers took this standard with them from England, where it had arisen from the people's struggles against the Crown. It provided protection against the Crown's use of the criminal courts to sanction critics or rebels. Today, it guards against similar abuses. It protects against the conviction of people merely because they are viewed as unpopular, rebellious or even dangerous—whether they be chief executives of a failed company accused of fraud, partisan government officials accused of leaking national security secrets, or college athletes accused of raping a woman of a minority race.

The formulation of the standard varies from state to state and court to court. Almost all formulations include something like the standard jury instruction from a well recognized treatise:

> [T]he defendant, although accused of a crime in the indictment, begins the trial with a clean slate—with no evidence against her.... The presumption of innocence alone, therefore is sufficient to acquit the defendant.
>
> The burden is always on the prosecution to prove beyond a reasonable doubt. This burden never shifts to a defendant for the law never imposes upon any defendant in a criminal case the burden or duty of calling any witnesses or producing any evidence. The defendant is not even obligated to produce any evidence by cross examining the witnesses for the government.
>
> It is not required that the government prove guilt beyond all possible doubt. The test is one of reasonable doubt. A reasonable doubt is a doubt based upon reason and common sense—the kind of doubt that would make a reasonable person hesitate to act. Proof beyond a reasonable doubt must, therefore, be proof of such a convincing character that a reasonable person would not hesitate to rely and act upon it in the most important of his or her own affairs.[1]

[1] 1 A O'Malley, et al., *Federal Practice and Instructions*, 5th Ed., § 12.10.

In another well recognized treatise of jury instructions, the writers define the concept a little further.

> The words almost define them-
> selves. It is a doubt based on reason
> and common sense. It is a doubt that a
> reasonable person has after carefully
> weighing all the evidence. It is a
> doubt which would cause a reasonable
> person to hesitate to act in a matter
> of importance in his or her personal
> life. Proof beyond a reasonable doubt
> must, therefore, be proof of such a
> convincing character that a reasonable
> person would not hesitate to rely on
> and act upon it in the most important
> of his own affairs.[2]

Thus, a reasonable doubt need not be the kind of doubt which would altogether prevent a person from proceeding with a decision. It need only be the kind of doubt which would cause that person to pause or hesitate before proceeding in a matter of great personal importance.

Translating this concept to the real world is the job of defense lawyers. For the sake of our clients, we try to make jurors understand that, although the government is not required to prove absolute certainty, it must prove something very close to it. Our clients—many of whom are wrongly accused or face unfair consequences—need jurors to understand that their belief that the defendant is probably guilty or possibly guilty or even most likely guilty is not enough upon which to render a guilty verdict.

I find most helpful the analogy to a decision by parents whether to approve a life-threatening surgery on their child. Naturally, the parents will be (and indeed should be) predisposed against the surgery and the risk at which it will place their child—just

---

[2] 1 L. <u>Sand, et al.</u>, Modern Federal Jury Instructions—Criminal § 4-2 (Matthew Bender).

as jurors must begin their inquiry presuming the defendant innocent and predisposed against conviction. The parents will not change their mind unless they become satisfied that the diagnosis is correct, that the surgery is necessary, that alternatives are even worse, that the child's current doctors are worthy of their faith, etc. If they doubt whether the surgery is necessary, they will hesitate. If they doubt the qualifications of the doctor, they will hesitate. If they have any other reasonable concern or question, they will hesitate. After all, the future of their child is at stake.

Under the law, the decision to abandon the presumption of innocence, to convict a human being of a crime, and to set in motion the process of stripping that person of his or her liberty is of equal gravity and must be treated with the same level of caution, if not even greater caution. Parents may hesitate, but nevertheless opt to proceed with the surgery on their child. If, however, after paying the same degree of scrutiny parents pay to a life or death decision relating to their child, a juror should hesitate, he or she may not proceed with a conviction. The juror simply must acquit.

Persuading a jury of this should be simple. It should be simple enough to explain that the same kind of hesitation one might experience in deciding whether to submit a loved one to a serious surgical procedure is the same kind of reasonable doubt that must require an acquittal.

In practice, however, this task is not so simple. We live in a "rush to judgment" era—where, often by virtue of media coverage, the accused is convicted in the court of public opinion before he even steps foot in a court of law. We live in an era where we believe an accused is guilty simply because our government says so in an indictment—a belief the exact opposite of which is the basis of our very Constitution. In our current climate, our rights have grown unpopular. We fear that at some level if we put the reasonable doubt standard to a popular vote, the proponents of more aggressive law and order systems might outnumber those who believe it should be retained to protect the innocent.

The requirement that the government establish guilt by proof beyond a reasonable doubt is nevertheless a fundamental element of our constitutional system. Although not explicit in the Constitution itself, the Supreme Court has held that it enjoys constitutional status, as indeed it should. (See In Re Winship, 397 U.S. 358.) It protects us all even from ourselves.

It falls upon our shoulders—the shoulders of defense attorneys—not only to explain to jurors in plain terms what this concept of reasonable doubt means and how to apply it, but also to convince them to set aside their modern-day inclination to rush to judgment and instead to honor this bedrock principle of our Constitution.

TV trial shows almost never portray the defense attorney arguing reasonable doubt...perhaps because the media folks think it sounds technical and apologetic. The real drama goes on every day in the criminal courts of the cities and towns across the country. We entrust the liberty of our citizens to ordinary people who, when they take their job seriously, struggle to restrain revulsion at a crime and do justice—which means that they sometimes must let people who they think are probably guilty go free just because the government's proof does not erase all reasonable doubt. That is the choice we have made and it is the only choice in a free society.

EDGAR H. HAUG, a founding partner, now managing partner, of Frommer Lawrence & Haug LLP, is a specialist in intellectual property litigation. Mr. Haug specializes in complex intellectual property litigation in pharmaceuticals, biotechnology, semiconductors, e-commerce and consumer electronic devices. He has successfully litigated against major pharmaceutical companies, paving the way to bringing affordable medicines to the market, including such blockbuster drugs as Zantac, Prilosec, Paxil, Ultracet, Claritin and Neurontin.

His representative clients include Fujitsu Limited, Merck KGaA, NEC Corporation, Sony Corporation, Tiffany & Co., Tokyo Electron Limited, Toshiba Corporation and Yahoo! Inc. Recently, Mr. Haug has won multi-million dollar jury awards in patent infringement and theft of trade secrets cases.

Mr. Haug received a B.S. in chemical engineering from the University of Notre Dame and a J.D. from St. John's University. He has studied law at the University of Exeter in England. In 2005, Mr. Haug was invited to the CEO Roundtable and is on the program committee and a speaker for the Federal Circuit Bar Association. His Bar admissions and qualifications include: New York State, U.S. District Court for the Southern and Eastern Districts, Court of Appeals for the Federal Circuit, U.S. Supreme Court and U.S. Patent & Trademark Office.

A Courtroom Standard
Full of Doubt?

By Edgar H. Haug

Though frequently equated with moral certainty, "beyond a reasonable doubt"—the guidance that all juries receive from judges in criminal cases in order to find a defendant guilty—remains one of those venerable legal concepts that too often is more honored in the breach than the observance. Its interpretation by jurors can be fraught with uncertainty. And small wonder! One juror's "beyond a reasonable doubt" may mean something entirely different to another sitting in the same jury box.

Far short of being a precise marker with an exact meaning for all, the concept of beyond a reasonable doubt has evolved over many centuries since it was promulgated in English common law and adopted by the framers of the nation's Constitution. In our criminal courts today, it is usually a highly subjective standard interpreted individually through the prism of a given juror's personal history, beliefs, culture, prejudices, experiences, race and gender. Different backgrounds and different lives equate to different standards.

Although a verdict based on beyond a reasonable doubt has to exceed that which is simply reasonable in a juror's mind, it has become a concept flexible enough to change from jury to jury. In an ideal world, it would fall just below absolute certainty about a defendant's guilt. "Beyond" is critical—the operative word. That is why a jury in a criminal case may entertain some reasonable doubt and properly still acquit. As an abstract ideal, such a high standard is wholly admirable, something few would dispute. In the real courtroom world, however, it is too often a notably problematic concept.

Fortunately, this kind of subjectivity is considerably less present in our civil courts where I have been practicing for many decades. There, the level of proof required to prevail in most cases is simply the "preponderance of evidence." The judge or jury must be persuaded that the facts more likely favor the plaintiff than the defendant or vice versa.

Such a preponderance is meant to reward the more convincing evidence—i.e., its probable truth or accuracy—not the amount of evidence. A single, clearly knowledgeable witness may provide a preponderance of evidence over a dozen opposing witnesses with hazy, uninformed testimonies. In a civil court, a defendant is also required to testify. Also, unlike in a criminal court, if the defendant pleads the Fifth, the jurors can assume he or she is hiding some damaging information. Unfortunately, what is sometimes the reality in a civil court is that jurors simply lack the knowledge or experience to make informed assessments of what is, and is not, true or accurate.

That a criminal court should demand a much higher standard for conviction is surely equitable and desirable from a societal perspective. The penalties meted out by our justice system to the convicted in criminal courts can be very severe and extreme up to and including capital punishment. That's hardly comparable to the monetary judgments that typically stem from civil actions. The flood of wrongfully convicted defendants (many on Death Row) in criminal cases that have come to light in recent years, thanks particularly to DNA testing, underscores both the failure and absolute necessity of the beyond a reasonable doubt standard.

Although juries do make mistakes—convicting the innocent and freeing the guilty—I remain a passionate believer in the jury system: a trial by a jury of one's peers. In a democratic society, a jury of equals rather than a judge or some legislative body should determine guilt or innocence.

But here, again, a never-ending debate in legal circles concerns just how one defines a "peer." In the final analysis, beyond a reasonable doubt depends on the composition of any given jury. As most skilled trial attorneys will tell you, selecting the "right" jury is the key to everything that subsequently happens in the courtroom. Every potential juror, being human, comes with baggage of some kind, and the best attorneys try to exploit that to their client's advantage.

The still-disputed O.J. Simpson double murder trial present-ed a classic example. Although the accused lived in one of Los Angeles' most exclusive sections, his lawyers were able to get the trial venue transferred to one of the city's most depressed areas from which the acquitting, largely African-American jury was drawn. Such a jury's perceptions of the world, including the concept of beyond a reasonable doubt, might vary considerably from those of Simpson's affluent neighbors in the posh Brentwood section of Los Angeles.

To them, the glove that didn't fit fell well beyond reasonable doubt. In the Simpson case, another factor that may have come into play is what legal scholars call jury nullification or willfully ignoring the evidence no matter how overwhelming—which a jury can do, if it arbitrarily chooses. In the first O.J. trial, quite obviously, some jurors felt that, even if they were wrong, the not-guilty verdict would send a powerful message to the L.A. police, and the D.A.'s office, often viewed in the black community as racially biased.

When the families of the victims later brought a civil action against the acquitted O.J. Simpson in a different venue and where the reasonable doubt standard did not apply, the jury found for the plaintiffs.

A criminal justice system like ours, resting on the doctrine of beyond a reasonable doubt, is designed to produce the best and most equitable of all possible outcomes—freeing the innocent and convicting the guilty. But we live in an imperfect world, peopled with imperfect, fallible human beings who often err. Yet for all its faults, that system, I believe, remains the gold standard in global jurisprudence.

COMMISSIONER DAVID A. ZISKROUT graduated UCLA School of Law in 1961. He was admitted to the California State Bar and to practice in the U.S. District Court in 1962 and to the U.S. Supreme Court in 1982. He was engaged in the general practice of law as a sole Practitioner from 1962 to 1968. He was selected as Juvenile Court Referee in 1968 and was appointed as Superior Court Commissioner in 1970, holding that position until his retirement in 2005. His Judicial assignments have included Civil, Criminal, Juvenile and Mental Health for the past 28 years.

Commissioner Ziskrout's Professional activities include: serving on the Federal Indigent Panel in defense of criminal defendants; lecturing before the Delinquency Prevention Control Institute on problems relating to the administration of Juvenile Justice; he was a Resource Trainer for California Attorney General's Crime Prevention Conference; participating Judge for the Roger J. Traynor California Moot Court Competition; discussion leader and author of an article on Juvenile Detention Practices for the Institute for Juvenile Court Judges and Referees and he is a member on Board of Directors of the California Court Commissioners Association. He has appeared as a guest speaker on radio, TV and on numerous occasions at schools, religious groups and service organizations relating to Juvenile and Mental Health matters.

Time for
Another Look

By Commissioner David A. Ziskrout

One's life is filled daily with countless decisions that require some introspection and thought. The decision that we ultimately arrive at is based upon on our life's experiences. But have we made the right decision and what is necessary to make the "correct" decision after drawing upon one's life experiences? These are questions asked by individuals as well as groups of people.

The term "beyond a reasonable doubt" is probably most often thought of as a group decision by individuals called a jury. The standard of proof in deciding a criminal case is beyond a reasonable doubt, that is, is the individual innocent or guilty beyond a reasonable doubt? The key words here are "beyond" and "reasonable." What is "beyond," is it forty, fifty or sixty per cent certainty or something else? And who decides what is "reasonable"? What affect does one's sex, race, age, nationality and countless other factors play in determining in one person's mind what is reasonable?

Having interacted for 35 years with judges, juries and countless lawyers, I have concluded that the definition given as to what is meant by being beyond a reasonable doubt is in need of clarity and repair. Given the severity of the consequences to an individual charged with a crime, the time has come to give more attention and certainty to this standard of proof. And did I fail to mention, that the decision has to be unanimous in order to find one guilty? Some might suggest that instead of a unanimous verdict, perhaps eleven of twelve people should be able to make that decision and thereby provide some margin of forgiveness because of the inadequacy of the definition. I am not in favor of this suggestion and believe with the talent and keen minds in the legal profession, we can and should do better.

But life is not only about lawyers and those charged with crimes; it is about the daily experience of leading a productive, useful and happy life. There are those among us that hold such strong views on a multitude of thoughts and beliefs that they proclaim that their conclusions are beyond a reasonable doubt, that is, they have no doubt. Men and women who devote their lives to a particular religious faith are examples of persons who have no doubt about the truth and certainty of those beliefs. Whether they are correct or not is not the question, the conclusion is that they believe there is no doubt.

For the majority of us, we make countless decisions with some doubt in the resolution of the issues that life presents. And that is OK; we don't have to draw on the legal definition or arrive at the certainty that others proclaim, we listen to our "gut" and then our "head." I might suggest that the majority of the time, we will dismiss the doubt and come up with the right decision.

For those who are in doubt after reading this, go outside and look at a tree, a flower or a child and have no doubt.

ADAM S. HOFFINGER has a litigation and trial practice with an emphasis on complex civil and white-collar criminal matters, including securities, money laundering, health care, qui tam, Foreign Corrupt Practices Act, antitrust, environmental, and RICO. He counsels corporations and individuals in compliance matters (including USA Patriot Act and Sarbanes-Oxley), internal investigations, and Congressional and regulatory matters. Mr. Hoffinger has represented clients in the Campaign Finance, Whitewater, Teamsters, Travelgate, Ruby Ridge, BCCI, and other government investigations.

From 1985 to 1990, Mr. Hoffinger served as an Assistant United States Attorney for the Southern District of New York; in 1990, he received the Director's Award for Superior Performance from the U.S. Department of Justice. He has been an instructor at Georgetown University Law Center, George Washington University Law School, George Mason University Law School, and the Federal Judicial Center. Mr. Hoffinger has been named by *Washingtonian* magazine and the *Legal Times* as one of the top lawyers in Washington, D.C., and is listed in *Best Lawyers in America*.

Reasonable Doubt

By Adam S. Hoffinger

The more I practice criminal law, the more I learn that there is very little I know "beyond a reasonable doubt." What I have learned about "beyond a reasonable doubt," however, is that, although the law requires it, no one really understands that in a criminal case the government must prove a person's guilt "beyond a reasonable doubt."

What is "beyond a reasonable" doubt supposed to mean in the criminal justice system? It means that we are supposed to give a person who has been accused of a crime the benefit of the doubt when it comes to guilt or innocence. It means that when a person enters the courtroom charged with a crime, the jury is supposed to "presume" that he or she is innocent. And the jury is supposed to cling to that presumption throughout the trial unless and until the government proves guilt "beyond a reasonable doubt."

But when jurors look around the courtroom, in its majesty and formality, ringed by armed uniformed guards, presided over by a "justice" sitting high on a pedestal festooned in billowing black robes and armed with an oversized wooden mallet to keep "order in the court," and see a lone, despondent human being flanked by dour grey-suited lawyers seated at a table separate from that of the white-shirted, blue-suited, red-tied, fresh-faced (often young) prosecutors, flanked by solemn law enforcement officers, steel carts and cardboard boxes of what can only be "incriminating" evidence, how can they be expected to think anything other than "this person must be guilty of something, otherwise why would all of these important and serious people be here?" What would judges, prosecutors, law enforcement officers, private lawyers and others be doing here if someone didn't do something wrong? And since there is usually only one "someone" in the courtroom, repeatedly referred to as "the defendant," it is not difficult to figure out who the wrongdoer is supposed to be.

Under such circumstances, can we really expect twelve men and women picked from the voters' rolls to give the defendant the "benefit of the doubt" by insisting that the government prove guilt "beyond a reasonable doubt?"

The answer to that question is "No." And that is something I believe "beyond a reasonable doubt."

CAROL ELDER BRUCE is a white-collar criminal defense attorney and a complex commercial civil trial lawyer who represents corporations and individuals in many forums, including federal and state courts, grand jury proceedings, Congressional hearings, federal agency enforcement actions, and internal corporate investigations. She is a partner in the law firm of Venable LLP. in Washington, D.C. Ms. Bruce has been named by *Legal Times* as one of the top 20 litigation lawyers in Washington, D.C.; by *Washingtonian* magazine as one of the top criminal defense lawyers in Washington, D.C., and has been listed for several years now (including in its current 2006-2007 listings) as one of the best criminal defense attorneys and commercial litigators in America in *Best Lawyers of America*. She is a fervent believer in the American legal tradition of due process and fairness in legal proceedings and currently is representing pro bono three Egyptian detainees in Guantanamo Bay, whom she believes have received neither.

Ms. Bruce's public service includes her work as the Independent Counsel in the investigation of matters relating to Secretary of the Interior Bruce Babbitt; and the Deputy Independent Counsel in the investigation of matters relating to Attorney General Edwin Meese. Before those investigations, she served for ten years as an Assistant United States Attorney for the District of Columbia where she investigated and prosecuted hundreds of criminal cases, and was lead counsel in over 100 jury trials. In 2001, she became the fourth woman lawyer in Washington, D.C. to be inducted into the prestigious American College of Trial Lawyers, where she now serves as Chair of the International Committee of the College. Ms. Bruce is a charter member and Master in the Edward Bennett Williams American Inn of Court; and is the Vice President of the of The Lawyers' Club of Washington. She obtained her college and law degrees from George Washington University, where she now serves on the Law School Dean's Board of Advisors. The mother of three grown children, she is married to another lawyer, James T. Bruce III.

Reasonable Doubt
in Moscow

By Carol Elder Bruce

There was no hiding the fact that it had started snowing outside the first floor offices of the American Bar Association Central European and Eurasian Law Initiative ("ABA CEELI") office on that late afternoon in Moscow in November 2003. The window shades were up, the streetlights bright on the quiet block of three-storied, upscale, old office row houses. A steady, silent, full-screen snowfall had begun, adding to our sense of urgency to finish our work. We needed to wrap up anyway, take a much needed break, and enjoy our last night in Moscow.

Our team from the U.S.—a Midwestern law professor, a New York state trial judge, and me—a Washington, D.C. criminal defense attorney—sat inside the front conference room in the CEELI offices facing this unfolding, lovely Moscow winter scene. Across the large conference table from us, with their backs to the street, was a Russian interpreter and one of President Boris Yeltson's top law reform experts. The latter—a lawyer himself—spoke some broken English and the professor was fluent in Russian, but we all leaned heavily on the skilled Moscow interpreters who had accompanied us on our ten day trip to Moscow as part of the ABA CEELI Jury Trial Program. We had all worked hard together on this trip to conduct adversarial trial and mock jury trial sessions with many of the judges who would preside over the first jury trials in Russia in 70 years. We had trained many of the criminal defense attorneys who would, for the first time in their professional careers, actually play an active and central role in the trial of their clients. This trip was no junket. And, we were near the end of our stay. Tonight was our last night in Russia. We'd fly home the next day.

CEELI started its Rule of Law program in Russia in 1992, one year after the first direct election of a president in Russia under the 2001 glasnost and perestroika movement that accompanied the crumbling of the Soviet Union. Boris Yeltsin had been elected President in the summer of 2001, and surrounded himself with bright, young, idealistic men and women as well as many former Communists from the old guard. The ABA was quick to seize the opportunity to share with the new Russian government the conceptual and structural frameworks of our legal institutions in many realms—commercial and private. It was now our turn to play our small part in the wholesale export to Russia of due process and fundamental fairness concepts in the conduct of jury trials.

We were one of a number of teams that CEELI had put together to assist the Russian government with the reintroduction of trial by jury in Russia for the first time since its elimination during the Bolshevik Revolution in 1917. With generous funding behind CEELI, teams of volunteers like us were helping the Russian law reform leaders construct from ground up a U.S.-style adversarial criminal justice system with the right to a trial by jury for the most serious offenses. For the first time since 1917, a defendant could elect to have the facts in his criminal case determined by his peers and a truly independent judge and not by a judge and two lay assessors (or "nodders" as the lay participants were derisively called, because these non-lawyers would perch on either side of the judge and just nod obediently in assent with whatever decisions the Communist party controlled judge made in a case). The judge-lay assessor system had existed since 1917, under the Soviet state. The system had provided no role for a defense attorney other than to plead for mercy and even prosecutors had little function as the judge would take the prosecution's dossier and examine all the witnesses himself. Conviction rates did not disappoint the State: they were virtually 100%.

The jury trial would be the cornerstone of a new criminal justice system in 1993. U.S. and Russian scholars alike were singing its praises. A jury trial represented one of the best ways to promote citizen involvement in government. Citizen jurors would feel they were a part of the system of justice, would now understand the role of the judge and lawyers in society, and would begin to believe and take pride in and ownership of the justice system through the jury trial process. The people would witness the elimination of the old, disdained, rigged ways of doing things. There would be no more "show trials" and arbitrary justice with predictable results (guilty!), and the citizenry would come to relish their new-found confidence in their judicial system and in themselves as decision-makers on juries. They would begin to feel qualified to make decisions on a jury panel about the merits of the State's case and about the guilt/innocence of their fellow man. And, a jury trial would force the government into actually proving that someone committed the crime with which he/she was charged. Powerful, intoxicating aspirations.

Our hosts lightened the historic nature of our work by joking with us about how, in 1917, the Bolsheviks had eliminated jury trials believing the Tsarist juries were a bourgeois institution and, besides, "there'd be no crime in the perfect state!" Jury trials had existed only for 50 years (having been introduced as part of Alexander II's judicial reform in the famous "Judicial Statutes" in November 1864) in Russia's 500-year history of authoritarian rule, before they were cast aside by the Bolsheviks. So, here we were, in 1993, almost 70 years later, bringing back the jury trial as the centerpiece of the Russian legal and political reforms taking place after the collapse of the Soviet Union. Our respect for the enthusiastic, bright young law reformers was matched only by our hope that their embrace of many Western criminal justice concepts—respect for individual rights, due process, and fundamental fairness for all—would last beyond our visit.

In July 1993, just a few months before our arrival in Moscow, the Supreme Soviet of the Russian Federation had adopted laws providing for dramatic changes in the Russian Federation Law on Court Proceedings. Revisions also appeared in the criminal procedural code and the criminal code itself. Jury trials would occur only in the highest level trial courts in Russia—the Russian regional courts—for only the most serious offenses.

Jury trials would start in early 2004 once all the preparatory steps and the training of judges and defense attorneys concluded (and I had the unqualified pleasure of participating actively in such training on three separate occasions). Reportedly since then, the majority of jury trials have been in premeditated murder cases and in rape cases. Acquittal rates would rise to a figure of approximately 20%, considerably higher than the .5 or 1% acquittal rate under the Soviet system. But, no matter how much well-intentioned American lawyers tried to persuade Russian officials to adopt virtually all of our fundamental constitutional rights and procedural practices, Russian law professors and legal experts resisted many of the suggestions and revived some of the Tsarist judicial practices in this new criminal justice experiment.

These professors and experts also insisted, as was their right, on improvising procedures to conform their new jury trial system with Russian legal and cultural traditions, thereby moderating what they perceived to be the more radical aspects of our American criminal justice system.

For example, under our American system of justice, the jury must consist of 12 persons and their verdict must be unanimous, otherwise it's a "hung jury," and the judge must declare a "mistrial." Under the new Russian system being devised in some other Moscow building as we visited Russia in November 2003, jurors would have only three hours to reach a unanimous verdict. If they failed, they would be allowed to convict the defendant on a majority vote and that verdict would hold as much weight as if it were a unanimous guilty verdict.

Another peculiarly Russian feature of the new system of justice was *the retention of the Soviet practice of returning cases for additional investigation in the middle of a trial if a prosecutor unilaterally determined that such further investigation was in the interests of justice.* This practice seemed to us inimical to the whole concept of a fair jury trial and, not incidentally, the practice was a real bonanza for prosecutors. I'm a former Assistant United States Attorney; a federal prosecutor. Every prosecutor would dearly love to pull the plug mid-trial on a case that was not going well for the government and send it back for further investigation to avoid these deficiencies in a second trial. But our system recognizes and embraces a cherished concept called "double jeopardy." It's enshrined in the Fifth Amendment to our Constitution: "nor shall any person be subject for the same offence to be twice put in jeopardy of life or limb."

The way double jeopardy operates is that once a jury is empanelled and sworn in, jeopardy "attaches." The government then, absent the declaration of a mistrial based on "manifest necessity" (such as a hung jury or the consent of the defense after a mid-trial unexpected development like the illness of a crucial defense witness), has one chance to get it right in its presentation of the evidence. One trial. So, in our system, the government can't decide to return a case for further investigation once a jury trial has begun or after a jury has delivered a verdict of "not guilty."

Thus, the double jeopardy clause protects the defendant from the government re-prosecuting him once he's been acquitted by a jury, regardless of why the jury voted to acquit. Indeed, it's the double jeopardy clause that gives such powerful weight and finality to our juries' verdicts of "not guilty." That is, even if the jury "nullifies" and acquits a man or woman in America based on factors other than a so-called rational evaluation of all the evidence and a thoughtful application of our reasonable doubt standard of proof, the government has no authority to retry the defendant for the crimes with which he/she had been charged and tried. In short, the double jeopardy principle is a real testament to the importance with which we hold the jury trial system in our country. There's no way to force a jury to reach a particular verdict or even to apply a particular standard (i.e., "reasonable doubt") to their deliberations about the facts. As one well-regarded and prolific jury commentator put it recently in his blog,

> ...the Double Jeopardy Clause of the Constitution prevents the Government from re-prosecuting anyone who has been acquitted by a jury—no matter how irrational, arbitrary, or bizarre the jury's reasoning in finding the accused not guilty. Even if the jury foreman scribbles the words "because your law sucks" under the words "not guilty"...[1]

Unbeknownst to us as we pondered our task that winter night in Russia, others in the Russian government had already given, or soon would give, another concession to the Russian prosecutors who were hell bent in opposition to the whole jury trial concept. That is, the *Russian experts decided they would allow the appeal of a jury's "not guilty" verdict to an appellate court.* So, an appellate court could reverse the jury's acquittal and force a new trial in complete derogation of any right against double jeopardy and the finality of the "not guilty" verdict. Under our system in the United States, a judge may set aside a jury verdict of guilty and enter an acquittal, and the judge may even dismiss the case with prejudice (so it cannot be brought again) before the case goes to the jury, if the judge concludes the government's case is insufficient. A judge may, in short, direct a verdict of "not guilty." But a judge in the U.S. may *never* take a case away from the jury and direct a verdict of "guilty" no matter how overwhelming the evidence may appear to be, and a "not guilty" verdict in the U.S. may *never* be appealed on any grounds whatsoever.[2]

---

[1] Clay S. Conrad. Http://jurygeek.blogspot.com (January 18, 2006). Mr. Conrad, who has written a respected book on *Jury Nullification: The Evolution of a Doctrine* (Carolina Academic Press, 1998), compared our reverence for the jury's verdict with what has actually happened in Russia in many trials under their jury trial initiative: "Consider the situation in Russia, in which jury acquittals are nothing more than speed bumps for prosecutors."

[2] If it turns out that the "not guilty" verdict was procured by corruption—e.g., jury tampering—people could be prosecuted for such corrupt behavior separately, but the not guilty verdict itself would remain nonetheless—a powerful testament to the power and the independence of the jury.

Nor, after a January 2005 Supreme Court decision in <u>United States v. Booker</u>, may a judge even sentence a defendant to additional time in jail based on evidence not proven beyond a reasonable doubt to a jury or admitted by a defendant.

Contrary to these cherished due process and double jeopardy practices in the U.S., the new Russian system under consideration in 1993, would allow for the appellate reversal of "not guilty" jury verdicts, placing some criminal defendants in an endless cycle of appeals and reinvestigations and retrials until the prosecutors could succeed in persuading some jury somewhere that the defendant is guilty.[3] In Russia, in short, the Soviet era belief in the importance of maintaining checks on the process to ensure getting the "correct" outcome (i.e., the "correct" verdict of guilty) still appears to hold more caché than ensuring fundamental fairness or due process to individual defendants in serious criminal jury trials or in showing faith and confidence in the new juries.

On this November 2003 night, we were unaware of these forces in opposition to our quest for fundamental fairness and the consequences of the ultimate decisions made in these debates had not played out yet in practice in the new jury trial system. These debates and issues were far from our thoughts as our challenge that evening was limited to advocating the acceptance and implementation of only one feature of the new Russian system of criminal justice—the adoption of jury instructions. These instructions would include an instruction to the jury that the Russian prosecutors would, in each and every criminal jury trial, have to prove each and every element of each charge brought against a defendant "beyond a reasonable doubt." Sound familiar?

Before coming to Moscow, I had put together a small team of people as part of the CEELI Jury Trial Project to draft a Russian Bench Book—a manual to assist Russian judges in the trial of criminal cases under the new jury trial system being inaugurated under the law reforms of 1993. The 207-page Bench Book consisted of three how-to chapters and a set of sample jury instructions. We lifted some of the

[3] One statistic had the reversal rate for acquittals in 1998, at 50 of 86 acquittal verdicts.

"standard" instructions from the Bar Association of the District of Columbia's Criminal Jury Instructions for the District of Columbia. And we drafted some of the other instructions from scratch. These instructions dealt principally with describing the elements of the offenses that we knew the Russians would bring before juries— Treason, Espionage, Bribery, Intentional Homicide under Aggravating Circumstances, Aggravated Rape and a host of other offenses against the State. We had submitted the Bench Book to translators weeks before we arrived in Moscow and all but some of the jury instructions were almost completely translated when we arrived.

Chapter One of the Bench Book dealt with general jury management and covered such nuts and bolts topics as how to create a general list of potential jurors that will ensure a random, fair selection of a group of qualified people who can serve on juries. This chapter also covered how, once the jury arrives at the courthouse, you provide juror education and orientation, compensation, and tend to their transportation and employer notification needs, while making them as comfortable as possible in the courthouse and giving them a private room for their deliberations. It all seemed so intuitive and self-evident to those of us who had worked in the trenches of criminal jury trials for decades. But it was brand new in Russia and, we think, of great assistance to them.

We then had a hopeful second chapter on the importance of excluding evidence—statements and objects—unlawfully seized by the police. The third chapter gave helpful suggestions on how to conduct a voir dire of a jury panel so that the 12 jurors and 2 or more alternates selected to hear a particular case would be competent, fair-minded jurors. Finally, the fourth chapter was the proposed jury instructions.

The judge and professor indulged me and my pet project this snowy late afternoon and I didn't want to abuse their patience. However, the judge grew increasingly anxious that if we didn't finish soon with the law reform expert, we would not have enough time to go to a decent restaurant before attending a 19th century opera based on a Pushkin work. We had tickets to a very popular opera in the Bolshoi. "I am NOT going to eat at McDonald's," the Judge pronounced firmly, laying down his pen and straightening himself in a huff. "Judge," I pleaded in my calmest, lowest monotone, barely moving my lips to avoid alarming the interpreter that something was amiss with the American legal team. "With respect, I think this is a little more important than whether we have a first class meal tonight or a burger and french fries." The professor stood, stretched, smiled knowingly and sighed, "Carol, besides, this is not going to work. They're never going to buy it." "Let's at least try," I begged. "Just this one and we're done."

We had already had a very promising and lengthy discussion earlier that afternoon with the law reform expert of the chapter (already translated) on excluding unlawfully seized evidence. And, we had covered all the preliminary jury instructions and then had skipped to some of the actual offense instructions. We were now back on two of the most important general instructions: Burden of Proof and Reasonable Doubt. We had an opportunity I didn't want to miss—discussing our proposed jury instructions that had not yet been translated with this top Russian law reform expert. He had read the first three chapters of the translated Bench Book and had many questions and suggestions for edits. When we got to these jury instructions, though, the interpreter had to read them to him in Russian for the first time, since they had not yet been translated in writing into Russian.

The judge and the law professor relented, and the interpreter read aloud in Russian to the Russian law reform the Burden of Proof instruction. That was easy because this topic, along with the "presumption of innocence" was in the new Russian Constitution—the defendant in a criminal case is presumed innocent and the government has the burden of proving the defendant's guilt; the defendant has no burden to prove his own innocence. Then the interpreter began reading aloud in Russian to the law reform expert the Reasonable Doubt instruction—Instruction No. 16. The judge, law professor and I exchanged glances. This was amazing. Is this how history is made?

The interpreter read Instruction No. 16:

REASONABLE DOUBT

Reasonable doubt, as the name implies, is a doubt based on reason, a doubt for which you can give a reason. It is such a doubt as would cause a juror, after careful and candid and impartial consideration of all the evidence, to be so undecided that he or she cannot say that he or she has an abiding conviction of the defendant's guilt. It is such a doubt as would cause a reasonable person to hesitate or pause in the graver or more important transactions of life. However, it is not a fanciful doubt, nor a whimsical doubt, nor a doubt based on conjecture. It is a doubt which is based on reason. The government is not required to established guilt beyond all doubt, or to a mathematical certainty or a scientific certainty. Its burden is to establish guilty beyond a reasonable doubt.

None of us on the American side of the conference table said a word to each other, but each of us smiled quietly, independently having the same thoughts as we heard the words read slowly and aloud in Russian for the first time to the law reform expert. What lay in part behind our collective smiles was the knowledge that, although we did not regard these words as a mindless incantation or tautology as some have argued, we weren't sure we were up to the task of explaining the history of the concept or its place in a trial, or in the context of other jury instructions. The truth is that Reasonable Doubt is such a part of the American criminal jury trial fabric that we take it for granted, as if its place in the scheme of life and in the instructions is obvious. Reasonable Doubt defines our criminal justice system and us as a people, even if it defies critical analysis upon careful parsing. Defense attorneys have argued to thousands, perhaps millions, of American juries for over two centuries that the government had failed to meet its high burden of proof in this or that criminal case—from shoplifting to first degree murder—so, "ladies and gentlemen, you must acquit!" Yet, many of these lawyers hadn't a clue as to what the term really meant. How were we going to handle President Yeltsin's law reform expert's hard questions that would surely follow his first hearing this term and the proposed jury instruction that purported to explain it?

We knew we'd each probably fall back clumsily on stock phrases and restatements of the instruction itself. "The instruction is a good way to avoid whimsical or fanciful verdicts; it gives the jury some guidance as to what 'reasonable doubt' means." We'd probably stumble about how, of course, reasonable doubt wasn't subject to quantification or to precise measures of metaphysical certitude (huh?). But we'd nevertheless speak hurriedly—as if to change the subject—about the different, lesser quantities of proof that exist in most civil justice adversarial trial systems. (This was such a huge subject with volumes of scholarly writings about it; who were we to presume to explain it before dinner?) We'd surely talk about standards of proof, for example, in civil fraud cases where "clear and convincing" evidence was required (where the fact trier must believe that it is highly probable that the facts exist or are true). Reasonable Doubt definitely required more proof, we'd surely say, than a "preponderance of the evidence" standard (where all that was necessary was to show that it is more probable that the fact is true or exists than it is that it does not exist) that was used in most all other civil cases. We'd end with some profundity about how the reason we in America insist on such a high level of certainty of proof—beyond a reasonable doubt—in criminal cases, is to protect innocent defendants from being wrongly convicted by erroneous guilty verdicts. We smiled as the interpreter read aloud for the first time the reasonable doubt instruction to the Russian law reform expert because we knew that Justice Antonin Scalia had just written in <u>Sullivan v. Louisiana</u>, five months earlier in June 1993, that "[d]enial of the right to a jury verdict of guilt beyond a reasonable doubt is certainly an error" of constitutional proportions, dooming any conviction obtained without such a verdict. Justice Scalia ended that Opinion by stating that "[t]he right to a trial by jury reflects, we have said, 'a profound judgment about the way in which law should be enforced and justice administered.'" It seemed so self-evident to us that it was the right and just thing to do for the Russians to adopt this high standard of proof in their jury trials, too. But, at the same time, it seemed wildly ambitious of us to make the suggestion. Reasonable doubt in Moscow? Ha!

On a mundane level, we were also mindful that state court jurists and federal circuit courts in the U.S. had written conflicting opinions for years about whether a jury instruction *describing* "reasonable doubt" should even be given at all, let alone what it should say. Many felt it was not necessary to define it. And, some of the different definitions used were vague or imprecise or required a lesser measure of proof than the words "reasonable doubt" implied. We, on the American side of the conference table anyway, were in agreement that a definition was a good thing and that the one we offered here would help jurors to better understand the concept of reasonable doubt. But we figured we'd have to defend it with our Russian law reform expert who had proven himself already to be smart, quick and wise beyond his young years. It might take a while. And the snow had now completely cloaked the cars outside our window.

As soon as the interpreter finished reading aloud her interpretation of Instruction No. 16, the Judge, the law professor, and I all leaned expectantly forward waiting for the expert to ask the interpreter to read it once more; waiting for his searching questions. Finally, after a short pause that seemed like an eternity, the law reform expert nodded his head, broke the tension, and spoke.

"Yes, I like that. We'll use it."

As simple as that.

We all rose and agreed we had done enough for one day and needed dinner (alas, at McDonald's, given the shortness of time left to us before the Opera). We shook hands with the law reform expert and the interpreter and said our thanks and farewells. We never were to see him again, but we later learned that a Reasonable Doubt instruction survived the final cuts of the Bench Book by the numerous Russian professors and law reform experts who took over the job from us. We later learned, not to our surprise or chagrin, that our Bench Book itself was apparently never published in the form it initially took. That was fine with us. At least we got the conversation going. And, many of the ideas—none original to us, yet all deeply ingrained in our American system of justice, due process and fundamental fairness, including the concept of "reasonable doubt"—are now an accepted part of the Russian law and practice and the Russian jury trial system. Indeed, in one respect you could say that they now go further than us: Russian jurors are now instructed to interpret all doubts in favor of the defendant.

Within a matter of minutes, we were each bundled up and trudging through the snow to drop our briefcases off at our Russian hotel a few blocks away before grabbing a bite to eat and catching a cab to the magnificent Bolshoi. As we walked away from the CEELI offices, our spirits were high. We were delighted about a job well done. Our persistence in pressing forward with the Reasonable Doubt instruction had paid off and made our entire trip feel like a surreal success. We agreed it would be a wonderful achievement if the Russian law professors and law reform officials, who would take charge of this project, would obtain confirming legislation or produce their own book and instructions to guide their judges and juries, and would actually adopt such a high standard of proof for their prosecutors.

Even if it takes them years of false starts to get the jury trial system working fairly for all, this high standard of proof—a reasonable doubt—would force prosecutors to think twice before bringing weak charges. This high proof standard would make the prosecutors do a proper job of preparing and presenting their case. That had to be a good thing and would protect more than a few Russian defendants from the arbitrary and predictable convictions their fathers and grand-fathers were exposed to under the Soviet system.

Our self-congratulations finished, we continued silently on our trek. The enormity of the moment was great and we were savoring it by losing ourselves in our own individual remembrances of what had just happened and of the entire amazing trip to Russia. But, here we were, just three nondescript Americans making our way on a gorgeous Moscow winter night. I broke the snowy silence with a little humor about our Reasonable Doubt accomplishment to bring us back down to a state of humility. I slapped the law professor on the back and quipped, "Hell, their juries won't understand it any better than ours do!"

EQUAL
JUSTICE

Lanny J. Davis
Alexander S. Volokh
Phillip Margolin
Sheldon Siegel
Roscoe C. Howard, Jr.
Robert Sanger
Bernard S. Grimm

"It is better to risk saving a guilty man
than to condemn an innocent one."
—Voltaire 1694-1778

LANNY J. DAVIS, a graduate of Yale College and Yale Law School, is a partner in the Washington, D.C. office of the global law firm, Orrick, Herrington & Sutcliffe. Between 1996-98, Mr. Davis served as Special Counsel to President Clinton. He now leads Orrick's unique law practice group, "Legal Crisis Communications," advising public and private companies how to deal with high-profile legal crises in the media and among political, shareholder, and other stakeholders.

Mr. Davis's memoir of his work as President Clinton's crisis communicator was published in 1999 and titled *Truth to Tell: Tell It Early, Tell It All, Tell It Yourself: Notes From My White House Education*. Tom Brokaw, formerly of NBC News, said, "Lanny Davis has written a book that should be required reading for all Washington officials and journalists alike. It's an instructive and cautionary tale of the constant struggle to know the truth of what is going on at the highest degree of government."

Davis is also the author of *Scandal: How 'Gotcha' Politics Is Destroying America*, published by Palgrave Macmillan in September 2006. Harvard Law Professor Alan M. Dershowitz wrote this about Davis' latest book: "Davis is that rare insider who is capable of being fair to all sides. He is willing to cast blame on his own party, his own candidates and even his own self, along with those on the other side who deserve blame. This perceptive look into the Washington world of equal opportunity scandal mongering must be read by Democrats and Republicans alike—and by all fair minded people who want to end the politics of mutually assured destruction."

Davis has appeared many times as a political commentator on every major network and cable Sunday morning and evening political talk show and has authored numerous op-ed columns and pieces in national newspapers and magazines. His unique "Legal Crisis Management" law group has been featured in *Forbes*, *Fortune*, and *USA Today*. He lives in Potomac with his wife, has four children and five grandchildren.

Beware Today's
Presumption of
Guilt Culture

By Lanny J. Davis

The famous principle that any person accused by the government of a crime must be presumed innocent until proven guilty beyond a reasonable doubt surprisingly appears nowhere in the U.S. Constitution. The Supreme Court in 1895, in <u>Coffin v. United States</u>, first articulated it as inherent in the meaning of "due process" rights as guaranteed in the Fifth and Fourteenth Amendments. But the Court also pointed out that this principle could be traced back to Ancient Greece, Ancient Rome, and even to Deuteronomy. Yet today more than ever that principle, rooted in long-held notions of fundamental fairness and civility, appears in greater danger than ever. In its place, in too many places, is the exact opposite—a culture based on the presumption of guilt.

Today former prosecutors become cable television talk show hosts who use rudeness to increase their ratings. They rant to an all-too-willing viewing audience that the accused must be guilty or why else would he or she be accused? As noted, this debate began a very long time ago. For example, a Roman historian, Ammianus Marcellinus, describes when Emperor Julian, who reigned from 361-363 AD. Numerius contented himself with denying his guilt—that there was not sufficient evidence against him. His adversary, Delphidius, seeing that his prosecution case would fail, pleaded with the Emperor, "Oh, illustrious Caesar! If it is sufficient to deny, what hereafter will become of the guilty?" To which Julian replied: "If it suffices to accuse, what will become of the innocent?"

Flash forward about 1,300 years to 1692; the place is Salem, Massachusetts. On January 20, nine-year-old Elizabeth Parris and eleven-year-old Abigail Williams began to exhibit strange behavior, such as blasphemous screaming, convulsive seizures, trance-like states, and mysterious spells. These girls accused three women, including Tituba (Parris' Caribbean Indian slave) and two other local women, Sarah Good and Sarah Osborne, of being witches who communed with Satan to produce their troubled state. Other young girls came forward to make accusations against other Salem women. For the next ten months, more than 20 people were hanged based on "spectral evidence": the assumption that the Devil could assume the "specter" of an innocent person. Many of the more fanatical members of the small community of Salem were convinced these hangings were just. Others who were not convinced remained silent. Finally, the Governor of Massachusetts dissolved the local Salem courts and instituted a special General Court of the colony to try the remaining witchcraft cases, which took place in May 1693. This time no one was convicted.

Flash forward another 260 years to the early 1950s. A demagogic U.S. Senator from Wisconsin named Senator Joseph McCarthy created headlines by accusing individuals and groups of being "communists" or "fellow travelers." The media uncritically reported those accusations. Most of them turned out to be false. But millions of Americans came to assume that if McCarthy made the accusation and it made it into the headlines, there must be some truth there. That presumption of guilt ruined reputations, created blacklists and misery, and in some cases, resulted in suicides.

Since Watergate up to the present day we have once again seen the evolution of a new atmosphere of presuming guilt. This time it is based on the powerful combination of hyper-partisanship, scandal, and the technological power of the Internet and cyberspace, where misinformation is spread in seconds around the globe and lives on forever in its search engines. And as most Americans wallowed in Watergate, so we wallow in this new scandal culture, with food fights on nightly cable television shows and extremist ranting on daytime radio talk shows. Of course in recent years we have also seen significant examples of real political and corporate corruption, from the serious crimes of Watergate to the sleazy bribery conspiracies of Jack Abramoff and his corrupt crew of lobbyists. But, given the power of the Internet to spread misinformation in seconds around the globe, the dangers of excess and the shattering of reputations of innocent men and women, are even greater today than they were three centuries ago in Salem, Massachusetts. That is why now is the time, more than ever, for each individual to take responsibility and resist the pressures to rush to judgment. Unfortunately, this will not happen until each of us sees danger not just for the unjustly accused but, ultimately, for ourselves.

Nothing compares to the Nazi terror and the Holocaust, but the indifference and blindness of individuals who witnessed that terror hold important lessons for today. Pastor Martin Niemoller, an anti-Nazi activist, made a now-famous comment about the phenomena of silence in the face of injustice to others:

> In Germany, they first came for the Communists, and I didn't speak up because I wasn't a Communist. Then they came for the trade unionists, and I didn't speak up because I wasn't a trade unionist. Then they came for the Catholics, but I didn't speak up because I was a Protestant. They came for the Jews, and I didn't speak up because I wasn't a Jew. Then they came for me—and by that time no one was left to speak up.

We know that in today's presumption of guilt culture we can no longer be silent. We know that the scandal and partisan attack machinery have gotten out of control. We know that the haters of the airwaves and on the blogs on the Internet have gone unchallenged, indeed rewarded, for too long. We all must know that it's time to say: Enough. We know this beyond a reasonable doubt. Before it is too late and there is no one left to speak up.

Born in Kiev, Ukraine (former U.S.S.R.), **ALEXAN-DER SASHA VOLOKH** emigrated to the United States with his family when he was two. He graduated from UCLA in 1993 with a B.S. in mathematics/economics and a B.A. in English/world literature. He received his J.D. from Harvard Law School in 2003 and his Ph.D. in economics from Harvard University in 2004. He clerked for Judge Alex Kozinski on the U.S. Court of Appeals for the Ninth Circuit, and for Justices Sandra Day O'Connor and Samuel Alito on the U.S. Supreme Court. He is now a visiting professor at Georgetown University Law Center. He is married and lives in northern Virginia. His essay is based on his article "n guilty men," published in 1997 in the *University of Pennsylvania Law Review* (vol. 146, no. 1, p. 173).

"Better that
ten guilty men..."

By Alexander Sasha Volokh

"Better that ten guilty persons escape, than that one innocent suffer," said English jurist William Blackstone. The ratio 10:1, now known as the "Blackstone ratio," expresses the classic Anglo-American ideas of the presumption of innocence and (insofar as the statement speaks of "guilt," "conviction," "imprisonment," and the like) the burden of proof "beyond a reasonable doubt" that prevails in criminal law.

But why ten? Other eminent legal authorities through the ages have put their weight behind other numbers. "One" has appeared on *Geraldo*. "It's better for four guilty men to go free than one innocent man to be imprisoned," says basketball coach George Raveling. However, "it's better to turn five guilty men loose than it is to convict one innocent one," according to Mississippi's former state executioner, roadside fruit stand operator Thomas Berry Bruce, who ought to know. "It is better to let nine guilty men free than to convict one innocent man," counters Madison, Wisconsin, lawyer Bruce Rosen. Justice Benjamin Cardozo certainly believed in five for execution, and allegedly favored ten for imprisonment, which is a bit counterintuitive. Benjamin Franklin thought "that it is better a hundred guilty persons should escape than one innocent person should suffer." Mario Puzo's Don Clericuzio heard about letting a hundred guilty men go free and, "struck almost dumb by the beauty of the concept...became an ardent patriot." Denver radio talk show host Mike Rosen claims to have heard it argued "in the abstract, that it's better that 1000 guilty men go free than one innocent man be imprisoned," and says of the American judicial system, "Well, we got our wish."

And it's not just the number of guilty men that varies from formulation to formulation. Even the number of innocent men depends on the speaker. A Georgia circuit court held in 1877 that it was "better that some guilty ones should escape than that many innocent persons should be subjected to the expense and disgrace attendant upon being arrested upon a criminal charge." Moreover, in Judge Henry J. Friendly's opinion, "most Americans would agree it is better to allow a considerable number of guilty persons to go free than to convict any appreciable number of innocent men." It is unclear whether a "considerable" number is greater or less than an "appreciable" one.

* * *

A British editorial recently surmised that the "bias against punishment" has its roots in "the most famous of all miscarriages of justice: Christ's crucifixion." In fact, however, people have been mulling over the innocent-guilty tradeoff at least since the ancient Greeks. Aristotle allegedly wrote that it is a "serious matter to decide [that a slave] is free; but it is much more serious to condemn a free man as a slave," and gave the same judgment about convicting innocents of murder. Others date the maxim to the codes of Athens. Deposed Panamanian leader (and perhaps amateur classical scholar) Manuel Noriega has claimed the saying went back to Socrates (though he did not provide a citation).

According to some researchers, though, the maxim is considerably older. According to Ninth Circuit Judge Alex Kozinski, this "popular notion" is just something "we have always said." Benjamin Franklin claims that the maxim "has been long and generally approved; never, that I know of, controverted." A then-future U.S. president, John Adams, dated the saying (using a variety of numbers between five and twenty) back to the beginning of law itself, saying that "there never was a system of laws in the world, in which this rule did not prevail."

And, on some accounts, the precept was handed down from Someone who was around "in the beginning." Consider the following haggle between Abraham and God in Genesis 18:23–:32:

> And Abraham drew near, and said, Wilt thou also destroy the righteous with the wicked? Peradventure there be fifty righteous within the city: wilt thou also destroy and not spare the place for the fifty righteous that are therein? That be far from thee to do after this manner, to slay the righteous with the wicked: and that the righteous should be as the wicked, that be far from thee: Shall not the Judge of all the earth do right?
>
> And the Lord said, If I find in Sodom fifty righteous within the city, then I will spare all the place for their sakes.
>
> And Abraham answered and said, Behold now, I have taken upon me to speak unto the Lord, which am but dust and ashes: Peradventure there shall lack five of the fifty righteous: wilt thou destroy all the city for lack of five?
>
> And he said, If I find there forty and five, I will not destroy it.
>
> And he spake unto him yet again, and said, Peradventure there shall be forty found there.
>
> And he said, I will not do it for forty's sake.
>
> And he said unto him, Oh let not the Lord be angry, and I will speak: Peradventure there shall thirty be found there.

And he said, I will not do it, if I find thirty there.

And he said, Behold now, I have taken upon me to speak unto the Lord: Peradventure there shall be twenty found there.

And he said, I will not destroy it for twenty's sake.

And he said, Oh let not the Lord be angry, and I will speak yet but this once: Peradventure ten shall be found there.

And he said, I will not destroy it for ten's sake.

What a lawyer! As it turns out, even the requisite ten were lacking. Nor were any innocents killed: There were only four righteous people in the city, and they were all saved, though they lost their real estate. Previously, God had killed the entire human population of the Earth because of its wickedness (except for Noah and his family) in a mass capital punishment which, although carried out without the benefits of a jury or any other due process protections, apparently also produced neither false positives nor false negatives. It is said that one day there will be another massive (post-) capital punishment, which will also produce neither false positives nor false negatives. These methods, however, may only be acceptable criminal procedure for God Himself, Who may do whatever He likes.

Commandments to man can be found in Exodus 23:7, by the same Author, in which God rejects the tradeoff between convicting the guilty and convicting the innocent, and simply commands, "the innocent and righteous slay thou not." Despite the seeming absoluteness of this command, the twelfth century Judeo-Spanish legal theorist Moses Maimonides interpreted it to imply that "it is better and more satisfactory to acquit a thousand guilty persons than to put a single innocent man to death once in a way." He called this the "290th Negative Commandment" and argued that executing an accused criminal on the basis of anything less would lead to a slippery slope of decreasing burdens of proof until convictions would be merely "according to the judge's caprice. Hence the Exalted One has shut this door" against the use of presumptive evidence.

Not all gods, however, are as strict as the Exalted One. The Roman emperor Trajan, who was later deified, wrote—in much looser terms—that a person ought not "to be condemned on suspicion; for it was preferable that the crime of a guilty man should go unpunished than an innocent man be condemned."

The most celebrated divine commandment related to punishing the innocent comes, of course, from Blackstone himself. Evidence of Blackstone's divinity is provided by an Arkansas district court, which ruled in 1991 that "Blackstone is, in the law at least, immortal," and evidence of His miraculous works is supplied by Lord Avonmore, who wrote: "He it was that first gave the law the air of science. He found it a skeleton, and clothed it with life, color and complexion; he embraced the cold statute, and by his touch it grew into youth, health, and beauty."

The maxim is also valid in Islam, according to Ayatollah Hossein Ali Montazeri, who was first in line to become the leader of Iran during the mid-1980s. One British writer, commenting on the death of innocent bystanders at the hands of the police during anti-Irish Republican Army crackdowns, wrote, "for a Catholic, oddly enough, it may be better to be shot suddenly like that if you are innocent, than if you are guilty." This view, however, is either out of the ordinary or not widely advertised.

To date, no major religious wars have been fought over the precise acceptable number of guilty men.

*   *   *

While the maxim of the guilty men has had wide currency throughout English and American law, it has not been without its detractors. For instance, Jeremy Bentham, founder of utilitarianism, warned against the warm fuzzy feeling that comes from excessive regard for protecting hypothetical innocent defendants:

We must be on our guard against those sentimental exaggerations which tend to give crime impunity, under the pretext of insuring the safety of innocence. Public applause has been, so to speak, set up to auction. At first it was said to be better to save several guilty men, than to condemn a single innocent man; others, to make the maxim more striking, fix the number ten; a third made this ten a hundred, and a fourth made it a thousand. All these candidates for the prize of humanity have been outstripped by I know not how many writers, who hold, that, in no case, ought an accused person to be condemned, unless evidence amount to mathematical or absolute certainty. According to this maxim, nobody ought to be punished, lest an innocent man be punished.

Some less theoretical minds went somewhat further in their skepticism. German chancellor Otto von Bismarck is said to have remarked that "it is better that ten innocent men suffer than one guilty man escape." Ditto Feliks Dzerzhinsky, founder of the Soviet secret police: "Better to execute ten innocent men than to leave one guilty man alive." Major Nungo, a Colombian military prosecutor, explains the rationale: "For us military men, everybody is guilty until proved otherwise.... Better to condemn an innocent man than to acquit a guilty one, because among the innocent condemned there may be a guilty man."

*　　*　　*

It is probably fair to say, however, that (to put it mildly) these last authorities do not exactly come from the mainstream of the Anglo-American tradition. To those who accept the maxim's fundamental logic, Blackstone's "ten" still seems to be the most popular choice. All innocent readers who have never been convicted may now take a moment to thank Blackstone's maxim for having inspired American criminal law and the burden of proof "beyond a reasonable doubt." All guilty readers who have been acquitted may do so too.

Consider, however, the story of the Chinese law professor, who listened as a British lawyer explained that Britons were so enlightened that they believed it was better that ninety-nine guilty men go free than that one innocent man be executed. The Chinese professor thought for a second and asked, "Better for whom?"

PHILLIP MARGOLIN served as a Peace Corps Volunteer in Liberia, West Africa after graduating from The American University in Washington, D.C. and worked his way through the New York University School of Law by teaching junior high school in the South Bronx. After a clerkship with the Chief Judge of the Oregon Court of Appeals, he spent twenty five years practicing criminal defense. Phil has handled thirty homicide cases, including several where his clients faced the death penalty, he was the first Oregon attorney to use the Battered Woman's Syndrome in defense of a battered woman who was accused of killing an abusive spouse and he has argued in the United States Supreme Court.

Phil is also the author of *Proof Positive* and eleven other legal thrillers, all of which have been *New York Times* bestsellers. He is the President of "Chess for Success," a non-profit that provides free after-school chess programs to children in more than fifty Title I elementary and middle schools in Oregon. The program uses chess to teach learning skills that can be used in the classroom and life. Most important, he has been married to his fantastic wife, Doreen, since 1968 and is the father of Ami and Daniel, the world's best children.

"How Can You
Represent Someone if You
Know They're Guilty?"

By Phillip Margolin

"How can you represent somcone if you know they're guilty?" is the first thing many people ask me when they find out I was a criminal defense attorney for twenty-five years. I never take offense at the question because I know that this is genuinely puzzling to those who are not aware of the way our remarkable American justice system works.

When I was in the seventh grade—probably as a result of an overdose of Perry Mason novels—I decided that I wanted to be a criminal defense attorney when I grew up. I wasn't attracted to this profession for any deep philosophical reasons. Trying murder cases just sounded exciting. It wasn't until I served in the Peace Corps that I began to truly understand what the American justice system was really all about and why being a defender of the accused—even those who were truly awful people—was such a noble profession.

When I arrived in Liberia in 1965, I was twenty-one years old and Canada was the only foreign country I'd ever visited. During my two-year tour, I saw first hand what it was like to live in a nation that did not have the Rule of Law. When Liberians did something that displeased the government, the secret police came in the middle of the night and dragged them away to a concentration camp in the bush, where they were tortured or killed. These accused did not have a right to an attorney, the right to remain silent or the right to due process of law, all of which Americans take for granted.

Countries like China and Iran use their legal systems to oppress their people. America uses it to protect our citizens. That's not to say that the system is without flaws. Any system in which humans are involved will have flaws because the people who run it don't always live up to the high ideals of the people who proposed it. But considering how powerful our government is and how oppressive it could be if the people in power wanted to abuse that power, it is pretty amazing. No event brought this home to me more than the resignation of President Richard Nixon. Here was a man who was facing impeachment for running a burglary ring. He had all of the character traits we find in dictators who routinely arrest judges and politicians who displease them. Yet President Nixon never tried to suspend the Constitution or close down Congress. Instead, he resigned his office, permitting a peaceful transfer of power to his Vice-President.

When I returned to America from Liberia I was a flaming patriot who truly appreciated the greatness of our system of government. The area where that greatness is highlighted is in the criminal justice system. When our founding fathers developed the American justice system they could have devised a system that assumed that those arrested by the authorities were guilty and which put the burden of proving innocence on the accused, but they didn't because they had just broken free from an oppressive government that did not value the rights of the colonists. The founding fathers viewed government as evil and wanted to make certain that the power of government was not misused, so they put in place safeguards to protect the innocent victims of government oppression or those who were simply accused by mistake. The greatest of these safeguards is the presumption of innocence.

When a person stands trial, the jury must begin with the assumption that the accusations against him are false. A juror can only find for the government at the end of the trial if the prosecution has erased all reasonable doubts about the defendant's innocence from that juror's mind. This is a very high burden, and it should be. There are occasions when a person is arrested in good faith but is factually not guilty and other situations where the government misuses its power and arrests innocent people to punish them for their political beliefs. Whenever I am asked how I can represent someone if I know they are guilty I explain that the guilt or innocence of a defendant is never an issue in a criminal case: In every case, the only question is whether the Government, which has accused the defendant of wrongdoing, can support its accusation with proof that erases all reasonable doubts about the innocence of the accused. When I selected jurors to hear a case I asked them if they understood that my client and I could go to a movie during the trial and only return for the verdict, because my client had no obligation to put on evidence or examine the evidence presented by the Government, which had the sole burden of presenting a case.

When I returned from Africa, I understood the importance of the safeguards provided by our justice system. During my years in practice I saw these safeguards work to prevent injustice. I represented roughly thirty individuals charged with homicide, including many who faced a death sentence. Of all my cases, the two that made the greatest impression on me were two murder cases that I was hired to handle on appeal after the defendants had been convicted of murder and sentenced to life in prison. In both of these cases I discovered—to my horror—that the defendants had not committed murder and had not been involved in any way with the death of the victim. Those who have not experienced it cannot imagine the emotional burden on a defense attorney in this type of situation. I was able to overturn these convictions on appeal and free both men from prison when their cases were tried again. My clients and I appreciated a system of justice that provides opportunities to correct injustices.

I get very upset when I hear politicians malign attorneys. In every profession—politicians, bus drivers, doctors, television repairmen—there are a few bad apples, but most attorneys—like most people in general—are hardworking, decent individuals. The outrage in the public against criminal defense attorneys and the criminal justice system usually reaches a peak when there is an acquittal in a high-profile case. Ask anyone who is really involved in the system how often justice is thwarted and they will tell you a just result is reached in all but a handful of cases. Any District Attorney whose office isn't running a conviction rate of ninety percent or more should be looking for another job. That's because the police are usually right when they arrest someone and they usually can produce the evidence to support the arrest. Most defendants plead guilty. Of those who go to trial and are guilty, most are convicted. Then there are those who should be acquitted, either because they are innocent of the charges or the government failed to prove guilt beyond a reasonable doubt. These cases represent a miniscule percentage of the cases brought against those charged with crime, but they are very important.

In America, a jury of people who don't know anything about the case and are not acquainted with the defendant, the prosecutor, the defense attorney or the witnesses screen the government's accusations. Anytime jurors acquit because they have a reasonable doubt they are obeying the law. Anytime jurors have a reasonable doubt but convict to please the public they are worse than the most horrible criminal because they are undermining the system of justice that makes this country great. It is very important that a serial killer like Ted Bundy or a despised terrorist receive a fair trial. If our system can give a fair trial to someone who everyone hates then the average citizen can feel secure about receiving justice if he is ever charged with a crime.

So, the answer to the question, "How can you represent someone if you know they are guilty?" is "Easily and with a clear conscience." Every time I did my best for anyone charged with a crime I was helping to maintain one of the greatest systems of justice ever devised.

San Francisco attorney **SHELDON SIEGEL** is the *New York Times* best selling author of five critically-acclaimed courtroom dramas: *Special Circumstances, Incriminating Evidence, Criminal Intent, Final Verdict* and *The Confession*. A graduate of Boalt Law School at the University of California at Berkeley, Mr. Siegel has been in private practice for more than twenty years. He is currently with the San Francisco office of Sheppard, Mullin, Richter & Hampton LLP. His books have sold millions of copies worldwide and have been translated into seven languages. Mr. Siegel is a frequent lecturer and panelist. He lives in Marin County, California, with his wife, Linda, and their twin sons, Alan and Stephen. He is currently working on his next novel.

Reasonable Doubt:
Challenging Times Test our
Fundamental Principles

By Sheldon Siegel

Whether you've been cited for a minor traffic violation or arrested for first degree murder, it is a cornerstone of our criminal justice system—however flawed—that the prosecutors must prove your guilt beyond a reasonable doubt. Even the most strident critics of our legal system find it difficult to question this basic right.

We live in challenging times in which our fundamental principles—including legal concepts such as due process and reasonable doubt—are tested every day. In the rapidly-changing post-9/11 world, we have been forced to sacrifice some of our basic freedoms in the interest of public safety. From the enhanced security at airports to the increased military presence in various parts of the world, we must draw increasingly difficult lines as to how much we are willing to compromise our principles in order to thwart potential threats.

The ramifications take many forms. A stark and highly-publicized example of the complexity of this issue is our government's treatment of the detainees at Guantanamo Bay. A second and equally compelling issue involves the treatment of accused war criminals—the most notable of which is former Iraqi leader Saddam Hussein. One can only begin to imagine the difficulty of bringing Osama bin Laden to justice if he is ever captured. Are individuals dubbed "enemy combatants" entitled to the presumption of innocence and the other legal protections generally afforded to American citizens? Are deposed dictators who are accused of war crimes entitled to the same legal rights as other criminal defendants? Does the threat of terrorism and the desire for public safety outweigh the basic civil liberties that we've accepted for more than two centuries? Where do we draw the lines?

These issues are hardly new. From the American Revolution War to the Civil War to the two World Wars to the modern conflicts in Vietnam and Iraq, there has been a compelling need to bring certain combatants (or former combatants) to justice. This is inherently tricky in that the practical realities dictate that the victors of such conflicts set the rules. In the modern era, the U.S. and its allies set the rules for highly-publicized war crimes tribunals such as the Nuremburg trials. In more recent times, the U.S. government is setting many of the ground rules for the logistics of the trial of Saddam Hussein. For obvious reasons, the U.S. Military must handle all aspects of the operations at Guantanamo Bay.

Of necessity, the individual cases require different ground rules. In the case of Saddam Hussein, there are compelling reasons for his case to proceed in Iraq and for justice to be handled within the framework of the Iraqi legal system—such as it is. The practical reality is that the U.S. has a vested interest in concluding these proceedings. It also raises some difficult and fundamental questions as to whether a deposed dictator and accused war criminal is entitled to any conventional due process rights that we take for granted under U.S. law (even where such rights are generally not available under Iraqi law).

The U.S. has a substantial interest in demonstrating that even a deposed dictator who is accused of war crimes is entitled to some degree of legal process. Our democratic institutions rely on the principle that we operate within the scope of the law. The concept of reasonable doubt—even for Saddam Hussein—separates our legal system and our values from totalitarian regimes. I would argue that even though Saddam Hussein did not afford any constitutional rights to the people of Iraq, a budding democracy (hopefully) must operate under fundamental rules of law. That rule of law would include basic rights such as due process and reasonable doubt.

The situation involving the detainees at Guantanamo Bay is equally difficult. We have limited information about many of the detainees. It appears that some have been detained because of an alleged association (however tenuous) with terrorist elements. What is certain is that their legal status remains murky. The Bush administration quickly dubbed them as "enemy combatants," an amorphous concept that appears to have no legal meaning. Does this mean that they are prisoners of war (who are entitled to the benefits of the Geneva Convention)? Does it mean that they are accused criminals (who are subject to the rights afforded accused criminals)? Many of these individuals have been in legal limbo for three years.

The Bush administration originally proposed trying the detainees in newly-formed military tribunals where the rights of the accused would have been severely curtailed. The U.S. Supreme Court rejected this proposal and refused to deprive the detainees at Guantanamo Bay of certain fundamental rights. The administration has also recently (and grudgingly) acknowledged that detainees are entitled to the benefits of the Geneva Convention.

The harsh realities of our increasingly-complex world make "bright-line" answers to issues involving accused war criminals and terrorists elusive. Those of us who fancy ourselves as civil libertarians reflexively argue that even accused terrorists should be entitled to certain fundamental rights such as due process and reasonable doubt. I would also acknowledge, however, that it is a lot easier to be a civil libertarian when you aren't guarding a cell block at Guantanamo Bay. I would postulate that certain base-line civil rights are so fundamental that they should not be compromised unless absolutely essential to promote public safety and the safety of our military personnel. The concept of proving guilt beyond a reasonable doubt is one of those principles.

Ultimately, the final answers will come down to a question of how much we are prepared to compromise our values for safety, order and predictability. It is a fundamental issue of our times and the stakes are high. If we give up these fundamental principles, we risk losing what generations of Americans have fought so dearly to preserve for more than two hundred years. And I believe that beyond a reasonable doubt.

ROSCOE CONKLIN HOWARD, JR. is a partner in the Washington, D.C. office of Troutman Sanders, LLP where he specializes in white-collar criminal matters, corporate compliance and ethics issues, and complex litigation.

Mr. Howard served as the United States Attorney for the District of Columbia from August 2001 until June 2004. He was a tenured, full professor at the University of Kansas School of Law from 1994 until his appointment as United States Attorney. Mr. Howard has also twice served as an Associate Independent Counsel in the investigations of Samuel R. Pierce, Secretary of Housing and Urban Development under President Reagan and A. Michael Espy, Secretary of Agriculture under President Clinton. Mr. Howard previously served as an Assistant U.S. Attorney in the District of Columbia from 1984 to 1987, and in the Eastern District of Virginia from 1987 to 1991 in both the Richmond and Alexandria offices.

Mr. Howard served as a Staff Attorney for the Federal Trade Commission's Bureau of Competition from 1981 to 1984 and was an Associate in two District of Columbia law firms after his graduation from the University of Virginia School of Law in 1977. He served as a law clerk to the Honorable Raymond L. Finch of the Territorial Circuit in St. Croix, U.S. Virgin Islands immediately following law school. He is a 1974 graduate of Brown University and a 1970 graduate of Culver Military Academy in Culver, Indiana.

Mr. Howard is a member of the Editorial Board of the National Law Journal and is a member of the Virginia and District of Columbia Bars. He is currently on the Board of Directors for the Canada-United States Fulbright Committee and Roger Williams University School of Law in Bristol, Rhode Island. Mr. Howard was named as one of Washington's Top Lawyers, by *Washingtonian* magazine in December 2004, and was honored as one of America's Top Black Lawyers in *Black Enterprise* magazine in November 2003.

Reasonable Doubt
in a Nation of Immigrants

By Roscoe C. Howard, Jr.

We are a nation of immigrants. Yet, immigration has become a matter of intense social and political focus in America; nonetheless, its effects in our criminal justice system have received little attention. The task is not to enact more laws to criminalize the drive to become a contributing citizen; it is to assure that our justice is truly blind to their origins when they are forced to confront accusation of a crime.

As millions of individuals from a vast array of backgrounds, cultures, races and educational backgrounds continue to flock to this country, they inevitably come into contact with our criminal courts. Fair assimilation of new arrivals in those circumstances is not only uncertain, it is sadly improbable; for our history manifests a persistently unbalanced burden on minorities confronted with our criminal law. We are, therefore, challenged to overcome the inertia of imposing that burden on new arrivals who are wholly unaware of their rights in the face of investigation or prosecution. We have endured shameful periods in our history. Too often we have endured legally abhorrent institutions predicated on ethnicity and origin—slavery, racial segregation, "Jim Crow" Laws, lynchings—a murderous act named for a judge— and the World War II internment camps. The trappings of law won't do. The question is whether the protections enjoyed by our longer-term residents will be a reality to our new ones.

If you don't speak English, and come from a country lacking the common law—to say nothing of the elements of the Bill of Rights and western democracy—you have no concept of the predominant protecting principle of our criminal law—that the government cannot impose any criminal sanction upon you unless it can prove—without any assistance from you—that you are guilty of a specifically defined offense beyond a reasonable doubt. Concepts of reasonableness, doubt, relative levels of proof and the right of an accused to put the government to its proof are natural to those of us raised, trained and skilled in our system. How do we pass on those crucial precepts to someone faced with a criminal charge who has no grasp of their meaning?

Immigrants often believe courts serve a very different purpose than seeking truth and determining guilt. As an individual is faced with the prospect of prosecution in this country, the question he or she often asks is how do I prove my innocence? Or, more importantly, how do I make a jury, in this country, understand my values? As the United States Attorney for the District of Columbia, I investigated violence between married individuals who came to Washington, D.C. from other countries. It was often "explained" to me that the type of violence we prosecuted was tolerated and even taught in the native lands of some defendants. Recently, I listened to a radio interview of a Muslim man who had recently immigrated to the United States. The man stated that he will not tolerate a woman who disobeys the wishes of her husband or father, or who works, or appears in public without certain clothing. He said that he was raising the "standards" of his adopted country and he would not abide by the laws of the United States.

The challenge with such defendants is to use the tools of the accused's protection while allowing her or him to express their cultural values. Where those values conflict with our laws, the task is particularly difficult.

I do not write to defend these positions, or condone them. However, in any criminal trial, it is the job of the attorneys to ensure that their clients are understood. It is the prosecutor's task to determine what constitutes a crime and to gauge what the appropriate disposition or punishment should be. As we become a more diverse society, our halls of education do not follow. In making a judge or jury understand a potential foreign born defendant, we often have lawyers who have no clue what many immigrants in this country have faced, have been taught or believe in, trying to guide them through our judicial system.

Just after the horrific day of September 11, 2001, federal prosecutors and agents across this country were asked to go into Muslim neighborhoods to talk to the communities, interview its residents and learn what they could about individuals who might be pursuing the same goals as the September 11th hijackers. Our ranks were woefully thin of any person who could inform me or my colleagues of what to expect once we entered such a community. How should we approach these individuals? Will they speak English since we did not speak Arabic? Will they trust us or turn on potential targets? We were ill equipped for this assignment, and had no guide for our efforts.

Our burden of proof in the criminal justice system is a heavy one: beyond a reasonable doubt. Nevertheless, that standard is appropriate for a government that professes fairness and equality. However, for those people who are caught in the system, the struggle is how to make oneself understood and how to explain one's actions?

We must understand that one way to make the criminal justice system responsive to the society we are becoming, is to recognize our obligation to enrich the ranks of attorneys and law enforcement with those who now make up our society.

The result will be a more just criminal justice system. When I was a law professor, just before my appointment as United States Attorney, I often asked my students to imagine that they found themselves in an African-American neighborhood where they were the only white person. You are arrested by a group of African-American police officers and charged with a horrendous crime in which the victim is an African-American child. Immediately, you are taken to jail and then a courtroom, where you are confronted by an African-American judge, faced with an all African-American jury, and appointed an African-American attorney to represent you. You are then told your trial is about to start. My question to my students was: "Do you think you will get a fair trial?"

That scene is played out many times over in this country, but only in reverse. The African-Americans could be replaced by almost any racial minority. When you live in a country where unfairness to minorities has been documented and proven, it is hard for minorities to believe that justice will prevail when they encounter a system devoid of diversity.

An easier case can be made in the context of gender diversity. A female rape victim will not want to come forward to tell her story when the person that is listening to her, embarrassing, terrifying experience is a male. It is imperative that women populate the ranks of prosecutors. Therefore, another reason to encourage diversity is to increase the chance that all factors bearing on a case have a reasonable chance to come out in a courtroom.

In the same vein, it is important that all minorities have options when seeking counsel. Individuals should have the chance to explain to law enforcement, a judge, or a jury the circumstances that brought them before the court. They will feel that their stories have been told, if they can be represented by competent counsel who come from their background.

By the same token, minorities should be encouraged, prodded and recruited to join the ranks of prosecutors so that individuals who wish to explain their actions by pointing to the values they were taught in a far different culture have that opportunity. When the putative defendant comes from a "diverse" background, the "whys" of many crimes can be better understood when the prosecutor shares that background.

A more diverse justice system will not, and should not, change what constitutes a crime under the laws of this nation. But when "reasonable doubt" is the applicable standard, a system that allows a potential defendant the opportunity to be represented by someone whom he or she trusts and understands, and who understands him or her and can explain his or her plight, is a more just system. In turn, prosecutors who also share the background of a defendant, and can even sympathize, may make it easier for a jury to understand why the prosecution, nevertheless, is necessary.

We talk about assimilation of newly transported immigrants to this country, but if we are to be a "justice" system, some of the assimilation should be taken on by us. We are a long way from a perfect justice system, and we must heed the lessons of the past. Bringing people of diverse backgrounds into our criminal justice system will provide more comfort that when a jury finds guilt "beyond a reasonable doubt" it truly means it.

ROBERT SANGER has been a criminal defense lawyer in Santa Barbara, California for over 32 years. He has been certified as a Criminal Law Specialist by the State Bar for 25 years. Mr. Sanger has defended people accused of crimes in high-profile cases—he was co-counsel with Tom Mesereau on the Michael Jackson case—as well as cases of little interest beyond that of the parties. He has handled a number of capital cases and has been active in attempting to bring legal and public attention to the abolition of the death penalty. Mr. Sanger recently published a law review article on the legal flaws in California's death penalty which has given rise to the current California State Senate investigation of the capital punishment system. He is a partner in the Santa Barbara firm of Sanger & Swysen and lives on a small ranch with his wife and youngest daughter.

Human Dignity
and Respect

By Robert Sanger

I believe beyond a reasonable doubt in standing up for the dignity of the human beings who I come to represent in the criminal courts. I believe in demanding respect for them from the system that is prosecuting them. Some of my clients have been famous, most have not. I have represented the truly innocent and some who have not been innocent, whether or not they were guilty as charged. I have represented the incredibly wealthy and the abjectly indigent. All of my clients suffer the embarrassment of being accused and the murmurs behind their backs that, at least, where there is smoke there is fire. Some of my clients, perhaps charged with a heinous murder or other crime of violence, may be regarded by society as lacking any dignity or as being unworthy of any respect whatsoever.

In fact, any criminal defense lawyer will tell you that the most frequently asked question at a cocktail party is, "How can you defend those people?" The question is asked again and again. I have heard other lawyers give responses, for instance, "To stand up for the rights of the guilty is to secure the rights of the innocent." Or, "You wouldn't ask that question if the person accused were your son or your daughter." Or, "It is an adversarial system and I am just doing my job." None of these answers are incorrect.

But none of these answers captures the essence of why I get up in the morning and come to work. I still have an enthusiasm for my part of the legal profession after over three decades of defending the accused. And I have a sense that what I do—or try my best to do—is not only correct but is at the core of my beliefs. It is my belief that it is my job to stand up for the dignity of the accused, no matter who she or he is, no matter what the charge is and no matter what she or he actually did. It is my belief that my duty is to demand respect for that human being.

No doubt, these beliefs meet with skepticism, hence the incredulous looks on the faces of those cocktail party interlocutors. But those interlocutors have not lived a day, let alone a life, in the criminal justice system. My strong beliefs are based on a lifetime of standing beside "those people"—those human beings accused by the government of crime. Let me tell you what I see and perhaps my belief in standing up for their dignity and in demanding respect for them will not be so unintelligible.

Let us take the paradigm case imagined by those skeptical interlocutors. Assume that I am representing someone who is charged with a serious crime. For our story, let us say, he is a man, he is poor, he is unkempt, he lacks social graces and he is angry. He has been to prison before and he remains in the custody of the Sheriff because high bail has been set, perhaps for good reason. My job is to stand up for his dignity—something he may think he lost long ago—and to demand that the system accord him respect. Why?

Well, when I walk into the courtroom, there is the prosecutor wearing a pin-striped suit seated at the counsel table on the side closest to the jury. He has little regard for my client as a person and sees it as his job to put him in prison. Next to the prosecutor is the arresting officer in full uniform who sees my client as the collar she made and wants to see him go to prison. The bailiff, a deputy sheriff who has the assignment only because he injured his knee wrestling some other "crook" to the ground, is waiting for the order to transport him to prison. The judge, seated three feet higher than everyone else with the Great Seal of the government and a couple of flags behind her, is more than likely a former prosecutor. The court clerk and the court stenographer go to lunch with the rest of them.

My client is handcuffed, chain wrapped and clad in an orange jump suit. He is seated in a plastic chair that does not swivel, farthest from the jury and hovered over by the armed bailiff and his backups. The only person in the world—and certainly the only person in the courtroom—there to stand up for the dignity of the accused and demand that he be treated with respect, is the defense lawyer.

This view of the courtroom may sound a bit cynical but is remarkably accurate. Even under the best of circumstances, with the most enlightened participants, the process is stacked against the accused. A wealthy person, perhaps someone theretofore loved and respected by the community, faces some level of animosity, distrust and suspicion once they become the accused. The presumption of innocence is a goal but it is not real. It is counter-intuitive. The reality is a presumption of guilt. It is the solemn duty of the criminal defense lawyer to reverse that de facto presumption of guilt and to stand up for the dignity and respect due to the accused. Only with that beginning can the system be expected to accord justice.

The criminal justice system is like a train. It is ponderous; it has a lot of momentum and processes a large number of people in an impersonal way. There are plenty of participants in this railroad to see that the criminal justice train runs and keeps moving. And, like the train conductor, even the good people in the criminal justice system start to impersonally punch the tickets of the passengers aboard. The judges, prosecutors, clerks and bailiffs do not see people, they come to see "cases," case numbers or code sections: "Call up that murder case." Or, "Let's take CR975874." Or, "Where is that Penal Code 187 case?" The defense lawyer is the person in the room to remind them that, "This is an accusation against Mr. ____, who is a human being." It requires slowing the train down so that the system can acknowledge the dignity and respect due the client—the same respect shown the prosecutor and any other civil litigant who comes before the court.

Standing up for the dignity of, and respect for, the criminally accused involves investigating and re-investigating every case thoroughly, poring over the reports and documents, re-testing the scientific evidence and rethinking the prosecution's theory of the case. It involves listening to the client and his or her family; learning about who the client really is. It may also manifest itself in little things, sometimes as simple as forcing the judge to order the bailiff to remove the client's handcuffs and let him or her sit, like any other litigant, at the counsel table. Sometimes, it is buying a suit for an indigent client. Sometimes it is helping a more prominent client maintain the sanctuary of his or her home in the months leading up to trial. It is helping each client realize some sense of that elusive presumption of innocence despite public opinion and sensationalist reporters. It is recognizing that the client—wealthy or indigent, famous or infamous, out on bail or in custody—must be treated with dignity and respect, first by his or her own lawyer, and then by the system.

So that is what the true defense lawyer faces every day. There are plenty of people with plenty of power who will see that the guilty are convicted and punished. The power of the government is awesome and no "dream team" will ever have the resources to match the international network of law enforcement officials, computers and resources at the hands of even local prosecutors. What gives any accused person a chance against this system is the commitment of his or her criminal defense lawyer to stand up for the client no matter what it takes. There are a few committed and often courageous defenders, private and public, who do not themselves become so cynical that they cannot stand up for the accused no matter who that accused may be. I believe—and I believe it beyond a reasonable doubt—that it is a privilege to be a member of that part of the legal profession whose duty it is to stand up for the dignity of the accused and to demand that the system accord that human being respect.

BERNARD S. GRIMM graduated from Kings College in Wilkes Barre, Pennsylvania in 1979 with a 3.98 G.P.A. National Honor Society, Summa Cum Laude. From 1980 to 1983 he was a student at Antioch School of Law, Washington, D.C. From 1984 to 1989 he was a Trial Attorney at the D.C. Public Defender's Office, Washington, D.C. Since 2004, he has worked at the Law Office of Bernard S. Grimm.

Mr. Grimm tried over 200 jury trials. He was voted top 100 Best Lawyers in America and was selected by *Washingtonian* magazine as one of Top 100 Lawyers in the Metropolitan Area 2004-2005. In 2004 he was awarded the Kenneth R. Mundy Trial Lawyer of the Year by Superior Court Trial Lawyers Association. He has successfully tried: <u>United States v. Johnson</u>, Judge Lee, 5 Count Death Penalty case Eastern District of Virginia, Alexandria, VA, 1998; <u>United States v. Armand Parker</u>, Judge Stewart, Rock Hill, South Carolina, 1997; 26 Defendant/Rico Drug Conspiracy, Judge William Nickerson, U.S. District Court, Baltimore, Maryland, 1995, 6 Month Trial. Mr. Grimm often appears as a Legal Commentator on FOX News, CNN and Court TV. He teaches at the Georgetown University Law Center Clinical Program, New Jersey Avenue.

Justifying Justice

By Bernard S. Grimm

My practice principally involves representing murderers, drug dealers and everyone in between. These are people who have decimated their own communities with violence and peddled poison in the streets of our nation's Capitol. Nonetheless they are entitled to the presumption of innocence and that the case against them be proved beyond a reasonable doubt. Unfortunately, since the advent of the War on Crime, many prosecutors and police officers have lost sight of these principles, which serve as the bedrock and pillars of our system. Although this may sound trite or corny, it is the system of Justice created over 100 years ago and at a great cost to many.

Today, prosecutors routinely withhold evidence of a client's innocence on a regular basis; police officers lie in court on a daily basis. This is what fuels my passion. Not a week goes by in court, where I don't witness an injustice being committed upon some alleged criminal. With that being said I believe that people who commit serious crimes belong in prison; it's how you convict them that troubles me.

Many of my cases come to mind. I will highlight just one. Unfortunately this case is by no means representative of all prosecutions and unfortunately it is not the worst abuse of police lawlessness.

Last year I represented a young man named Donnell Vaughn who was arrested and charged with two counts of attempted murder. Mr. Vaughn was 24-years-old and had no prior criminal record.

Briefly, according to the police, this is what happened:

On June 25th at about 3 a.m. two police officers, sitting in a squad car, heard the sounds of gunfire. Moments later they observed a red sedan speed by with the rear windshield shot out. They followed and a chase ensued. After a mile the car screeched to a stop and three young black men jumped out. Mr. Vaughn, my client, was the only one caught.

He told the police that he was riding in the backseat of the car when suddenly the back window was shot out. Minutes later the police received a radio transmission that two young women had been shot several blocks away five minutes earlier. The police brought the victims back to where my client was. In handcuffs and standing next to the red car. Neither victim could identify him but reiterated that the red car sitting in the middle of the road was involved in the shooting. Specifically they said that the driver pointed a gun at them and fired into their car, injuring both of them.

The police later admitted they had no evidence that my client was the shooter but they arrested him anyway. He was brought to the police station, remained in handcuffs or shackled to a wall and interrogated for over four hours.

He maintained that he was in the back seat when the gunshots rang out.

Multiple police officers and Detectives confronted him. They cursed at him and told him he was a liar. Specifically they told him the following:

1.   That witnesses had seen him throw a gun from the car and that his fingerprints were on it. This was a lie.

2.   That if he cooperated he would in all likelihood be given community service and have his record expunged. A lie.

This went on for over an hour; my client maintained his innocence. Finally the lead Detective (who knew my client had been raised by his grandmother) told Mr. Vaughn that within an hour after his arrest the police executed a search warrant at his grandmother's house looking for evidence. The Det. informed my client that when the police entered, at about 5 a.m., *they kicked down the door, his grandmother, unaware of what was happening, collapsed on the floor and suffered a massive heart attack. Also a lie.*

My client began to sob and pleaded with the Detectives to call his mother so he could check on the condition of his grandmother. The police agreed to do so only after he admitted his involvement in the crime. He maintained his innocence. It is important to note that during this four-hour interrogation my client was handcuffed to a wall in a 5-by-14 foot room with no windows and no ventilation.

He continued to cry and the police left the room, watching him on the TV monitor.

He laid his head on a steel table and appeared to be resting while crying.

The lead Det. came in, kicked the table and said, "This isn't no Mother fuckin' hotel—wake up!"

Fifteen minutes passed and a second officer walked in and said, "I'm sorry to be the one to tell you this but your grandmother died on the operating table." Obviously a lie since she never had a heart attack to begin with.

Mr. Vaughn began to sob and banged his head against the table.

The Detectives saw this and believed they could exploit his fragile emotional state.

They explained that the funeral services were that Tuesday (it was Sunday night) and if my client cooperated and admitted his involvement in the shooting they could try to arrange a police escort to the funeral. A lie.

Darnell said he wanted to go to the funeral but he was innocent. The Det. stated that he obviously didn't love his grandmother, since he would not admit to the crime, and as a result he, the Det., would see that my client would spend the rest of his life in jail. A lie, since the maximum penalty did not carry life in prison.

Darnell explained to the police as he was crying because his grandmother's death was entirely his fault, since the police would have never gone to her house if he had not been arrested. He said "she was everything to me I have nothing else to live for… I feel like just killing myself." The Det. took him up on his offer and said, "You know, you're right, you should just go ahead and do it. I agree you were responsible for your grandmother's death."

Mr. Vaughn renewed his request to call home over five times. Each time the Det. said he would give him a phone call if he admitted to his involvement in the crime. Specifically saying, "I know what you did. I just need to hear it out of your mouth." The Detective had no idea who did it. Another lie.

Thirty minutes passed. The Det. exited the room and returned, saying, "We caught one of your buddies who was in the car with you and he said that you had done the shooting." Another lie.

Despite this my client maintained his innocence.

Into the third hour the Supervising Sgt. with over 20 years on the force came into the room. He asked my client if he believed in God and if he did that my client needed to come "clean with the Lord." Mr. Vaughn said he believed in God but was innocent. The Det. said, "We know you're not innocent so don't even talk about that. Put it this way, what would you say if your grandmother was here?"

"I would tell her I was innocent."

"Well," the Det. said, "now you are disrespecting your dead grandmother."

It was now almost 10 a.m. My client had been in custody for over six hours and interrogated for over four. Nothing to eat or drink, other than a bag of potato chips and a soda, no bathroom break, no phone call.

He told the police he was sick and wanted to lay down. The police said he could lay down only after he admitted his involvement in the crime. If he did he would go to court the next day and be released. Another lie.

He said, "OK, I shot the gun." At this point they formally charged him with two counts of Assault with Intent to Kill, based on a single piece of evidence, his own statement.

He spent 13 months in jail. The Judge, who denied three requests to release my client, heard my motion to throw out the confession. The Det. didn't have much room to lie at the hearing since everything was captured on videotape. After a six-hour hearing the Judge, widely regarded as a pro-government judge, threw the confession out. The law really didn't give him much of a choice.

Mr. Vaughn was released two days later after spending over a year in jail.

Days before the hearing the prosecutor informed me that he had recently re-interviewed the two arresting officers and they both stated that when the red car stopped, my client was the last out, since he came out of the back seat. No one in the back seat ever fired a gun. So in the end my client confessed to a crime that he never committed.

A crime was in fact committed; it was committed against my client. I don't fight to "get people off"; I fight for fairness. Each day I think about whether it's worth fighting this fight, given that the odds are stacked against me and certainly against my clients. I quickly remind myself that these days I am not fighting for individual clients, I am fighting, I hope, to preserve and protect the Constitution against these abuses. The work is exhausting but my passion never fades. Ironically it's the government who provides the fuel.

QUEST
for TRUTH

Philip K. Howard
Blair Berk
Daniel M. Petrocelli
E. Lawrence Barcella, Jr.
Roger C. Spaeder
Robert S. Bennett
Dick Thornburgh
William Deverell
Richard Ben-Veniste
Daniel B. Spitzer
Martin Garbus
Michael D. Hausfeld
Allison B. Margolin
Reid H. Weingarten
Roger Zuckerman
Lynne Bernabei
Elaine Charlson Bredehoft
Paula Canny
John Kenneth Zwerling
Karen Patton Seymour

"Equal and exact justice to all men of whatever state or persuasion,
religious or political...freedom of person under the protection of the habeas corpus;
and trial by juries impartially selected. These principles form the bright
constellation which has gone before us, and guided our steps....
They should be the creed of our political faith, the text of civic instruction,
the touchstone by which to try the services of those we trust."
—President Thomas Jefferson, First Inaugural Address, March 4, 1801

PHILIP K. HOWARD is a well-known leader of legal reform in America. He is the author of the bestseller *The Death of Common Sense* (Random House, 1995) and *The Collapse of the Common Good* (Ballantine, 2002), and he is a periodic contributor to the op-ed pages of *The New York Times*, *The Wall Street Journal*, and *The Washington Post*. He advises leaders of both parties on legal and regulatory reform issues. A practicing lawyer, Howard is Vice-Chairman of the law firm Covington & Burling LLP.

In 2002, Howard founded Common Good (www.cgood.org), a national bipartisan coalition organized to restore common sense to American law. The Advisory Board of Common Good is composed of leaders from a broad cross-section of American political thought including, among others, former U.S. Senators Howard Baker, Bill Bradley, George McGovern and Alan Simpson.

Howard has long been a civic leader in New York. He is Chair of the Committee that installed the "Tribute in Light" Memorial for those who died on September 11th. He is also Chairman of the Municipal Art Society of New York, a leading civic group that spearheaded initiatives to preserve Grand Central Terminal.

Making Civil Justice Sane

By Philip K. Howard

In many ways, the tort reform movement has succeeded. Over half the states have damaged limits, kangaroo courts no longer exist in Mississippi and Texas, and, thanks to the class action reform that Congress passed last year, some obscure county court can no longer bankrupt entire industries. Supreme Court rulings have limited punitive damages and charged federal judges to guard against "junk science" by dubious experts.

But a lawsuit culture still corrodes daily relations throughout society. Doctors practice defensive medicine to ward off patient lawsuits and hesitate to intercede against inept colleagues, fearful of years of litigation. Businesses won't give job references. Teachers have lost control of the classroom—78 percent of middle and high school teachers surveyed recently reported that students had threatened them with lawsuits for violating their rights. Distrust of justice may be at a new low: only 16 percent of Americans said that they would trust the justice system if someone brought a baseless claim against them.

Hardest hit are activities that are optional. Fun, for example, is fraught with fear. Schools ban dodgeball and tag. Jungle gyms, diving boards, and seesaws seem relics of some past civilization. Meanwhile our children, rescued from the risks of roughhousing and accident, suffer from the far greater risk of obesity, now at epidemic proportions.

The direct costs of this approach to justice are large (about twice the percentage of the GDP than in other developed nations). But the indirect costs are debilitating, infecting daily dealings with distrust and defensiveness. What's at stake is the functioning of society.

Last summer, Lord Hoffmann, a judge on Great Britain's highest court, noted that the U.K. was the dream of every U.S. tort reformer—no punitive damages, limits on pain and suffering, no contingency fees, loser pays, no juries in most civil cases, and a trial bar with almost no political influence. Yet, he remarked, England increasingly suffered from the pathologies of what the British call the "compensation culture." The problem, he argued, was that judges had to come to view litigation merely as a way of resolving private disputes and no longer appreciated that the proliferation of lawsuits affects the behavior of everyone in society. If judges don't act as gatekeepers, drawing the boundaries of claims on behalf of broader society, then the mere possibility of a lawsuit will end up "diverting resources from activities where they are most needed and...restricting the liberty of individuals to enjoy their lives in their own way."

Lord Hoffmann put his finger on what's missing in American justice: judges don't exercise their discretion to protect against abusive or unreasonable claims. The goal of civil justice is not merely to provide a forum to resolve disputes but to provide legal guideposts defining right and wrong. Law is the foundation of freedom in part because people know where they stand—they have confidence that our system of law will enforce contracts and require someone who's negligent to compensate the person injured. Law is supposed to protect the good as well as condemn the bad. Citizens in a free society should be confident that courts will affirmatively defend them if they act reasonably.

Today America's civil justice system is not providing these guideposts of right and wrong. People believe, on the whole accurately, that any aggrieved person can haul another into court over an accident or disagreement and put his claim, in almost any account, before a jury. Because one jury can't bind the next, civil justice has become an ad hoc process, without meaningful guidelines or limits.

Restoring freedom in social interaction requires a basic shift in the goals of civil justice. Judges must see their role not as referees of a neutral dispute-resolution system but as guardians of reasonable choices, constantly making rulings that draw boundaries of reasonable dispute.

An important decision by the Law Lords began pushing Britain back in the direction in 2003. The case at issue could have come from many courts in America. On a hot day in Cheshire, an 18-year-old named John Tomlinson went for a swim in the lake of a local park. Racing into the water, he dived too sharply and broke his neck on the sandy bottom. He was paralyzed for life.

Tomlinson sued the Cheshire County Council for not doing more to protect against the accident. The Council, he discovered, knew about the risk. Three or four near-drownings occurred every year. NO SWIMMING signs had been posted—and widely ignored—for over a decade. The popularity of the park, with over 160,000 visitors a year, made effective policing almost impossible. Fearful of liability, the Cheshire Council had decided to close off the lake by dumping mud on the beaches and planting reeds. But before the reeds were planted, Tomlinson had his accident. The Council should have acted sooner, his lawyer argued, to prevent "luring people into a deathtrap" and to protect against a "siren call strong enough to turn stout men's minds." Because the county obviously knew the danger, the lower court accepted this argument.

The Law Lords took the appeal and ordered the case dismissed. The lead opinion by Lord Hoffmann declared that whether a claim should be allowed hinged not just on whether an accident is foreseeable but "also the social value of the activity which gives rise to the risk." Permitting Tomlinson's claim, the Law Lords held, means that hundreds of thousands could no longer enjoy the park: "[T]here is an important question of freedom at stake. It is unjust that the harmless recreation of responsible parents and children with buckets and spades on the beaches should be prohibited in order to comply with what is thought to be a legal duty."

The country's ineffective effort to prevent swimming, instead of establishing negligence, the Lords held, demonstrated how a misguided conception of justice hurts the public. "Does the law require that all trees be cut down," Lord Hobhouse asked, "because some youths may climb them and fall?" Lord Scott added, "Of course there is some risk of accidents.... But that is no reason for imposing a grey and dull safety regime on everyone."

The <u>Tomlinson</u> decision highlights the forgotten goal in American justice. Judges have forgotten that lawsuits concern not only the parties to the dispute but everyone in society. The mere possibility of a lawsuit changes people's behavior. That's why judges must draw boundaries as a matter of law.

Today in America, such a solution would be practically unthinkable. We look to the jury as our guarantee of fairness and see judges as mere neutral referees. The phrase "the right to sue" has magical powers—and the jury is an essential ingredient of that right. All the trial lawyers need to do is pound the table—"they're trying to take away your right to sue"—and instantaneously reformers are on the defensive, muttering about the need to curb frivolous cases.

Access to courts is indeed a core value: even a frivolous claim requires someone with authority to decide that it's frivolous. But the "right to sue" has come to mean not just getting inside the courthouse door but going all the way to the jury as the ultimate decision maker. Any other conception of justice, the trial lawyers tell us, would mean that the system is rigged. As leading trial lawyer Richard Scruggs put it: "I trust the jury system and I trust the American people and their common sense far more than the National Association of Manufacturers to protect the American public."

The populist appeal of juries is easy to understand. The idea of the jury—a randomly picked group of citizens—seems like the model of American fairness. Former senator John Edwards, who made millions suing hospitals in the South, summarized the prevailing sentiment toward juries in a *Newsweek* essay, "Juries: 'Democracy in Action.'" Its gist: freedom's flag waves in the breeze, as jurors, summoned from all walks of life, come to do their civic duty. The vision is so powerful that we don't look back to consider what the role of the jury is supposed to be.

But is civil justice supposed to be a kind of mini-election, where 12 (or six) voters decide, case by case, what's right and wrong? "The basic moral principle, acknowledged by every legal system we know anything about," Yale law professor Eugene Rostow once observed, "is that similar cases should be decided alike." The rule of law—the very *idea* of the rule of law—is that it is supposed to set and apply standards of conduct evenly.

It is impossible to reconcile these two ideas. Under the "democracy in action" conception, each jury decides a case as it sees fit, whatever the verdict in similar prior cases. This model not only tolerates but encourages decisions that vary wildly from case to case. Fairness is defined largely by the neutrality of a randomly picked group of jurors, not consistency among similar cases.

If fairness were the only issue in a particular case, why *not* let the jury make the choice? Somebody has to decide. But litigation, as Lord Hoffmann observed, affects people not in the courtroom. Derek Bok, Harvard's former Law School dean and its once and future president, observed that lawsuits "often have their greatest effect on people who are neither parties to the litigation nor even aware that it is going on." The news last year that someone received a large verdict in a sledding accident had the natural effect of causing other towns to bar winter sports from town property. No legislature or judge, however, made a decision that sledding is an unreasonable risk. Who represents the interests of the citizens who want to enjoy winter sports? One jury decides that an activity is safe; the next jury decides that it is not. What is a prudent person supposed to do?

The rule-of-law model, by contrast, aspires to guidance and predictability, to fairness to society as a whole, not just to the individual parties. Its main tools are statutes by legislatures and written rulings by judges. By setting boundaries that people can rely upon, the rule of law promotes the freedom to interact honestly and take reasonable risks.

But doesn't the Constitution require juries to make such decisions? The answer is a qualified no. If the case turns on a question of law, rather than a question of fact, then the judge should make the final decision. In our constitutional framework, juries have the job of deciding disputed facts—who is telling the truth, say, or who ran the red light. But juries are not supposed to interpret the law—that's the judge's job. Many cases turn not on factual disputes but, as in the Tomlinson case, on whether the conduct at issue was reasonable. This allocation of responsibility between judge and jury has distinguished Anglo-American jurisprudence for centuries. To quote the landmark Jacobean common law treatise by Sir Edward Coke: "Judges do not answer questions of fact... [and] jurors do not answer questions of law."

The Seventh Amendment, though hardly a model of clarity, defines the jury right by incorporating common law practice, and it explicitly invokes the fact-law distinction: "In suits at common law...the right of trial by jury shall be preserved, and no fact tried by a jury shall be otherwise re-examined...than according to the rules of the common law." In the debates over ratification of the Constitution, future chief justice John Marshall stated categorically: "What is the object of a jury trial? To inform the Court of the facts."

Popular confusion over the jury's role probably stems from the distinction between civil and criminal cases. Under the Sixth Amendment, only a jury has the power to convict. Juries in a criminal case are our protection against abuses of state power. But a private lawsuit, we seem to have forgotten, is a use of state power against another private citizen. Filing a lawsuit is just like indicting someone—it's just an indictment for money. Without the protection of a disinterested prosecutor and a grand jury, the defendant needs the protection of the judge to decide whether the claim has legal merit, leaving the jury to decide disputed facts.

The use of a jury in a particular civil lawsuit should depend on whether the case hinges on a factual dispute—who's telling the truth, for instance. But in other cases, the judge should decide. If the claim implicates the functioning of society—say, a claim that a seesaw or jungle gym is unreasonably risky—juries can resolve specific factual disputes (using what are known as special interrogatories), but the

judge should then rule as a matter of law whether the activity constitutes an unreasonable risk.

Cases that turn on acceptable standards of medical care almost
always have broader social ramifications—for example, whether it's
appropriate for a doctor to prescribe aspirin for a bad headache and
then wait to see how the patient progresses. Once in a while, that
headache will be a tumor. Is the doctor liable for not immediately
ordering a battery of tests? If so, then doctors will continue to squan-
der billions on unnecessary procedures, driving up costs and thereby
causing others to go without care altogether. To avoid this result, the
legal system must draw boundaries of reasonable risk. Doctors need to
know what's expected of them.

Prominent trial lawyers whom I debate typically argue the jury
system is our best form of regulation. But in that case, where does the
doctor go to find the rule? It doesn't exist, because the "regulation"
varies from jury to jury. That's why Oliver Wendell Holmes, Jr., perhaps our most eminent common law thinker, believed that what constitutes reasonable conduct was a question requiring a ruling of law:
"Negligence... [is] a standard of conduct, a standard by which we hold
the parties bound to know beforehand...not a matter dependent upon
the whim of the particular jury or the eloquence of the particular
advocate."

California Supreme Court chief justice Roger Traynor, a liberal innovator, emphasized the need for judges to declare rulings even
in the simplest accident and not to leave standards of reasonableness
to the "oscillating verdict of juries." When a woman hit her head on a
slanted ceiling while walking down a staircase, Traynor insisted that
the judge determine whether the ceiling was an unreasonable hazard
or whether "the danger is so apparent that visitors could reasonably be
expected to notice it."

In commercial law, where the focus is predictability and efficiency, it is a well-established principle that judges, not juries, have the
obligation to interpret the standard language of contracts. The
Uniform Commercial Code was a legislative effort to achieve consistency. Its core concepts—including ones that look very much like

those of tort, such as reasonableness—are often decided as a matter of law. America's system of commercial law, generally considered the most consistent and predictable in the world, is a bedrock of America's economic strength.

Just imagine the mischief if parties to a commercial deal could make up theories about the unfairness of a particular contract. That's what's happened in social relations in America.

The rights that our founders gave us were rights against state power. The modern conception of the "right to sue" allows a claimant, more or less at his whim, to threaten you with state power. The jury may uphold your conduct, or it may not. But there's no one on behalf of broader society who sees it as his job to keep claims within knowable bounds. This is not the rule of law, with predictable standards and guidelines, but something closer to the opposite.

Judges today give lip service to the distinction between fact and law, but, as one scholar put it, there's "a strong tendency to let all issues go to the jury without discriminating among them." Letting the jury decide is easy—it "reduces judicial effort and the risk of reversal." Prior to the 1960s, judges didn't need to keep tight reins on hot-coffee claims or multi-million-dollar personal-injury lawsuits. There weren't any. People didn't have the idea that they could use litigation as a lottery.

In the 1960s, legal theorists reconceived civil justice as a neutral process, telling judges that their first duty was to avoid asserting judicial values. Who knows what bias lurks in the heart of the judge? Appellate courts admonished judges not to dismiss any claim unless "it appears beyond doubt that the plaintiff can prove no set of facts in his support of his claim which would entitle him to recover." The standard is almost like that required for a criminal conviction: judges won't dismiss a claim (or, for that matter, a bogus defense) unless there is virtually no room for argument. Since most accident cases involve interpreting standards of conduct in factual circumstances—what are known as mixed questions of law and fact—judges believe that their main job is to read legal instructions to the jury, and leave it to the jury to apply the law in each case instead of applying it themselves.

The effect was not to achieve the ostensible goal off neutrality, however, but to leave a vacuum that has been filled by an ever-broadening range of private legal claims and threats. Lawyers began pushing the envelope, and they haven't stopped.

Like the rest of us, judges have witnessed this vast expansion of legal exposure, and many don't like it. But they feel powerless to do anything about it. Making a legal ruling based on broader social effects of a lawsuit—say, whether seesaws are a reasonable risk—is inconceivable to most judges. A few years ago, when debating the judge in the McDonald's hot-coffee case, I suggested that the reasonableness of selling hot coffee from a takeout window should be decided as a matter of law. His response perfectly captured current judicial orthodoxy: "Who am I to judge?"

But what about judicial activism? In this same period, judges around America were taking control of schools and prisons and causing riots when they ordered children bussed to different neighborhoods. Judges felt just fine making rulings as a matter of law that effectively preempted the legislature. How can we come to terms with this Jekyll and Hyde performance?

The common thread is a judicial preoccupation with the plight of the individual, coupled with a distrust of business, professionals, and democracy itself. The jurisprudence of our era is not, in fact, based on principle of neutrality but on active antagonism to the establishment. Someone feels aggrieved? Let him sue for the moon. The Kansas City school board isn't doing a good job educating students? Let the court take over the schools. Courts in the 1960s embraced the judicial philosophy of championing anyone claiming victimhood.

What judges forgot in their preoccupation with fairness to the particular claimant is that the impact of lawsuits goes beyond the particular verdict and affects society as a whole. An overly activist judicial approach to social issues preempts the legislature and distorts public priorities in areas not even considered by the judge. A passive judicial approach to private lawsuits, leaving most decisions to the jury, creates an open season for anyone who wants to use state power to threaten another person. Social policy in these areas ends up being made by lawyers like Dickie Scruggs and whoever else comes up with a theory of liability.

Rulings by the Supreme Court in the past ten years suggest that it is pushing judges in the same direction as the British Law Lords. The Court has repeatedly instructed judges to assert their power in a wide variety of civil cases, with the goal of restoring legal consistency.

Several important decisions exhort judges to use summary judgment to make rulings as a matter of law. In <u>Celotex v. Catrett</u>, a wrongful-death asbestos case, the Court starkly shifted direction from the presumption that judges should avoid summary dismissal if there is a "scintilla of evidence": "Summary judgment procedure is properly regarded not as a disfavored procedural shortcut, but rather as an integral part of...rules...designed 'to secure the just, speedy and inexpensive determination of every action.'"

Justice Souter, in <u>Markman v. Westview Instruments</u>, explained the importance of judges making rulings of law to achieve consistency in patent cases. A legal system that creates a "zone of uncertainty," Souter cautioned, "would discourage invention."

In <u>Cooper v. Leatherman</u>, the Court held that judges should decide the upper limits of punitive damages as a matter of law. "Requiring the application of law, rather than a decision maker's caprice, does more than simply provide citizens notice of what actions may subject them to punishment; it also helps to assure the uniform general treatment of similarly situated persons that is the essence of law itself," the Court declared, quoting an earlier opinion of Justice Breyer. Going still further, in <u>State Farm v. Campbell</u>, the Court itself took responsibility for mandating a limit on claims for punitive damages, to bar plaintiffs from making outlandish claims to extort settlements. "Elementary notions of fairness enshrined in our constitutional jurisprudence dictate that a person receive fair notice not only of the conduct that will subject him to punishment, but also of the severity of the penalty that a State may impose," Justice Kennedy wrote for the Court.

In <u>Daubert v. Merrell Dow</u>, the Court shifted the responsibility of what constitutes credible expert testimony from jury to judge. On the authority of <u>Daubert</u>, a federal judge in Texas, Janis Jack, recently took it upon herself to investigate the validity of more than 9,000 silicosis claims. She found that the diagnoses were a sham and that the litigation had basically been mass-produced by lawyers who would advertise for potential plaintiffs, invite them to a mobile X-ray truck, and then pay doctors to sign their names on preprinted diagnoses. What was shocking about Judge Jack's 250-page opinion was not the details of this scheme—anyone associated with asbestos litigation has seen the scam in action for years—but that a judge actually took the authority to declare that the emperor had no clothes. Until her decision, judges overseeing several hundred thousand cases had basically taken the position that the plaintiffs had the right to submit these bogus claims to the jury.

Of course, legislatures, not judges, have the ultimate authority for drawing the boundaries of law in our society. So far, though, Congress and the statehouses have treated civil justice as a fight between special interests. Even when passing specific tort reforms, they have ducked responsibility for sorting out the underlying systemic flaws. While legislators cannot crowd into the courtroom to make rulings of reasonableness in a particular case, they can certainly direct judges to take responsibility, and they can provide appropriate goals and guidelines. Judges need such help: after four decades of letting trial lawyers argue almost anything, they have no idea how to draw the required legal boundaries.

Legislators should pass laws giving judges the responsibility to safeguard our freedom to act reasonably. In November 2005, the House of Lords introduced a bill on civil liability that, among other changes, would make the <u>Tomlinson</u> ruling law, granting broad authority to judges to consider whether allowing a claim might "discourage persons from undertaking...a desirable activity." Congress and individual states could enact a similar bill directing judges to act as gatekeepers of the reasonableness of claims, perhaps along these lines: "Judges shall take the responsibility to draw boundaries of reasonable dispute as a matter of law, applying common law principles and statutory guidelines. In making these rulings, judges shall consider whether allowing a claim or defense to proceed to the jury, and the exposure of others in society to similar claims, might undermine the ability of citizens to engage in reasonable or productive activities."

Congress has before it a number of bills that would accomplish this result in specific areas. In the wake of Hurricane Katrina, for example, Senator John Caryn (R, TX) introduced a bill to shore up the toothless Volunteer Protection Act by giving judges the responsibility to decide as a matter of law whether claims fall within the scope of the act. Arkansas governor Mike Huckabee, concerned about the chilling of children's recreation and the crisis of obesity, is considering proposals shifting responsibility to judges to decide whether a particular activity is unreasonably risky.

Some areas of society are too far gone. Health care is in such disarray, and involves such complexity, that a broad coalition, including patient advocates, has endorsed the idea of a new system of health courts. Although the idea of an expert court may seem radical, America has a long tradition of special courts in areas needing specific expertise— admiralty courts, tax courts, drug courts, bankruptcy courts, and administrative tribunals in areas ranging from workers' compensation to vaccine liability. In the Senate, Michael Enzi (R, WY) and Max Baucus (D, MT) have introduced a bipartisan bill to authorize and fund pilot health courts, with hearings planned later this term.

Restoring reliability to civil justice is a radical idea, but that just shows how far we've fallen. Why are there frivolous and extortive cases? Because judges don't think they have the authority to decide what's frivolous. Why are daily choices riddled with legal fear? Because judges won't draw the boundaries of reasonableness.

Probably the hardest part for judges will be the idea that they have an important role as protectors of society's values. They must understand that if a claim will affect the conduct of people not in the courtroom, they have they duty to assert the reasonable values of society. The hardest part of this reform for the rest of us, in this age of distrust, is that we don't trust judges. And almost certainly judges will make a certain number of bad rulings. But at least the rulings will be in writing for all to see and can be appealed and, if really stupid, overturned by the legislature. But having no rulings—letting unreasonable claims go to the jury—is like having a perfect record of bad rulings. Most people will act as if they might be liable. Why take the risk?

The opponents of such a reform are not hard to identify. The American Bar Association recently passed a broad resolution condemning special health courts, even pilot projects, declaring that "it is against ABA policy related to juries." Other factors may influence their position as well. More than 60 percent of the total cost of the malpractice system is consumed by lawyers' fees and administrative costs. The lawyers portray themselves as a kind of Robin Hood for injured patients, but the modern twist is that they keep most of the money. This trial-lawyer wealth comes in handy politically and, indeed, has become an opiate to one of our political parties.

The lawyers' most powerful weapon, however, is their rhetoric. No one wants to give up the "right to sue." What the public needs to understand is that the right to sue has no substance without the rule of law. Rights without law do not protect freedom but undermine it—causing disorder in schools, contributing to unaffordable health care, and putting a pall over life's simple pleasures. Let the lawyers, increasingly isolated by their self-interest, talk about the right to sue. We should talk about the rule of law and how it should support the functioning of a free society.

BLAIR BERK, a partner in the nationally prominent law firm of Tarlow & Berk in Los Angeles, is considered one of the most gifted criminal lawyers of her generation. In 2005 and again in 2006, she was selected by her peers in Naifeh & Smith's *The Best Lawyers in America* as well as by *Los Angeles Magazine* as one of the "Top Criminal Lawyers" in California. A graduate of Harvard Law School who studied under Professors Laurence Tribe and Alan Dershowitz, Ms. Berk defends complex criminal cases ranging from homicide and sex crimes to computer hacking and white-collar matters.

Among Ms. Berk's most important cases, her pro bono Habeas Corpus representation of Clarence Chance, an individual whose freedom was won after being framed, wrongfully convicted and imprisoned for over 17 years for the homicide of a deputy sheriff he did not commit. Ms. Berk regularly lectures on criminal justice and public affairs issues and is frequently consulted by the nation's leading newspapers, including *The New York Times*, *Los Angeles Times* and *The Washington Post*. Ms. Berk also specializes in the representation of individuals and companies in the entertainment industry and her clients have included a number of well-known public figures. A native of North Carolina before moving to Los Angeles in 1990, she lives in Beverly Hills with her husband Daniel and their daughter Blythe.

Ruminations on
a Doe-Eyed Puppy

By Blair Berk

We Americans embrace a system predicated on the principle that "truth" in a criminal case is rarely as simple as a DNA test. Who is ultimately charged with a crime, with what crimes they are charged, and for what offenses, if any, they are ultimately convicted, are decisions historically determined by our adversarial process—a carefully calibrated system that works hard to preserve objectivity and fairness as the only reliable benchmarks to uncover the "truth" as to guilt or innocence.

Prosecutors representing the community's interest wage battle against the advocate for the accused before a judge and/or jury with the goal that only through a confrontation of competing positions of fact and law will the guilty be convicted and the innocent walk free. Admittedly easier said than done in a nation where we all agree the quality of justice is too readily dependent on the symmetry of the playing field in which that battle takes place. Where the pitch of that adversarial field has far too much to do with whether a defendant can possibly compete with the unlimited resources and deep bench of government prosecutors—always a fundamental challenge to the fairness of the fight.

We find ourselves presently in an era, however, when our politicians cynically suggest that the constitutional rights solemnly guaranteed by our founders to every citizen may well be up for discussion. Where our elected leaders, both Republican and Democrat, frantically search for new and different ways to appear tough on crime to their constituents and knock each other out of the way to win the "who cares more about crime victims" trophy.

We are glued to television shows about criminal justice that are wildly popular in a "feeding the Christians to the lions" kind of way. Entertainment news shows about crime abound, anchored by utterly graceless personalities who cynically hackle at the presumption of innocence and whose angry and hysterical voices daily rail against the inconvenience of due process. Trotting out their own victimhood, real or imagined, often as an impenetrable shield against any and all criticism of the unconscionable fear they are peddling. Their most perverse guarantee of a high Nielson rating, the exploited victims themselves beamed into our homes as if they are all being dug from shallow graves in our own backyards. Graphic images designed as daily emergency alerts interrupting regular programming after every commercial, showing the sweet face of the braided kidnapped girl sexually tortured and buried alive—making us feel as if she actually lived just down the street of every one of us.

It is with this sensationalized backdrop that our scales of justice find themselves in grave danger of forever losing their balance. Scales exquisitely designed to maintain equilibrium between the interests of society and the rights of an accused are increasingly weighted against fairness and due process by the emergence and awesome political power of the "victim" as a new adversary in the system. A "victim" improperly elevated to the role of an actual party to a criminal case is the proverbial "wolf" in the softest and most empathetic of sheep's clothing. An unlikely enemy to justice who in the minds of the public is every kind-hearted person's friend, a sweet lamb often with a name like "Meghan" or "Jessica"—yet in reality as easily and often a false victim like Tywanna Brawley or an abusive husband whose battered wife has finally bested with a knife to the bullying arm. But it is the seductive siren call of the alleged victim as a party to a criminal case who could likely become the ultimate saboteur of a fair justice system in this country.

Our founders knew the dangers of giving too much power to the accuser in a criminal case. Importantly, in our system of justice it is the community and not the accuser who prosecutes the accused. There is a very good reason for that. Subjectivity and vengeance are antithetical to fairness and due process, for the very reason that neither—as eloquently put by the conservative former Congressman Bob Barr—can ever be persuasively countered by actual fact or logic. Our long and shameful history of lynch-mobs and the wrongfully-convicted, spending years in prison or even being executed before exoneration would hopefully give us pause here at the precipice of this brave new world of justice, where "victims" rule supreme. The loss of objectivity replaced by subjectivity, dispassion in arriving at a just result replaced with the hunger for vengeance driving those who believe they have been wronged. All will inevitably conspire to send us right back to the tree in the field at midnight as the accused is strung up by those convinced of his guilt before anyone has bothered to hold up the actual evidence to the reflective light of day.

But before a jury renders its verdict in a criminal case, the accuser under law should be nothing more than that. As a matter of law, there is no "victim" unless and until a jury decides that a crime has been committed and the person accused is the wrongdoer. Where our forefathers thought it crucial for an accuser to be named publicly so that any previous false allegations or bad conduct on their part could be properly brought forward, we now find ourselves making more and more incremental concessions to the right of confrontation, allowing, in some states, accusers to remain anonymous and be instead identified as John or Jane Doe. Prosecutors are now allowed to refer to the accuser as "the victim" throughout a trial, before there is ever any determination made by a judge or jury whether that person is actually a "true" victim at all. The liberty/order equation is both delicate and complex. Yet while the balance naturally shifts slightly as the political winds blow, we are witnessing not a breeze but a blustering gale force of reckless political opportunism demanding a new model of "immediate gratification" justice.

A proposed Victim Rights Amendment to our rarely amended Federal Constitution continues to be aggressively pushed by both sides of the aisle in our Congress as well as our current President. Such an Amendment would dangerously allow an alleged victim of a crime to dictate to a criminal prosecutor, among other things, whether there will be any plea bargain in a criminal case at all. Imagine the grieving parent of a slain child being given the power to call the shots as to the extent of due process afforded the accused. Good luck with that.

It is fashionable these days to go so far as to call into question a criminal defense lawyer's cross-examination of an alleged victim as being unnecessary and rude. This author was recently condemned by a syndicated columnist as attempting to "destroy the victim" by being so bold as to dare to even cross-examine a complaining witness in a sex case by asking her to specifically describe what she claimed happened.[1] As if the claims made by an alleged victim of certain crimes are per se "truth" and prevent all but the equally victimized from approaching and asking any indelicate and specific questions.

When our government, with all of its resources and power decides to accuse one of its citizens and take away their liberty, I am very proud of what I do and the role I play as the advocate for the accused. I am a criminal defense lawyer. I defend vigorously and without apology. I am convinced to a moral certainty that elevation of the accuser in a criminal case to the constitutional status of a party in the adversarial system will render the presumption of innocence meaningless and any semblance of justice a vague afterthought. The awesome power of the government as accuser I can fight. But if we succumb to the prevailing winds and show the back of our hand to our beloved Constitution by reshaping it as a contest instead between the accuser and the accused, lady justice might as well take her blindfold off and toss in her towel. A criminal defendant will never have justice competing against a doe-eyed puppy, no matter how innocent that defendant turns out to be.

---

[1]Estrich, Susan. *Every Defendant Deserves the Best Defense* (7/27/06); *The Mentor From Hell* (7/22/06)

DANIEL M. PETROCELLI, a partner in O'Melveny & Myers' Century City office, has a national trial practice representing clients in major litigation in a wide variety of areas, including entertainment, intellectual property, unfair competition, business torts, securities, employment law, and criminal defense. Daniel is Chair of the firm's General Trial & Litigation Practice and a member of The American Lawyer's 2004 "Litigation Department of the Year." Mr. Petrocelli first gained national media exposure in 1997 when he represented Fred Goldman, the father of murder victim Ron Goldman, in a wrongful death civil suit against O.J. Simpson, resulting in judgment of $33.5 million. In what has been called the most important while-collar case of our time, Mr. Petrocelli was lead trial counsel for Jeffrey Skilling, the former President of Enron Corporation, in the recent federal criminal trial against Mr. Skilling and former Enron Chairman Kenneth Lay in Houston, Texas.

Mr. Petrocelli is the author of the international bestseller *Triumph of Justice: The Final Judgment on the Simpson Saga*, Random House (1998); *"Effective Witness Preparation," California Litigation*, (Spring 1999) and *"Opening Statements under California Law," Los Angeles Lawyer*, (March 1989).

Mr. Petrocelli is the recipient of numerous awards, including Southwestern University Alumnus of the Year; Century City Bar Association Litigator of the Year; Malibu Bar Association Trial Lawyer of the Year; San Diego Trial Lawyers Association Trial Lawyer of the Year; one of Los Angeles' Top 50 Litigators by the *Los Angeles Business Journal*; one of the Lawyers of the Year by *California Lawyer* and Southern California Super Lawyer by *Los Angeles Magazine*.

Outside
the Courtroom

By Daniel M. Petrocelli

I've had the privilege to have played a role in two of the more celebrated cases in recent history. In 1996, following the criminal murder trial and acquittal of O.J. Simpson, I represented Fred Goldman in the civil trial against Simpson for the wrongful death of Fred's son, Ron, and Simpson's ex-wife, Nicole Brown Simpson. This time, a civil jury unanimously found Simpson responsible for both killings. Ten years later, I argued to a federal criminal jury in Houston, Texas, that my client, Jeffrey Skilling, the former President of Enron Corporation, was innocent of all crimes charged against him in connection with Enron's spectacular demise and ensuing bankruptcy in late 2001. The jury disagreed, convicting Mr. Skilling on 19 criminal counts while acquitting him on 9 others.

The two cases could not have been more different, yet in my view, they share one tragic thing in common. In both criminal trials, the wrong result was reached. In the Simpson case, the jury acquitted a guilty man. In the Skilling case, the jury convicted an innocent man.

Admittedly, many will disagree with these views, and it is not my purpose to argue the merits of the cases. I do suggest, however, that these two cases exemplify the serious challenges in getting to the truth in highly visible trials, where the weight of public opinion, interest, and scrutiny can overwhelm cases and produce aberrational results.

This occurs not so much because the legal system is flawed, but because participants in high-profile cases too often yield to external temptations. Media interest, public attitudes, political agendas, and personal ambitions all can combine to veer the conduct of trials off course. These pressures operate on everyone in the process—law enforcement investigators, prosecutors, private lawyers, judges, witnesses, victims and their families, the media, and, of course, jurors.

No case has ever been more publicized than the Simpson criminal trial. It captivated the nation and dominated the news from the first day of the investigation when the slain bodies of Ron Goldman and Nicole Simpson were found outside Nicole's condominium; through the surreal spectacle of watching Simpson's white Bronco leading a parade of police cars as Simpson sat in the back with a .357 magnum in his hand; through the gavel to gavel coverage of nine months of primetime trial beamed across the country and around the world; through the broadcast of audiotapes from the courtroom—out of the presence of the jury but for a transfixed public—bearing proof that a police detective uttered racial slurs; to a nation and world paused as the verdict was read.

Obscured in the spectacle of all this was the evidence. Simpson's blood was found at the murder scene, as were his shoeprints, hat, fiber from his clothing, and one bloody glove. At his nearby home, the matching glove was found stained with the victims' blood, as were drops of Simpson's blood and blood from both victims on his driveway, floor, and socks. Simpson's white Bronco also was smudged with his blood and his victims' blood. Simpson had no credible alibi; no witnesses could account for his whereabouts during the time of the murders. After he was arrested the next day, Simpson's hands displayed nearly a dozen cuts, consistent with the wielding of a knife used to kill the two victims. All this evidence of guilt and much more were not enough for Simpson's criminal jury. It took them only three hours to acquit Simpson and send him home to a hero's welcome.

Many critics say the trial never should have been televised. Perhaps so. But the fault lies not with the camera, but the people in front of it. Lawyers argued, acted, and even dressed for it. Witnesses with no bona fide evidence raced to get in front of it and capture their minutes of fame. Witnesses with real evidence ran away from it to protect their privacy. The trial judge, who authorized televising of the trial, seemed to relish it all, prolonging the trial with too few restrictions on the evidence and too many dangerous detours from the pivotal issues in the case. No wonder, then, that a clear-cut double murder case could turn into a trial on police conduct and referendum on race relations in this country. In the process, the truth was compromised.

In contrast, the Simpson civil trial managed to avoid many of these pitfalls. The credit goes primarily to its trial judge, who refused to bow to external interests and pressures. There was no camera in the courtroom. There was a strict gag order banning the parties and lawyers from talking to the press. The evidence was confined to the essential facts. Issues of racial animus, which inflamed the criminal trial, played no role. These trial conditions contributed to a neater, more efficient trial, requiring about half the time of the criminal trial.

To be sure, the civil trial enjoyed another crucial advantage that, in my view, helped produce the correct result. It was conducted under rules governing civil cases, which are aimed at maximizing the discovery, exchange, and presentation of evidence at trial. Unlike the criminal system, civil cases permit a lengthy period before trial where both sides can subpoena witnesses to give sworn testimony in the form of oral depositions. In criminal cases, the defense has no such power, although the prosecution can do so at secret grand jury proceedings at which neither the defendant nor defense counsel can attend or otherwise participate. So, for example, the plaintiff in a civil case can take the pretrial deposition of the defendant to find out what he knows and intends to say at the time of trial and then at trial can call the defendant to the stand. If the defendant refuses, the plaintiff can take the defendant's default and proceed to get a judgment against him.

In criminal cases, the Fifth Amendment protects the defendant from giving compelled testimony; the defendant only testifies if he wishes to do so in his own defense. This constitutional right, together with other legal requirements such as proof beyond a reasonable doubt and juror unanimity, are all designed to pose formidable obstacles to the government's ability to successfully prosecute and deprive a person of liberty or life. But they come at the expense of obstructing an unfettered flow of relevant evidence. For that reason, many agree that civil cases and trials represent a more pure search for the truth than criminal cases.

The two Simpson trials bear this out. In the criminal case, Simpson exercised his Fifth Amendment right not to testify, depriving the prosecution of a chance to cross-examine him. It was a wise decision on Simpson's part, because his testimony would not have been credible. In the civil case, forced to appear for a pretrial deposition, O.J. Simpson was required to answer questions for 13 days. This deposition provided the building blocks that enabled the plaintiffs to call Simpson to the stand in their case and cross-examine him. The jury was able to assess Simpson's credibility in the face of all the other evidence presented at trial. If Simpson were an innocent man, he would have no reason to lie on the stand. If he were guilty, he would have every reason. The jury concluded he was not truthful.

The trial of Jeff Skilling also was swayed by powerful external forces. During the 1990's, Enron skyrocketed in growth to become the country's seventh largest company. Then, in a matter of weeks in the fall of 2001, the company spiraled into bankruptcy. Thousands of people lost their jobs. Billions of dollars of shareholder value in Enron stock disappeared. Images of Enron employees, standing dazed outside the Enron towers holding only boxes of belongings from their offices, appeared everywhere. Accusations of fraud and impropriety abounded. Investigations from all levels of government ensued. Private lawsuits multiplied daily. Congressional hearings on television were the leading news story for months.

The public outcry was matched only by the political response. The President formed a special corporate fraud task force, assembled from prosecutors with the United States Department of Justice. Their primary targets were Jeff Skilling and Ken Lay, Enron's former Chairman, who was jointly prosecuted and tried with Skilling. (Mr. Lay passed away shortly after the jury's verdict.) After three years of massive investigation, the Enron Task Force, as it became known, separately indicted Skilling and Lay in 2004, claiming they misled the public about the company's financial health. The indictments against the two men were announced in nationally broadcast press conferences by the Department of Justice, SEC, and FBI, publicly labeling Skilling and Lay corporate crooks.

The condemnation in Houston was unlike any place else. Prior to its demise, Enron was a dominant force in Houston. With its innovative and highly successful businesses, Enron helped pull Houston out of a deep economic recession in the mid-80's brought on by the collapse of energy prices. Enron's rapid growth through the 90's produced great economic benefits to Houston—thousands of new jobs, billions of dollars of new shareholder value, and the emergence of other successful energy companies all contributed to restoring Houston as the energy capital of the world. Local businesses, from car dealerships to restaurants to vendors, flourished with Enron's success. Enron lavishly supported charities, music and the arts, advancement of medicine, and many other community causes. It was instrumental in building the new baseball park, which took its name from the company. Enron was truly the toast of the town.

But all this good will erupted into bitterness, anger, and even rage when Enron suddenly collapsed. With deep financial and psychological wounds, Houston perceived itself as a victim of Enron's fall. Against this backdrop, the Enron Task Force sought trial in a federal district court in Houston, Texas, just blocks away from the empty Enron towers. Both Skilling and Lay argued to the court that Houston was not a suitable trial venue, asking that the trial be moved to a city outside of Texas, such as Phoenix, Denver, or Atlanta. Extensive evidence and data were submitted to substantiate the intense anger toward Skilling and Lay and the widespread effects of Enron's collapse on Houston, including surveys in which Houston residents described Skilling and Lay as "evil," "pigs," "snakes," and "economic terrorists," likened them to "Al Qaeda," "Hitler," and "Satan," and declared them "definitely guilty." The trial judge refused to change venue and ordered trial to proceed in Houston.

When prospective jurors were summoned with lengthy questionnaires asking for their views about the case, the results confirmed the pervasive hostilities in Houston against Enron and Skilling and Lay in particular. Another request to change venue was made, but it was turned down. So, too, was the defendants' request to individually examine prospective jurors to better identify and select jurors with little or no biases regarding the case. (By contrast, the trial judge in the Simpson civil trial permitted nearly one month of such individual questioning to pick the jury.)

Forced to defend themselves in front of a Houston jury empanelled without a full and vigorous selection process, Skilling and Lay's chances of receiving a fair trial were compromised before the first witness was called. Despite their best intentions, the jurors could not help but be influenced by their community's attitudes, beliefs, and expectations—the same community where they all returned when the trial was over. While this is true in many cases, the trial against Skilling and Lay pushed the limits beyond the breaking point. The jurors were fully aware that their community was watching and united in anticipating just one outcome. Only by convicting both men could the trial jurors vindicate the community. In this environment, there was little chance they would do otherwise.

Whatever one's views about the outcomes in these cases, the Simpson and Skilling trials are vivid reminders of the difficult demands and challenges posed by trials of great public interest. When the outcome of a case can depend more on what happens outside rather than inside the courtroom, justice is jeopardized. There is no easy solution or remedy for this problem. It is not about the system. In the final analysis, it is about the character, responsibility, and obligation of all of us in the system to do right by it.

E. LAWRENCE BARCELLA, JR. has been a successful and highly regarded criminal trial lawyer for over three decades. For 16 years, he was one of the most successful and highly decorated federal prosecutors in the country, serving as an Assistant United States Attorney in Washington, D.C., where he prosecuted a diverse variety of matters, including murders, rapes, robberies, narcotic offenses, bribery, political corruption, fraud, and securities violations. He also was responsible for investigating a number of high visibility terrorism cases, including the assassination of former Chilean Foreign Minister Orlando Letelier, the hijacking of TWA 847, and the hijacking of the Achille Lauro cruise ship.

As a defense attorney, he has represented a wide range of individuals and organizations. His recognized investigative talents have resulted in the representation of numerous clients for whom charges were never brought. He also served as Chief Counsel to the U.S. House of Representatives for the October Surprise Task Force, investigating allegations that William Casey and others delayed the release of the U.S. Embassy hostages held in Iran to deny reelection to President Jimmy Carter. Additionally, he served as Special Master to two federal judges regarding sensitive law office search issues. As well as being past Vice Chair of the American Bar Association's White Collar Crime Committee, he is a Fellow of the American College of Trial Lawyers.

Unbalanced Justice?

By E. Lawrence Barcella, Jr.

With at least a moderate touch of nationalistic arrogance and philosophical superiority, we Americans have long prided ourselves on our sense of justice and fair play. Perhaps because we are, at our core, a diverse mix of nationalities, cultures, religions and beliefs, and because many of our forebears arrived here to escape repression and injustice, we believe that the body of laws we have developed are as sound, just and protective as any in the world.

We enjoy a robust legal system at the federal, state, and local levels. We have laws, statutes, rules and regulations that fill vast libraries. We are particularly proud of our court system. We learn in junior high civics classes that this system may have its flaws, but it is the best in the world. On the civil side, an aggrieved party can file a complaint for virtually any perceived wrong and have the case reviewed at some level at least by a judge and perhaps by a jury. On the criminal side, we proudly talk about the Constitutional rights and legal protections our defendants enjoy. To a large extent, in both criminal and civil matters, the parties enjoy a right to a trial by jury, a system in which each side can present its version of the facts and let a cross-section of the community decide who is right and who is wrong.

There are grave imbalances, however, in access to those facts. In civil cases, where money is usually at stake, there is virtually open discovery between the plaintiffs and defendants as to what the likely evidence would be. In criminal cases, on the other hand, where an individual's liberty is at stake, the government is in almost singular control of the evidence. What does it say about our society that the scales of justice seem far more balanced when tangible things are at stake than when the most important of intangibles—freedom—is at issue? As is often the case, history provides context, but not always rationale.

Up through the early part of the 20th century, civil and criminal proceedings were essentially alternative ways for victims of wrongs to seek redress. It may be hard to believe now, but the idea of a government-funded prosecutor is one of relatively recent vintage. Before the advent of public prosecutors, a victim often sought a private prosecutor to gather evidence and prosecute an action seeking both civil and criminal penalties. As a result, real and perceived differences between civil and criminal justice were minimal. Today, civil practice is dictated almost exclusively by private lawyers, with virtually no government involvement, while criminal process is dictated almost exclusively by the government, with little input from private lawyers. While politicians in Washington regularly decry the power of civil trial lawyers and attempt to legislate limits to their effectiveness, they also regularly augment the already incredible powers of prosecutors in criminal cases.

So how do these differences affect an individual's access to information? On the civil side, any citizen or organization that feels victimized can file a lawsuit which, with certain minimal exceptions, triggers a process known as discovery. During discovery, lawyers for both sides can demand that all the documents and evidence supporting the plaintiff's claim or the defendant's defense be produced to the other side, and can compel the testimony of witnesses that may tend to support one side or the other. The process of discovery can be time-consuming, onerous and occasionally used to try to bring one side or the other into submission. At the end of the day, however, lawyers on both sides are in a position to know most of the facts, circumstances and evidence surrounding a claim. If one party or another is taken by surprise, it's usually because that party didn't take full advantage of the liberal rules of discovery. Given this broad access to the evidence, those civil cases with a sufficiently strong factual basis usually end up settling. Such settlements are very often quite private, with the world never knowing their precise terms.

In criminal practice, on the other hand, the prosecution virtually controls the arsenal of discovery. Prosecutors and police have wide investigative powers, including the ability to obtain arrest warrants, search warrants, wiretaps, as well as subpoenas from grand juries empanelled to enable prosecutors to investigate possible criminal activity. They can make people stand in line ups, provide fingerprints, and supply blood and DNA samples. The most skilled criminal defense attorneys and private investigators can compel none of those things during the course of an investigation. Even after charges are brought against someone, the rules of criminal discovery limit a defendant's access to evidence that the prosecution determines will be used at trial, allowing the prosecutor to weed out anything that might not be helpful to their case. The timing of production of that evidence, moreover, may be long after charges are brought and only shortly before a trial begins. While prosecutors are obligated to produce all evidence tending to show that a defendant did not commit the crime with which he or she is charged, it is the prosecutor who decides what constitutes evidence that would assist the defense, and the timing of such disclosures, again, often makes its utilization less than helpful. In a reality theater played out thousands of times throughout the country each day, judges quietly accept the rote representation of prosecutors that "We are well aware of our obligations [to produce favorable evidence] and will act accordingly." While most prosecutors are well meaning, since they investigated and brought the case in the first place, their view of what evidence might be material to the defense can be narrowly colored.

In recent years, the distinction between criminal and civil discovery has become more prominent because of the emergence of what are known as parallel proceedings. As has been observed in many of the recent corporate scandals, it is common for a criminal investigation to take place at the same time as a civil investigation by the Securities and Exchange Commission as well as civil lawsuits by private plaintiffs. In high-visibility cases, you can also add Congressional subpoenas and hearings into the mix. This scenario has played out in virtually all of the recent highly-publicized scandals, such as Enron, Worldcom and Adelphia. These parallel proceedings very often put targets of a criminal investigation in a remarkably uncomfortable position, while rarely giving them the advantages that one would think they could obtain in civil discovery. The Fifth Amendment to the U.S. Constitution provides that no one can be compelled to say anything that might tend to incriminate him. No defendant in a criminal investigation can be forced to testify against himself. Prosecutors cannot ask a jury to draw any adverse inference against a defendant because he pleads the Fifth Amendment; in fact, you normally can't even tell a jury that a defendant has taken the Fifth. This is great protection in a criminal case. But if that same defendant is simultaneously under investigation by the SEC, or if there is a civil lawsuit pending, he may be noticed to provide a deposition, and if he invokes that beloved Fifth Amendment privilege, an adverse or negative inference can be drawn against him, and he may lose on the civil side whatever the plaintiff is suing for.

So can a defendant caught in parallel proceedings deal with this apparent imbalance? Not easily. A defendant under criminal investigation is unlikely to prevail on a motion to stay a pending civil action unless and until criminal charges are actually filed. Nor does a defendant have the ability to seek a delay in the criminal investigation. If a defendant cannot delay, then logic might suggest under these circumstances that the individual under investigation should at least be able to use the civil discovery process to find out what evidence there may be against him. Unfortunately, this rarely happens. While prosecutors almost always succeed when seeking stays of civil discovery in order to prevent defendants from seeing the evidence against them, defendants under criminal investigation who seek meaningful discovery in civil cases are usually viewed as meddlesome by judges. Oftentimes, counsel for such defendants are told (not just by prosecutors, but frighteningly by judges as well) that they don't need discovery because they can simply ask their clients what happened. If we pride ourselves, as we do, on providing criminal defendants with the presumption of innocence, being told to ask the defendant turns that venerable concept into meaningless drivel.

Many will argue that this view that criminal and civil discovery should both be open and full is simplistic and naïve. Most criminal defendants are, after all, viewed as criminals as soon as charges are brought. Just look at the spectacle surrounding the brief arrest of John Karr in the JonBenét Ramsey case. Then the DNA results came in! The laws are not designed, however, for the purpose of helping criminals, but rather with the goal of protecting us all. If they do not protect the worst of us, they cannot protect any of us.

In a scene from Robert Bolt's *A Man for all Seasons*, Sir Thomas More, England's Chancellor, refuses to endorse Henry the VIII's wish to divorce his aging wife so that he can marry his mistress. In trying to explain the importance of laws, he's asked whether he would give the Devil the benefit of law. His accuser says that he would cut down every law in England to go after the Devil. More's response eloquently explains his principles:

> Oh! And when the last law was down,
> and the Devil turned round on you, where
> would you hide, Roper, the laws all being flat?
> This country's planted thick with laws from
> coast to coast—Man's laws, not God's—and if
> you cut them down—and you're just the man
> to do it—do you really think you could stand
> upright in the winds that would blow then?
> Yes, I'd give the Devil the benefit of law, for
> my own safety's sake.

ROGER C. SPAEDER, a lawyer and former federal prosecutor, is a partner in the firm of Zuckerman Spaeder LLP, headquartered in Washington, D.C. His practice concentrates on the defense of federal enforcement investigations and includes service as Special Counsel to the Executive Office of the President of the United States. He successfully defended a former U.S. Secretary of Energy on bribery allegations under the Independent Counsel Statute and represented the former General Counsel of the CIA in an investigation of unauthorized release of classified information. His post-Enron experience includes the representation of high-profile public company executives before the SEC and federal grand juries.

A native of Ohio, Mr. Spaeder attended college and received his undergraduate degree in mathematics in 1965. For the next three years, he was a mathematician with the U.S. Central Intelligence Agency. Following law school, he was a law clerk in the office of U.S. Attorney (now Judge) Thomas A. Flannery, and from 1971 to 1976, he served as an Assistant United States Attorney for the District of Columbia. Mr. Spaeder has been a faculty member of the Attorney General's Advocacy Institute and the National Institute of Trial Advocacy. He was an adjunct faculty member at the Georgetown University Law Center and the Harvard Law School Litigation Program. He was Cardozo Prize Judge at the Yale Law School in 1992, and his articles have appeared in *The National Law Journal, American Banker, Corporate Criminal Liability Reporter,* and *Criminal Justice* magazine.

An Inequality
of Forces

By Roger C. Spaeder

"A doubt for which you can give a reason." For centuries we have asked juries in criminal cases to decide the guilt of a defendant by requiring proof "beyond a reasonable doubt." When asked for a definition of "reasonable doubt," judges have given this one. It emphasizes that the jury must acquit a defendant if any juror has a doubt about guilt for which the juror can articulate a reason.

Our justice system distinguishes itself in another important way. We begin our criminal trials with a legal presumption that the defendant is innocent. We tout this presumption as representative of our system of democratic government with its respect for the rights of individuals as its core value. We say that it is better that one hundred guilty persons go free than one innocent person be convicted. Many of the Constitution's provisions are intended to increase the likelihood that our criminal trials will be fair.

In the resolution of criminal cases, we often visualize the Constitution as an "invisible thumb" on the scales of justice, pushing down on the accused's side to ensure that before he is found guilty, the government's evidence must be strong enough to overcome the presumption of innocence and leave no reasonable doubt of guilt.

While these requirements speak eloquently to our highest aspirations, they overlook the realities of our criminal justice system. We may hold the government to the highest burden of proof, and we may presume the defendant innocent until proven otherwise, but we often fail to ensure justice for all because we neglect the basic requirements of a fair trial.

This neglect permeates our criminal justice system. It derives from the imbalance of forces that exists in a typical trial. The theory of our adversary system is that truth is more likely discovered if both sides are given equal resources and then battle one another in the arena of the courtroom. We believe that with each side firmly committed to the interests of its respective client, the contest that comprises a trial will result in an accurate finding of guilt or innocence. The presumption of innocence and the burden of proof are procedural rights that contribute to but do not guarantee a fair and accurate trial outcome.

In the real world of criminal justice, where the vast majority of defendants are poor, we almost never find equality of resources in the courtroom. Even in capital cases, we rarely provide indigent defendants with counsel having the same qualifications and receiving the same compensation as the prosecution. The documented history of countless capital cases demonstrates that the accused is typically represented by inexperienced counsel with inadequate resources. We pay lip service to the ideal of a fair trial, but without a true equality of resources, we can never be certain that the adversary system is working as intended.

Efforts to address this imbalance have been only marginally successful. For the indigent defendant charged in the federal criminal justice system, judges are empowered to appoint counsel from the office of the Federal Public Defender. These lawyers are usually well qualified but are overburdened with cases. There is no parity, for example, between the staffs of the United States Attorney's offices and those of the Federal Public Defender, even taking into account the fact that the prosecutors' offices must be larger because they investigate crimes as well as bring them to trial. If a Federal Public Defender is unavailable, judges can appoint private attorneys to represent the indigent accused, but the compensation is low and payment is slow. In state criminal justice systems, where the vast majority of defendants in this country are prosecuted, the problem is much worse.

In the modern courtroom, the use of scientific or forensic evidence is commonplace, and the government typically has unlimited resources in this respect. The same can not be said for the indigent defendant, who in some states is forced to defend himself with virtually no access to talented investigators and qualified scientific experts. The prosecutor is free to hire any specialist deemed necessary for a successful prosecution, yet the indigent defendant must petition the court for every dollar needed to pay for similar services.

In the last two decades, the effects of this imbalance have reached even the middle class. A business person or civil servant charged with a crime quickly learns that the financial resources necessary to mount an adequate defense often exceed his net worth. And very recently, the government has exploited this financial imbalance by actively discouraging employers from funding the costs of employees' defenses. The government contends that, although presumed innocent, the defendant should not receive financial assistance from his corporate employer because such assistance by the employer would be inconsistent with the employer's obligation to "cooperate" with the government's investigation.

The middle-class defendant confronts a truly horrific situation. Because he does not meet the legal definition of an indigent defendant, the middle-class accused is ineligible for court-appointed counsel. But without financial assistance, he will likely be unable to engage qualified defense counsel. At least if he were indigent, he would qualify for appointment of counsel paid by the state. Often, the middle-class defendant has been charged with a crime arising out of his employment and is entitled by state law to a defense funded by his corporate employer. This frequently occurs if the employer is a business corporation. By discouraging the employer from advancing the costs of the employee's defense, the government effectively deprives the defendant of his right to counsel. This alone can dissuade a middle-class defendant from exercising his right to a trial by jury and instead coerce him into entering a guilty plea when, if properly defended by a lawyer with adequate resources, he would be acquitted. This is the most acute example of the government's overt tampering with the balance of resources and directly interfering with a defendant's right to a fair trial.

All of us must strive to oppose any government policy or practice that threatens our process of fairly determining guilt or innocence. Given the critical role played by the balance of forces in our judicial system, we must protect this equilibrium. Whether the issue is adequate funding of government programs to compensate counsel for the indigent accused or ensuring the rights of defendants to receive reimbursement of legal fees by their employer, we must resist any effort to tamper with the balance of forces in our courtrooms.

ROBERT S. BENNETT is a partner of Skadden, Arps, Slate, Meagher & Flom LLP. He is a former federal prosecutor, renowned for being one of the nation's most influential and successful trial attorneys. In addition to the representation of Enron, other successful recent corporate representations include HealthSouth in connection with a criminal investigation being conducted by the United States Attorney's Office for the Northern District of Alabama. Mr. Bennett was also lead counsel in the KPMG tax shelter investigation being conducted by the United States Attorney's Office for the Southern District of New York. In KPMG, Mr. Bennett successfully obtained a deferred prosecution agreement which was a significant victory for the nation's fourth largest accounting firm.

Mr. Bennett successfully represented two former Secretaries of Defense, Clark Clifford (Democrat) and Caspar Weinberger (Republican). His extensive experience includes representing clients before Congressional committees; Mr. Bennett Has served as Special Counsel to the United States Senate's Select Committee on Ethics in several major investigations. He was President Clinton's personal attorney in the Paula Jones case and, most recently, he represented Judith Miller in the CIA leak investigation. In 1981 and 1982, he served as a legal consultant to the Senate Foreign Relations Committee regarding the appointment of Alexander M. Haig, Jr. as Secretary of State.

Robert Bennett has written extensively on complex criminal and civil matters and crisis management issues.

It is Beyond a
Reasonable Doubt—
Be Fair to Judges.
Judicial Independence Requires it!

By Robert S. Bennett

As a Washington lawyer for over 40 years I have observed our three branches of government—Congress, the Executive and the Judiciary—up close. My legal practice has enabled me to work with all three branches. As a result, it is absolutely clear to me that the federal judiciary is the jewel of our system of government. Our federal judicial system is the envy of the world. One major reason our capitalist system thrives and attracts foreign investment is because of the stability, integrity and independence of our federal judiciary. The world knows that you will get a fair shake in our federal courts. Moreover, respect for the independence of the federal judiciary guarantees that issues will be resolved by law and not violence. When the Supreme Court decided <u>Bush v. Gore</u>, which handed the Presidency to Mr. Bush, a diplomat friend from the former Soviet Bloc said to me "You Americans are remarkable. Had our court decided a presidential election, the tanks would have been in the streets within hours." The reason that this did not occur in the United States was because of the respect most Americans have for our federal judiciary, which is based on their belief that it is truly independent.

The Founders emphasized in the Federalist papers the importance of an independent judiciary. Mr. Hamilton in The Federalist No. 78 observed that "The complete independence of the courts of justice is peculiarly essential in a limited Constitution" and Mr.

Madison, often described as the Father of the Constitution, described an independent judiciary as "an impenetrable bulwark against every assumption of power in the Legislative or Executive." Unfortunately, in recent years, that independence has come under attack by members of Congress. The attacks take several forms. Some Congresspersons condemn the judiciary in vicious terms for specific decisions. This usually is nothing more than Congressional pandering to a political base. Frequently, in order to pass legislation, Congress avoids dealing with the tough issues and leaves them for the courts to decide and then bashes them when they do not like the decisions. Other attacks include proposals to limit jurisdiction of the federal courts or legislation to create an inspector general for them. These are foolish and destructive attacks on judicial independence.

While judges should not be above criticism, they should not become battering rams for Congresspersons who are unable to resolve issues in the political process. If legislators did their jobs, many of the most emotional issues of the day such as the right to die, or gay and lesbian issues would not be dumped on the Courts. In the Terri Schiavo case, which dealt with a hopelessly brain damaged young woman, 11th Circuit Court Judge Stanley F. Birch, Jr. in rejecting the claims of Terri's parents said "In resolving the Schiavo controversy it is my judgment that, despite sincere and altruistic motivation, the legislative and executive branches of our government have acted in a manner demonstrably at odds with our Founding Fathers' blueprint for the governance of a free people—our Constitution." Following the Court's decision, House Majority Leader Tom DeLay, made the outrageous and inflammatory statement "Mrs. Schiavo's death is a moral poverty and a legal tragedy. This loss happened because our legal system did not protect the people who need protection most, and that will change. The time will come for the men responsible for this to answer for their behavior, but not today." Such attacks only encourage disrespect for the courts and increase the risk of threatening conduct and even physical threats towards judges and their families.

A more subtle, indirect but arguably more damaging threat to a strong and independent judiciary is the failure of Congress to raise the salary of judges which really means the lowering of salaries because of the rise in the cost of living and the decreasing value of the dollar.

Chief Justice Roberts in his 2005 Year-End Report on the Federal Judiciary reported to the public that:

> A more direct threat to judicial independence is the failure to raise judges' pay. If judges' salaries are too low, judges effectively serve for a term dictated by their financial position rather than for life. Figures gathered by the Administrative Office show that judges are leaving the bench in greater numbers now than ever before....

> There will always be a substantial difference in pay between successful government and private sector lawyers. But if that difference remains too large—as it is today—the judiciary will over time cease to be made up of a diverse group of the Nation's very best lawyers. Instead, it will come to be staffed by a combination of the independently wealthy and those following a career path before becoming a judge different from the practicing bar at large. Such a development would dramatically alter the nature of the federal judiciary.

In 2006 the Chief Justice of the United States was paid $212,100 and the Associate Justices $203,000. Judges of the United States Court of Appeals were paid $175,100 and Judges of the United States District Courts were paid $165,200. When you consider the fact that young lawyers without any legal experience, except for judicial clerkships, often make more than the experienced judges they worked for, something is wrong. A law clerk to a Supreme Court

Justice in today's market can command a salary of close to $200,000 a year and on top of that receive a signing bonus in the range of $240,000. That a young lawyer, without any real experience, can start a career making approximately $400,000, almost twice what the Chief Justice of the United States earns, is a cause for concern.

No one, I think would argue that judges should earn as much on the bench as they could at a law firm. Public service always carries a price. But the gap between private sector pay and judicial salaries has grown too large. Not only is it unfair to current judges, but it will inevitably hurt the ability of our nation to attract to the judiciary the brightest and the best members of the legal community. Do we really want a system in which only independently wealthy individuals choose to take the bench, or those who see a judgeship as providing a substantial pay raise?

In order to protect the long-term health of the judiciary, Congress must rise to the occasion. Congress has shown an unwillingness to raise judges' salaries above its own (and, for political reasons, has generally been unwilling to give itself meaningful raises).

The linking of judges' salaries to those of members of Congress makes no sense. Unlike members of Congress, federal judges do not have well heeled lobbyists doing all that they can to help with various forms of financial assistance. Federal judges have a unique role under our Constitution. They have life tenure, and, for the most part, we want them to assume the bench and stay there and do nothing else but judge. Judges are not expected to serve for a few years and then cash in in the private sector—as members of Congress and high-ranking executive officials routinely do. Nor do we want them writing books or giving speeches to supplement their salaries. Federal judges—because of very strict rules not applicable to Congress—are very limited in their ability to supplement their income.

Not only should judges receive a hefty raise, but Congress should ensure that they receive automatic cost-of-living adjustments, just as virtually every other government employee does. The constitutional guarantee of a judicial salary that "shall not be diminished" is of substantially less value if that salary can be eaten away by inflation.

A pay raise and automatic cost-of-living adjustments are the only way to go.

Our federal judiciary is the jewel of our system. Common sense and fairness dictate that we protect this great treasure.

DICK THORNBURGH was elected Governor of Pennsylvania in 1978 and was re-elected in 1982; the first Republican ever to serve two successive terms in that office. During his service as Governor, Thornburgh balanced state budgets for eight consecutive years, reduced both personal and business tax rates, cut the state's record-high indebtedness and left a surplus of $350 million.

After his unanimous confirmation by the United States Senate, Thornburgh served three years as Attorney General of the United States (1988-1991) in the cabinets of Presidents Reagan and Bush. He mounted an unprecedented attack on white-collar crime as the Department of Justice obtained a record number of convictions of savings and loan and securities officials, defense contractors and corrupt public officials.

The *Legal Times* noted that Thornburgh as Attorney General "built a reputation as one of the most effective champions that prosecutors have ever had." He was instrumental as well in the passage of the Americans With Disabilities Act. His 25-year public career also included service as the highest-ranking American at the United Nations. He is presently a lawyer in Washington, D.C. with Kirkpatrick & Lockhart Nicholson Graham LLP and an occasional guest on *Larry King Live*.

What I Believe
"Beyond a Reasonable Doubt"

By Dick Thornburgh

A professional life in the practice of law and in holding public office has taught me the absolute necessity of societies and systems of government being based upon the Rule of Law. Our experience in America has demonstrated "beyond a reasonable doubt" just how vital this principle is to human progress. To accomplish justice and enhance human rights anywhere requires the structure and discipline that can only flow from rigorous application of the Rule of Law.

The Rule of Law is not a set of beliefs rooted in prayer or devotion. Nor does it provide the basis for the observance of secular holidays where politicians orate and high school bands play. It is much more subtle and more sophisticated that that. The Rule of Law provides the very framework within which government and individuals exist in a democratic society.

To what end is the application of the Rule of Law pursued? What specific gains to humankind come from strict adherence to the Rule of Law? What are the consequences of its absence from any society? Here the answers are clear and they derive from examination of our very first collective legislative enactment, the Constitution of the United States.

Today the United States stands throughout the world as the prime exemplar of the advantages of the Rule of Law and of a democratic political system. We are the envy of most other nations and their people for characteristics which, frankly, we all too often take for granted. Consider, for example, what our Constitution's Bill of Rights guarantees to every citizen:

• The right to free speech, no matter how unpopular the views expressed may be.

• The right to peaceably assemble and petition our governments for the redress of our grievances, real or imagined.

• Absolute freedom of the press, to spread its views among the populace, regardless of whether or not they hew to the "party line."

• The right to worship if, and as, we please.

• Equal opportunity for advancement, regardless of race, religion, creed, gender, ethnic origin or, most recently, disability.

• Due process of law to ensure that our property is free from unlawful seizure and our persons are protected from the arbitrary exercise of police power.

Sustaining and supporting all of these is an independent judiciary, part of a legal system, which is designed to enforce all these rights on a neutral basis—the very essence of the Rule of Law.

Our political system is also distinguished from the majority of those around the world. We have the absolute right to vote to elect and un-elect those who hold public office at all levels of our government. It has been said that the beauty of our system is not that it is always right, but that it is usually responsive. Indeed, there is built into that system, as in no other, a high degree of accountability of public servants to those whom they serve.

While we are accustomed to thinking of the Rule of Law in its important role as a protector of civil rights and civil liberties, it is also a major factor in promoting economic growth and job creation in our country and elsewhere. It guarantees a competitive environment. It ensures full access to the courts to enforce contractual undertakings and to prevent government expropriation of business assets. These features are notably absent in countries where the Rule of Law is not enshrined, where arbitrary decisions by faceless functionaries are the rule and prospects for economic growth are correspondingly stifled.

In all of these areas, what we enjoy in our nation is looked on with covetous eyes by most of the world's people—especially those still living under despotic rulers, fearful of the knock on the door at night, unable to speak out against injustices, mired in poverty and laboring within backward economies which are often corrupted by their leaders. Worst of all, too many of the world's peoples today are denied the means at the ballot box to effect necessary changes in their political and governmental systems. Progress in all these areas, I suggest, must be founded on a firm adherence to the Rule of Law.

Thus the Rule of Law is no mere principle. It has real world every day consequences. And its absence or failure of full implementation can well consign those who do not enjoy its beneficence to permanent second-class status in the world community.

One of our greatest presidents, Abraham Lincoln, was first and foremost a man of the law. A superb legal practitioner himself, he revered the law and its values as a guide for his fellow Americans. Early in his public career, in January 1838, he laid out his beliefs in no uncertain terms:

> Let reverence for the law, be breathed by every American mother, to the lisping babe, that prattles in her lap. Let it be taught in school, in seminaries, in colleges;—let it be written in primers, spelling books and almanacs;—let it be preached from the pulpit, proclaimed in the legislative halls, and enforced in the courts of justice. In short let it become the political religion of the nation.

The Rule of Law today is being sorely tested at home and abroad by fanatic terrorists, corrupt politicians and corporate wrongdoers in ways never before experienced. Our journey may at times seem challenging. But so long as we adhere to the principles inherent in the Rule of Law, I have no doubt that we can move toward a productive future with energy and confidence.

This is why it is Abraham Lincoln's "political religion"—the Rule of Law—in which I today believe "beyond a reasonable doubt."

WILLIAM DEVERELL was a journalist for seven years and a trial lawyer for twenty, as defender or prosecutor in more than a thousand criminal cases, including thirty murder trials. His first legal thriller, *Needles*, won the $50,000 Seal Prize and the Book of the Year Award. His subsequent 12 novels include *Trial of Passion*, which won the Dashiell Hammett Award for literary excellence in crime writing in North America. In 2006, a sequel, *April Fool*, earned him his second Arthur award for best Canadian crime novel. His novels have been translated into fourteen languages and sold worldwide.

He is also the creator of CBC-TV's long-running series, *Street Legal*, which has run internationally in more than 50 countries. He has served as Visiting Professor in the Creative Writing Department, University of Victoria, has been twice Chair of the Writers' Union of Canada, and is an honorary director of the B.C. Civil Liberties Association. He lives on Canada's Gulf Islands and, in winter, Costa Rica.

His life and works can be viewed at www.deverell.com.

Reasonable Doubt—
a Canadian Perspective

By William Deverell

From my twenty years as criminal counsel (before I escaped the clutches of the law and became a novelist), I can't count the times a jury collectively popped back into court to ask: "Could you define reasonable doubt again?" The judge would patiently, in mantra-like syllables, repeat the lesson. (I've also known judges who by tone, emphasis and even facial expression—all missing from the record on appeal—might as well be saying to the jury: "I'm compelled to recite all this la-di-da about reasonable doubt, but you'd be out of your minds to acquit this liar.")

If jurors show themselves to be grappling with the notion of reasonable doubt, that's good, they're doing their duty. It's not easy for members of the public to cast aside a typical tendency to seek belief and certainty, or to let emotion thwart reason. It is notable that in Canada the Supreme Court has held that proof beyond a reasonable doubt lies much closer to absolute certainty than to a mere balance of probabilities, suggesting that one must be almost absolutely certain of guilt before convicting.

The time-tested standard of criminal proof works well in normal times, but in this Age of Terrorism the worry arises that citizen juries may allow emotion to prevail. I hope not. I trust juries, but do not trust legislators who peddle fear, who would limit our traditional freedom under the banner of the so-called war on terror. Much depends on a sensible citizenry unwilling to be cowed by the climate of fear and retribution.

In an age when broad anti-terrorism laws have been galloping through the world's legislatures (and merely crawling through the courts), reasonable doubt and even our traditional concept of fair trial wither when trials are secret, when defense counsel are unable to examine proofs or even consult their clients. (An egregious example is India's Prevention of Terrorism Act, which subjects suspects to six months without charges being laid and shifts to the defense the burden of proving innocence.)

Apropos are remarks of Justice David Davis in a unanimous ruling of the U.S. Supreme Court in freeing an alleged terrorist unlawfully tried during the Civil War (the Milligan case). "It is the birthright of every American citizen when charged with crime, to be tried and punished according to law.... By the protection of the law human rights are secured; withdraw that protection, and they are at the mercy of wicked rulers, or the clamor of an excited people.... The nation...has no right to expect that it will always have wise and humane rulers, sincerely attached to the principles of the Constitution. Wicked men, ambitious of power, with hatred of liberty and contempt of law, may fill the place once occupied by Washington and Lincoln; and if this [broad power of martial law] be conceded, the dangers to human liberty are frightful to contemplate."

Some would suggest that defendants in emotionally laden trials are safer opting for trial by a judge alone, who is presumably able to resist his or her own biases (though there are some judges who wouldn't recognize a reasonable doubt if it landed screaming on their head).

Here's a striking example in a Vancouver terrorism case of a judge grappling with the tenets of reasonable doubt:

Until the attack on the World Trade Towers, the 1985 bombing of Air India 182 remained the most ghastly terrorist act of modern times, and still holds the repellent distinction of being history's worst airline mass murder. The flight from Canada was bound for Mumbai but ended 31,000 feet above the Ireland coast in an explosion that murdered 250 adults and eighty children. All the world grieved—except a cell of fanatical Sikh extremists based in Vancouver.

It took prosecutors fifteen years to assemble a case against two suspected ringleaders, one a millionaire. What followed was probably the most complex criminal case in Canadian history. It ended in March 2005, after 115 witnesses were heard over 233 trial days.

Mr. Justice Ian Bruce Josephson said in his judgment: "Words are incapable of adequately conveying the senseless horror of these crimes." Those who perished "were entirely innocent victims of a diabolical act of terrorism...finding its roots in fanaticism at its basest and most inhumane level.... The horrific nature of these cruel acts of terrorism cry out for justice."

Despite that, he added, "There can be no lowering of the standard of proof from that required in any criminal trial. Justice is not achieved if persons are convicted on anything less than the requisite standard of poof beyond a reasonable doubt. Despite what appears to have been the best and most earnest efforts by the police and the Crown, the evidence has fallen markedly short of that standard."

The trial ended with two highly controversial acquittals. Mind you, much of the case stank. The prosecution produced a plethora of snitches with histories of lies and perjury or with revenge motives against the defendants. One of them, pulled from the FBI's roster of informants, was paid $300,000 by the RCMP to testify, and then demanded $200,000 on the eve of his court appearance.

The defendants' counsel chose not to elect trial by jury, and that may have been wise: a public opinion poll found that 68 per cent of those who followed the case disagreed with the verdict. But of course they hadn't taken the crash course in reasonable doubt that judges must give juries.

The doctrine of reasonable doubt and its sister precept, presumption of innocence, are the linchpins of our democratic justice system—we must always be wary of attempts to chip away at them.

RICHARD BEN-VENISTE is a partner in the Washington, D.C. office of Mayer, Brown, Rowe & Maw. He was Assistant Special Prosecutor and Chief of the Watergate Task Force, and prosecuted the principal Nixon Administration defendants in the Watergate cover-up trial. As Chief of the Special Prosecutions Section of the United States Attorney's Office, Southern District of New York, he successfully prosecuted a wide variety of fraud, official corruption, organized crime and labor racketeering cases. Mr. Ben-Veniste has served as Special Counsel to the Senate Subcommittee on Governmental Operations and as minority Chief Counsel to the Senate Whitewater Committee.

In 2002, Mr. Ben-Veniste was appointed to the National Commission on Terrorist Attacks on the United States. In July 2004, the 9/11 Commission issued its Report and recommendations. Mr. Ben-Veniste is a Presidential appointee to the Nazi War Crimes and Japanese Imperial Government Records Interagency Working Group, which is mandated to declassify secret documents relating to World War II era war crimes. Since 1998, the IWG has supervised the declassification of more than 8 million pages of previously classified documents.

While in private practice, Mr. Ben-Veniste has represented clients in a broad array of white-collar criminal investigations and trials including securities fraud, mail and wire fraud, bank fraud, conflict of interest, tax evasion, antitrust, false statements, bribery, foreign payments and RICO violations. Additionally, he has been involved in a wide range of civil matters including class action securities fraud, RICO, congressional investigations, Lanham Act, FHA and ADA breach of contract, internal investigations, licensing and intellectual properties, civil rights, law firm and oil and gas partnership disputes, and trade secrets litigation.

Mr. Ben-Veniste is the co-author of *Stonewall: The Real Story of the Watergate Prosecution* (Simon & Schuster). During the Congressional hearings on the Iran-Contra affair, Mr. Ben-Veniste was NBC's on-air legal consultant, and has been a frequent commentator on current affairs involving the intersection of law and politics. Mr. Ben-Veniste has been listed in *Who's Who in America* since 1975, *The Best Lawyers in America* since 1983, and *Washingtonian* magazine's Top Lawyers in Washington, D.C. since 1992, when the list first appeared.

In the end
we must all be partisans—
for the truth

By Richard Ben-Veniste

What is it about exposing the hypocrisy and mendacity of public officials that continues to get my juices flowing? Perhaps a combination of the idealism taught me in the New York City public schools, a mother who reflected the edgy skepticism of a childhood in foster care, and a patriotic father who served overseas in the Army Air Corps during WWII got me started in believing that our nation's leaders owe us a duty of telling the truth.

Examples of a politician making puffed-up campaign promises, exaggerating his record, or minimizing extracurricular sexual liaisons are hardly remarkable. But those in high office who make false and misleading statements about matters of life and death or our constitutional protections, while at the same time proclaiming their moral rectitude, invariably make me see red. Over the course of my career, I have sometimes found myself in a position to do something about it.

As a young federal prosecutor in New York City, I cut my teeth on organized crime and labor racketeering cases. Usually, the major villains were "honest" about their crimes. If caught and convicted, they did their time as the cost of doing business.

I soon gravitated to the investigation and prosecution of corrupt officials. In the late 60s, a crooked lawyer named Nathan Voloshen was found to be operating an influence-peddling ring out of the office of Speaker of the House, John W. McCormack (D-MA).

We soon linked Voloshen to McCormack's longtime Administrative Assistant, Martin Sweig. Regularly, Voloshen would fly the shuttle from New York to Washington, where he would install himself behind McCormack's district office desk, with full access to staff, phones and stationery. His requests for special consideration for his well-heeled clients at various federal agencies, were accompanied by calls from Sweig, who could mimic the Speaker's voice perfectly, expressing the Speaker's personal support for whatever favor Voloshen was asking.

What got my particular attention were the cases in which the Speaker's office interceded on behalf of young men drafted into military service. The Speaker was a voluble and consistent hawk on the Vietnam War. But having the office of the second most powerful elected official in government win discharge and other favorable treatment for the rich and well-connected, while others by the tens of thousands were giving their lives and future well-being to the war effort, was a truly reprehensible piece of hypocrisy. I prosecuted Sweig in two separate cases involving favors for servicemen, convicting him of bribery and perjury. Voloshen pleaded guilty and died shortly thereafter. While no evidence was produced implicating Speaker McCormack in the scheme, he surrendered his office by not standing for reelection.

Given my role in investigating the office of a powerful Democrat, it was mildly surprising that President Nixon's political spin machine branded me (along with Archibald Cox and the rest of the Watergate Special Prosecutor's staff) as a political partisan out to get Nixon. In the end, it was hubris and hypocrisy—tied to a plethora of criminal and constitutional violations—that brought Nixon down. Had he accepted responsibility early on for his underlings' criminality instead of launching a massive cover-up, Nixon's presidency might well have survived. In the end, Nixon's outright lies to the American people about his role in the conspiracy to obstruct justice— proved irrefutably by his own secretly tape-recorded conversations— made for a choice between certain impeachment or resignation.

An independent, bipartisan commission to investigate the 9/11 attacks was created over President Bush's initial opposition. We were determined to be as transparent as possible in disclosing to the public as much of the 9/11 story as our investigation revealed. Along the way, it became clear that the Administration was unwilling to provide the 9/11 Commission a critical document that showed that the President was warned by CIA, in an ultra-secret briefing more than a month before the 9/11 attacks when our intelligence agencies were anticipating an imminent "spectacular" attack by al Qaeda, that bin Laden was determined to strike at the American homeland. It would appear that political embarrassment—rather than legitimate concern over national security—motivated the effort to keep the contents of this briefing secret. Similarly, statements professing that "no one could have anticipated commercial planes being used as weapons," and claims that Saddam and Iraq were involved in the 9/11 attack were shown to be misleading, at best.

As we face ever more creative forms of manipulation and disingenuousness by those in power, I believe, beyond a reasonable doubt, that the American people have a right to know the truth and, that the quality of our democracy depends on it.

In the end we must all be partisans—for the truth.

DANIEL B. SPITZER practices in the areas of business litigation, real estate law, and mediation in Encino, California. Born in 1953, Spitzer is a graduate of UCLA, where he spent 12 years completing undergraduate studies, a Masters Degree in Comparative Literature, and law school. Mr. Spitzer has written on a variety of topics, ranging from the treatment of retirement trusts under the Bankruptcy Code, to unlawful detainer issues, to the most recent changes in the Bankruptcy Code.

Among the published cases Mr. Spitzer has successfully litigated are the United States Bankruptcy Court's decision in In re Bosse, 122 B. R. 410 (Bankr.C.D. Cal. 1990), and the California Court of Appeals decisions in Okrand v. City of Los Angeles (1989) 207 Cal.App.3d 566 and Leasequip v. Dapeer (2002) 103 Cal. App. 4th 394. Spitzer has been designated as an expert witness in several legal malpractice matters, and condominium disputes.

Mr. Spitzer has a long commitment to pro bono activities as part of his practice. He has represented, among others, the Valley Beth Shalom Day School, Friends of Lubavitch, Chabad of Simcha Monica, Catholic Relief Services and Project New Start. He has served on the Board of Directors and Board of Governors of the Jewish Federation-Council of Greater Los Angeles, and until 2004 served as the Vice-President for Legal Affairs of the Valley Beth Shalom Day School.

Beyond a
Reasonable Order

By Daniel B. Spitzer

To this child of the late 1950s and 1960s in the United States, it was clear, beyond a reasonable doubt, that the world was a well-ordered place.

I suppose that politics, economics and science all lent themselves to that gauzy sense of security. The United States was the greatest country in the world, a fact my father, a veteran of the Pacific Theater in World War II, constantly impressed upon us. Hitler and his minions were dead. Our leaders seemed trustworthy, even heroic—the commanding Eisenhower, the professorial Stevenson, the energetic young Kennedy. Even our enemies seemed predictable, with the world evenly stacked between our friends, and those other, darkened souls beyond the Iron Curtain of Communism. The economy was expanding, rapidly, and there were jobs and opportunities to be had. We believed that all problems could be resolved with enough work, enough research, enough understanding.

Many of my generation have written about the crystallizing impact of the Kennedy assassination. "Where were you when…?" was a question posed thousands of times, an emblem of our bonding as a generation and as a nation. To me, however, the more formative moment came 11 years later, with the resignation of Richard Nixon. Can you imagine anything more frightening than that moment, when these noisy adolescents, who had turned "Tricky Dick" into the symbol of everything wrong, everything they hated about America, were actually proven right? Even more vividly than the Kennedy assassination, I recall the Nixon resignation speech, the sour, sickening feeling that our world had now truly begun the descent into chaos and disorder. The veneer of a well-ordered world had been entirely stripped away and I, for one, felt no joy at Nixon's humiliation.

My choice of law as a profession came late, after seven years of a Ph.D. program in Comparative Literature. Law was immediately refreshing. For years, I had toiled endlessly with literary texts, constructing, dissecting, deconstructing, and had written voluminous, very bad critical studies. In law, my words had a concrete reality, which I had never experienced before. It seemed like the highest form of imitatio dei: speaking words, and having them spring into being; creating order where chaos had reigned before. A client's rambling story was distilled into charging allegations; causes of action were researched, complaints were drafted, litigation and change ensued. An idea became a contract and gave rise to a new business. A loan agreement took material form as a new building was erected. I was enthralled.

The nagging sense of chaos, however, remained. My first day on the job as a new lawyer, fresh out of law school, still awaiting bar results, the managing partner of my first firm met with all of the new hires. He told us five words to guide ourselves in the practice of law: "Assume nothing. Trust no one."

That moment marked the beginning of my professional law practice. It also haled my dawning recognition that chaos, not order, would more often than not be the leitmotif of my practice.

For what brought me into law was a love of order and predictability, the sense that one can, through study and perseverance, arrive at clarity and truth and the right result. Moses the lawgiver had given tablets of truth, and it was for us to discern their true meaning; the Founding Fathers, likewise, had given us a Constitution to interpret, so as to discover their truth. Yes, the representation of a client is the lawyer's immediate task, but the higher purpose is supposed to be a search for truth.

Isn't it?

I could not have been more wrong, at least in practice. Order is illusion. Predictability is a function of politics and spin and the color of one's tie. Truth, I was about to learn, is flexible, the lessons of Rashomon brought into the courtroom.

During my first year of practice, one of the firm's senior partners outside my practice group took me under his wing. In retrospect, I think he was more in need of a drinking partner than impressed with my intellect or wide-eyed enthusiasm for the practice of law. For my part, I was content to drink his wisdom, along with whatever else he was buying.

One night, I shared my frustration at a particularly difficult deposition in which our client's testimony had contradicted the essential details of a transaction, as she had painstakingly related them to us for months previously.

He turned to me and smiled. "Everybody lies," he said. "It's the one fundamental principle you can rely on. Everybody lies."

Assume nothing; trust no one. Everybody lies.

And without a doubt, these verities have stood me well in my law practice. By assuming nothing, I have learned to anticipate, and not to fear, the unexpected. By trusting no one, even myself, I have learned to discount the statements made to me by everyone, knowing that for the purpose of practicing law, the only "truth" which matters is the final determination by a judge or jury. I have learned that there is nothing intrinsically predictable or orderly about the practice of law. I have learned that our legal system depends on fairness and justice, upon the goodwill of jurists and common citizens, and not on some innate attribute.

This all sounds very dark and somber. To the contrary: I do not find myself becoming more cynical and detached. I have simply come to understand that the skills of a lawyer are neutral tools which may be used well, for good or not, depending upon the proclivities of the practitioner. The moral lessons I attempt to impart to my own children derive more from the mythos of the law—due process, equal justice for all, and that vaunted sense of order and predictability—than from its reality.

I am still passionate about that sense of order, and I still suffer outrage when a particularly galling result occurs. More and more, however, I am impressed with the organicism of the law. Even when a jury returns the wrong result, or a judge decides a question of law against me, I recognize that there is a process—perhaps not entirely to my liking—in the making. In this chaos, a sense of order still manages to bubble up to the surface.

MARTIN GARBUS is a partner with the law firm of Davis & Gilbert LLP. One of the country's leading First Amendment trial lawyers, Martin Garbus has tried First Amendment civil and criminal cases, as well as media cases, in many states. He has appeared before the United States Supreme Court as well as the highest state and federal courts in numerous states on many occasions.

He has represented most of the major book publishers, movie companies and media conglomerates in the United States and abroad in media actions. He has also represented major entities in new media, Internet companies, networks and cable television and radio industries, including Channel 4, PBS, Pearson and Penguin-Putnam Books in the United States and Australia, Fox and Warner Bros., and Michael Bloomberg. As part of his First Amendment practice, he has represented the publishers of Salman Rushdie and Henry Miller, has personally represented actors such as Spike Lee, Al Pacino, Richard Gere, and Robert Redford, authors such as David Halberstam, as well as such well-known political dissidents such as Vaclav Havel, Nelson Mandela and Anatoly Sakharov. Garbus has also served as a consultant and lectured on the free speech sections of the Constitution and communications law in Canada, England, Australia, the former Soviet Union, Czechoslovakia, Poland and Hungary.

Mr. Garbus is the author of six books: *Ready for the Defense*; *Traitors and Heroes*; *Tough Talk: How I Fought For Writers, Comics, Bigots,* and *the American Way*; *Courting Disaster: The Supreme Court and the Unmaking of America Law*; *The Next Twenty-Five Years* and *China on the Precipice* (2008).

Time magazine described Garbus as "legendary" and "one of the country's foremost trial lawyers." *New York Magazine* called him "one of New York's most prominent lawyers," and he is listed in "The Best Lawyers in New York."

Rush to
Judgment

By Martin Garbus

There has long been a desire and movement in America for restrictions on democratic rights, for an authoritarian government propelled by a combination of religious and nationalistic fervor. The helplessness caused by the events of September 11th and the international war against Muslim "terrorists" deepened a felt need. What has led to a rush to judgment, on Iraq, on the war on terror, on how to satisfy our need for roil and on every aspect of our foreign policy?

A set of needs in Germany, long before Hitler came to power, ultimately resulted in a totalitarian state. There are similarities and of course significant differences between America in the 21st Century and Germany in the 1920s.

Bush has spoken of God as choosing him to destroy those who planned September 11th 2001; he said God chose him to be President when it was time to decide whether to go to war against Iraq, and God chose him again to lead America in its war against Iraq, a war that the administration justifies with nationalistic rhetoric and the hope of spreading the faith, of a God-fearing Christian democracy. Germany, too, had a messianic leader.

I am not alone in using the word "fascism" in trying to see what can happen in this country. Scholars and commentators from the Left and Right agree. Professor Fritz Stern, professor of German studies at Columbia University, noted the similarities, pointing out

Hitler saw himself as "the instrument of providence," who fused his "racial dogma with Germanic Christianity," who then capitalized on the longing and discontent of the people. Paul Craig Roberts, an arch-conservative, a senior fellow at the Hoover Institution and a former Wall Street editor wrote of the "brownshirting" of American conservatism, by the use of Gestapo tactics and permissive laws—he says the hype about terrorism serves little or "no purpose other than to build a police state that is far more dangerous to Americans than terrorists."

The pressure for fascism comes not just from the top. A substantial portion of America has always wanted a simpler state, one not burdened with true democracy, the trappings of a totalitarian state. When America was first being created, a number of our founders distrusted the masses, did not truly believe in democracy and wanted to call the President "His Excellency."

Authoritarian tendencies exist in this country (as well as in others); fascism can develop faster here if the President is given the unlimited power he wants to run the "war on terror" and avoid the processes of our democracy, the system of checks and balances. Never before was there such a possibility of such constitutional violations, because there has never been such an open-ended war.

The expansion of Presidential powers and the expansion of police powers is the single most important issue facing this country. How much power this President gets depends in large part on Congress and the new Supreme Court. It is safe to say a majority of Congress (both Democrats and Republicans) is prepared to give him a nearly blank check in the war on terror. Carl Levin, the liberal Democratic Senator from Michigan, an opponent of the war, sponsored legislation upholding Bush's created legal system. The Senate vote was 79-16 in favor.

The Pentagon already has expanded its domestic surveillance activity, breaks into homes, wiretaps and eavesdrops at will, and builds secret dossiers on citizens while arguing that there can be no judicial review of their activities. The President has argued there can be no judicial review of any decision he makes when he decides whether an alien or American citizen is, and is not, an enemy combatant. For years our Democratic leaders, aware of these illegal programs, said nothing.

Supporting the President, we presently have in the United States a secret Court created by the Foreign Intelligence Services Act. It is not surprising that very few people know of its existence. The courtroom is in a vault-like chamber, a windowless room on the top floor of the Department of Justice. It meets in secret, with no published opinions or public records. Nearly all of those spied upon never knew they were under surveillance. No one, except the judges involved and the John Ashcroft Department of Justice knows what it does. No one, except the government and FISA judge, knows who the warrants are aimed at. There is no review of its decisions. Over 12,000 search warrants, permitting eavesdropping, surveillance and break-ins, have been sought by the government. Although the FISA court is required to determine if there are enough facts to justify a warrant, only once has it ever denied a warrant sought by the government. There are more warrants issued by the FISA Court than by the over 1,000 district judges in the Federal system.

If there is another terrorist attack (and it is very likely there will be), the government will seek more powers, claiming that it shows the present laws on the books are inadequate. We will certainly see, as we recently saw in Britain, the head of government ask for 90-day detentions without access to court. The end of habeas corpus started at Guantanamo; it will spread to the rest of America.

Five years after we started Guantanamo, not one person in that prison has been found guilty of anything. Not one person has been convicted in an American court of terrorism. Even though there have been many, many court orders, not one detainee, either in the United States or Guantanamo or the CIA overseas bases, has been better for it: the detainees continue to be showpieces for the war on terror.

The legal system to treat the new prisoners of the war on terror, created out of thin air, disgraces us. No one ever before suggested such a legal system—not during the Civil War, not during both World Wars and not during the Cold War with Russia and China.

We are better than military commissions, Abu Ghraib, Guantanamo, the Patriot Act, and "rendition"—the sending of prisoners overseas to be tortured at CIA-controlled prisons—practices justified by the Attorney General, Vice President, the CIA and others in the administration. No previous administration ever sought to justify such practices. No previous American government has been so criticized and seen as so radical and dangerous to the rest of the world. Skepticism or disbelief about anything we or the rest of the world is told is appropriate when a potential police state starts talking about spreading its democracy.

How we conduct the "war on terror" tells the American people who we are and what this country stands for. For me it is beyond a reasonable doubt that the people who presently control the country, the politics and the corporate interests, would prefer a presidency of unlimited powers.

I also believe America, who has the oldest and most dynamic democracy in the world, can right itself. Let's immediately change course.

MICHAEL D. HAUSFELD is one of the country's top civil litigators; his career has included some of the largest and most successful class actions in the fields of human rights, discrimination and antitrust law. Hausfeld litigated such historic matters as the Holocaust/Swiss Banks cases, Texaco race discrimination, and represented native Alaskans in the Exxon Valdez suit. He is actively involved in ongoing investigations into antitrust cases abroad, and was the only private lawyer permitted to attend and represent the interests of consumers worldwide in the 2003 closed hearings by the EU Commission in the Microsoft case.

The Price
of Liberty

By Michael D. Hausfeld

Fundamental human rights law condemns genocide, systemic racial discrimination[1] and murder[2], disappearances, torture, and rape[3] committed by government officials. Those associated with these crimes are deemed "enemies" of all humankind.[4] Whoever commits or aids such violations not only affronts his or her victims, but "also hurts the common safety and well-being of all nations." They are guilty of "a crime against the whole world."[5]

But who is accountable for these atrocities? The government and its officials, the members of the military, the security and other law enforcement agencies, and, in general, the ruling political party are the obvious perpetrators of arbitrary exercises of power. They are the ones who pass the laws, pull the triggers, and torture, rape, humiliate, and dominate. They are the true faces of abuse.

But they do not act alone. As observed by the Judicial Tribunal at Nuremberg, atrocities committed by governments need:

[1] Such as in South Africa during Apartheid.
[2] The Khmer Rouge regime killed approximately 1.7 million people in a sweeping genocide between 1975 and 1979. Yale University, *The Cambodian Genocide Project*, http://www.yale.edu/cgp (last visited November 18, 2005).
[3] In Columbia, a company hired paramilitary gunmen to torture, kidnap, and murder union leaders. Rodriguezo v. Drummond, No. CV-02-BE-0665-W, 2003 WL 1889330 (N.D. Ala. April 14, 2003). In Argentina, the military engaged in arbitrary detention, disappearance, torture and murder. Forti v. Suarez-Mason, 694 F. Supp. 707 (N.D. Cal. 1988).
[4] Filartiga v. Pena Irala, 630 F.2d 876, 890 (2d Cir.1980).
[5] Respublica v. De Longchamps, 1 U.S. 111 (Pa. 08 T 1784).

> ...the cooperation of statesmen,
> military leaders, diplomats and busi-
> nessmen. When they, with knowledge of
> [these] aims, gave their cooperation,
> they made themselves parties to the
> [inhumane] plan.... They are not to be
> deemed innocent...if they knew what
> they were doing.[6]

Globalization has aggregated the concentration and exercise of economic power, enabling some international businesses to pose as great a threat to individual liberty as any rogue government. Most businesses do not place democracies in a position of choosing between economic welfare and individual well-being. Unfortunately, history is replete with tragedies of the exceptions—among others: slavery, trafficking, child labor, sweatshops, and apartheid. Although episodic, there is a legacy of those who have sought to extract too great a benefit for too few, at the expense of too many, who were made to suffer too much.

In South Africa, for example, for over four decades the Apartheid regime received the willing cooperation and help of certain businesses in violating the fundamental human rights of black South Africans. These businesses saw opportunity where others suffered the pain of oppression. Infringements on individual well-being and dignity were collateral and subservient to economic investment and development. After the Sharpeville massacre in 1960, for example, a top official of UBS, the largest Swiss bank, was asked, "Is Apartheid necessary or desirable?" He responded, "Not really necessary, but definitely desirable."[7] Similarly, IBM, which supplied the Apartheid regime with the computer equipment used to establish the hated national identity card system, conceded that the Apartheid government used its

---

[6] The Nürnberg Trial 1946, 6 F.R.D. 69, 112 (1946).
[7] Truth and Reconciliation Commission Final Report, Vol. 6, Sec. 2, Ch. 5 at 18 (Mar. 21, 2003).

equipment for repression but stated, "[I]t's not really our policy to tell our customers how to conduct themselves."[8]

There is an inherent tension between capitalist principles of economic welfare and democratic principles of human well-being. Slavery, for example, is inconsistent with democracy, but compatible with capitalism. Individual liberty is essential to democracy, but irrelevant to profit.

The root causes of this tension arise from the nature of business itself. As expressed in the seminal work of Milton Friedman almost a half century ago in *Capitalism and Freedom*: "Freedom is a real and delicate plant. Our minds tell us, and history confirms, that the great threat to freedom is the concentration of power."[9]

Power, Friedman noted, was a two-sided coin. "The power to do good is also the power to do harm; those who control the power today may not tomorrow; and, more important, what one man regards as good, another may regard as harm." [10]

Friedman addressed the relationship between capitalism and freedom as reflected in the balance between business and government. Freedom blossoms, he claimed, when government did not interfere with business. Free markets and free business strengthen democracy, he wrote, as well as individual freedom. According to Friedman, "there is one, and only one, social responsibility of business—to use its resources and engage in activities designated to increase its profits...."[11] Individuals, Friedman implies, like governments, prosper best when they leave business unrestrained.

Some in the business community, including large multinational corporations, urge avoidance of these legal obligations. A former senior vice president of global affairs for a major international corporation stated: "For years the multinational business community has strongly supported the development of a new 'global financial architecture' to protect capital flows and property rights. But it has

---

[8] Erin MacLellan. "U.S. Business Debates South Africa Ties Limits on Computer Exports are Difficult to Enforce," *Wash. Post* (Aug. 25, 1985).
[9] Milton Friedman. *Capitalism and Freedom*, 2 (University of Chicago Press, 1962).
[10] Id. at 3.
[11] Id. at 133.

adamantly opposed creating a complementary 'international social framework' of corporate responsibility...." Why? The same corporate official answered, "Litigation threatens to breach barriers that have historically shielded multinational corporations from liability."[12]

But unrestrained and unaccountable business is incompatible with individual freedom. Indeed, the knowing exercise of pure business power, without conscience or regard to its consequences, carries within it the seed for unparalleled personal loss.

Only a rule of law respecting fundamental human liberty, however, "...will drive companies to adopt global standards for their behavior...."[13] As the Minister of Trade and Investment for the United Kingdom recently expressed,[14]

> We believe that the most effective means of achieving the goal (of combating impunity for human rights violations) is the strengthening and developing of credible national justice mechanisms that conform to international human rights standards.

Although accountability for human rights abuses is not in the nature of business, it is in the nature of law. No one could claim today, without shame, that Germany or South Africa was better off because they had more business under despotic regimes than they now have under democracy.

All people of all societies must be secure from the exercise of arbitrary or abusive power—whether committed by government officials, or knowingly aided by natural or corporate persons. There must be accountability to a rule of law which defines and proscribes that conduct. The cost of failing to recognize and enforce that rule is the loss of liberty.

[12] Elliot Schrage. "A Long Way to Find Justice," *Wash. Post* (July 14, 2002).
[13] Id.
[14] Baroness Symons of Vernham Dean, Address at The United Kingdom Parliament (July 17, 2003).

ALLISON BRANDI MARGOLIN is a criminal defense attorney in Los Angeles. She grew up there, attending Beverly Hills High School, before leaving at age 17 for Columbia University. Allison graduated from Columbia College in 1999 with a B.A. in Political Science and a certificate in the Creative Writing Program. While at Columbia, Allison served as Editorial Editor of the *Columbia Daily Spectator*, the newspaper there, and taught a class in judicial politics through a fellowship. Allison attended Harvard Law School after Columbia and graduated in 2002. She spent her third year in an exchange program at Boalt Hall, where she studied the implementation of a new drug sentencing scheme.

After graduating from law school, Allison spent a year in Flint, MI with her now-husband as he participated in his medical internship. During her stay in Flint, Allison flew home to take, and ultimately, pass the California bar. After returning to Los Angeles in 2003, Allison worked for her father shortly before starting her own practice.

Allison was featured in the *Daily Journal* newspaper (the official court paper for California) and on the front page of the *Los Angeles Times* for her criminal defense work. She has also been on the radio advocating the legalization of drugs and prostitution. Allison blogs at www.allisonmargolin.com. You can also see her YouTube video at that web address.

Jury Nullification
and Reasonable Doubt:
the People's Check on
the Government's War on
Victimless Crimes

Federalist Paper 420

By Allison Brandi Margolin

In the American system of jurisprudence, government actions, like police and prosecutors, make life-changing decisions at every turn. When a police officer is confronted by a man on the street smoking a joint, that officer has the power to allow that person to go on with his day or face months of anxiety awaiting a court date and proceedings.

If that officer decides to detain the man, send the paper work off to the District Attorney's office, the filing deputy of the D.A.'s office is then the one with the "power" to decide to pursue charges or to give the guy a break.

Sounds like a scenario from a different era? Haven't heard that people are still getting into trouble for what many consider victimless crimes involving marijuana or prostitution?

The enforcement of state and local marijuana laws annually costs U.S. taxpayers an estimated $7.6 billion, approximately $10,400 per arrest. Of this total, annual police costs are $3.7 billion, judicial/legal costs are $853 million, and correctional costs are $3.1 billion. In both California and New York, state fiscal

costs dedicated to marijuana law enforcement annually total over $1 billion. [1]

"Around 500,000 people are
arrested a year for possessing marijuana."[2]

"Prostitution cases have accounted
for 90,221 arrests in the United States in
2003."[3]

Despite the fact that much of society does not want the government to focus on the arrests of individuals for victimless crimes
(like drugs and prostitution) and to refocus their energy on the prosecution of "terrorists," the government's arrest data reveals that thus far
nothing has checked the relentless war against victimless crimes. The
answer is jury nullification—a form of reasonable doubt whereby
jurors exercise discretion (just as the police and filing deputy attorneys) to do justice by not enforcing a criminal law against a particular
individual.

In my paper "The Right to Get High," I present a thorough
argument on the unconstitutionality of criminalizing drugs. The government's illegalization of the use of drugs violates our fundamental
right to control, stimulate and manipulate one's own brain and body;
the right to cognitive liberty. This right is that upon which the Bill of
Rights is based.

There is no reason to make a drug
criminal when you can simply make the
behavior criminal, even if we were in a hypothetical universe where prohibition would
actually deter people who really wanted to get
hold of a drug.[4]

[1] 2005 report issued by NORML Foundation, available at http://www.norml.org
[2] John Tierney. *New York Times*, "The Czars' Reefer Madness," (August 26, 2006).
[3] FBI, Uniform Crime Reporting
[4] Allison Margolin. "On the right to get high," http://leda.law.harvard.edu, 2002, p. 11-12

BEYOND a REASONABLE DOUBT

Furthermore, it cannot be proven that the use of a drug does produce harm inherently to anyone but its user or that drugs are different in kind from any other thing, like food or sex, that may become the subject of an addiction.

To quote Richard Glen Boire,

> ...The so-called war on drugs is not a war on pills, powder, plants, and potions, it is war on the mental states—a war on consciousness itself—how much, what sort we are permitted to experience, and who gets to control it. More than an unintentional misnomer, the government-termed war on drugs is a strategic decoy label; a slight-of-hand move by the government to redirect attention away from what lies at ground zero of the war—each individual's fundamental right to control his or her own consciousness.[5]

In order to convict someone, a jury must find, beyond a reasonable doubt, that a crime has been committed. Many feel that drug crimes and prostitution do not deserve the moral condemnation for which conviction of a crime entails. For those people, there is reasonable doubt that a crime has been committed. The people deserve the opportunity to make the decision that the law in this instance is obsolete and that this person does not deserve the conviction that following the law would otherwise command.

Jury nullification is defined, according to *Black's Law Dictionary*, as "the de facto power a jury in a criminal case possesses to acquit a defendant, regardless of the strength of the evidence against him or her."

Many people, including the courts, have opined on the propriety and use of jury nullification. The Supreme Court of Indiana offered an

---

[5] Richard Glen Boire. "On Cognitive Liberty Part II," http://www.cognitiveliberty.org (2000)

interesting and thorough discussion of the history and ideas animating the debate about jury nullification in <u>Holden v. Indiana,</u> (788 N.Ed.2d 1253, Indiana Supreme Court, 2003). That court (Id. At 1254) quoted Clay S. Conrad's definition of jury nullification in his 1998 *Jury Nullification: The Evolution of a Doctrine* as the "right to refuse to convict if they believe that a conviction would be in some way unjust."

Conrad's definition is the one I would hope the public would take, were the notion of jury nullification to become more etched into the popular psyche through the media or otherwise. Of course, the nether side to jury nullification is the notion that racist and other prejudiced individuals will be inspired to apply those beliefs to the jury experience because they know they have the right to nullify. Such a concern is valid.

The arrest figures have shown that this country's war against drugs and individuals who have committed victimless crimes is not abating. In a time where our civil liberties continue to be threatened by a government truly more interested in legislating supposed morality than in protecting the country, there is no choice but to turn to the people. Jury nullification needs to be the people's answer to the continued enforcement of draconian laws against its citizens.

REID H. WEINGARTEN is a partner with the Washington, D.C.-based law firm of Steptoe & Johnson LLP and is head of the firm's White Collar Crime Defense group. Prior to joining the firm, Mr. Weingarten served as a trial attorney for the Public Integrity Section of the United States Department of Justice and as a deputy district attorney for Dauphin County, Pennsylvania.

Mr. Weingarten represents clients in complex criminal matters in both state and federal courts at the pre-trial, trial and post-trial stages, including cases involving public corruption, the Racketeer Influenced and Corrupt Organizations Act, bank fraud, bribery, government procurement fraud, antitrust, health care fraud and tax and securities fraud. He has gained national recognition for his representation of many high-profile individuals such as Secretary of Commerce, Ronald H. Brown; Secretary of Agriculture, Michael Espy; former Teamsters president, Ron Carey; Treasury Department Chief of Staff, Joshua Steiner; Charlie Trie; Pauline Kanchanalak; and clients involved in the Archer Daniels Midland, Drexel, Salomon Brothers, Ill Wind, BCCI, G.E./Israel, FDA/generic drug, tobacco, House Bank, and Columbia HCA investigations.

Mr. Weingarten has served, by special appointment, as Special Counsel to the Senate Foreign Relations Committee, Subcommittee on Near Eastern and South Asian Affairs, to head the "October Surprise" investigation in 1992; Associate Independent Counsel in the Iran-Contra affair in 1988 as lead counsel in the prosecution of <u>Major General Richard v. Secord</u>; and Special Prosecutor, United States Attorney's office for the District of Alaska, for <u>U.S. v. Dischner, et al.</u> in 1988.

The Criminal Justice System:
Stronger than
Human Fallibility

By Reid H. Weingarten

I have been a trial lawyer in the criminal justice system for almost 30 years—about half on the prosecution side and half as a defense attorney. At times, I have appeared before arrogant judges, political judges and ignorant judges. There have been occasions when I have been up against ambitious prosecutors, lazy prosecutors and unethical prosecutors. There also have been times when I have been in court with unprepared defense attorneys, incompetent defense attorneys and egomaniacal defense attorneys.

And yet, I believe in our judicial system. I love working in it and I believe that it produces a fair and just result in almost every case. How can that be given my experience? Our justice system works despite the imperfections of its human participants. The reason it does is that over many, many years, protections have been built into our criminal justice system that allow for and correct when necessary the inevitable human errors. These protections are the cumulative work of the legal community—judges, practitioners, scholars and lawmakers—all dedicated to the proposition that justice must be done in every case. The ignorant judge gets reversed on appeal. The ambitious prosecutor runs for governor. The unprepared defense counsel gets disciplined by the bar association. Wrongs wrought by human imperfections are regularly righted by the justice system.

There are always new pressures that threaten the system and there are some powerful ones at play today. September 11th has produced an environment in which the federal government holds suspected terrorists for years without charges and with no access to lawyers, judges or any process at all. The Enron/WorldCom environment has produced monstrous prison sentences that have caused defendants to plead guilty to avoid lengthy prison exposure even when they believe they have not committed crimes.

I also believe, beyond a reasonable doubt, that we have a responsibility to right these wrongs and to continue the centuries-old tradition of making our justice system stronger than the human imperfections of our day.

ROGER E. ZUCKERMAN is a trial lawyer. He is a founding partner of Zuckerman Spaeder LLP, a firm of approximately 100 lawyers located in six cities that specializes in complex litigation. The firm was selected in 2005 by the publication *The American Lawyer* as one of the top five litigation boutiques in the United States.

Mr. Zuckerman is a 1964 graduate of the University of Wisconsin and a 1967 graduate of Harvard Law School. From 1968 to 1972, he was an Assistant United States Attorney in the District of Columbia. He is a member of the American College of Trial Lawyers and various other professional societies.

His firm and he have been involved in many of the most significant cases of the last several decades. He and his wife live in Potomac, Maryland. They have two daughters, Laura and Nina, who are both lawyers.

Passion Tempered

By Roger Zuckerman

I have spent the last 38 years in and around courtrooms, judges, and combatants engaged in the adversary process. I have represented the guilty who swore they were innocent, the innocent who felt they were guilty, and a surprisingly large number of people who—in the confused climate in which corporate executives are often prosecuted—simply didn't know. My early years were spent as a prosecutor. It was a good training ground and gave me a sense of perspective and of the importance of being fair.

These experiences have given me a sense of how people ought to behave and how disputes of all kinds ought to be resolved. As a trial lawyer, one is a combatant, a professional adversary. The adversary process—the trial and resolution of disputes in a legal forum—is the place in which legalized combat occurs. Developed over the ages, it mediates the passions that people of differing views rightly feel and reaches a result that is about as close to the truth as one can get. As societies and legal systems have evolved, verbal sparring of professional advocates has replaced other forms of dispute resolution now considered universally to be primitive and barbaric. In medieval times, legal systems throughout Europe sanctioned as just trial by combat: litigants themselves, or in some cases champions defending the interests of certain litigants, such as the elderly, women, or children, would battle one another under the view that justice would be done because God would empower the victor.

That we now prefer resolving our disputes by means of discourse rather than force does not mean that the passion of battle is entirely lost. Our adversarial process embraces passion and values it. However, it tempers that passion, mediates it, and ultimately utilizes it for the benefit of its participants and the correctness of its result. And passion is the stuff of the modern adversary process. It is a part of its core psychology and characterizes virtually all of its participants. In my own life, as a young prosecutor, I "knew" that my positions were correct. I "knew" that justice would not truly be done unless I obtained convictions. My life as a prosecutor spanned the late 1960's and early 1970's in Washington, D.C. My colleagues and I prosecuted homicides, drug conspiracies and a variety of frauds. We believed we were doing God's work.

After my experience as a prosecutor, in the normal progression of things, I moved into the private sector and began a long career as a defense attorney. As if magically, the passion that I felt to obtain convictions as a prosecutor vanished. I was a defense attorney, after all, and I came to embrace my clients' innocence as the sole worthy objective that I was to pursue. I got an early education as a defense attorney in the Glen Turner Dare to Be Great mail fraud trial in Jacksonville, Florida, where I met F. Lee Bailey. Lee and I came to be lifelong friends and professional colleagues. Lee's passion in defense of his clients was largely unrivaled. I understood it and learned from it. It is the oxygen that feeds a defense attorney in all of his trials, but particularly in long, trench warfare cases (my longest has been nine months) that are brutal in a variety of ways and that take an exacting toll. One cannot function as a defense attorney, at least to the maximum, without being a "true believer" and without passionately embracing the client's innocence.

So, at the end of the day, the trial process is (and ought to be) a clash of passionately held views, those of an equally motivated prosecutor and defense attorney. The structure that mediates these views is, quite obviously, the adversary system. Neither the prosecutor nor the defense attorney, after all, gets to choose the final result. That is the product ultimately of a judge or a jury. It is they who determine what justice is. This process is not perfect, but it is as fine a system as we know. It produces results that are accepted as legitimate and fair. It has characterized the growth of our culture and our values for almost a thousand years, since the Magna Carta and the development of the common law, and it is in many respects one of the most civilizing institutions that we have developed. Our adversary system functions to mediate passion—the claims of innocence and the claims of guilt that "true believers" on either side rightfully advocate with fierce commitment.

Having been a part of this process for 38 years now, I have a worldview that has very much been shaped by the values that underlie it: tolerance, civility, open debate, respect for the views of others, and a healthy pluralism. These are essentially values of openness and temperance. They underlie much of that which has brought us where we are today: empiricism, the scientific method, and our most fundamental democratic institutions. In all, they have worked for centuries to mediate the most difficult disputes that we as humans have had and to produce the fairest, best and most reliable answers to many of the core questions that we as humans pose. While the answers are not perfect, the process is the best that we can divine. It is a process that embraces "passion," but it tells us at various points that passion is best tempered in the resolution of human disputes and the pursuit of the truth.

The truth is, after all, fundamentally elusive. The ancients believed the world was flat or that it sat on a turtle, that the sun circled the earth, that gladiatorial contests were the highest form of entertainment, that trial by ordeal was the way to demonstrate innocence (you had to be a good floater) and that various indigenous populations were themselves "primitive" and their colonizers "civilized." History is littered with these kinds of worldviews and values, all now regarded as flawed. What of ours will future generations place in that category? Surely many, for we are far from knowing fully and perfectly the truth about our existence and the proper norms by which to govern it.

With deference to those who profess to have firm answers to profoundly metaphysical questions, our presence here as sentient beings is an existential absurdity. We all make sense of it and the wonder of our existence differently. We occupy a small island in space and time, on a planet about 6 billion years old in a universe about 13 billion years in age and of vast and almost immeasurable proportions. The cosmic coincidence that has put us all together at close quarters for a small sliver of time is almost beyond comprehension. If one accepts that reality, one comes to understand that the values of temperance serve as the appropriate foundation for the resolution of our most volatile issues; those values allow us to embrace and cherish one another to the fullest for the tiny slice of time that we share with one another on this island.

So to all of those who have received "the truth" and know it "beyond a reasonable doubt," one may say in equal parts congratulations and temper your epiphanies with respect for "the truth" of others. It is the ability to temper and the fulsome embrace of the values of temperance that have brought us to a good place in this world and will bring us to even better places in times ahead. And that, my friends, is the real truth, from the perspective of a trial lawyer who has spent the last 38 years searching for it.

LYNNE BERNABEI has been practicing civil liberties/public interest law since 1979, after clerking for U.S. District Court Judge William B. Bryant. Since 1987, she represented plaintiffs in employment discrimination cases, and high-profile whistleblowers in private industry and government employment. She also represents physicians, lawyers and other professionals in civil rights and civil liberties cases. She has regularly appeared on national television and radio programs, and in print media to speak about a range of civil rights issues. She is recognized as one of the nation's leading lawyers in her areas of specialty.

New Age
Cross-Examination

By Lynne Bernabei

Cross-examination of a hostile witness is a mystery, even to trial lawyers who do it quite effectively. The lawyer needs to establish a rapport with the witness so that he or she tells you his illegal motivation in acting against your client.

How do you do that? How do you learn how to know what answers you are going to get from a witness before he gives it? Trial lawyers say it is instinct and studied preparation. Both are needed for those magical moments when a witness makes the case for the opposing side by confessing something terrible.

Malcolm Gladwell calls this ability to read minds "thin-slicing" or the "ability of our unconscious to find patterns in behavior based on very narrow slices of experience," in his popular book *Blink*. However, I believe that it is not that an observation of a small number of factors that help a trial lawyer pose the right question at the right time. It is connecting to the witness' energy in a way that can be done before you ever see him.

While this sounds very New Age, we do it all the time. One needs to get into the present, aware of all your senses. You close your eyes, become aware of the sounds that come to you, the smells you pick up, the air on your face, what you are sitting on, and when you open your eyes, let the colors, sensations and sights come to you. Once you are in the present with a vibrant sense of what surrounds you,

you'll be able to sense the person's energy and what the witness wants to tell you. Once you key into the witness' energy and not your own, it becomes fairly easy to know what he wants to tell you.

Despite the imposition of legal rules designating that the witness is on the opposite side of the case from you as the lawyer, the underlying harmony or connections between you as human beings do not disappear. Once you learn to access those, you can easily communicate on a level with the witness where he will want to tell you exactly why he did the things he did, which often reveals the illegality of his actions.

The following is an excerpt from the deposition of Dr. Raymond Patterson, a psychiatrist who was head of forensic services for the District of Columbia public mental health hospital. Our client claimed Dr. Patterson destroyed her career as a psychologist, because as the primary mental health professional treating John Hinckley, Jr., she was prepared to testify that Hinckley's disease was in remission, and he was ready for unsupervised visits with his parents. Her superiors, under pressure from the United States prosecutors, pressured her to change her testimony. She refused, and later reported to the media their attempts to force her to perjure herself. Dr. Patterson, as the chief witness for the U.S. government, sought to discredit her by bringing a series of false disciplinary and ethical charges against her. Her suit settled for $800,000, and a dismissal of all the charges against her in late 2005.

Dr. Patterson testified in his deposition that he had falsified his application for employment at the hospital, a federal crime. The following are my questions and his answers:

> Q: Dr. Patterson, take a moment to look at Patterson Exhibit 4.... This is a document from Howard University College of Medicine that indicates the class rank you held during the four years you were there, is that correct?

A: It looks like it. Yes.

Q: It says the first year you were 97 in a class of 109, is that correct?

A: That is what it says.

Q: So, that would indicate that you were approximately in the bottom ten percent?

A: ...That seems about right.

* * *

Q: Then we have the second year you were 97 in a class of 111, is that correct?

A: That is what it says.

Q: So, that would be approximately the bottom ten percent again?

A: Some improvement.

* * *

Q: Well, if we did it [the math] and it turned out to be approximately 10, 15 percent, would you argue with that?

A: Not if you did the math....

* * *

Q: Now, in the fourth year it indicates you were 73 in a class of 98, is that correct?

A: That is correct.

Q: So, that would be approximately the bottom 30 percent, is that correct?

A: ...That is probably about right.

Q: ...So, if these figures are correct, it would indicate that you were never above the bottom third of your class, is that right?

A: That is probably what it indicates.

***

Q: Take a look at the next document that follows. This is a Personal Qualifications Statement.

A: Yes.

Q: If you take a look at the last page, your signature appears below that, May 1, 1983, is that right?

A: Yes.

Q: And you understood when you were signing...that a false answer might be punishable by fine or imprisonment?

A: That is what it says.

***

Q: Now, if you take a look at the top...it asks you about the professional training you have, the type of degree and your class rank or standing, is that correct?

A: Yes.

Q: Then it asks for your class rank and standing, and you put top 50 percent, is that correct?

A: That is what is says.

Q: Now, that is in fact not accurate, is that right?

A: Well, based on what we just looked at....

***

Q: ...you answered the question you were in the top 50 percent, even though you didn't know what your rank was at that time?

A: That is what I thought.... Because I had a difficult start to medical school with punching, as we called it, failing two courses, but I had a great deal of success in my clinical clerkships the third and fourth year. ...So, I thought that they thought highly enough of me for me to come and work for them.... Which made me feel that my class rank must be in the top half of my class.

***

Q: In fact, you didn't know at the time you said you were in the top

```
50 percent, you didn't know what your
rank was?
```

***

```
A: I did not know the fact.
```

***

Dr. Patterson, a very experienced and sought after expert witness, has testified hundreds of times in court. So, why did he testify to a federal crime? Because in his way of seeing the world, the correct answer to any important question is not factual, i.e., what his grade point average was, but is a measure of his charm, popularity, or ability to manipulate the system. This way of seeing the world is the reason he destroyed our client's—not because she had done anything wrong or unethical, but because he needed to destroy her credibility to bolster his public standing as the only mental health professional who really knew Hinckley. He was being truthful in explaining why he lied on his application for federal employment, and thought I would understand why he did it.

In an early AIDS discrimination case I litigated, the head of a start-up telemarketing firm admitted that he stole commissions owed to our client, an HIV-positive employee. He testified that he did that because, he would rather use the commissions to grow his business than have them go to our client's estate. In that one moment, the witness revealed his entire world view, and made our case. He testified truthfully because he thought I would understand and sympathize with him. While I did understand his testimony, I certainly did not sympathize, and found his actions despicable. It was by connecting to his energy as a human being that I could get him to open up and tell the truth.

It is the same practice as that of tae kwon do masters. If one is able to access the energy of an opponent and repel it back toward him, one can vindicate an important public interest, using the opposing force to do it. This is what I believe beyond a reasonable doubt.

ELAINE CHARLSON BREDEHOFT is a principal and founder of Charlson Bredehoft & Cohen, P.C. in Reston, Virginia. Ms. Bredehoft practices civil litigation, with an emphasis in employment and business law, primarily in Virginia and D.C. federal and state courts. Ms. Bredehoft has been listed in *The Best Lawyers In America* since 1997. She was named by *Washingtonian* magazine as one of the "Fifty Best Lawyers in Washington" in 1997, one of the "Forty Top Lawyers Under 40" in 1998, one of "75 Best Lawyers" in 2002, and one of the top Employment Lawyers in 2004. Ms. Bredehoft was recently featured in *The Legal Times* as one of "Twelve of the D.C. Area's Top Labor & Employment Litigators." In 2003, Ms. Bredehoft was inducted into the American College of Trial Lawyers, an organization electing and limiting its membership to the top one percent of trial lawyers in each state, and in 2005, Ms. Bredehoft was inducted into the International Academy of Trial Lawyers, an honor reserved for only 500 trial attorneys under age 70 in the United States. Ms. Bredehoft is also a permanent member of the Fourth Circuit Judicial Conference. Ms. Bredehoft is a frequent lecturer at CLEs and bar association sponsored seminars.

Trial by Jury:
America's Tried and True
Political Orthodoxy

By Elaine Charlson Bredehoft

We have the fairest judicial system in the world. Standing on the Sixth and Seventh Amendments, we resolutely guard the right to a trial by our peers. The Virginia Constitution suggests that the right to a trial by jury "ought to be held sacred."

A jury represents common sense and uniquely possesses a full appreciation of a litigant's life experiences. Jurors are our neighbors, customers, bosses, local mail carriers, trash collectors, bus drivers, referees, and our consciences. In their mission of rendering a fair and impartial verdict in a particular case, jurors are unspoiled by overt monetary contributions, political debts, or religious control. Their collective anonymity creates a natural insulation from retaliatory consequence. A jury, regardless of its diversity, strives to make the right decision and to ultimately apply the law fairly to the facts. While juries have occasionally given us pause because of seemingly bizarre results, those instances pale in comparison to the sound verdicts rendered daily in every city, county, state, and federal court across the country. We never hear about these verdicts, because the juries simply take their jobs seriously and crank the wheels of justice to a successful conclusion. Statistics overwhelmingly favor the strength and fairness of the jury system.

I have represented clients in over 100 jury trials. I have appeared before most tribunals, including the United States Supreme

Court. For eight years, I have also served as a substitute judge in courts without juries. I have voted for Republicans, Democrats, and Independents. I am a wife, a mother, an athletic coach, a business owner, and one who seriously questions the wisdom of those who dragged and arranged the rocks at Stonehenge. The wisdom of the inalienable right to a jury trial, however, I do not question.

I believe passionately in the right to a jury trial because of the life experiences each juror brings to each case and the unspoiled, collective quest to be fair and impartial. They display a seriousness to their task, listen intently to the evidence and arguments, and reflect a genuine desire to determine the truth, apply the law to the facts, and render a verdict that is the product of fairness, impartiality, and justice.

Unfortunately, the "independence" of our judicial branch is rapidly eroding. Our politicians scathingly and hypocritically threaten judges applying the law as it is written. Like the emperor's subjects in *The Emperor's New Clothes*, mindless herds, including many in the media, follow these politicians and chant their mantras. We witness with angst religious groups (each of whom claim to be the sole religion granting eternal salvation) wielding their influence to select judges "like them." This homogeny often translates into bigotry, chauvinism, and the loss of freedoms guaranteed by the Constitution.

We hold our judiciary to a very high standard to ensure that both sides receive a fair trial. Replacing the jury with an omnipotent judge subjects both parties to the mercy of a randomly selected single person's reasoning, prejudices, and political or religious obligations. A juror, however, must answer to their fellow jurors if attempting to apply prejudice or flawed reasoning. A jury's strength in numbers reflects an internal check and balance system.

In the judicial system, jury selection motivates an individual to apply fairness and reason to redress a wrong. In our democratic form of government, witnessing multiple acts of injustice motivates that same individual into action in the voting booth as well, ultimately representing common sense and reason in both places. This sets into motion the circular process of restoring the integrity and independence of the entire judicial branch, offsetting undue political and religious influences. Perhaps the next motivator will be the noticeable dearth of qualified female and minority appointees to the Courts.

Without the protections of the jury system, we are subject to select political and religious doctrines in a system propounded to be free of prejudice and guaranteeing justice for all. Without the protections of the jury system, we are not the advanced, enlightened, and fair United States that we have thus far proudly presented to the world.

May we, like our forefathers, never lose sight of the importance of trial by jury as a key component to our integrity and independence as a Nation. I believe in our system of justice, and particularly the right to a jury trial, beyond a reasonable doubt.

PAULA CANNY has practiced law in California for over twenty-five years. She began her career as an intern at the State Public Defender's Office doing indigent appellate work including death penalty defense. After graduating from the University of San Francisco School of Law in 1980, and a brief stint in a civil law firm, she worked as a deputy District Attorney for Ventura County and San Mateo County, California. As a San Mateo County prosecutor she never lost a jury trial including winning the first state armor piercing bullet prosecution. In 1984 Paula went into private practice. Until that time Paula had identified herself as Paula K. Canny. But when she opened her own office, she dropped the initial "K," reasoning if Perry Mason did not need a middle initial she did not need one either.

Paula Canny has since represented people from all walks of life accused of all types of illegal conduct, from misdemeanor driving offenses to death penalty murder cases. She has tried many, many cases with very good results. She won the first three strikes case in her home county of San Mateo, California. She works with the San Mateo County Drug Court and is on the Board of Directors of Women Defenders. Paula has become a frequent legal analyst on local, cable and national television. She began her legal analyst career when the Scott Peterson case arrived at her doorstep in San Mateo County. Paula Canny has provided legal analysis on the Scott Peterson and Michael Jackson cases, as well as the Susan Polk case to name a few. Some of Paula's clients are famous and some are not. But regardless of stature or accusation Paula Canny's commitment to a client is fierce. That is what makes her such a good lawyer.

Beyond a Reasonable Doubt

By Paula Canny

"Beyond a reasonable doubt" is the level of proof required to establish guilt in all criminal cases in the United States. When I hear the term "beyond a reasonable doubt" I do not think of "level of proof." What I think of is a jury trial and talking to jurors about what "beyond a reasonable doubt" means. Each case has its own set of facts and each case requires application of the principle "beyond a reasonable doubt." This is what good lawyering is about—applying the reasonable doubt standard to the facts of the case. In my experience it is the ability to explain not just the facts of the case but the term "beyond a reasonable doubt" to the jury that determines the outcome of my case.

The term "beyond a reasonable doubt" is explained in conjunction with the other cornerstone term of the criminal justice system, "presumption of innocence." Each term is used repeatedly during the course of a trial. The jurors are first told about them during jury selection. Either the judge or the lawyers (prosecutors and/or defense attorneys) ask potential jurors how they feel about the presumption of innocence and proof beyond a reasonable doubt. Usually a potential juror asks, "What is beyond reasonable doubt?" In California there is a book of jury instructions and the judge reads the definition contained therein.

Reasonable doubt is defined as follows:

> It is not a mere possible
> doubt, because everything relating to
> human affairs is open to some possi-
> ble or imaginary doubt. It is that
> state of the case which, after the
> entire consideration of all the evi-
> dence, leaves the mind of the jurors
> in that condition that they cannot
> say they feel an abiding conviction
> of the truth of the charge. (Caljic 2.90)

Reasonable doubt does not exist in a vacuum. It is contextual. Reasonable doubt is established, or not, with reference to evidence. Reasonable doubt is not susceptible to any concrete explanation. That is both its beauty and its failing depending upon your perspective. If I have won a trial, I love it. If I have lost, I hate it.

Luckily, of the many times I have spoken to jurors about reasonable doubt in the context of the evidence in the case, I have lost only occasionally. I do not try as many cases as when I first began practicing. I try every way I know, every procedure, every tactic to get my client's case not filed, or dismissed—by filing Motions, doing investigation, and engaging in bargaining—to avoid the risk of a jury trial.

Jury trials are expensive, time-consuming, and risk filled. A jury trial for a criminal defendant is a zero-sum situation. With many charges carrying mandatory minimum sentences, the stakes, in terms of time in prison, are often very high. Before any jury trial there are many court appearances and discussions between prosecutors and defense attorneys. During these proceedings the matter of plea bargaining arises. Plea bargaining is the process by which a prosecutor and a defense attorney resolve a case without a trial. The process results in the defendant's pleading to an agreed-upon charge(s) for some agreed-upon punishment.

Going to jury trial necessarily means rejecting the plea bargain offer and the set sentence that goes with it. The decision to forgo the known outcome of a plea bargain for the unknown outcome of a jury trial is oftentimes very difficult. For example, I had a client who was charged with arson, a very serious felony, and yet was offered a plea bargain to plead to a less serious charge of misdemeanor vandalism, with a set county jail sentence of a few weekends. Both the client and I had to weigh the risks and the future consequences of each strategy. The process is stressful to me and my client. I very much want to do right by my client. Sometimes it is difficult to know what the right thing is. The pretrial plea bargain offers are not discussed with the jury. The jury does not know of such things. But I know. And I always want to do better for my client than whatever the plea bargain offer was.

Regardless of the crime charged, the burden of proof is the same. Whether the accused faces charges of murder or petty theft, the prosecutor's burden is to establish guilt beyond a reasonable doubt. I tell the jurors that. I also tell them that each person must decide for themselves if the prosecution has met that burden; that a jury verdict is the decision of each individual, and not the collective conscience of the group. The importance of the individual's decision is my favorite aspect of the jury system. Unanimity is required for a verdict. One person holding true to their belief about the state of evidence, whether it be to support not guilty or guilty, results in a mistrial. And the whole trial process can be forced to begin anew.

Whether it is Henry Fonda in *12 Angry Men* as the holdout who turned the jury around, or an anonymous citizen who refuses to give in to the pressures of the others to reach some collective agreement, the term beyond a reasonable doubt is both a sword and a shield. Again, it is a matter of perspective.

Twenty plus years ago, very early in my career I tried a "drunk driving" case. I thought I tried a good case, but I lost. My client was convicted. One of the jurors called me the next day. A second juror called. Each juror wanted to retract their guilty verdict. Each person told me they had given in to the bullying of the others. Each person told me they felt ashamed for having given in. I felt really bad for them. I felt worse for my client who had been wrongly convicted. It is from that experience that I came to understand the meaning of the term "proof beyond a reasonable doubt" in the context of group dynamics. Until that trial I did not understand the power of a group to bully an individual; I did not understand the toll an individual juror suffers in succumbing to the bullying.

So now, when I talk to a jury I tell them that I believe in the power of the individual. I believe in the sanctity of the phrase "to thine own self be true." I believe that a decision in a jury trial for a juror, is one of the most important decisions, if not the most important decision, they will make in their life. It is a decision that will have a huge impact on the life of another. It is also a decision that for all intents and purposes is irreversible. There are no "take backs." They cannot come back in a month or a year, or in ten, and tell the Judge after further reflection they were wrong. A juror will live with that decision for the rest of his or her life. I tell them that. And I remind them that after they are excused from their jury service, they will go their own way, alone with their decision, no longer 1 of 12, but forever as one with their decision.

I believe that. I have learned that over my 25 years doing jury trials and some 50 years of living, that living with regret is terrible. Not being true to myself is equally terrible. And that a decision in a jury trial is a decision fraught with potential future consequences of regret and self-loathing for everyone involved.

So I think of all of that and of all my cases when I hear the phrase "beyond a reasonable doubt." I think of my many clients—people with families and lives, and the impact a given result of a case has had on their life. I do not remember the cases I have won as much I regret the cases I have lost. I have much feeling and judgment wrapped up in my work. I hope more than anything that I have done the right thing. I think that is really what each of us wants. I want the jury to do the right thing as well. So I close my argument to the jury with a statement of absolute truth—that the best pillow is a good conscience. "Beyond a reasonable doubt" is that standard, when properly applied, that will allow an individual juror a good night's sleep, and peace with their decision, for the rest of their life.

JOHN KENNETH ZWERLING practices law with Zwerling, Leibig & Moseley, P.C. in Alexandria Virginia.

For the past 36 years, Mr. Zwerling has been defending individuals and corporations who have run afoul of the law in the trial and appellate courts of state and federal judicial systems. His clients include the famous and the infamous. Rock stars, lawyers and doctors; politicians and protesters; the innocent and the not so innocent on charges ranging from murder to misdemeanors, including espionage, terrorism, mail fraud, bribery, cyber sex and unwanted sex.

He is a nationally recognized and respected criminal defense attorney. His ability to speak persuasively to prosecutors, judges and juries has yielded the type of success that resulted in his peers evaluating him as one of the Best Lawyers in America, a Pre-eminent Lawyer, and a Super Lawyer. He is sought out on the CLE lecture circuit and well as the national media including *The Today Show*, *Firing Line* and the NBC, ABC and CBS evening news.

Some of his and his firm's better known clients include the Red Hot Chili Peppers, Lorena Bobbitt, Daniel Elsberg, Peter Max and Dominick Dunne. He has represented defendants and subjects of the grand jury investigations of The Church of Scientology (United States v. Mary Sue Hubbard et al.); and government employees caught up in the special prosecutors' cases involving the White House e-mails; the mismanagement of the Indian trust funds by the Department of Interior (Cobel v. Norton) and Vernon Belicourt, Russell and Bill Means of the American Indian Movement.

Mr. Zwerling served in Vietnam prior to attending the American University's Law School. He is the past President of the Alexandria Bar Association, the founding President of the Virginia College of Criminal Defense Attorneys, and is currently a member of the Virginia State Bar Counsel.

The Right to a
Fair and Impartial Jury
of One's Peers

By John K. Zwerling

One of the most important safeguards to our liberty that the Founding Fathers incorporated into our Bill of Rights is the Sixth Amendment's guarantee to a fair and impartial jury of his peers. Before the sovereign may deprive a person of his life or liberty, the sovereign must prove the guilt of the accused beyond a reasonable doubt and must do so to an impartial jury, not just a judge.

VOIR DIRE

Clearly, the right to a fair and impartial jury will not be provided to the accused, if it is comprised of jurors who are not able to be fair and impartial or are unable to vote not guilty even if the government has not proved the accused's guilt beyond a reasonable doubt.

There is a procedure that takes place in every court room in the United States before the start of a jury trial. It is known as Voir Dire. It requires the jurors to answer questions placed to them. In some jurisdictions the judge and the attorneys for both the prosecution and the accused are allowed to ask questions, but in most jurisdictions only the judge asks the questions. The purpose of Voir Dire is to identify potential jurors who are not able to be fair and impartial, or are unable to provide the accused the constitutional protections of the presumption of innocence and government's burden of proof beyond a reasonable doubt.

Voir Dire when conducted solely by the judge is simply ineffective in helping the prospective jurors recognize their unsuitability
to serve on the particular case or to feel comfortable to state that they
are unsuited to serve on that case.

There are many reasons that this is so. For example, as a general rule judges ask questions to the entire panel at one time and if no
one responds, no one is disqualified. This is the "silence is golden
school" of Voir Dire.

Judges ask generic questions such as can they give both the
government and the defendant a fair trial. Since virtually no one views
themselves as a biased person, the predictable result is that virtually no
one admits that they are a defective human being. This is the "who
among you are so stupid or prejudiced that you can't follow my
instructions and fairly try this case" Voir Dire.

To bring this problem to life, I offer the following Court-con-
ducted Voir Dire in a recent case that eliminated no potential jurors:

> THE COURT: The Defendant is accused
> of using a computer to solicit a minor
> for sex acts that violate Virginia law.
> He will be pleading not guilty, and we
> will be having a trial by jury here
> today. Are any of you aware of any bias
> or prejudice that you might have against
> either the Commonwealth or the accused
> in this case?
>
> JURY PANEL MEMBERS: No.
>
> THE COURT: Do each of you under-
> stand that the Defendant is presumed to
> be innocent?
>
> JURY PANEL MEMBERS: Yes.
>
> THE COURT: Do you understand that
> the Commonwealth must prove the

Defendant's guilt beyond a reasonable
doubt?

    JURY PANEL MEMBERS: Yes.

    THE COURT: Do any of you know any
reason whatsoever why you could not give
a fair and impartial trial to both the
Commonwealth and the Defendant based
solely on the evidence that you will
hear in this courtroom over the next two
days and the law of Virginia as I will
instruct you later on?

    JURY PANEL MEMBERS: No.

    THE COURT: Those are all the ques-
tions I have.

The following defense attorney Voir Dire just moments later
resulted in one-third of the potential jurors telling the judge that they
were not suited to serve on the jury. This case involved the defendant
exchanging IM's, or Instant Messages, with a police officer who had
assumed the personae of a thirteen-year-old girl on the Internet.

    DEFENSE ATTORNEY: The question
that you're going to be presented with
is whether or not the defendant believed
it was a thirteen-year-old child, a
juvenile, or whether he believed he was
dealing with an adult who was playing a
role. Now, this type of a case, I'm sure,
brings up strong feelings in many people, and the purpose of the question
that we're going to ask you and that
you've been asked already is really to

help both sides decide whether or not
we're comfortable having you sit on this
jury and also to help you focus on
whether you're going to be comfortable
sitting on this jury, and therefore, be
able to provide a fair and impartial jury.
There is nothing wrong in a particular
case with a person not being cut out for
that case. We all have cases that we
shouldn't sit on, and there's nothing
shameful about that even though we all
want to be impartial. So please, it's
important. This will get me to a question I really need to put to all of you.

I appreciate your candor. That
is this:

In a case such as this where the
allegations are that the Defendant is a
sexual predator seeking a child to have
sex with, can you still acquit him if you
believe he's probably guilty, but you
aren't sure; the Commonwealth hasn't
proven its case? In other words, having
reasonable doubt about his guilt, but
knowing that if you acquit him, and he
did do it, he is a sexual predator, that
you'd be letting him out on the street.
Is that going to make it hard for you to
find him not guilty?

MR E: Yes. I couldn't—if I didn't
fully think he was guilty, but I par-
tially thought he was guilty, then I'd
vote that he was guilty.

MR. T: I would too.

Mr. ZWERLING: Anybody else?

MR. B: (Indicating Yes)

MR. ZWERLING: Anybody else sitting
in the jury box that feel that way?

* * *

Even when the prosecutor tried to "rehabilitate" the juror with the "Can't you keep an open mind and follow the judge's instruction" technique, she failed because the jurors were comfortable with their biases because they understood that it was acceptable and being truthful was preferable.

PROSECUTOR: And knowing now that
it is the Commonwealth's burden to prove
the case beyond a reasonable doubt,
would you be able to keep an open mind
during the case and look at the instructions of law and really judge the evidence and be able to find a person not
guilty if the Commonwealth hasn't met
its burden? Would you, knowing now that
that's your responsibility today, think
you'd be able to do that?

MR. E: I don't think I could objectively look at it. I think, in the back
of mind, I would always be thinking
about my daughter.

One third of the jury panel disqualified themselves after the defense attorney was allowed to question them. There is a movement to do a way with attorney Voir Dire. This will also do away with fair and impartial juries.

> MR. T: If I were to err, I would err on the side of saying "he would be guilty."

> PROSECUTOR: And Mr. B?

> Mr B: I'd say the same way. I mean, I think I would see him as guilty.

> PROSECUTOR: So you're basically all saying that your personally held views would make you unable to hear the case fairly for the Defendant, basically?

> MR B: In my situation I think so.

The next group that was called to replace these jurors had witnessed these exchanges and was ready to admit their unsuitability to be jurors in this case.

> THE COURT: Ms. L, would you have wanted to discuss any of the questions that have been asked?

> MS. L: Yes. I have a fourteen-year-old son that lives at home with me, and I would find it very hard to find the Defendant not guilty.

> MR. ZWERLING: Ms. V, Do you feel the same way, ma'am, or not?

> MS. V: If they haven't proven it

beyond a reasonable doubt, then I would
hope that I could make an impartial—I
would try to.

MR. ZWERLING: The question is, do
you believe that you could if you had a
reasonable doubt but you felt that the
Commonwealth had established to your
satisfaction that he probably did it—

MS. V: Guilty.

MR. ZWERLING: What?

MS. V: He'd be guilty. Yeah, he'd
be guilty. If I could save another child.

Clearly these individuals were not suited to serve on this jury and the accused would not have been tried by a fair and impartial jury if only the judge had asked the questions.

Three weeks later we were in Federal Court about to start a similar case. The Federal Court in the Eastern District of Virginia, as in most federal courts, has a custom and practice that only the judge asks the jury questions during Voir Dire. Our Judge even refused our request for him to ask questions similar to the ones listed above. He refused, even after we shared with him our experience with the jury responses just weeks before. He simply stated that he will instruct them on the government's burden of proof and he is confident that they will follow his instructions. I am not—are you?

Lawyer conducted Voir Dire is a crucial tool for ensuring that the concept of proof beyond a reasonable doubt survives in the twenty-first century. There is a movement afoot to restrict the conducting of Voir Dire to judges, as well as to completely dispense with Voir Dire. Either of these changes would be severe blow to the Sixth Amendment's guarantee of a Fair and Impartial Jury.

KAREN PATTON SEYMOUR is the head of Sullivan & Cromwell LLP's Criminal Defense and Investigations Group. Her practice focuses on white-collar criminal defense and internal investigations. She has represented clients in state and federal investigations and proceedings involving allegations of securities fraud, money laundering, obstruction of justice, insider trading, violations of the Foreign Corrupt Practices Act, health care fraud and criminal antitrust violations. She has tried numerous jury and bench trials in federal court and has argued many appeals before the U.S. Court of Appeals for the Second Circuit. Ms. Seymour served as Chief of the Criminal Division of the U.S. Attorney's Office for the Southern District of New York from February 2002 through November 2004. In that capacity, she supervised 165 federal prosecutors and oversaw all criminal investigations and prosecutions in the District, including the investigations of corporate fraud involving WorldCom, Adelphia, and ImClone. She was lead trial counsel for the Government in the prosecution of Martha Stewart and Peter Bacanovic. During her first tenure in the U.S. Attorney's Office from 1990-1996, she served as Chief of the General Crimes Unit. Ms. Seymour has been recognized in *Chambers USA: America's Leading Lawyer's for Business* as a Leading Litigator in White Collar Crime and Government Investigations; by *New York Super Lawyers* in the field of Criminal Defense: White Collar; and by *Lawdragon* magazine as one of the top 500 lawyers in the U.S. Ms. Seymour serves on the Federal Bar Council's Inn of Court. She is a frequent lecturer and speaker on topics such as business ethics and corporate fraud.

It is Beyond a
Reasonable Doubt that Our Nation's Prosecutors and Judges Deserve a Raise

By Karen Patton Seymour

Every year, hundreds of the nation's most talented and experienced prosecutors quit. Men and women who have devoted years of their lives to making our streets safer, our financial markets more secure, and our public officials more honest give up the fight. Not because they feel that the cause is unworthy or hopeless—indeed, the astonishing success of United States law enforcement in reducing crime over the last two decades has been widely praised and studied. Nor do our nation's prosecutors leave because they have grown weary of seeking justice from our judges and juries—to the contrary, I have never known a prosecutor who didn't love the job from the first day to the last. Rather, most of the prosecutors I know who leave to return to private practice do so for one reason: they can't afford to stay. And when they leave, they take with them knowledge, skill, and experience that their offices are hard pressed to replace.

At the same time, the judiciary before whom our nations' prosecutors appear, face financial challenges of their own, as they watch their salaries shrink relative to the cost of living and the pay scale of the private sector. Whether appointed to life tenure or elected or appointed to a term of years, our nation's judges are called upon to decide nearly intractable questions of limitless variety, from interpreting complex statutes and regulations to resolving heartbreaking family disputes—and to do so unerringly, with limited time and resources, and under the scrutiny of the media and special interest groups looking to score partisan points. The compensation for such service? Less than the starting salary at most large national law firms. It is no surprise that the prospect of such great responsibility for such modest pay, prompts some of our best judges to leave the bench and persuades many of our most talented private attorneys to remain in private practice.

The numbers are striking. A newly graduated lawyer can earn $165,000 a year at a large national law firm. With just a few years' experience, that lawyer's pay can increase to more than $200,000. Meanwhile, a partner at the same firm can comfortably pull in seven figures.

By contrast, in 2005, a federal judge presiding over the cases brought and defended by those same law firms received $162,100 for her efforts—less than everyone on the law firms' legal teams except the paralegals. And for this, the federal judge can consider herself lucky—just six years ago, her salary had been stuck at about $136,000 for the preceding seven years. On the federal courts of appeals, the judges do only slightly better: in 2005, the men and women who serve as the final arbiters in the vast majority of federal cases—and who likely underwent the most intrusive of background checks before they were confirmed—made only $171,800, less than the salary of a second-year associate at a large law firm.

And that salary has to last a lifetime: unlike the members of Congress, whose salaries are linked to the pay of federal judges by law, a federal judge is appointed for life. And for good reason. Judicial wisdom comes with experience, and judicial independence is safeguarded by lifetime tenure. It would plainly threaten that independence if the federal bench became just a career stop on the path to lucrative job offers in the private sector. Notably, more judges are leaving the bench than ever before. According to Chief Justice Roberts' 2005 Year-End Report on the Judiciary, out of the 92 judges who left the bench since 1990, 59 have stepped down to enter private practice. And since 1969 the real pay of Federal judges has declined by 24% while the real pay of the average worker in America rose by more than 15% during this period. Further, few private attorneys can apply to the bench unless they've first amassed a comfortable nest egg in the private sector. And while successful private attorneys may be fine candidates for judges, certainly the ideal composition of the judiciary includes those drawn from a broader and more diverse talent pool.

And yet, from the perspective of a career prosecutor, a federal judge has it pretty good, and not just because of the prestige and other trappings that go with the bench. The salary of a U.S. Attorney is capped below that of a district judge, and the assistant U.S. attorneys—the line prosecutors who handle the bulk of all federal prosecutions—make substantially less than that. As an example, a young prosecutor a few years out of law school having just left a private firm can expect to make perhaps $75,000—about a third of his or her law firm salary. Obviously, not everyone can afford to make such a move in the first place, especially given that many young lawyers carry with them six-figure debt from their law school educations. Those that do make the switch frequently find their economic difficulties compounded once they start families and face increasing financial commitments.

In New York City, where I live and practice law, the problem is particularly acute. Soaring real estate prices have made living in already-expensive New York City beyond the means of many. When I was the Chief of the Criminal Division of the U.S. Attorney's Office for the Southern District of New York, I saw many of my best prosecutors leave because they simply could no longer afford to support their expanding families on their salaries. Men and women who had spent years unraveling sophisticated financial fraud or becoming experts on terrorist organizations, street gangs, or mafia families were constrained to take that knowledge and expertise with them to the private firms that offer double or triple the income. As a result, U.S. Attorneys' Offices like mine play a constant game of catch-up, trying to replace seasoned veterans with new prosecutors who, for all their intelligence, talents, and enthusiasm, need years of training and experience to reach the same level of mastery—only to leave themselves when they can no longer afford to stay.

The situation is even worse for the states. The starting salary in New York for assistant district attorneys and assistant attorneys general—less than $50,000 a year—make those of federal prosecutors seem high by comparison. State court judges similarly struggle to keep up with their federal brethren. Recently, Chief Judge Judith S. Kaye of the New York Court of Appeals submitted a request to increase the pay of New York State judges to the level of federal judges. If her request is approved, it will mark the first salary increase for New York State judges in six years.

It doesn't have to be this way. No one believes that public service should be a path to riches, but the pay gap between our public servants and the private sector has grown too big. The independent judiciary is the crown jewel of our constitutional system, and the men and women who represent our federal, state, and local governments in the nation's courts are the front-line soldiers in the cause of justice. Increasing the salaries of federal judges by $100,000 a year would cost the government about $125 million—a tiny fraction of the federal budget. Raising the salaries of assistant U.S. attorneys by $25,000 would similarly cost only about $138 million. Such a small investment in the pay of these servants of the public good will help ensure that these men and women are the best able to seek and administer justice.

MEDIA and the JUSTICE SYSTEM

Michael Cardoza

Claudia Cowan

Eric J. Dubin

James Bastian

Jayson Blair

Kenin M. Spivak

David Margolick

Brian Oxman

Les Whitten

"We have a criminal jury system which is superior to any in the world; and its efficiency is only marred by the difficulty of finding twelve men every day who don't know anything and can't read."
—Mark Twain

MICHAEL E. CARDOZA, a San Francisco native, is a high-profile defense attorney and has a criminal law background that spans over thirty-five years. Mr. Cardoza spent the first half of his career as a prosecutor in Los Angeles, San Francisco and Alameda Counties. After 14 years of prosecutorial experience, he established the highly successful criminal defense and business litigation firm, The Cardoza Law Offices, located in Walnut Creek, California.

In addition to his law practice, Mr. Cardoza is currently a leading legal analyst for television and radio programs commenting on such cases as Scott Peterson, Michael Jackson, Robert Blake & JonBenét Ramsey among others. His legal commentary credits include: CNN's *Larry King Live* panel, NBC's *Today Show*, MSNBC, Fox News and Court TV. Cases that Mr. Cardoza have been involved in such as the San Francisco Dog Mauling and Barry Bonds steroid scandal have been featured on the *Oprah Winfrey Show*, *Good Morning America*, *60 Minutes*, HBO, and *48 Hours* as well as in print in such publications as *Time* magazine and *Sports Illustrated*.

Mr. Cardoza acts as a faculty member of the trial advocacy program at Stanford University Law School. He also volunteers his time as a Judge Pro Tem in Santa Clara County, and acts as an appointed arbitrator for the Superior Court of the City and County of San Francisco. He frequently guest lectures at the San Francisco District Attorney's Office, numerous District Attorney's Associations and private firms. He resides in Walnut Creek, California with his wife and children.

Troubling Changes
in the Prosecution of Cases.
How Prosecutors have allowed
the Media and Politics
to affect their Discretion

By Michael Cardoza

In my 35 years as a California prosecutor, criminal defense attorney and commentator on legal affairs I have seen tremendous changes in the criminal justice system. Our system of justice usually works well, and I cannot conceive of a better one for our country. Nevertheless, I am deeply concerned about the way in which political pressures and the intensified glare of media scrutiny have combined in recent years to influence how our system functions.

I began my career in 1971 as a deputy district attorney in Los Angeles, and then worked as a prosecutor in San Francisco. In 1973 I crossed the Bay to Oakland and joined the Alameda County District Attorney's Office, where I was mentored by some of the best prosecutors in the country. There I was taught the guiding principles which have shaped my career: that while people may not remember whether you won or lost a trial, they will remember whether you acted ethically; that legal decisions must be based on the merits, and not on political or media concerns; and most importantly, that a prosecutor's job is to do justice and not necessarily to convict.

As a true believer straight out of law school, I wanted only to make people safe from criminals. The young deputy district attorneys I worked with in those days all seemed ethical and honest, and in Oakland they were given significant control over the cases to which they were assigned. In that time and place, prosecutors were taught how to evaluate each case they were assigned, and then they were allowed to exercise their own discretion as to whether it should be dropped, plea bargained or taken to trial. This is not to say the District Attorney himself did not have input on these important decisions, but micro-managing was rare. In those days, the position of District Attorney was far less politicized than it is today. It was far less likely that an ambitious lawyer might challenge an incumbent District Attorney in an election based on an unpopular decision in a high-profile case or a spike in the local crime rate.

It's a different story today, when District Attorneys routinely face tough reelection campaigns that can turn on the blare of headlines about the DA's win-loss record and other crime statistics as opposed to whether he has been doing a good job of seeking real justice for the community. While voters may be influenced by crime statistics, the stats do not tell the whole story.

On many occasions a police report will suggest that a case can be proved beyond a reasonable doubt, and so charges will be filed against the suspected criminal. But sometimes, when the prosecutor interviews the witnesses or does further investigation, it becomes clear that the evidence is insufficient to prove the case beyond a reasonable doubt.

In the past, the prosecutor assigned to the case would dismiss it without fear of repercussion. But in today's politicized, media-driven climate, many District Attorneys are loath to use their discretionary powers to get rid of a weak case. They fear that the dismissal of a filed case will negatively affect their offices' conviction rate, and that the offices' supposed failures will attract media coverage, and that they will be attacked as "soft on crime" in the next election. And so a great many of those weak cases are prosecuted.

Sometimes in a weak case the District Attorney will try to squeeze a guilty plea from the defendant, knowing that innocent people will often plead to a crime if the offer involves no state prison time. Rarely, police and prosecutors may adopt an "ends justify the means" mentality when prosecuting weak cases. Since I became a defense lawyer, I have seen prosecutors fail to reveal exculpatory evidence to defendants, disingenuously claiming that the evidence was not relevant. I am convinced I have also seen prosecutors call police officers to the witness stand with the expectation that they would lie under oath, all to ensure a conviction and to pump up the stats of the office.

The cynical rationalize such tactics: after all, isn't any defendant who is booked for a felony almost certainly guilty of something? But I guarantee you that if you or someone you love were charged with a crime, you would expect an honest prosecution above all. As the English jurist William Blackstone explained it, the underlying premise of our justice system is "better that ten guilty persons escape than that one innocent suffer."[1] Some prosecutors have lost sight of that very basic premise.

I recently represented a young man who was charged with a home invasion robbery in a county known for being "tough on crime." The victim was a methamphetamine addict with many prior felony convictions. She identified my client as one of the robbers. But police found no corroborating evidence and other witnesses gave a far different description of her assailants. When my client learned he was under investigation, he went to the police station, told the investigator that he had several alibi witnesses, and volunteered for a polygraph test to prove his innocence. But the investigator refused to give a polygraph and failed to contact the alibi witnesses. Instead, my client was arrested. He sat in jail for four months while the prosecutor ignored our attempts to point out the problems with his case—the shaky identification, the victim's questionable past, my client's strong alibi. Finally the case went to trial. The prosecutor offered an eight-year state prison plea bargain. We refused. After my opening statement, the prosecutor lowered his plea bargain offer to one year in the county jail. We again refused. The prosecutor then dismissed the charges, saying the victim was no longer sure of her identification. My client spent four months in jail when he should never have been charged in the first place.

Sometimes the combined pressures of politics and media coverage finds its way into a criminal courtroom in unforeseen ways.

[1] William Blackstone. *Commentaries* *35

Recently I represented a 61-year-old retired Marine with no criminal record who had a hobby of collecting U.S. military gear, much of it purchased on the eBay Internet auction Web site. Among his many purchases were tactical vests used by U.S. soldiers, and the ceramic plate inserts used to protect them from enemy fire. Thousands of these items were bought and sold on eBay prior to the U.S. invasion of Iraq. But starting in late 2003, the national media began reporting that U.S. troops in Iraq were not being supplied with sufficient body armor. Newspaper stories described families who went to the internet to buy body armor—including vests and ceramic plates—and then sent the items to their sons and daughters fighting in Iraq. These stories were deeply embarrassing to the U.S. military and the government. And so the Department of Defense began investigating the people who bought and sold this equipment online, and caught my client in their dragnet. I firmly believe that the federal government's decision to indict my client was influenced in large part by the media's criticism of the Bush administration's conduct of the Iraq war.

Intense media coverage can make it nearly impossible for a prosecutor to drop a bad case. It's a nationwide trend, as I have learned in recent years as I have worked as a legal commentator on high-profile trials: The Duke University lacrosse team rape case is the latest illustration. Based on everything I have learned in connection with my television commentary on this matter, the prosecutor in Durham County, N. C. does not have a strong case against any of the Duke students accused of raping the victim. But the prosecution has gone forward anyway, motivated by the political concerns of a District Attorney running for reelection in a primarily African-American community, where the victim was black and the alleged perpetrators were rich, white college kids. Given the intense media coverage the case has generated, the prosecutor's decision to file the case seems set in stone. Apparently he prefers to go to trial and lose rather than dismiss the case and lose face.

The prosecution of Michael Jackson was a slight variation of this. An earlier child molestation prosecution in 1993 was thwarted when Jackson made a multi-million dollar civil payout to the victim and his family. This was a very public outmaneuvering of the District Attorney by Jackson and his attorneys. The intense coverage of that investigation and settlement spurred the prosecutor in Santa Barbara County to pursue a weaker second prosecution with less evidence and weaker witnesses whose motives were very suspect, with the result being an acquittal.

Of course it's impossible for us to return to an era when District Attorneys rarely faced electoral challenges and media coverage of the criminal justice system was more measured. Still, prosecutors could do a great deal to enhance public confidence in the system if they embraced the prosecutorial values I encountered early in my career. Make decisions about cases on their merits, and not through political calculation or the intensity of the media firestorm. Better yet, empower your experienced and ethical trial prosecutors to make the decisions for you, and don't micro-manage or second-guess them. Justice, and the public, will be better served.

CLAUDIA COWAN joined FOX News Channel as a San Francisco correspondent in April 1998. Before that, she was a reporter with KRON-TV, the top-rated NBC affiliate in San Francisco, and an anchor/reporter at KOVR-TV (CBS) in Sacramento and KMST-TV in Monterey, where she also spent time producing and editing.

A graduate of UCLA, Cowan began her career at KTTV-TV (FOX) in Los Angeles, where she worked as a messenger. Among the hundreds of stories she's covered while at Fox News, Claudia has reported on the Middle East conflict, California's recall election that saw Arnold Schwarzenegger become governor, and the Scott Peterson trial.

She and her husband, sports agent Steve Baker, live with their young twins in the Bay Area of California.

"Lights, Cameras...
Lawyers!"

By Claudia Cowan

After spending two years covering the search for Laci Peterson, and the ensuing arrest, trial and conviction of her husband, Scott, I witnessed a legal phenomenon that unfolded, not inside the courtroom, but outside, in front of the TV cameras, lights and microphones.

Celebrity lawyers are nothing new. But today, more than ever, high-profile cases foster legions of legal eagles willing to travel far distances to appear on various cable news channels, and weigh in with their law-minded opinions. For most, these appearances offer incredible, and free, publicity.

For rookie analysts, it's often just 15 minutes of fame. For a rare few, legal commentary can lead to bigger opportunities...even their own prime-time cable TV show.

During the Peterson trial, every cable news outlet had at least one panel. On Fox News, Greta Van Susteren—a veteran lawyer herself—started out with defense attorney Mark Geragos, who famously said on her show, "You'd be hard pressed to find a prosecutor who couldn't put together an indictment against Peterson, let alone a conviction." Shortly thereafter, Geragos was hired to represent the accused wife- and baby-killer. With Geragos muzzled by the judge's strict gag order, Greta turned to former San Francisco prosecutor, Jim Hammer, and legal analysts Ted Williams and Bernie Grimm, among others.

Larry King had San Francisco defense attorney, Michael Cardoza, and trial lawyer, Chris Pixley, out of Atlanta. During the trial, Geragos hired Cardoza to do a "mock" direct examination of Peterson, after which Geragos decided not to put the defendant on the witness stand. Other attorneys-turned-cable-talk-show hosts had other attorneys-turned-analysts. On Court-TV, Nancy Grace had well-known trial lawyer Daniel Horowitz. On MSNBC, Dan Abrams had defense attorney Paula Canny. The on-air debates about Peterson's fate were often lively, sometimes funny, and usually informative...a winning recipe for good TV and high ratings.

The legal discussions also helped fuel the story. In the early months following Laci's disappearance, the media onslaught put pressure on police and galvanized volunteers to help in what became a nationwide search. During the trial, viewers learned more about the justice system and the nuances behind everything from the many motions to dismiss the case to why Justin Falconer, the infamous Juror #5, was kicked off the panel for making a comment to the victim's brother while cameras were rolling. With the lawyers in the case unable to talk to the press, these experienced trial lawyers were more than willing to step in, offer analysis, and get their face on TV.

The notable exception to the rule was prominent L.A. attorney Gloria Allred. Along with being a ubiquitous TV analyst, Allred happened to represent the trial's star witness: Peterson's secret lover, Amber Frey. Geragos tried mightily to have Allred gagged along with the rest of the key players, but the judge repeatedly said no dice. That gave Allred leeway to appear on various legal panels and, in equal measure, slam Peterson and fiercely defend her client. Moreover, she made no attempt to shield her contempt of Geragos. At one press conference in August, 2004, she held up a plastic bag to make her opinion of the lead defense counsel crystal clear. "I have a trash bag with me, a garbage bag actually, because I think a lot of the arguments that Geragos engaged in were total garbage," Allred said.

The media ate it up and sure enough, inside the courtroom, Frey emerged as the heroine of the trial. While she said relatively little on the witness stand, excerpts of Frey's secretly recorded conversations with Peterson were played for the court, giving the jury a unique window into his complex—and pathological—soul. Ultimately, prosecutors used the affair to show a motive for murder.

But this story wasn't about Amber, and I tried to make sure it wasn't only about Scott. In every report, I tried to make sure I got Laci's name and picture on the air, so that viewers would remember why we were all there. A beautiful, innocent young woman was viciously killed, on Christmas Eve of all days. Her lifeless, pregnant body was dumped into the San Francisco Bay to rot. Her seemingly "perfect" husband thought he'd get away with murder. He didn't.

Reporting for Fox News Channel, my job was to deliver hourly updates on the day's proceedings, ending with a full re-cap of events to lead off *On The Record with Greta Van Susteren*. In every way imaginable, this was a plum assignment. More than a million viewers watched Greta's show, and the ratings during the Peterson trial were among her highest. But at times, doing my job became slightly awkward. In Modesto, the weather was sometimes so cold we had to cover our laps with blankets. And every night without fail, a loud locomotive would roar by in the background, finally prompting Greta to ask us, on the air, "What is up with those trains?!" The actual reporting could cause uncomfortable situations, too. In addition to my trial reports, Greta asked me to do profiles of the main players: Geragos and Allred among them. I remember the night I profiled Allred, who's as quick with a smile as she is with a press conference; she was a guest on the legal panel. There I was, reporting live, coast to coast about Allred's legal career and headline-making cases, while standing inches away from her. While not everything I said was necessarily positive—Allred has often been accused of seeking publicity—she was gracious and understanding as she watched me deliver that report.

Off camera, all these legal commentators could find themselves at the center of network TV politics. Every day, one or more would be asked to stand before a microphone outside the courthouse, and answer questions about everything from courtroom testimony, to the demeanor of the jurors, to the reaction of emotionally fragile family members. Scores of reporters assigned to cover the trial were allowed to use this "expert sound" in their reports that aired on the local news.

But it didn't always work smoothly for network correspondents. Jim Hammer, in the employ of Fox News, was not to appear on CNN—or anywhere else. I was not to use any sound bites from reporter Ted Rowlands, who was covering the case for CNN, and sometimes was tapped as the so-called "pool reporter." The same went for me when it was my turn to report the action unfolding in the courtroom. When it came to using another channel's "trial observer," we had to be careful, get clearance, and keep it short.

The personalities who became legal celebrities during the Peterson trial continue to intertwine. For a time, even as he defended Scott Peterson, Mark Geragos represented Michael Jackson, while Canny, Cardoza, Hammer and the rest provided regular analysis from outside the courthouse in Santa Maria, California. Currently, a federal grand jury in San Francisco is looking into whether baseball slugger Barry Bonds committed perjury in 2003, when he testified under oath that he'd never knowingly used steroids. Bond's former trainer, Greg Anderson, the person prosecutors suspect of delivering the steroids, is represented by none other than Mark Geragos. In the summer of 2006, Anderson was sent to jail on contempt of court charges for refusing to testify against Bonds. When he was released on July 20th, 2006, it was Paula Canny who picked him up and drove him home. Bonds is also being investigated for tax evasion—and his former business partner, who could be a key witness, is represented by Michael Cardoza. As for Gloria Allred, she represented another girlfriend in another murder case...that of 17-year-old Scott Dyleski, convicted of the 2005 Bay Area murder of Pamela Vitale, the wife of attorney and TV legal analyst...Daniel Horowitz.

While the legal spin zones swirled outside the Peterson trial, the justice system hummed along inside the courtroom. Twelve jurors and a few alternates sat through nearly 6 months of testimony and reached a verdict despite several shake-ups on the jury, including a change of foreman. In the end, I believe, beyond a reasonable doubt, that America's trial courts are the best in the world. Up against one of the most famous attorneys in the country, two unknown prosecutors from a small town, Rick Disasto and Dave Harris, won the case, and in a sense, helped rebuild some of the trust many Americans had lost after another California jury acquitted O.J. Simpson. The system worked because counsel on both sides chose a jury of smart people. A highly respected and experienced judge was called out of retirement to preside. It worked because key witnesses stepped up and did the right thing. Single mom Amber Frey preserved her testimony, even though tabloids were offering her big money for exclusives...and hung tough when, in retaliation, those same tabloids published nude photos of her. Despite the public spectacle that befalls many high-profile cases these days, I believe the justice system can still prevail.

ERIC J. DUBIN is a California trial lawyer who gained national acclaim after winning a thirty million dollar jury verdict in the Wrongful Death lawsuit against Robert Blake. Having trained with the legendary Gerry Spence, Eric was recently named one of the "Top 20 lawyers" in the State of California by the Los Angeles and San Francisco *Daily Journal*, at the age of forty. In 2006, *Super Lawyers* magazine honored Eric with its "Rising Star" award, after he obtained one of the largest jury awards in California history. Eric has been featured in hundreds of publications around the world, including a prestigious profile in the "California" section of the *Los Angeles Times*. Eric has been a frequent guest on NBC's *Today Show*, and has also served as a legal expert and commentator for the Fox News Channel and Court TV.

Eric lives in Orange County, California, with his wife and two young children, where he was featured by *Orange Coast Magazine* in 2005 as one of the communities "Great Guys." Eric's law practice focuses on helping victims and their families of terrible tragedies, and he is currently representing the family of the multi-platinum rock band "LIT" for the Wrongful Death of their father caused by a mislabeled motorcycle helmet. Eric began his career working as a judicial clerk for the California Court of Appeal, participating on several published opinions that are still California law. Eric has been a law professor at Whittier Law School, teaching both Ethics and Legal Remedies, as well as hosting the CBS Radio Talk Show *Legally Speaking with Eric Dubin*. His first book *Hardball with Blake* is expected to be released in early 2007.

The Power
of Celebrity Silence

By Eric J. Dubin

The day after I won the 30 million dollar jury verdict in the Robert Blake Wrongful Death case, an absurd headline ran in papers all across the world: O.J. SLAMS THE BLAKE VERDICT. I thought "Wow, here is a man who has twice used fame and fortune to sidestep the American Justice System now trash-talking the same system he manipulated." The true irony? O.J. Simpson is free to say anything he wants because our Constitution gave him the right to remain silent at his double murder trial.

The winning formula is simple and virtually unbeatable in modern law, the Fifth Amendment right to remain silent *combined* with the power of celebrity equals *"reasonable doubt."* The power of the Fifth Amendment for a celebrity is a trap door that every prosecutor has fallen through. Silence is why Robert Blake is free to "cowboy" across the desert and O.J. is free to talk smack from a Florida golf course after both faced evidence that surely would have convicted you or me.

The Fifth Amendment forces a jury to judge and convict a beloved celebrity without ever getting to ask the most important question of all, "Did you do it?" Throw in "fame's" twin brother "fortune," and a celebrity defendant can hire extremely talented lawyers, the end result being an unfair legal fight over the phrase "reasonable doubt" Richard Steel would surely step in and stop.

When you think about it, it makes perfect sense that these celebrities are winning freedom despite the outward appearance of guilt. Asking a jury to put a major celebrity away in prison is really no different than asking them to convict a long beloved friend. We grow up watching and following celebrities, and equate music and movies with key moments in our own lives. Celebrities are really America's royalty, with a dozen or so magazines devoted each week to telling us all the juicy details of their private lives. We know everything from their marital woes/relationship history, dining favorites, vacation spots, and even where they live. In short, we are invested!

Much like a close friend who is suddenly and uncharacteristically charged with a horrific crime, friendship and goodwill would lead you to look your friend in the eyes and give them the chance to explain exactly what happened. After 10, 20, 30 years of following a celebrity's life and work, do they not deserve the same fairness? Is that not *"reasonable?"* If you were never given any chance to hear your friend's side of the story, you would always harbor at least some *doubt* of your friend's or beloved celebrity involvement.

Can you say "REASONABLE DOUBT?" And even though you would *never* be allowed to serve on a jury involving a friend or acquaintance, celebrities *do* get to stack the jury with "fans" and this is where the unfixable problem begins. The "Reasonable Doubt" burden of proof hurdle is raised dramatically, because many jurors have known about, and maybe even loved, the work of the defendant.

Celebrity silence at trial allows a jury to look across the counsel table at a famous defendant and envision O.J. running down the sidelines in his complete glory in snowy Buffalo, or Blake in his grey short sleeve sweatshirt as "Barretta," the coolest TV cop ever. A conviction would inherently mean we were all bad judges of character by devoting years of our time, love and attention. In essence, our own personal history and memories are sitting alongside the celebrity being judged and questioned.

The charm, history, and instinct to ask for an autograph simply does not exist for the average defendant charged with murder. The average accused murderer who takes the Fifth Amendment is viewed as guilty, and unable to withstand a cross examination by a prosecutor. A celebrity simply looks like they are following the advice of their high-powered lawyer, a point usually hammered home by the lawyer at a press conference to defuse blame.

The power of silence gives the celebrity a legal opportunity to cash in years of accumulated good will chips of fame. It is saying to the jury through silence "I am not even going to talk about these ridiculous charges against me, you all know me and know I would never do something like this!" The "fame" gets you the opening to overlook otherwise obvious/overwhelming evidence against you, while the "fortune" gets you the gifted lawyers to get you home.

Much like a close friend, your natural inclination would be to give a beloved celebrity every benefit of the doubt. To a talented lawyer, this advantage alone should be enough to win any circumstantial case. It would also make it very easy for a juror to believe your expert witnesses' explanations with respect to any physical or scientific evidence. "Fame" gets you the benefit of the doubt; "fortune" will get you any expert opinion you need on the planet.

Suddenly, the rules have changed, and the burden of proof is unrealistically elevated. What prosecutors miss is the absolute backwardness of a celebrity trial. The mistake is treating a celebrity case "like any other case," when it clearly is NOT. Jurors WANT to be on high-profile celebrity cases, and "Reasonable Doubt" becomes elevated to "No Doubt."

This is why real justice for these celebrity cases is Civil Court. Because the Civil Trial stakes are money v. "life and liberty," a celebrity is forced to take the stand and discuss the hard facts and evidence without Constitutional protection. Many jurors said I won the 30 million dollar judgment against Robert Blake based on my cross examination of him on the stand. He simply could not talk or charm his way around my hard questions, and I was able to expose his dark and violent side the criminal jury in his murder trial never heard or experienced. I took away the power of celebrity silence and won the case.

I am confident that, had the State of California had the opportunity to put Robert Blake and O.J. Simpson on the stand, they would both be living in the same place and wearing the same prison-issued clothing. Michael Jackson I am not so sure about. How can you convict a guy who can pull off satin PJ's in a Court of Law?

Great movies and music are pure magic, and really are some of the best things life has for us to enjoy. They give us a lifetime of enjoyment and bliss, and we reward the best with all the fame and fortune America has to offer. Even when our celebrities fall from grace, we usually give them a second chance to show us the magic we loved in the first place. True celebrities are special, and most understand their power and privilege and use it to promote charity and a better world. A few bad apples benefit from the collective goodwill of the rest, which is why you see the well-deserved relentless late night jokes turning on their own.

I will say the bubble of celebrity protection seems to be deflating with time; it appears our sports stars may be the first wave to lose the unspoken immunity. And hey, we even put the armed and dangerous Martha Stewart in the slammer for a few months (while Jason Williams avoided any real time after blowing away his limo driver with a shotgun).

One thing we do know beyond a "Reasonable Doubt," being charged with murder doesn't seem to be a problem for a celebrity—just don't "five finger discount" the merchandise at Saks Fifth Avenue!

JAMES C. BASTIAN, JR. is a partner with the Southern California law firm Shulman Hodges & Bastian LLP and specializes in business law, litigation and bankruptcy matters. Prior to joining SHB, Mr. Bastian served as judicial law clerk to the Honorable Kathleen Thompson, United States Bankruptcy Judge for the Central District of California. Mr. Bastian received a B.A. in Political Science from UCLA in 1991 and his J.D. from Southwestern University School of Law in 1994.

Mr. Bastian has represented nearly every type of party in a Chapter 7 or Chapter 11 bankruptcy proceeding in every district in the State of California and has been specially admitted to represent parties in additional jurisdictions nationwide. Currently, Mr. Bastian and his firm are representing the estate of Bonny Lee Bakley in the bankruptcy case of Robert Blake.

Mr. Bastian lives in Coto de Caza, California with his wife Elizabeth and their three children.

The Reasonableness
of Doubt

By James Bastian

Before I started law school, life was simpler. Things seemed much clearer to me. There were more blacks and whites and fewer shades of grey. Sure, it was because I was younger and my life experiences and responsibilities were fewer. But in addition, my view of things was often shaped by my tendency to categorize them in absolute terms: right or wrong, good or bad, Democrat or Republican, guilty or innocent.

My time in law school changed all that—for two reasons. First, as most lawyers will tell you, law school can be a time for analysis and true study—an opportunity to ask and learn why our laws are what they are, as opposed to simply learning and reciting the rules. Next, and more importantly, I attended law school in a city at a time when the law, especially criminal law, became the focal point of American pop culture through some of the most high-profile cases in the history of our criminal justice system. These cases created an entire industry and made celebrities out of formerly unknown and ordinary lawyers. The unprecedented media attention, the impact on people and society in general and the outcomes of each case, arguably did more to affect our understanding and perception of what it means to have proof beyond a reasonable doubt than anything else in American jurisprudence.

After graduating from UCLA in 1991, I enrolled at Southwestern University School of Law in Los Angeles. Southwestern sits just off Wilshire Boulevard and Vermont Avenue, a couple of miles west of downtown in the middle of various ethnic communities, and has produced many prominent players in the world of criminal justice. As all students do, I took Criminal Law in my first semester, Criminal Procedure in my second semester and Evidence in my second year. After my first class session in Criminal Law, I remember thinking how hard it must be to convict anyone of any crime. So much had to be shown—from the defendant's *mens rea* (his state of mind) to the acts he committed. Then to compound matters, you had to prove all of this "beyond a reasonable doubt." After breaking down every nuance of a crime, I saw nothing but opportunity for doubt. Yet people were convicted all the time. How could that be? The key, I came to understand, was the word "reasonable."

The most common thread in all law school classes is the application of the word "reasonable." You learn of the reasonable person standard, reasonable interpretation of contract terms, reasonable actions, reasonable force and of course, reasonable doubt. Reasonableness is intended to create an objective standard to apply to a given set of facts. The reasonable person is supposed to be purely objective. Whatever he or she would do, that is the standard that governs. When "reasonable" is interjected into anything, however ironically, the door to subjectivity is opened. This was never more in evidence than during the first trial of the officers in the Rodney King case and in the O.J. Simpson case.

In late April of 1992 I was preparing for final exams at the end of my first year of law school when the verdicts came back in the state court trial of the officers accused in the beating of Rodney King. To most people who saw the video of the incident there was really no doubt (reasonable or otherwise) that something criminal took place. However, when twelve men and women, most of whom were white, were presented all the evidence in a court room in suburban, fairly affluent Simi Valley, California, reasonable doubt existed and the accused were found not guilty of any crime. Protests, then riots and looting, ensued and my school was shut down as buildings in and around the neighborhood burned and chaos reigned. Final exams were delayed over a week and I watched in dismay as the city unraveled. The not guilty verdict led to an outpouring of disenchantment with the legal system and spurred initial protests that authorities in Los Angeles could not or would not prevent from spinning out of control.

In the King case, there was no daily broadcast of proceedings so we could not see and hear everything presented to the jury—but we didn't need to, we had the tape. We saw all we needed to see and most of us concluded there was a crime committed. But under the pressure of a courtroom proceeding, the jury reached a different conclusion and found reasonable doubt. How could that be?

I had just graduated and was beginning preparation for the California State Bar Examination when Nicole Brown and Ron Goldman were brutally murdered. The investigation, the famous low-speed chase, the plea and the pundits provided me with an interesting diversion from my studies. As I reacquainted myself with the rules I learned in my first year Criminal Law and Procedure courses, I had a real life demonstration playing out before me. As I began my legal career, I was able to witness the application of the law to a set of facts on a grand scale. Again, all the evidence appeared to point to Mr. Simpson's guilt beyond any doubt, yet the jury failed to convict.

While some have argued that both cases were the product of jury nullification, I would argue that the verdicts reflected a proper finding of reasonable doubt, in all its subjective glory. To some, it may not be reasonable to doubt the guilt of the officers who were caught on tape in the Rodney King case; but to a jury comprised of people whose demography suggests they held a high opinion of the police, never had any reason to question the actions or intentions of the police, and may have believed Mr. King was in the wrong to begin with and thus, responsible for what occurred, there may have been reasonable doubt. Similarly, the presence of substantial DNA and blood evidence, motive and opportunity to kill and too many coincidences to explain, may have eliminated any doubt of Mr. Simpson's guilt for many people. On the other hand, if your life experiences caused you to question the integrity of police, if you considered Mr. Simpson an icon and incapable of such crimes or believed his counsel's catchy lines that appeared to be based on simple, visible facts (the glove did not fit), then it might have been entirely reasonable to doubt his guilt.

Do these cases illustrate the ultimate flaw in our criminal justice system, or do they represent the very best the system has to offer? The defendants in these cases were tried by a jury of their peers, who were able to find doubt, which to them was reasonable. What may be reasonable to you or me, may not be reasonable to someone else. That may very well be the beauty of our system—it affords a great measure of subjectivity hidden in objectivity's clothing. And in the case of most criminal trials, twelve individuals' subjective experiences are brought into the mix and if they come to an agreement, it is called a verdict. If the state cannot do enough to overcome this hurdle, then it should not be able to deprive someone of life, liberty or property.

Before law school, I did not pay much attention to these issues and, in retrospect, I took things like burdens of proof and due process for granted. In that way, I don't think I am too different than most people. That all changed for me once I had the opportunity to study these issues and appreciate their importance when I was in law school. I believed it was next to impossible to convict someone of a crime and today, while I am a little older and hopefully a little wiser, I share the same view. Moreover, I believe the threshold *should be* very high to convict someone of a crime. If we are going to take away rights that are guaranteed by our constitution, we had better be damn sure there is a good reason to do so.

Because of the Simpson and King cases, and the many cases that have followed, Americans have received lessons similar to the ones I learned in law school. Before these cases, these issues may have received attention, but nowhere near what is seen today. We now have entire television programs and networks devoted to the study of the criminal justice system in America. As a result, regular people get to learn and appreciate everything that goes into a criminal conviction and jurors appear to take their jobs more seriously. We may agree or disagree agree with the juries in the Michael Jackson or Scott Peterson cases, but at least we have a better understanding of what is involved. And while many defendants are, no doubt, wrongly convicted or improperly set free notwithstanding the attention that these cases have received, at least there has been a focus on these issues, and that, to quote a defendant who recently learned a great deal about this, is a good thing.

JAYSON BLAIR is the president and chief executive of Azure Entertainment Corporation and a former reporter for *The New York Times*. He has written for *The Washington Post, The Boston Globe* and more than a dozen other newspapers.

Blair is the author of *Burning Down My Master's House: A Personal Descent into Madness that Shook The New York Times* and is heavily involved in advocacy for those with bipolar disorder and other mental illnesses.

Beyond a
Shadow of a Doubt

By Jayson Blair

My view of reasonable doubt was influenced, like many young Americans of my generation, by the events of October 3, 1995. That was the day that jury of nine people in Los Angeles County returned a not guilty verdict in the case of <u>The People of the State of California v. Orenthal James Simpson</u>.

Not long after I watched O.J. Simpson lead the Los Angeles Police Department on the famous white Bronco chase around Southern California, I came to the conclusion that it appeared that O.J. Simpson had killed his wife, Nicole, and Ron Goldman. I was working as a reporter for Capital News Service the day that verdict was announced and was on a tree-lined street of shops in Annapolis, Maryland when I heard the news from an antique shop where customers and workers had crowded around a television. I was so shocked I cried that day. Something about truth and justice, the righteous avenging nature of the American justice system, shattered for me that day. I listened to the lawyers, the jurors and everyone else who thought the acquittal was the correct decision and still find it incongruous with my sense of right.

I believed, like many do, that a guilty man should not get away with murder.

That was until years later when, because of the efforts of Barry Sheck, one of the lawyers with the Simpson defense, I was exposed to a number of innocent men who were in prison. As a crime reporter at *The New York Times* during the late 1990s and early part of this century, Mr. Sheck's team was constantly pointing out examples of how DNA was proving dozens of convicted men and women innocent, something that collectively shook my faith in the reasonableness of the results produced by our modern criminal justice system.

That's when I realized that a legal system can only work as an instrument of justice when it is so difficult to convict someone of a crime that many guilty parties go free and innocent parties rarely are put away. At the heart of the presumption of innocence—at least for it to work in practical terms—is the notion that it is better that five, ten, twenty or one hundred guilty men go free than one innocent man spend a day in jail. It was a principle I learned from Mr. Sheck's co-workers at the Innocence Project, based in New York, was embodied in the 1895 Supreme Court decision in <u>Coffin v. United States</u>. In that case, the Court traced this presumption of innocence to England and then to ancient Rome, the laws of Sparta and Athens and even words in Deuteronomy.

Meeting men who had been convicted of crimes and later exonerated by DNA evidence told me that, if anything, we need a justice system in America that makes it even more difficult to convict someone of a crime. Marcia Clark and Chris Darden, the lead prosecutors in the Simpson case, convinced me that O.J. Simpson probably killed Ms. Simpson and Mr. Goldman. I hardly question that. But what those men who have been falsely convicted, some of them placed on Death Row, convinced me of was the fact that, based on the evidence, Mr. Simpson should have been acquitted. It was not that the evidence was not enough—it was convincing, as I said. But what it did not do was exclude alternative and plausible theories of the crime. The slim chance that Mr. Simpson was innocent was enough to create a doubt that would be reasonable in the mind of anyone who has seen a person who has been wrongly convicted.

I joke that a prosecutor would never allow me onto a jury. It is probably true. Perhaps the problem is that I do not believe that most people are reasonable, and I also believe that most people choose not to doubt those in positions of authority, especially when it comes to fear and safety. These days, with a little more life experience, I do not look at cases like I did the O.J. Simpson case—black or white, right or wrong. It would be nice if things could be black and white—but if I want to live in a world where all good guys get off and all bad guys go to jail, then I also would have to live in a world where we could presume to know the truth—something that is often elusive—and one where people do not make mistakes.

My new view of the criminal justice system was made clear to me in how I viewed two recent high-profile cases—the murder trials of Scott Peterson, in the death of his wife Laci, and the murder trial of Andrea Yates, who drowned her five small children in the bathtub.

Mr. Peterson denied involvement, but there was plenty of circumstantial evidence that suggested that he killed his wife. My problem with the guilty verdict in the Peterson case was that—despite the fact that there were many circumstantial facts suggesting that Peterson committed the crime—there was no evidence that he was the only one who could have killed Laci Peterson. In other words, there were other reasonable, albeit unlikely, alternative theories of the crime. When dealing with circumstantial evidence, jurors and prosecutors often push toward convictions because it suggests a person has committed a crime. Is that really enough? I firmly believe that circumstantial evidence should only be used to seal a conviction when the said information excludes all other reasonable possibilities. At that point, there can be no reasonable doubt, which there was a lot of in the Peterson case. I say this with the caveat that I believe Scott Peterson killed his wife. I also believe the prosecutors did not put on enough evidence to prove that case—at least not beyond a shadow of a doubt, and certainly not beyond reasonable doubt. I believe he did it. I also believe that justice dictates that he should be a free man today.

Ms. Yates admitted to the killing, so that was never a question. The issue in that case revolved around culpability, and I have a hard time seeing that nine reasonable people find Ms. Yates insane. She was seeing psychiatrists before the killings, was doped up on anti-psychotics and anti-depressants and had been taken off medications to prevent psychosis—ding, ding—in the days before the killings. Ms. Yates' husband left her home alone with the children for several hours as a part of the therapeutic process, working with Ms. Yates and her doctors to help her feel as if she could be responsible for the children. Part of the so-called circumstantial evidence—it was circumstantial but it surely was not evidence—was that Ms. Yates had seen an episode of the television program *Law & Order*, where a mother drowned her children and was acquitted of murder on an insanity plea. Forget the fact that Dick Wolf, the producer of *Law & Order*, says that he gets all his episode ideas from the front page of *The New York Post* and other real-life crime stories. Oh, wait, there was never such a *Law & Order* episode (although *Law & Order: Criminal Intent* featured a similar storyline after the Yates trial). Is this the type of flimsy evidence we use to put people to death? Perhaps Ms. Yates is not the only one who is insane.

The death penalty itself raises numerous questions. Recent research has raised the questions about the integrity of eyewitness identifications, laboratory procedures, evidence collection, witness statements and law enforcement. Research at the Benjamin Cardoza School of Law in New York has shown that the primary causes of wrongful convictions are mistaken eyewitnesses, negligence, misconduct, poor training in forensic laboratories, false confessions, deceptive jailhouse informants and incompetent defense lawyers. For psychological reasons we need to believe that our justice system is just; but all the real evidence suggests that the most reasonable doubt anyone could have would be to question the effectiveness of the our criminal justice system. It all makes me feel that the legal standard should not even be reasonable doubt, but beyond a shadow of a doubt. Perhaps that would not be practical, but it would come closer to guaranteeing that no innocent man went to jail.

KENIN M. SPIVAK is chairman and CEO of wireless technology pioneer Telemac Corporation, author of the thriller, *The Karasik Conspiracy* (with Julie Chrystyn), co-editor of *The Knowledge Exchange Business Encyclopedia*, a blogger for Huffingtonpost.com, and CEO of Spivak Management Inc. which manages entertainment industry clients. Kenin was COO of major studio MGM/UA, CEO of independent film company Island World, chairman of publisher Knowledge Exchange, chairman of the Paul Mitchell cosmetology schools, vice chairman of hair care leader John Paul Mitchell Systems, an investment banker at Merrill Lynch, an attorney, and a director of media, banking and consumer goods companies. Kenin produced feature films for Twentieth Century Fox, and produced and hosted radio and television series. He holds multiple patents for wireless billing technologies. Kenin received his A.B., MBA and JD from Columbia University.

Of Celebrities, the Infamous,
Scott Peterson
and No Possible Doubt

By Kenin M. Spivak

Recent events have amply demonstrated the advantage celebrities enjoy when they have the misfortune of participating in America's criminal justice system. From O.J. to Robert Blake, Michael Jackson, Kobe Bryant, Snoop Dogg, Puff Daddy (a/k/a Sean "P. Diddy" Combs a/k/a Sean John Combs), and William Kennedy Smith, celebs appear to enjoy a presumption of innocence so strong that prosecutors are seldom able to motivate 12 jurors to convict. Even when convictions or pleas are obtained, the courts are consistently lenient when it comes to celebrity justice.

Just look at Winona Ryder (probation for stealing $6,000 of clothes), Zsa Zsa Gabor (three days for striking a policeman), Robert Downey, Jr. (repeated probation) or Russell Crowe (probation for assault). And this isn't a recent trend. Witness Fatty Arbuckle, Errol Flynn and Norman Mailer, among many others.

Though the advantage of fame in our celebrity-obsessed society is not limited to the criminal justice system, it finds its most odious manifestation when it incapacitates the reason of those who have sworn to uphold impartiality and justice. Too many jurors and judges just can't separate fact from the fiction of celebrity publicity machines, or even if they can, the possibility that they might enter their beloved icon's orbit has them bewitched, bothered and bewildered.

Celebrity nullification of the State's prosecutorial efforts has been well covered by the celeb-hungry media, but the corollary nullification of the fundamental right to a fair trial for the infamous has not. Yet, their plight is growing at an alarming rate. Thanks to 24-hour-a-day cable networks, thousands of television and radio stations, and the public's insatiable appetite for someone to despise, the abhorrent stench of infamy, once limited to just a few mass murderers like Genghis Khan, Hitler or Stalin, now oozes from increasing numbers of run-of-the-mill predators and alleged predators.

Seemingly every few weeks, the media picks one gruesome crime or another to highlight with intense round-the-clock coverage. When the story clicks with a public impatient for the next Jack the Ripper, the coverage goes into hyperdrive, demonizing the alleged culprit. Whether it's the McMartin pre-school trial, Joey Buttafuoco and Amy Fisher, Unabomber Theodore Kaczynski, Lyle and Erik Menendez, British au pair Louise Woodward, Scott Peterson, or any of the dozens of other alleged murderers, pedophiles, and rapists plucked from obscurity by the rapacious media pack, these once nobodies become instant household names. But, unlike O.J. or Kobe who entered our consciousness as icons, these apostates are instantly infamous. Within minutes after their names come screaming across the airwaves, and over the ensuing days and weeks, they are convicted over-and-again by the media of horrendous crimes. No matter that there has been no trial. Often, there hasn't even been an arrest.

Of course, the public has a right to know and advertisers covet an inquisitive public. Combining three public services in one with comprehensive 24-hour coverage, the media not only keep us safe and satiate our need to know, but also educate us about erectile dysfunction and athlete's foot.

The criminal justice system argues that a fair and impartial trial can still occur. Carefully screened jurors will simply ignore all they have read, heard and discussed. All rumor and innuendo will disappear from their psyches when they begin deliberations.

Not in the real world.

Reason and countless studies demonstrate that it is nearly impossible for informed Americans to ignore the media, particularly when a story is pervasive and compelling. Not only do the media make stars of these hapless unknowns, but it zealously convicts them, while parading every purported detail of their allegedly sordid lives in front of the public in a frenzy that can last from a month to well over a year if the defendant is foolish enough to enjoy the macabre adulation that often ensues. With each story on *Inside Edition*, *Entertainment Tonight*, the local television and radio news, and each article in *USA Today* and, all too frequently, *The Washington Post*, *The Los Angeles Times* and yes, save us all, *The New York Times*, CNN, *Newsweek* and *Time* magazine, the allegations take a step closer to being perceived as fact and the alleged predator is transformed into Lucifer.

Now, we all enjoy a little devil here or there. When the devil is played by Al Pacino or Elizabeth Hurley, we flock to his (or her) side. Just put Pacino or Hurley on trial and no doubt a juror or judge will fondly find the celeb innocent of all charges and probably even apologize for the inconvenience. As the late comedian Flip Wilson often proffered in his own defense, "The devil made me do it."

But, our enjoyment of the devil inside extends only to beloved actors, professional athletes and cute kids. Our view of the media-designated Satans-of-the-moment is entirely different. Suddenly, the lessons we learned in church come to the fore. These murderers must burn in eternity for they have forsaken the laws of God and Man. The reaction is of fire and brimstone vanquishing Hester Prynne, John Scopes, Sacco and Vanzetti, and the Rosenbergs in one fell swoop.

Even better if our latest Lucifer is good-looking and shows no remorse. And nothing can tamp down the inexorable drum beat for death and dismemberment if our evil-doer *du jour* has the unmitigated lack of judgment to hire a celebrity lawyer. Many believe that Mark Geragos, Robert Shapiro, Leslie Abramson and their ilk are only called in when the defendant is guilty. There is considerable sentiment that these camera-loving media jockeys aren't there to help find the truth. Rather, their job is to razzle-dazzle the press, the jury and possibly even the judge. They no longer have to make their clients stars;

the media has already done that. Rather, they have to mesmerize the jury into missing the obvious, believing the improbable, and considering the implausible.

That's why, once these fiends hire a celebrity lawyer, the media crescendo climaxes. Soon, Nancy Grace, Greta van Susteren and Dan Abrams are explaining to us in meticulous detail just how Rick Tabish and Sandy Murphy supposedly suffocated Las Vegas mogul Ted Binion, which drugs Andrea Yates took and why, and how Scott Peterson lied to his mistress, Amber Frey. They also will explain to us the deceptive tactics Jo-Ellan Dimitrius, F. Lee Bailey, or Mark Geragos will use to trick the jury. They will explain this to us day after day, in print, on cable, and on talk-radio.

By the time our celebrity lawyer and his well-coiffed client show up to select a jury, every potential juror who knows how to read and think has been schooled not just on the dastardly pre-meditated atrocities so coolly committed by the unrepentant atheist before them, but also on all of the lies and deceptions his $1,000-an-hour mouthpiece will be espousing. The jurors are ready and many are convinced.

Most in the potential jury pool don't want to serve. They know how to get off. "He done it." "He must die." "It happened to my niece."

Others are just lying in wait. "Yes, it is true I have my bachelor's degree in political science from Yale, my law degree from Columbia and I served in the Massachusetts legislature for nine years before relocating here as the Stanford University Randolph Hearst Professor of Know Everything. Somehow, I guess I just missed all newspapers, magazines, radio and television over the last two years. I just don't know anything about this defendant. And I think his lawyer is swell." Yeah, we believe the professor knows nothing. And we also believe the other 11 jurors and the alternates.

I know I can be too practical. I really wish I were better at being academic and theoretical so I could prattle on about how the jurors can put aside their prejudices and form unbiased opinions. But, I can't help myself. I've got to be me. The truth is, when a defendant has received as much unremittingly negative publicity as, say, Scott

Peterson (more than 1.3 million stories on the Web alone), with the rarest of exceptions, there are only two possibilities when it comes to the jury pool, especially in the community in which the crime occurred: either the juror has already convicted the defendant and the celebrity lawyer he rode into court with, or the juror is so unaware and stupid that he can't find his way to the bathroom in the apartment he has shared with his mom and their booze for the last 40 years of his deplorable life. Not that he may not be a really swell guy, of course.

So, given the absolute incontrovertible fact that except for a few iconoclastic skeptics, any jury in Northern California empanelled to try the guilt or innocence of Scott Peterson could be filled with only three types of jurors—those who told the truth but were inexplicably permitted to serve, those who were secretly confident that he was guilty and *lied* to get on the jury in order to see him fry, and those who were too stupid to decide whether another human should live or die— just how was Scott Peterson supposed to get a fair trial?

In 2004, Peterson could not have received a fair trial in Northern California, even if the Court had tried to shield the jury from on-going media coverage and the public, which it did not. Because Peterson could not get a fair trial at the time and in the location of his trial, particularly given the Court's *de facto* refusal to shield the jury from press coverage and the public, it means he did not get one. Manifestly, Peterson's conviction should be overturned.

Scott Peterson's extended 15-minutes of infamy began on Christmas Eve in 2002, the day 27-year-old Laci Peterson disappeared. Because Laci was pregnant, the case immediately caught the media's attention. The attention focused on Laci's husband, then 30-year-old Scott, a fertilizer salesman who claimed to be fishing at the time of Laci's disappearance. As the evidence would soon show, just weeks before his wife and unborn son's disappearance, Peterson had started an affair with single mother and massage therapist, Amber Frey.

Three months later, on April 13, Laci's body washed ashore in San Francisco Bay. Within five days, Peterson was arrested and charged with two counts of murder, one for Laci and the other for their unborn son. At the time of his arrest, Peterson was carrying $10,000 in cash and had grown a beard and dyed his hair.

After briefly being represented by public defenders, Peterson retained high-profile lawyer Mark Geragos. Geragos earned his media credentials representing Winona Ryder on shoplifting charges, Susan MacDougal on Whitewater-related charges, and former Congressman Gary Condit after his mistress, intern Chandra Levy, disappeared. He joined Michael Jackson's defense team as the Peterson trial was still in progress.

One of Geragos' first acts was to request that Peterson no longer appear in court in a red jail jump suit, bound in handcuffs, shackles and waist chains. Geragos appropriately complained that the media's frequent publication of such images labeled Peterson as a "monster." The Court granted his motion.

Geragos' next steps seemed more geared to the court of public opinion than to the court in which his client's future would be determined. Geragos spent a considerable amount of time giving interviews and seeking to create doubt in the minds of the public—the jury pool—about the procedures followed by the police and his client's presumed guilt.

Much of Geragos' early efforts were probably undone when the media covered a memorial service for Laci with all the fervor usually reserved for a head of state. Prison officials refused to permit Peterson to attend the service.

Then, after more than seven months of intense publicity, the Court imposed a "gag" order on counsel. That order meant that the defense would have no further opportunity to undo the damage already done.

The next battle was over where the trial would take place. That battle was surreal. Trial was scheduled for Modesto, California, Laci's home town. Geragos moved for a change of venue, claiming that as a result of the publicity, Peterson would be unable to receive a fair trial there. The prosecution conceded the jury pool in Modesto was tainted, but asserted that as a result of widespread publicity, a change of venue would be pointless. They were right.

The prosecution's solution was to use the jury selection process to weed out those who had already decided on Peterson's guilt. The prosecution contended that could be as easily accomplished in Modesto as in the nearby Northern California town to which the Judge considered moving the trial. Again, the prosecution was right, sort of. The reality was that the selection process in any other Northern California town was as equally incapable of producing an impartial jury as the process in Modesto. Given the widespread publicity, there likely was no place in California in which an impartial jury then could be empanelled, unless that jury was filled with members either too unintelligent or too indifferent to rule on matters of life and death.

As jury selection proceeded, Geragos requested that the pool be released and that the trial be moved to Los Angeles. Geragos argued that the pool in Northern California was filled with "stealth" jurors who had already made up their minds and that the larger pool of potential jurors available in Los Angeles offered a greater possibility of obtaining an impartial jury. The court rejected Geragos' motion, ruling that the publicity would be as intense in Los Angeles as it had been in Northern California. On May 11, 2004, jury selection concluded. A jury of six men and six women, as well as six alternates were chosen from an initial panel of some 1,600, many of whom were excused after admitting they had already made up their minds that Peterson was guilty.

The Judge next abandoned any real effort to shield the jury from the intense media coverage, when he rejected the defense's plea to sequester the jury. The Judge sighed that he could not "control the whole world" and instead instructed jurors to avoid the news.

Following a 23-week trial and 184 witnesses, the case went to the jury on November 8, 2004. Long after jurors had been irretrievably biased by 23 months of saturation media coverage, the Court finally sequestered the jury during their deliberations. After seven tumultuous days that included the removal of two jurors and a mutiny against the foreman, Peterson was convicted of first-degree murder in the slaying of his pregnant wife and second-degree murder in the death of his unborn son. After the verdict was announced, the jury was released from its brief sequestration and left the courthouse to the rousing cheers of more than a thousand fans. The same jury was due back in court to decide whether Peterson should be put to death.

Geragos then launched an unusual effort to seat a new jury to decide whether Peterson should be executed. Geragos argued that as a result of "unprecedented" levels of adverse publicity, the jury pool was already tainted against Peterson before the trial and the community's sentiment impermissibly had been a factor taken into account by the unsequestered jury. He also argued that by allowing the jury to bask in the public's adulation after their verdict, any possibility for impartiality had been lost. In rejecting Geragos' motion, the trial court again bemoaned the hopelessness of the situation as "a problem without a solution."

Promptly after the appeals court and the California Supreme Court affirmed the trial court's decision, the same jury that convicted Peterson voted to impose the death penalty. A month later, the Judge sentenced Peterson to death.

Peterson is appealing his conviction on numerous grounds, including the Court's refusal to address in any meaningful way the effects of the pernicious media coverage.

I don't know Scott Peterson. Like most, I don't like the way he treated his wife, or his mistress. I don't like his affinity for the media. He's smug and slimy. There is evidence supporting his conviction. But, the fact that he is unlikable and the probability of his guilt are not sufficient grounds to conclude that beyond *all reasonable doubt* he is a murderer.

Some trial observers have parsed the evidence and concluded that regardless of jury taint, Peterson's conviction should stand because they too have concluded he was guilty (or, as they more euphemistically and pedantically explain, a "juror acting reasonably" could have concluded that Peterson was guilty). These analysts' conclusions as to what the evidence reasonably *could* have proven, or what a reasonable juror *might* have concluded are possibly correct, and certainly irrelevant.

The Constitutional guarantees of a fair trial are not so trifling that they can be forfeited to an analysis of whether an impartial jury might have been able to conclude that the defendant was guilty. I concede that Peterson might have been convicted even if there had never been a single story printed about him. But, as a principled absolute, I can't countenance the trial court's miserable and hopeless surrender to the media's onslaught. I will not ignore the reality that the incessant coverage and public clamor had an insidious effect on the jury. There were many things the Court could have done to mitigate the problem, including moving the trial and sequestering the jury. Yet, the Court simply stuck its head in the sand and did nothing.

As the press dies down and memories fade, some place in America there likely will be 12 impartial and intelligent jurors who could consider Scott Peterson's guilt or innocence based solely on what they see and hear during the trial. To restore the integrity of our criminal justice system, they should be given the opportunity to do so.

DAVID MARGOLICK is a longtime contributing editor at *Vanity Fair*, where he writes about culture, the media, and politics. Prior to that, he served two tours at *The New York Times*: from 1981 to 1986, as a legal reporter on the metropolitan desk and, from 1987 to 1994, as national legal affairs editor, where he wrote the weekly "At the Bar" column. In the second position, he covered the trials of O.J. Simpson, Lorena Bobbitt, and William Kennedy Smith.

He is a graduate of the University of Michigan and Stanford Law. He is the author of *Undue Influence: The Epic Battle for the Johnson & Johnson Fortune* (1993); *At the Bar: The Passions and Peccadilloes of American Lawyers* (1996); *Strange Fruit: Billie Holiday, Cafe Society, and an Early Cry for Civil Rights* (2000) and *Beyond Glory: Joe Louis vs. Max Schmeling, and a World on the Brink* (2005).

A Jury of
Journalists

By David Margolick

The first question people invariably ask me when they learn I covered the O.J. Simpson case is "Was he guilty?" Invariably I say yes, partly because I believe it, partly because I sense it's what they want to hear—i.e., they feel the same way—and partly because it cuts off the conversation cold, allowing us move on to something more because the topic makes me squirm. The better question, at least to me, would be "Would you have voted to convict?" And the answer to that is a bit more complicated.

Perhaps it's the journalist in me. In fact, it certainly is the journalist in me. I've always wrestled with the phrase "beyond a reasonable doubt." I doubt for a living; I'm in the business of balance. My normal position when covering something isn't standing up straight, but bending over backwards. To me, therefore, almost any doubt is reasonable. I'd be a terrible juror, at least for the prosecution. All any halfway decent defense lawyer has to do for me is splatter doubt profligately all over a case, and hope that at least one dollop of it sticks on something crucial. My standard would be more like "beyond a shadow of a doubt." Even a scintilla of uncertainty would gnaw at me in the jury room.

This is what happened to me during the Simpson trial. Intuitively, I thought what every other reasonable person thought: that Simpson was clearly guilty. The motive was clear, the evidence overwhelming. Just as crucial, at least to me, was intuition: watching him come into court every day, he looked and acted and carried himself like a guilty man. And yet—and this was the genius of his defense, at least for someone like me—they raised all that doubt: most memorably, about the glove, and just as importantly, about the methods and motives of the Los Angeles Police Department. Had I been on that jury, I would have agonized. Perhaps someone could have convinced me that these caveats didn't matter, and remind me of how strong the case against him really was. Or perhaps I would have been carried along by eleven colleagues determined to convict; this is, of course, both the genius and the great danger of the jury system. I don't know how much Henry Fonda I'd have had in me. But it would have taken some time.

And that's my quarrel with the Simpson jurors. I think they acquitted a guilty man, but ambivalent me can't fault them for that. Instead, they reached what to me was the right result for the wrong reason. Given the haste with which they decided things, it was clear that they didn't weigh doubt at all, reasonable or otherwise, and that all that fancy footwork of the Simpson defense mattered little; they voted with, and acquitted from, their gut. More than sift through evidence, they wanted to make a point. They did not do what reasonable jurors, if not newspaper reporters, do all the time, lest our criminal justice system become paralyzed: carefully consider a case, realize that nothing in life can ever be entirely free of doubt, and make a common sense decision. To ordinary people, as opposed to journalists, that's "beyond a reasonable doubt."

So O.J. walked, and walks. And in the meantime, I will always wonder what would have happened had O.J. Simpson been tried in another part of town—or by a jury of journalists.

BRIAN OXMAN is an attorney with 30-years of experience and a member of the California Bar. He was has represented the Jackson Family for a decade and a half and was counsel for Michael Jackson in one of the most widely publicized criminal trials in American history. He has represented Amtrak, AT&T, Burell Restaurant Corporation, Cheseborough-Ponds, Chevron U.S.A., Creators Syndicate, General Motors, Ragu Foods, Inc., and others. He taught law school as an Associate Professor of Law specializing in corporate and commercial law and teaches continuing legal education for attorneys throughout the country. He has represented people from all walks of life, including former California Governor Jerry Brown, Denver Bronco's owner Patrick Bowlen, Supermodel Beverly Peele, Actress Cathy Lee Crosby, Apollo 12 Astronaut Richard Gordon, Apollo 17 Astronaut Ronald Evans, and others. Mr. Oxman has been a Member of the Democratic National Committee, Rules Committee, and Judge Pro Tem of the Orange County Superior Court. He has testified in court as an expert witness on the hedge fund and mutual fund trading scandals, and he has spoken across the country on corporate and celebrity scandals. Mr. Oxman has been a guest commentator on CNN, Fox News, MSNBC, Court TV, ABC, NBC, CBS, BBC, AM Canada, Fuji TV Japan, NHK Japan, Spiegel TV Germany, and others.

Our Free Press—
Riddled with Doubt!

By Brian Oxman

Conscience of the country, guardian against abuse, and marketplace of ideas—here were the roles of the press in America envisioned by the Constitution. "Mighty words" these are for a nation with a crisis of confidence in a press gone astray. Most disturbing is the realization that it is doubtful the press will recover its honored role as democracy's watchdog anytime soon.

Reasonable doubt? How about riddled with doubt!

Americans feel journalists can't be trusted and are only slightly more credible than used-car salesmen. Gallup Poll surveys find only 21 percent of Americans believe journalists have high ethical standards, which ranks them below auto mechanics. Only one in four believe what they read in the newspapers. Some 53 percent of the public view the press as out of touch with mainstream America, and another 78 percent think journalists pay more attention to the interests of their editors than their readers. A full 58 percent feel journalists don't care about inaccuracies. A Roper poll found 88 percent of Americans believed corporate owners improperly influenced news reporting.

We certainly are a nation of doubters, and the Fourth Estate, the press, is a prime target.

In his novel called *Scoop*, Evelyn Waugh weaves a tale about a rush of war reporters to a thinly disguised Abyssinia in 1938, and describes a reporter who files a story about a city on the brink of civil war. His dispatch in Latin, used to maintain secrecy, describes a body lying in the street like a broken doll. Its sensational publication in English causes a public uproar, including riots, a run on currency, and the outbreak of fighting. "That's the power of the press for you," a note-worthy colleague says in the book. The problem was the journalist had the wrong city, wrong country, and a made-up wrong story. Oh, what the heck!

But wait, ye of little doubt.

Newsweek published an article about U.S. soldiers desecrating the Koran at the Guantanamo, Cuba detention facility holding Muslim prisoners, by flushing the Holy Book down the toilet. In Afghanistan, riots broke out and Islamic fundamentalists charged the U.S. with blasphemy against Allah. Fifteen people died. The "heck" was that the Koran story was all made up—never happened. But the 15 lost lives were real.

The *Newsweek* story was only one in a string of incidents, which have led the media to take a deep look at its ethics with extraordinary doubt. When Dr. David Kelly committed suicide following the misreporting from BBC's Andrew Gilligan that the British government had "sexed-up" its claims on Iraqi armaments, the world started to wonder. Had the BBC fabricated a story about a source, "the good doctor," which so humiliated him that he took his own life?

Without a doubt!

The honor roll of journalists fired for fabrications or misconduct form a Discredited Journalist Club of strange proportions. Most of the banished offenders have later reappeared with major book deals or new high-powered positions. Strange how an ethical faux pas is rewarded in America. Jack Kelly, a *USA Today* war correspondent, resigned under accusations of fabricating numerous stories. Jayson Blair, the *New York Times* reporter, was fired when caught fabricating stories about the Washington-area sniper case and PFC Jessica Lynch. Christopher Newton, an Associated Press reporter, was fired for concocting sources in more than 30 stories. But the consequences of these transgressions have been minimal, and in fact, most of the offenders' bank accounts smiled at these sordid affairs.

In *Good Night and Good Luck*, famed journalist Edward R. Murrow, who sat on a London roof top during the "Blitz" in 1939 to bring the world some of the most enduring and chilling war images, was unceremoniously "dumped" by CBS. Politics, not honor, dictated whether Murrow was "axed" from prime time because he had the unpopular fortitude to stand up to government recklessness, including U.S. Senator Joseph McCarthy. His vision of a potent, responsible press lost out to *The $64,000 Question*—a quiz show. Who cares that television news programming would never again be at the pinnacle of the American conscience? The lesson is what we did to Murrow was shameful.

However, beyond a shadow of doubt, the lesson hasn't gone too far.

Norman Solomon's book, *War Made Easy: How Presidents and Pundits Keep Spinning Us to Death* sets out an important lesson for all members of the media. Journalists must not let pious proclamations from governmental, religious, or institutional sources intimidate them. Question the official story line. When a reporter sees suppression of human rights or policies that fuel disasters, they must not hesitate to expose the indignity. Remaining silent and letting it slide are the greatest of all sins.

No doubt!

Can you imagine someone like H.L. Mencken, a journalistic legend of bygone years, being a reporter today? He was irreverent, drank hard, smoked like an ocean liner in the fog, and swore at—no, he swore better than the President. He never used the remote to check out cable news as source material, and sitting on the couch eating "cheetos" while perusing the "blogs" for a story would have been heresy. In tune to *Monty Python's Flying Circus*, I can hear him now, "Today's journalists are bores and upper-class twits." That's right— give 'em H.L.!!!

He was the personification of Mr. Doubt; Fire and Brimstone too!

The fundamentals of ethical journalism have always been that reporting must be objective. Opinion should be saved for the editorial and op-ed writers. The days of yellow journalism are over, and modern journalism abides by a Code of Ethics with integrity as the cornerstone. Be skeptical—show your reasonable doubt. Teach it at the journalism schools, and pass it on to new reporters as a legacy where Edward R. Murrow, Walter Cronkite, and Larry King are icons.

In his Oscar-winning performance in *On the Waterfront*, Marlon Brando played a one-time boxer, Terry Malloy, who turned against his friends and brother in a corrupt union. In one of the most memorable scenes in cinema history, Malloy tells his brother, played by Rod Steiger, "You don't understand. I could have had class. I could have been a contender. I could have been somebody, instead of a bum—which is what I am."

Should the press take heed? You bet, beyond a reasonable doubt!

LESLIE H. WHITTEN, JR. is the author of 10 published novels, four other books, booklets of his own poems and of translations of Charles Baudelaire. He has also written other translations, numerous individual poems, book reviews, and articles—printed in magazines and newspapers. From 1953-97 he was a journalist with Radio Free Europe, INS, UPI, the *Washington Post, Hearst Newspapers,* and was a partner in the Jack Anderson column, a major column during the Watergate days. He was mainly an investigative reporter, but also covered national politics, wars, murders, floods and all the ills the press is heir to.

He appeared on various national TV shows and lectured at numerous colleges and other venues including the FBI Academy. He read to the blind, 1980-1987 and was a Hospice home-care volunteer 1987-2003. He attended Lehigh University, and got a B.A. journalism-English, magna cum laude in 1950; he received a Doctorate in Humane Letters from Lehigh in1989. He was a visiting professor at two colleges.

He was arrested and jailed by the FBI in 1973 in a controversial First Amendment case; the charges were dropped in 1972; he got a major ACLU award in 1974 for protecting his sources and was made a Blood Brother of the Iroquois in 1974; U.S. Army 1946-48 S/Sgt.

Under
the Nixon Gun

By Les Whitten

On January 31, 1973, at the height of President Nixon's hate campaign against those members of the press who had unsparingly told the truth about him, I was driving my little yellow Vega into downtown Washington to pick up a big batch of stolen papers. They had been "liberated" from the federal Bureau of Indian Affairs (BIA) by a group of angry militant Indians who had taken over the building. They wanted the files that would prove past wrongs against them by the government. These they would use to get redress from the Nixon White House for their grievances.

When finally the Indians agreed to leave the building they took hundreds of pounds of documents with them in sleeping bags and in the trunks of their dilapidated cars. My boss, and friend, was columnist Jack Anderson, a prominent name on Nixon's famous "Enemy's List" and we were hot to see those documents. Because of our long-time ties with the Indian tribes, we were secretly leaked a dynamite slew of these stolen papers and did a series of stories called "The Trail of Broken Treaties."

It was a risky business. There was no question that we might be committing a serious crime if the Nixon administration chose to get technical about it. And, in fact, a jury might well find we were culpable beyond a reasonable doubt in conspiring with the Indians to commit a federal felony. Besides, the FBI, which had been looking for the documents all over America, was furious that Jack and I had come up with them.

When more documents were smuggled by bus into Washington, to my Assiboine-Sioux friend Hank Adams, he tipped me off. We two and a Paiute Indian, Anita Collins, were loading the boxes of papers into my hatchback, when a band of FBI agents rushed like Comanches from hideouts in nearby buildings and surrounded us.

The FBI had infiltrated the Indian movement and hoped to nail Jack Anderson but, as so often with their informants, they had gotten their facts wrong. They found their perp (perpetrator) was the lamb and not the sheep. Nevertheless, they handcuffed my white hands in front of me and Hank's brown hands behind him.

After conferring with Nixon's minions in the Justice Department, the FBI charged us with possession of government property with intent to convert it to my own use, a felony generally reserved for "fences." It carried a penalty of ten years in a federal prison. Almost immediately I thought, there will not be a shred of reasonable doubt in any jurors' mind that we were guilty. I had the documents, which Jack and I had hoped would shed some more light on white men's unending crimes against the Indians.

What would I be doing with them if not converting them to our own use: turning them into stories in our columns that produced substantial income from some 900 newspapers? Besides, I had seen many a prosecutor willing to ignore or try to suppress defendants' sides of cases when I was covering the courts for *The Washington Post*, United Press, the Hearst Newspapers and our column. I was looking at hard time.

If I went before a judge sympathetic to the government, I could be unprotected from numerous filings by the government to suppress what little exculpatory evidence I might come up with. The grounds might be hearsay or irrelevance or the reputation of witnesses or legal technicalities. The rash of defendants' convictions being thrown out recently because of unjustified prosecutions, marks a shocking stain on our justice system. Yet prosecutors are seldom, if ever, punished for imprisoning these poor devils—often for a decade or more—on false charges.

"Beyond a reasonable doubt" is a phrase made for the prosecutors, as any criminal defense lawyer will tell you. Judges are more often drawn from the ranks of prosecutors than from those of lawyers working for the defense. And at trial, it is the judge who by accepted law defines the meaning of "beyond a reasonable doubt." When all the chips are counted the prosecution comes out ahead. Indeed, the mere fact that a defendant is facing criminal charges makes a conviction "beyond a reasonable doubt" easier. The jury's thinking, and often the judge's, is almost inevitably this: if he is innocent, what is he doing here? Already "reasonable doubt" is in trouble. The government's ability to use squads of lawyers and investigators is almost limitless. For a small operation like ours, the costs of a long trial could close us down and the Nixon bunch knew it.

The next two weeks were a hell. I did not have even a reasonable doubt that I would escape prison. I had a vivid memory of stories I had done on prison horrors: rapes, beatings by prison gangs, and the occasional violence against prisoners by vicious guards. I lost 12 pounds in those two weeks and was sleepless night after night.

Still, Jack and I were longtime scrappers. We worked tirelessly and ingeniously to prove before a jury that they must find a reasonable doubt of our guilt. Yes, our first evidence was flimsy. Hank had ascertained that there were no good stories in the papers, mostly useless land records plus some photos of Indians dancing for President Lyndon Johnson. It was our honest intent to take them back to the BIA that morning. Indeed, Hank had written on the boxes the name of the FBI agent who he hoped would look at them when they were back in the BIA's hands.

But we knew the zealous Nixon administration prosecutors could make our statements about the papers' lack of value and our mission to return them appear merely self serving. And Hank's writing the FBI agent's name on the boxes, they could argue, was simply a ruse to cover our possession of them.

Our first long footstep on the road to establishing reasonable doubt came with the discovery that an FBI supervisory agent, involved in the case, was reputed to defy the saying that, "there are old FBI agents, and there are bold FBI agents. But there are no old, bold FBI agents." I reached him by telephone and asked him about our chances. He damn well proved to be bold. He reflected a moment on what an honest answer would cost him and then said evenly that the FBI had found a slip of paper at the Bureau of Indian Affairs, stating that Hank Adams had called to say that he would be coming over early for a visit on the morning in question. This was close to proof that we were not taking the papers off to work on them, but, on the contrary, were bringing them back to the BIA. Yet, the prosecutors and FBI higher-ups continued to try to make a case against us. We remained only half-safe.

A few days later, a freak break shattered any chance that the Nixon crew could convict me beyond a reasonable doubt. Like a fool, I had forgotten that a trusted Defense Department source had called me early on the morning I was to pick up the papers. He had a good story for me and I had asked him to call me back later that afternoon (from a pay phone of course). He now reminded me that I had said I was in a hurry at the moment because I was driving off to take back some Indian papers to the BIA.

My source had a bad heart problem and volunteered that he would give me an affidavit about his call and my remark, in case he died before I was tried. I cried on the telephone both because this would clear me—no ten years in prison! And because of his brave decency. My source and his attorney met me that night at a safe site across the Potomac. The lawyer drew up the affidavit and we got it notarized at a nearby hotel.

With some confidence, Jack and I went before a federal grand jury, saying nothing about our sources, but telling our story. Although a grand jury need not meet the standard of "beyond a reasonable doubt" to indict, that thought is always on the minds of jurors and prosecutors alike. No one wants to indict or prosecute a defendant and then be a made a fool of when the case blows up at the actual trial.

Our fair-minded grand jury refused to indict us. The Justice Department, with reluctance, gave up at last and the ugly charges were dropped.

There remains a lovely Washington irony. Our lawyer Herbert "Jack" Miller, an ex-Assistant Attorney General who helped convince Nixon's prosecutors that their case was full of holes, later successfully represented Nixon himself in an unrelated case after he quit the presidency in disgrace.

PROTECT VICTIMS

Wayne Cohen
Jack H. Olender
Joseph Cammarata
Robert K. Tanenbaum
Steve Dettelbach
Billy Martin
Ronald Zonen
Owen LaFave
Michael A. Ramos

"Power is no blessing in itself, except when it is used to protect the innocent."

—Jonathan Swift (1667-1745)

WAYNE COHEN is the founder and managing partner of Cohen & Cohen, P.C. Mr. Cohen is an AV-rated lawyer, whose practice is concentrated in the areas of medical malpractice, wrongful death, automobile accidents, product liability, class actions, and other personal injury areas. In short, he has devoted his professional career to representing the rights of the injured. Mr. Cohen has appeared on numerous occasions in local and national television shows and print media. Mr. Cohen has been called one of Washington's "top 40 lawyers under 40," one of "Washington's top trial lawyers," one of "the 50 best lawyers in Washington," and "one of the city's most feared personal injury lawyers." (Washingtonian Magazine, July 2006, August 2004, April 2002 and June 2001 respectively). The Washington Examiner identified Mr. Cohen as a "prominent, personal injury lawyer" on January 31, 2006.

Mr. Cohen has been an Associate Professorial Lecturer of Law at The George Washington University Law School since 1993, where he currently teaches Trial Skills. He is also the former President of the Trial Lawyers Association of Metropolitan Washington D.C. (TLA-DC, D.C. branch of ATLA), is a former Board of Governor of the TLA-DC, a member of the Association of Trial Lawyers of America, former Chairman of the Litigation Section of the District of Columbia Bar Association, and the former chair of the Injury to Persons and Property Section of the D.C. Bar. Mr. Cohen also served a 2 year appointment to the Attorney Grievance Commission of Maryland, Peer Review Committee. Perhaps it was The Wall Street Journal in a feature article on Mr. Cohen which most clearly identified him, as "brash, aggressive, and enterprising." Mr. Cohen, who is a former amateur boxer, zealously pursues his cases and has won millions of dollars in settlements and verdicts for his clients.

Mr. Cohen is a graduate of the University of Michigan (with distinction-1988) and the University of Miami (cum laude-1991).

"No Tort Reform—
Beyond a Reasonable Doubt"

By Wayne Cohen

There are many things that I believe I know beyond a reasonable doubt, but I chose to write about an issue of the utmost importance to me professionally and personally. It is a topic that I am passionate about, and one that I believe is fundamental to the basic values of our civil justice system.

I know, beyond a reasonable doubt, that there is no need to alter our civil justice system to restrict the rights of innocent victims and protect negligent defendants. In short, there is no need for so-called "tort reform." The firmness of my opinion on this subject comes from over a decade of experience as a civil litigator. Before I get into the specific consequences of a few of the proposed changes to our civil justice system, I want to put a human face on this complex issue by offering a brief story.

In my line of work I deal with tragedy on a daily basis. Once in a while however, I come across a client whose story is particularly poignant. Such was the case about a year ago. My client's daughter went to the emergency room twice complaining of severe pain in her lower stomach. Both times the ER doctors made a simple diagnosis of constipation. They sent her home groggy with pain killers and hoped the problem would just go away. Just a few hours after the second diagnosis, it became clear that a terrible mistake had been made. It wasn't constipation. It was a small bowel obstruction, and an 11-year-old girl was dead.

This is a clear example of a medical mistake resulting in a tragic wrongful death. There is no mathematical formula that will provide an accurate assessment of the damages in a case of this kind. The most qualified entity to make such a judgment is a jury of the victim's peers. Proponents of tort reform, however, want to restrict the rights of juries to determine the proper amount of compensation. Capping jury awards, as most plans for tort reform call for, would take this right out of a juror's hands and replace it with an arbitrary ceiling on the amount a victim can recover. The only group of victims that this sort of plan has the potential to affect are the most seriously injured. Of all the parties involved in these sorts of disputes, the last group we should look to hurt is victims themselves.

Not only will capping jury awards harm victims, but it will also insulate the most negligent parties by limiting their potential payouts. In a capped jury awards system, negligent parties win and innocent victims lose. Our society needs to create incentives that encourage businesses and individuals to operate in a conscientious and safe manner. Limiting jury awards would work directly against this goal. A brief hypothetical will illustrate this last point.

A vitamin manufacturer produces a popular multi-vitamin. The company can save 25 cents per pill by substituting a cheaper synthetic version of one of the ingredients in the pill. The only problem is that the cheaper ingredient is fatal in one out of 100,000 people.

Under our current system, it would most likely take one lawsuit to convince the company to use the more expensive ingredient. A $10 million civil payout would completely wipe out any savings from using the cheaper, synthetic ingredient. If jury awards were capped, however, the maximum amount that a victim could obtain would be arbitrarily set at say $250,000. A one-time payout of this amount would probably not offset the increased profit from using the cheaper ingredient. Additionally, because the adverse reaction happens so rarely, it might make sense from a purely financial standpoint for the company to keep using the unsafe ingredient and make the $250,000 payout once or twice a year.

This is an extreme example, but it illustrates the underlying problem with tort reform. Not only does it hurt victims, it does this while protecting the assets of the negligent party. We need our civil justice system to be free to operate as a tool for redressing carelessness and encouraging safety. Proponents of tort reform say that jury awards are astronomically high and out of control. But I bet they have never sat across the table from someone who was paralyzed in a car accident or lost a loved one due to a medical mistake like I do every day. If we want to see these innocent victims get adequate compensation, and we want to create a society where people are held accountable for their actions, we must never limit the rights of juries in civil cases.

I know this beyond a reasonable doubt.

Since winning the first seven-figure obstetric verdict in the United States, Attorney **JACK H. OLENDER** has amassed a record that includes some 200 verdicts and settlements of at least one million dollars each. *The Washington Post and The Washington Times* have given Mr. Olender the title King of Malpractice. *Washingtonian* magazine notes, Of all the medical malpractice lawyers in the country, none is more recognized or feared than Jack Olender. *The Washington Business Journal* calls his firm the heavyweight malpractice firm. The Malpractice Law Firm Jack H. Olender & Associates consists of nine lawyers who are leaders in the legal profession. Two are nurse/attorneys and a physician/lawyer is of counsel.

Jack Olender has been honored as Lawyer of the Year by the Bar Association of the District of Columbia, and Trial Lawyer of the Year by the Trial Lawyers Association, D.C. He is recipient of the Washington Bar Association Charles Hamilton Houston Medallion of Merit and was inducted into the National Bar Association Hall of Fame. He has received numerous awards from local and national civic and legal organizations for his accomplishments as a lawyer and as a philanthropist. Mr. Olender is a frequent lecturer to medical and legal groups and is author of numerous articles on legal and medical issues. He has been published in *Trial* Magazine, *Everyday Law, Group Practice Journal, The National Law Journal* and other periodicals. Mr. Olender has appeared on numerous network, cable, and local television and radio programs, to discuss malpractice, high-profile trials, tort reform, personal injury disasters, and how to avoid malpractice. Appearances include ABC, CBS, NBC, and CNN News; CBS *60 Minutes*; CBS *48 Hours*; CNN *Larry King Live*, C-SPAN, and COURT-TV.

Mr. Olender is founder, director, and president of the Jack and Lovell Olender Foundation. The Foundation provides support to a wide array of local and national organizations that serve the public interest. The Olender Foundation gives scholarships to exceptional law students. Jack Olender received his A.B. from the University of Pittsburgh, where he graduated Summa Cum Laude in 1957. He earned his J.D. from the University of Pittsburgh in 1960, and his LL.M. in forensic medicine from George Washington University in 1961. He is admitted to the bars of the District of Columbia, Maryland, Pennsylvania, the Federal and D.C. Circuits and the U.S. Supreme Court.

What I Know
"Beyond a Reasonable Doubt"

By Jack H. Olender

There must be a thousand and one things I "don't know" beyond a reasonable doubt, but there is one thing I do know with the same degree of certainty with which I know the sun rises and sets every morning, regardless of storm clouds or high winds, etc.

I know that all life is sacred, no matter how battered, withered and unproductive it may appear to be to someone from the outside looking in. Working for over forty years as a patients' malpractice lawyer, I've had the fortunate/unfortunate opportunity to see life's mishaps up close and too, too personal. Fortunate in the sense that we were able to financially rectify some of the damage dealt to our clients, and provide them with a semblance of what had been taken from them. However, unfortunate in that we are witness to some of the most egregious and unnecessary suffering. The callousness with which these people were tossed aside after undergoing horrific medical mistakes still baffles me. The execrable care by medical professionals who had taken an oath to provide compassionate care, to *first do no harm*, is truly incomprehensible.

Thirty years ago, a child named Janetta taught me the importance of our work. Janetta's mother's family lawyer brought her and her mother to me when Janetta was a two-year-old with severe cerebral palsy. They had already been turned away by other, more experienced malpractice lawyers. I was their last hope.

At the time, I had never represented a child as badly damaged as Janetta. Her brain had been damaged by lack of oxygen near the time of delivery so she could not sit up, walk, talk, feed herself or do any of the things a normal child could do. She was, as lawyers sometimes say, "totalled out."

The work began. First, I recruited an "M.D./J.D.," a physician lawyer to obtain the necessary expert witnesses and help prepare the case for trial. The medical record from the hospital contained one entry by a nurse which gave us some hope. The nurse's note said that the resident obstetricians (obstetricians in training) saw that the baby was a breech baby with both feet down about to come out of the mother. The nurse's note said that the young doctors pulled the baby's feet out *in the labor room*. This is not to be done in the labor room because the baby's oxygen supply can be cut off if not delivered immediately. Such maneuvers should not be done until the mother is *in the delivery room* and ready to be delivered right away. In fact one of our obstetric experts who happened to be from England, told us the rule was "hands off the breech." The only problem was we could not locate the nurse who wrote the note. The suit was filed and we went through the "discovery" phase where we lawyers do such things as take oral testimony under oath from parties and witnesses in the case. Predictably, the two resident obstetricians denied that they had pulled down the feet in the labor room and testified the nurse was mistaken in her notes and that they pulled the feet down in the delivery room as part of the delivery.

Remember *The Verdict* with Paul Newman? Well, our trial preceded the *The Verdict* by a few years. The nurse was nowhere to be found until one day close to trial. I was in the Bronx, New York preparing one of our obstetric experts, the Chairman of the obstetric department, and I discussed the problem of the missing nurse. He looked at the medical record and exclaimed "She's here! She just started as a nurse midwife practitioner." It turns out the nurse had been in England for two years studying to become a nurse midwife. The case was tried before a jury, the young doctors still claiming they didn't do it and the nurse explaining that she remembered it well and that she had admonished the young doctors not to pull the feet in the labor room. The jury returned a verdict of $2.5 million for Janetta, the first obstetric malpractice verdict of seven figures in the U.S. Afterward, a hospital administrator said that the verdict was the best thing that had ever happened to clean up the obstetric department.

At the trial, there was medical testimony that Janetta, at that time four years old, would likely live only a few more years. However, with the money available to purchase the finest care, therapy and equipment for Janetta, she was taught to communicate by speaking, although difficult to understand. She learned to operate an electric wheelchair. She learned to operate a computer and she even painted a beautiful abstract artwork for me using a wand attached to her head. Janetta graduated college and became a counselor for other handicapped persons. Thank God we did not turn her away as the other lawyers had. Of course, luck always plays a role as it did when the key witness, the nurse, showed up, but good luck seems to come only after a fair amount of work.

I know the work we do helps victims and survivors obtain justice, brings order out of chaos, and puts injustice to flight. It is good.

To see parents weeping over impuissant, "damaged" children, to listen to brain-injured babies wail incessantly for hours on end, to watch a beautiful young child with no hips or legs scoot around the floor, balanced on her forearms, and see the heartache and misery endured by these families is something I will never forget as long as I live.

I have not always been able to give my clients redress. I haven't always ended a case with a satisfactory judgment or settlement, but the times I have done so are the times that bring me the most peace and gratification. To know that a child considered beyond hope and a "vegetable" is now living on her own, riding the buses and subway, and enjoying a small circle of friends, heartens me because God allowed me to touch her life in such a positive way. To know that a young boy's fate is now not confined to a group home because of his single mother's inability to provide for his catastrophic injuries, is a joy. To know that a widow and young children will never want because of the settlement provided to them, is why I keep going.

I know that the lame ones will probably never walk again. I also know the brain-damaged ones will probably, outside a miracle, never regain the full use of their senses. And while I accept that, I also know, beyond a reasonable doubt, these people are living, breathing, human beings, *valuable* human beings deserving of the same respect as the rest of us. Their lives, though "damaged," are just as worthy and sacred as that of presidents and senators. And I'm thankful I was instrumental in bringing dignity to the remainder of their lives.

JOSEPH CAMMARATA graduated from Georgetown University in 1980 and from the St. John's University School of Law in 1983. Mr. Cammarata also obtained a Masters of Law in 1987 from the Georgetown University Law Center.

During his professional career, Mr. Cammarata has been a champion for those who have suffered injury whether through the negligence of others, or as a result of discrimination and civil rights abuses. His pursuit of justice has resulted in litigation against governmental entities, corporations and even the President of the United States.

Mr. Cammarata is board certified by the National Board of Trial Advocacy, has been named in *Who's Who in American Law*, and has been repeatedly recognized by *Washingtonian Magazine* as one of the Washington Metropolitan region's top trial lawyers.

Mr. Cammarata is a partner in the Washington, D.C. based law firm of Chaikin & Sherman, P.C.

Access to
Justice

By Joseph Cammarata

Beyond a reasonable doubt, all individuals must be guaranteed full, prompt access to justice. Nothing less is acceptable in a civilized society.

In 1994, I represented a young mother against the most powerful man in the world. In the case of <u>Paula Jones v. William Jefferson Clinton</u>, my client, Paula Jones, claimed that she was sexually propositioned by Bill Clinton, when he was Governor of Arkansas. I filed a lawsuit on her behalf against Mr. Clinton, when he was President of the United States. Mr. Clinton responded to the lawsuit claiming that he was immune from suit, while President, because he was too busy and therefore, Ms. Jones' case had to be delayed until he left office. I urged the courts to reject the President's claim of immunity from suit to allow my client's case to be heard. The United States Supreme Court unanimously agreed with me that my client's case had to go forward immediately so as to provide my client with her timely day in court. The Supreme Court acknowledged that memories fade, documents may be lost or destroyed, and that witnesses may die if a case is delayed, thereby upholding and reaffirming the bedrock principle of our judicial system, that "Justice delayed is Justice denied."

However, what good is having the ability to have your day in Court if you cannot gain access to justice? Most individuals, untrained in law or court procedure, need an attorney to bring a meritorious claim on their behalf. This is especially true for those individuals who are injured, maimed or killed through no fault of their own, and they or their loved ones do not have the financial means to pay a lawyer an hourly rate regardless of the outcome of the litigation. On the other hand, the wrongdoer in such cases is usually represented by lawyers hired and paid for by large insurance companies with unlimited resources. The wrongdoer does not pay anything. Meanwhile, the innocent victim is left to hire a lawyer to take the case. So how can an individual afford to hire a lawyer to get justice against some person or entity with unlimited resources? The answer is the "contingent fee." Lawyers who work on a "contingent fee basis" only get paid if successful in obtaining compensation for the client. This provides a viable method for an individual to gain access to the courts.

There are those who want to limit our access to the courts by eliminating or limiting contingent fees. They argue that contingent fees promote frivolous lawsuits. However, bringing a frivolous lawsuit is bad business for a lawyer, especially on a contingent fee basis. A typical contingent fee agreement not only requires a lawyer to wait to get paid, if at all, but also requires a lawyer to pay the expenses of the case up front and hope to get reimbursed at the end of the case. It is hard to imagine a lawyer trying to make a living by spending valuable time and money to pursue frivolous lawsuits that are likely to be thrown out of court and to result in the lawyer being punished by the court. In reality, the only effect of eliminating or limiting contingent fees will be to eliminate or limit our access to justice by limiting our ability to hire a lawyer. This should not be tolerated.

However, what good is having access to the courts, if an individual's ability to obtain full and complete justice, when one gets there, is restricted?

Our modern-day jury system evolved after a long history of being beholden to kings, religious leaders, and politicians for the resolution of disputes. Our right to a trial by jury is guaranteed by our Constitution and State law. A jury is made up of citizens who are called upon to resolve disputes in society, such as those situations where an individual is accused by the Government of criminal wrongdoing, or accused by one individual of injuring another individual. Each side to the dispute is given a full and fair opportunity to present their claim, or defend against one, with the jury making the ultimate determination as to who is right and who is wrong based on all the facts presented. The jury system relies on the common man exercising common sense; a right which Thomas Jefferson believed to be America's greatest, and defining, right.

There are those who want to limit the common man's exercise of common sense. For example, when an innocent victim seeks compensation for injuries due to the wrongdoing of another, there are those who, in a "one size fits all" philosophy, seek to arbitrarily limit or cap the amount of non-economic damages (for payment of other than medical expenses or lost wages) available to the injured innocent individual, regardless of the circumstances unique to each case. Those people believe that right and wrong is best determined by politicians or by legislative edict, rather than by real people, a jury, which we have historically trusted to make fair decisions. Those people believe that there exists a "litigation lottery," and that insurance premiums must be reduced, and that capping damages is the only means to fix these "problems."

I doubt that any individual who is severely injured or paralyzed, or whose family loses a parent, spouse or child due to someone else's negligence believes they have won the lottery. In fact, the Department of Justice, Bureau of Justice Statistics reported that the median payout for all personal injury cases dropped 56.3% between 1992 and 2001 to $28,000.

Caps on non-economic damages punish those victims who have a diminished quality of life, such as a child paralyzed for life, a brain damaged baby, a grandmother abused in a nursing home, an individual who loses a limb or sight, or the family of a stay-at-home mom or child killed by someone's negligence.

The non-economic aspects of life are real, and reflect the human losses suffered by real victims in real pain.

Further, studies show that in states with caps on damages, insurance premiums continued to increase in real dollars and on a percentage basis more so than in states without caps. Also insurance company representatives are on record admitting that caps do not, and will not, lower insurance premiums. If insurance rates are an issue, why not enact insurance reform and pass legislation to require an insurance company to justify rate hikes, just like an injured victim must present his/her case to a jury?

We can all agree that if someone causes harm to another, the wrongdoer must be held accountable. Accountability requires that the wrongdoer be required to pay for all damages caused by the wrongdoing.

To arbitrarily limit or cap the amount of damages available to an innocent victim, provides less than full accountability and, in turn, victimizes the victim. This only serves to undermine our system of justice which operates on a belief and pledge of allegiance to a Nation that provides "justice for all."

If undermined, our system of justice will no longer be viewed as providing individuals with a forum where truth can be tried, a forum where disputes can be resolved without resorting to violence, and a forum where justice can be obtained. A civilized society requires redress of grievances in a civilized framework within a system perceived as fair.

Beyond a reasonable doubt, beyond all doubt, we must act to protect our right to full, prompt access to justice.

ROBERT K. TANENBAUM is a nationally known attorney and legal expert. As well as being a high profile defender, he is one of the most successful prosecuting attorneys, having never lost a felony trial.

As assistant D.A. in New York county, he ran the Homicide Bureau, served as Chief of the Criminal Courts Bureau and was in charge of the D.A.'s legal staff training programme. He served as Deputy Chief Counsel for the Congressional Committee investigation into the assassinations of President John F. Kennedy and Dr. Martin Luther King. He was a special prosecution consultant on the Hillside Strangler case; he defended Amy Grossberg in her sensationalized baby death case and represented eight black plaintiffs in a major racial profiling case.

He served two terms as mayor of Beverly Hills and is a member of the State Bars of California, New York, and Pennsylvania. He taught Advanced Criminal Procedure at his alma mater, the Boalt Hall School of Law, University of California, Berkeley.

Robert Tanenbaum is the author of eighteen novels and two non-fiction books. His non-fiction *Badge of the Assassin*, was made into a television movie starring James Woods as Robert Tanenbaum. His most recent book *Counterplay* was published by Simon & Schuster in August 2006.

The Insanity of
the Insanity Defense

By Robert K. Tanenbaum

The criminal justice system is suffering from a severe case of ineffectiveness and eroding credibility. The perception in our urban centers is that crime is spiraling out of control. There is a growing sense that the system is not representing the people in their desire to see justice done. One of the most corrosive aspects of the criminal justice system is the insanity defense, which provides an escape mechanism for wrongful violent misconduct. Basically, the insanity defense, for example, permits a mass murderer to beat the system by establishing that she was suffering from a delusional belief system that induced irrational motivations, which compelled her to act out her violent conduct.

Simply, based upon her mental disease/defect, she did not know or appreciate the nature and consequences of her acts or that they were wrong. Accordingly, she was not responsible when she executed her victims.

Recently, I witnessed in horror the not guilty by reason of insanity verdict granted to Andrea Yates. She murdered her five children in a particularly brutal, vicious and depraved manner. She forcibly drowned each child in the bathtub at her home and literally chased, grabbed and dragged her seven-year-old son, Noah, into the bathroom for his summary execution. The forensic evidence revealed that the children struggled mightily with their mother while she was forcibly keeping their heads under water during the course of snuffing out their lives.

The evidence clearly established that Andrea Yates, with premeditation and deliberation, planned to kill her children on the morning she executed them. The evidentiary basis for establishing her responsibility for vanquishing her five children is best established beyond a reasonable doubt by viewing objectively her own conduct:

1. Before drowning her children, she waited for her husband to leave the house to go to work;

2. She drew the bath water knowing that it would be used as the means to execute her babies;

3. She grabbed each of her children individually and held each child's head and face under water until each could breathe no more.

4. Her oldest child, Noah, seven years of age, fled. Recognizing that one of her potential victims might escape, she chased after him, grabbed him and dragged him back to the execution site where she forcibly drowned him.

5. After forcibly drowning each of her five children and knowing that she had accomplished her murderous design, she made two telephone calls: one to the police and one to her husband telling him to come home.

To be sure, Andrea Yates was suffering from a mental disease/defect from which was spawned a delusional mindset, false beliefs that impelled her to kill her children. She even believed "it was the right thing to do!" But should our criminal justice system allow individuals with a delusional belief system that induces irrational motivations that result in violent wrongful conduct be exonerated? Isn't one of the major purposes of the criminal justice system to incarcerate those violent criminals who cannot control, but act out their violent impulses? It offends notions of common sense that the criminal justice system creates, by use of the insanity defense, the very mechanism for these violent offenders to avoid responsibility and escape punishment.

Moreover, the insanity defense has been rendered farcical in its manipulation by so-called experts. A further exacerbating, corrosive aspect of the insanity defense, which increasingly erodes credibility of the entire system, is the nature of the conduct at trial of the so-called psychiatric experts. The farcical manipulation of the insanity defense by these alleged experts can be graphically illustrated by the following recap of an actual case that I prosecuted:

Charles Harrison was a titan of industry in his early 50s, who, on the last Friday of every month, dined with his wife and his middle-aged secretary, Helen Mullaney.

Afterward, the Harrisons would escort their guest to the downtown depot where she would board a bus for the 100-mile trip to visit her older brother, James.

One evening, James Mullaney was waiting at the depot for the sole purpose of executing his sister's boss.

Mullaney had been distressed for several months. He was convinced that his sister's disenchantment with practicing the rituals of their religion was due to Harrison's pernicious influence. Mullaney decided that, to salvage his sister's soul and avenge the corrupting agent, he would have to kill Harrison.

Earlier that day, Mullaney had purchased a 25-caliber automatic pistol, two clips and 20 rounds of ammunition. At 7:30 p.m., he parked across the street from the depot's main entrance. He loaded the pistol, left his car, walked across the street and stationed himself on a wooden bench facing the entrance. There he waited an hour and 20 minutes for his victim to arrive.

As Harrison walked into the depot, Mullaney withdrew the pistol from his pocket and fired one shot into Harrison's forehead. He immediately walked outside, told a police officer sitting in a squad car that he had just shot a man, handed the murder weapon to the officer and led him to Harrison's lifeless body.

James Mullaney was charged with murder, and responded with a plea of not guilty by reason of insanity.

After Mullaney was arraigned, his attorney hired a forensic psychiatrist. After several interviews with the defendant (whom the doctor regarded as his patient) he concluded unequivocally that, as a result of mental disease and defect, James Mullaney did not know or appreciate the nature and consequences of his acts or that they were wrong.

Not to be outdone, the prosecution employed another forensic psychiatrist who, after careful evaluation of the defendant, determined that indeed he was a paranoid schizophrenic, but added—with certainty equal to that of his adversary and colleague—that James Mullaney indeed was responsible for taking the life of Charles Harrison.

At the trial, the defense set its case on the persuasiveness of its psychiatrist. After he explained why Mullaney was not responsible for the murder, the prosecutor conducted intensive cross-examination, a portion of which follows:

> Q: Doctor, in arriving at your opinion, did you take into account the fact that the defendant had planned to kill the deceased for two months prior to the night of the murder?

> A: Yes.

> Q: Did you take into account the fact that the defendant purchased a pistol, not a banana, for the purpose of killing the deceased?

> A: Yes.

> Q: Did you take into account that the defendant loaded the clip with six live cartridges, not raisins?

A: Yes.

Q: Did you take into account that the defendant loaded the pistol by inserting the clip with live ammunition into the butt of the pistol, and not by placing a Hershey bar there instead?

A: Yes.

Q: Did you take into account that the defendant waited at the murder scene one hour and 20 minutes, during which time hundreds of people passed him?

A: Yes.

Q: Did you take into account that not until Mullaney observed the deceased, did he take the murder weapon out of his pocket, point it at the deceased and pull the trigger?

A: Yes.

Q: Doctor, do you agree then that the defendant, at the time he purchased the gun, knew and appreciated that the weapon was an instrument capable of causing the death of the deceased?

A: Yes.

Q: Further, Doctor, you agree that while the defendant waited at the depot he knew and appreciated that he was armed with a loaded pistol, not a Roman candle, and that he was waiting to shoot a person, Charles Harrison, not a paper target?

A: Yes.

Q: On the issue of wrongfulness, did you take into account the fact that, after shooting the deceased, the defendant immediately walked over to a police officer, not the ice-cream vendor sporting his Good Humor outfit, told him he had just shot a man and handed him the murder weapon?

A: Yes.

Q: Well, then, Doctor, please tell us when it was that Mullaney failed to know and appreciate the nature and consequences of his acts or that they were wrong.

A: Precisely at the time he pointed the pistol at the deceased and pulled the trigger. You see, at that moment, Mr. Mullaney thought he was killing the Devil!

This sketch of the Mullaney case serves as an illustration of the foolish nature of the insanity defense as well as the outrageousness of accepting psychiatric testimony as expect testimony in criminal cases. In virtually every "insanity" case that goes to trial, each side—the prosecution and the defense—hires its own so-called expert psychiatrist. Both psychiatrists then proceed to give ironclad divergent opinions regarding the defendant's state of mind.

Such testimony is at best conjecture, mere opinion and not scientific empirical truth. It mocks the truly expert opinion that derives from a reasonable degree of scientific certainty. And it betrays the purpose of a criminal trial, which is the search for truth under the rules of evidence and the meting out of justice. Instead, the insanity defense gives criminally violent and unpredictable individuals in our community an opportunity to avoid being held accountable for their actions. In effect, they are exonerated, not because they have provided a legitimate defense, such as justification, but because their hired-gun psychiatrists are more convincing than the ones testifying for the opposition.

The victims of crimes, their families and friends care precious little for such gamesmanship. They only want to see justice done. Eliminating the abuses of the insanity defense would improve the chances of that happening.

STEVE DETTELBACH is an attorney and a partner with the law firm of Baker & Hostetler, LLP., where he counsels and defends corporations and individuals that being investigated by regulatory and law enforcement officials. Previously, as a federal prosecutor for over 12 years, Mr. Dettelbach served as Deputy Chief of the United States Attorney's Office for the District of Maryland, Southern Division, as acting Deputy Chief of the Civil Rights Division, Criminal Section and on the Organized Crime Strike Force. During his time as a prosecutor, Mr. Dettelbach handled numerous high-profile matters, including the El Monte Slavery case, hate crime matters and public corruption and fraud cases involving elected officials and corporate executives.

Mr. Dettelbach has also worked in the United States Senate, serving as Counsel to the Senate Judiciary Committee from 2001-2003. There, he worked extensively on policy matters, including the Sarbanes-Oxley Act relating to corporate misconduct and the oversight of law enforcement activities after the 9/11 terrorist attacks. Mr. Dettelbach graduated from Harvard Law School and Dartmouth College and began his career as a law clerk to the Honorable Stanley Sporkin in federal court in Washington, D.C. He is married and has two children.

When the State
Helps the Underdog—
The Promise of Power
in the United States

By Steve Dettelbach

As Americans, we are fond of pointing out that "power corrupts." Indeed, during my career as a federal prosecutor, I heard constantly that the power of the government must be checked at every turn. While true, I believe that such adages can obscure another fundamental point—that at least here in the United States, the power of the state is often brought to bear in the most positive way and on behalf of the most powerless in our society. In those cases, I believe beyond a reasonable doubt that power does not corrupt—power purifies. It makes things as they should be, so that the good guys—not the powerful guys—win.

Indeed, it is an ironic quirk that as Americans, the most powerful and most privileged people on earth, we love to root for the underdog, even knowing that it will likely cause us heartache in the end. That is why it is such a wonderful thing when not only can we root for the underdog, but when we can bring the immense power of the state to the side of the weak to fight against the strong. Then we can tip the scales in favor of justice in a way that people in many nations cannot fathom.

Why is it that the American legal system lends itself to the government protecting the weak against the strong? After over a decade of trying cases all over our nation, one answer seems clear to me. The United States is blessed with a key institutional advantage—

its strong jury system. That system, where any individual from the community can decide the case—even cases involving CEO's and Congressmen—transports the American ethos of underdog rights into the courtroom itself. I have found, in fact, that there is nothing more frightening to a rich, self-dealing executive or a corrupt politician than the specter of facing a jury. Thus, our jury system creates a powerful incentive for law enforcement not to blindly take the side of the establishment, but to pursue investigations that help the vulnerable to stand up to power. As a prosecutor, I saw many examples of this, but one case sticks out in my mind.

Believe it or not, the case was a slavery action that I prosecuted in El Monte, California. The facts were shocking. In a predawn raid, the INS had uncovered a horrific situation just outside of Los Angeles. Over 70 Thai nationals, mostly women and all illegal aliens, had been found in a town house complex living in sub-human conditions. These people had been held against their will for years and forced to work over 18 hours a day, 7 days a week in a sweatshop. They lived on top of each other and just feet from their sewing machines. They were surrounded by barbed wire and constantly watched by armed guards. They spoke no English and many had been denied basic medical care for years. In short, it was a true nightmare.

Coming on this scene, the INS had no earthly idea what to do with these people. These women were victims by any common sense definition. On the other hand, they were illegal aliens and there was tremendous pressure on the INS to stem the tide of illegal aliens coming into California. In short, the Thai workers did not fit neatly into any legal category. Furthermore, the "owners" of the sweatshop were rich business people, also from Thailand, who were supplying clothing to very reputable manufacturers. They had the implicit backing of the Thai government and they hired reputable and capable attorneys to sort out any misunderstanding with the agents and prosecutors.

From the other side of the fence, the Thai workers also did not know what to do with us. They did not view law enforcement as their saviors, but as the enemy. From their earliest memories, they had learned that the authorities were tools of the status quo, used to protect the wealthy and to oppress the poor. They had been taught that power was inevitably corrupt. In addition, these Thai workers had been told by their captors that the American authorities were no different than the police at home—a lie that they accepted. After all, they were told, who would possibly take the word of a poor peasant girl, and an illegal alien to boot, over the word of a rich merchant backed by reputable lawyers?

This misunderstanding could have led to disaster. The defendants could have been allowed to skate, and the Thai women could have been quickly deported. Almost as bad, a few "sample witnesses" could have been retained to allow for the prosecution of a criminal case, and the rest of the women could have been shipped back to Thailand as illegal aliens, where they would have faced poverty and likely retaliation.

But that is not what happened. Instead, the United States government marshaled all its power and resources not only to prosecute the wrongdoers, but to help the victims. Although there were surely some setbacks, agency after agency saw past narrow legal definitions and bureaucratic "missions." They treated the Thai women as true victims. Law enforcement agencies and humanitarian groups worked hand-in-hand for endless hours to make sure that the workers were provided food, shelter (and not in some INS holding cell) and even proper authorization to work as the case was resolved.

From the victims' standpoint as well, an equally amazing thing occurred. After countless tearful interviews and court hearings these women slowly realized that, despite their lives on the harsh receiving end of power, this time the government was taking their side against their rich bosses. Slowly, these women began to trust the American police, and even to do the unthinkable, to like them.

For the victims it was a transforming experience. Moreover, I think it was a uniquely American one. The idea that the massive power of the state could be harnessed to help these vulnerable victims, all of whom were illegal aliens, to stand up to their rich masters was beyond their comprehension.

The women were not alone in being surprised. Even as a hardened prosecutor, earning their trust was transforming for me as well. I still remember that as the prosecution team left the courtroom, the victims lined up and bowed to us in respect. This remains the greatest honor I have ever received as a public servant.

When power intervenes to right the scales, the results are limitless. In this case, not only were the defendants successfully prosecuted (could they have ever won as slaveholders facing an American jury?), but the Thai victims were all accepted into a special immigration program authorized by Congress. They were provided a path to become permanent residents and eventually U.S. citizens. Recently, there was a 10-year reunion of the victims and law enforcement, and the overwhelming majority of these amazing women were contributing members of American society. Their nightmare had been transformed to an American dream, and along with their incredible spirit, it was the government that had made it possible.

I often ask myself why it seemed so impossible to these women that I would be on their side. After all, wouldn't any human being be sympathetic to their plight? The best answer I can manage is that many human beings would want to help, but most governments would not. These stories are all around us in the United States, every time a prosecutor goes to bat for a rape victim or cop risks his life to help a family imprisoned in their neighborhood by gang violence. It is so much a part of our heritage that we often forget the special character of the United States. We love our underdogs here, and once in awhile, with the help of American juries, we can use the government to rig a happy ending. Our government makes mistakes—whoppers—but I believe beyond a reasonable doubt that it is still the most powerful force for good that man has devised.

So when someone tells me that power corrupts or that the free market can handle things just fine without an overbearing government, I remember those brave Thai women and the all the good people who used their power to help them. It is true, power can corrupt, but be careful about bashing the government too much—someday you might need it too.

WILLIAM R. "BILLY" MARTIN is a seasoned trial lawyer and legal counselor with over 30 years' experience handling civil and criminal cases before federal and state courts throughout the country. His diverse trial practice has included representation of individuals and corporations in connection with federal and state criminal investigations, as well as in private disputes including allegations of financial fraud, improper employment practices and civil rights violations. During the course of his career, Mr. Martin has served as a counselor to Fortune 500 corporations, private citizens, political leaders, professional athletes, entertainment industry celebrities, and local and foreign governments. In addition to advising clients on ways to eliminate or reduce their exposure to criminal prosecution or civil litigation, Mr. Martin has substantial jury trial experience representing his clients in connection with both major criminal investigations and trials and private civil litigation.

Mr. Martin is a former attorney for the U.S. Department of Justice serving in Ohio, California, and Washington, D.C.. For the second year in a row, Mr. Martin has been ranked among *The Lawdragon* 500 Leading Trial Lawyers in America. By vote of his peers, he was one of 500 attorneys selected from over 15,000 nominations as one of the nation's leading lawyers. He was also ranked in Washingtonian magazine as one of the four top lawyers in Washington, D.C. in 2005. He was chosen from an elite group of lawyers who have "attained national and even world-class status in their fields." He is consistently recognized as an established legal expert, is invited frequently to appear to offer commentary and legal analysis on major television networks such as CNN, NBC, CNBC, Court TV and BET and has been profiled in the *Baltimore Sun*.

What do I believe
in "beyond a reasonable doubt"?
Justice.

By Billy Martin

Over my thirty years as a lawyer, I have been involved in a number of high-profile and even history-making cases, including the impeachment of President Clinton, the investigation and trial of U.S. Senators and Congressmen, state and local elected officials, the defense of some of our most famous athletes, and the defense of corporate officers accused of fraud or some other white-collar crime for decisions made relating to their business. Each case comes with its own compelling facts, and the outcome affects the lives of all those involved differently. I feel fortunate to have had the opportunity to act as a participant in our judicial system and not merely an observer because one thing I do believe, beyond a reasonable doubt, is that every person is entitled to a "fair trial," and most importantly, justice.

As a prosecutor, I earned the reputation of being a tough no-nonsense law-enforcement officer whose decisions ranged from whether there was sufficient evidence to charge an accused, to whether or not to seek the death-penalty. The answer to those type of questions was always governed by doing "what was in the best interest of justice." You see, in the end all lawyers, prosecutors and defense attorneys want the same thing, "justice." Like any other complex issue, the devil is always in the details. Defining or finding justice is much more difficult than seeking justice. All of the lawyers who know me personally, or who have been on the other side of a case against me know one thing: I believe in justice and I will fight to find it.

One of my most memorable representations involving a search for justice did not even involve a judge, jury, or a courtroom—at least not yet. In 2001, the family of missing Capitol Hill intern Chandra Levy approached my law firm and me to represent them. The Levy family was understandably grief-stricken over their daughter's disappearance, and they wanted two things above all: to find their daughter, and to find justice.

The Levy investigation was unlike any other trial or investigation I handled as a prosecutor or defense attorney. Chandra's family was concerned that the person responsible for her disappearance might be a Washington power broker and the authorities would be deferential to the powerful to the detriment of the investigation. Our challenge in the Levy investigation was to make sure that every lead was followed, that every witness was interviewed and forced to tell all that he or she knew, and finally to determine whether Chandra was still alive. As time passed, and we began to face the grim likelihood that Chandra had been killed, our goal became finding her body and the person responsible for her death. The Levy family wanted to ensure that Chandra was not forgotten and that her killer or killers were held accountable. After more than a year of searching and following countless potential leads, Chandra's remains were found in a wooded Washington, D.C. park. Five years later, her murder remains a mystery and her killer or killers remain at large. To the Levy family, there has been no justice and there will be no justice until the mystery is solved and the killer punished.

To this day, I am haunted by the fact that the circumstances surrounding Chandra Levy's death are still unknown, and her family's search for justice has not yet come to a close. I firmly believe that the Levys deserve to find justice, and I am hopeful that one day a witness will come forward with the information needed to solve the mystery of Chandra's death and bring her killer to justice.

The Levy case serves as a powerful reminder that justice sometimes is not easy to come by, but that fact only reinforces the importance of fighting for it. I approach all of my cases with that sentiment in mind and the understanding that there is no greater reward for the struggles along the way than finding justice for my clients in the end.

RONALD ZONEN has been a prosecutor in the Santa Barbara County District Attorney's Office for 25 years. He specializes in prosecuting sex crimes and crimes against children. He is currently prosecuting Jesse James Hollywood, who along with his four now convicted co-defendants, is alleged to have organized the kidnapping and murder of 15-year-old Nicholas Markowitz. He most recently delivered the closing argument for the prosecution in the case of <u>People v. Michael Jackson</u>.

Beyond a Reasonable Doubt

By Ronald Zonen

The first molestation case I prosecuted was many years ago and involved a high school coach who had a sexual relationship with a student, a 14-year-old boy. He was a popular coach who had taken the basketball team to a championship. The boy was awkward, very different from the other children. It was clear early on that there would be no "reasonable doubt" about the man's guilt or innocence as far as the school community was concerned. His colleagues, students and many parents had already decided to believe the man and not the child. The school actually held a fundraiser to help pay the coach's legal expenses. The boy, facing a very hostile environment from his teachers and classmates, dropped out and finished his education at a continuation school. I had thought the cards the coach had written the child or the hotel receipt where they had spent an afternoon would make a difference. Obviously they did not. The jury took less than a day of deliberation before acquitting the coach.

At best, children are difficult witnesses. But a child victim of long-term sexual abuse knows no peer in that regard. Child molesters know which children to pick. They look for the most vulnerable ones, often kids from broken homes. The more dysfunctional the home the easier it is to gain access to the child. Boys without fathers are particularly vulnerable. Predators capitalize on a mother's concern that her son is not getting the kind of attention only a male figure can give.

Experts call it "the grooming process." It begins with long periods of just being together. Pedophiles are nothing if not attentive. They will spend endless hours with children going places and doing things. They'll eat ice cream together, watch movies, play games, but mostly they will talk. They will talk about anything and everything. Pedophiles know how to talk to children, and perhaps more importantly they know how to listen to children, to get them to open up their innermost thoughts and dreams. The adult and the child will become best friends.

The predator will give the child gifts, video games, electronics and even money. He and the child will be intimate, sitting closely with one another. He will touch the boy's arms, shoulders, hands, hair and face, but nothing too obvious at first. He will kiss the child. He will introduce nudity into their relationship, stepping out of the shower just when his young friend arrives. He will assure the child that the naked body is natural and beautiful. He will show the child pornography. It's exciting and it lessens inhibitions. He may give the boy alcohol or drugs.

They will lie together and watch television, covered by a single blanket, arms around one another, feeling the warmth of each other's bodies. It will take weeks or even months but slowly and systematically he will bring the child into the world of adult sexuality. Pedophiles are marvelously patient.

It may start with a tickling game, the most innocent of touching, full of laughter, love and intimacy. The pedophile will carefully measure the response of the child to make sure he is comfortable being touched. They will talk about secrets and how important it is to "never tell" those secrets. He will assure the child of his love and demand total trust. That is, until the child gets too old.

Pedophiles have their preferences and older children are not among them. By age 13 or 14 most victims lose their appeal. A new child suddenly appears. There's always one in the pipeline, a new special friend. It is excruciatingly confusing and painful to the child when he is suddenly dropped by the only best friend he has ever known.

Kids who have been subjected to long-term sexual abuse are often problem witnesses. It is not unusual for child victims to act out in a variety of ways. They do everything kids with low self-esteem do. They hang out with the worst kids (often victims themselves), perform poorly in school, get in fights and talk back to their teachers. They may lie, steal or use drugs. They are sometimes sexually inappropriate and on occasion they may molest younger children. By contrast the adult is often seen as an upstanding member of the community. They may be married with children, gainfully employed, active within church and charity groups.

Defense attorneys have a field day parading a detailed list of a child's past bad performance before juries. They say the child is an experienced troublemaker and a liar. Some jurors intuitively understand how a child can be transformed so horribly. Many do not. I have watched many jurors watch many victims. I can almost measure the disbelief in their eyes when a child, already stretched to his emotional limit, becomes sullen and petulant after hours on the witness stand. No, he can't remember how many times it happened, what position he was in, whether it was the suspect's right hand or left, whether he gave the exact same accounting each time he was asked. No, he doesn't know why he didn't tell his mother, or why he did not run away, or why he continued to return. He can't explain why he once felt love for the man who he now says victimized him.

After prosecuting hundreds of cases of child sexual abuse I've noticed that after acquittals jurors often say the case was not proven "beyond a reasonable doubt." As often as not they are really saying the adult seemed more trustworthy, that they did not like the victim. Young victims of long-term abuse are not always likeable.

OWEN LAFAVE, 28, is a commercial real estate lender in Tampa, Florida. He has become an advocate for children since his now ex-wife, former teacher Debra Beasley LaFave, was arrested and pled guilty for sexually abusing a 14-year-old student at the middle school where she taught. Owen is currently working on a documentary titled *Afterschool*, examining the alarming trend of female teachers having sex with their students. Additionally, he is completing work on a book titled *Gorgeous Disaster*, examining the actions of his ex-wife and other similar offenders. Owen has appeared in over 40 national interviews, and has had numerous conversations with experts in the making of both the documentary and book. Many consider him to be an expert on the subject of teacher/student sexual relationships.

My Wife,
the Sex Criminal:
Why the Double Standard?

by Owen LaFave

There are times when a superficially compelling story catches national attention—even the attention of even a seasoned and wise interviewer like Larry King—and then spreads rapidly worldwide. On June 21, 2004, my wife of 11 months, Debra LaFave, was arrested for having a sexual relationship with a 14-year-old boy, a student at the middle school where she taught. For the media, the story offered ethical and moral elements wrapped around stirring details of a stunning hot young blonde one-time model who could have probably have attracted almost any man into a sexual relationship but chose a teenage virgin.

The LaFave story would also draw comparisons to Mary Kay Letourneau. Both were attractive; both were teachers, both were professionally admired, respected and liked by their colleagues. Both had suffered dramatic tragedy in their lives not long before: Mary Kay's father, a California state Senator, had died of cancer and Debbie's beloved sister Angie was killed in a car crash. Both would also claim they were bipolar, giving rise to battles of the experts on interview shows about whether this might have been a factor the courts should consider. Definitely a story not to be missed.

The media trumpeted the fact that the young beauty in each case was sentenced to no prison time (although Mary Kay would later end behind bars for violating her parole).

In interviews and articles, media people and experts pondered, as I did, about whether it made sense that they received no prison time when in the opposite situation—male teacher/female student—there would be a huge public outcry over letting any offender escape without a stiff prison sentence.

Since my then-wife was arrested, I've become sought after in unexpected ways, giving well over 40 interviews to some of the most respected personalities in the world of television news. I'm involved in a feature documentary, *After School*, about sexual abuse in our classroom, and as I write this am just finishing the manuscript for *Gorgeous Disaster*, a book about my wife's story, a search for the reasons, and an exploration of the larger issues.

None of that qualifies me as an expert on the subject but it has forced me to give a lot of thought to what's right and what's wrong about the sentencing pattern. I'm repelled by the responses of men who say something equivalent to a statement quoted to me by one of the prosecutors in my wife's case—a citizen had written to a local paper that the boy couldn't testify because he hadn't gotten the grin wiped off yet.

Why are we not outraged when an adult female sexually assaults a minor boy? Why are we not outraged when the female perpetrator receives no prison time for a crime that a man would serve years of hard time for?

In 2002, teacher Pamela Diehl-Moore pleaded guilty to having sex with a 13-year-old male student and was let off with probation. The judge, Bruce A. Gaeta, offered these shockingly irresponsible remarks: "I really don't see the harm that was done here and certainly society doesn't need to be worried. I do not believe she is a sexual predator. It's just something between two people that clicked beyond the teacher-student relationship. ...And don't forget, this was mutual consent."

Can you imagine if the teacher was male and a judge had said this? He would have been booted off the bench and crowds would have been protesting on the courthouse steps.

In September 2005, Sandra Beth Geisel pleaded guilty to three counts of child rape involving a 16-year-old. Sentencing her to only six months in jail, presiding Judge Stephen Herrick told her from the bench, "The 16-year-old ... certainly was not victimized by you in any sense of the word. ...You misunderstood attention as affection and failed to realize you were being manipulated and sexually abused, and you became a playmate."

Let me get this right. Geisel, 26 years the boy's senior, is the victim?

But yet somehow, as unsettling as these two judges' comments were to many, it seems to be a common view these days. With male perpetrators, the crime is referred to as rape or sexual abuse. With women, it's often an "inappropriate sexual relationship" (the *Herald Democrat* newspaper) or a "sexual affair" (ABC News).

Why the difference? The answer is as simple, but as complicated, as this: Society does not view a boy as a victim to the same degree as when the victim is a young girl.

The research for my book *Gorgeous Disaster* included discussions with several of the nation's leading experts on the subject of child sexual abuse and teacher sexual abuse. One of these experts, Dr. Leo Cotter, a Tampa therapist specializing in dealing with sexual offenders, says boys are taught by society that seeking sexual conquests is "normal and desirable," and that "a connection with any older woman, teacher or otherwise, may be seen to confer special bragging rights." These boys are championed as heroes for their so-called sexual prowess. The male goal of sexual success is to "score as many times as you can, double the number, and brag to your friends."

That attitude was reflected by the late-night talk show hosts. I had to stop listening when I heard cracks like Jay Leno's offensive quip, "Where were the teachers like that when I was in school?"

Sure, every boy fantasizes about older women and I hate to break it to the men reading this, but girls fantasize about older men, too. But the key is in the word fantasy. Fantasies are meant to remain in the imagination. Acting out a fantasy is, after all, what criminals do. When anyone crosses the line from fantasy to reality, people are hurt and lives are destroyed.

David Lisak, Ph.D. concluded in his research of 26 adult male sexual abuse survivors that boys who were abused were likely to exhibit anger, betrayal, fear, and problems with their sexuality.

Professor David Finkelhor, considered the leading authority in the field, says a boy victim may "have serious developmental reactions" that last for years.

While most of these boys in female teacher/male student sexual abuse cases are willing participants, what many fail to realize is that they are still children. Their bodies may be physically mature enough to respond but that doesn't equate to emotional maturity.

World Net Daily provided a list of almost 70 female teachers who garnered some media attention over the past two years, while the stories of male sex offenders hold little interest. The attitude about a male who has sex with a young girl is "Lock 'im up and throw away the key;" the female sex offenders become the subject of feature films, TV interviews…and books like mine. Clearly there is a double standard: you and I and a lot of other people are intrigued by the female sexual offender.

This crime is far more common than you think. A 2004 U.S. Department of Education study conducted by Professor Carol Shakeshaft of Hofstra University found that "More than 4.5 million students endure sexual misconduct by employees at their schools, from inappropriate jokes all the way to forced sex. About 7 percent report physical sexual misconduct." She also reports that about one-third of those cases are female teachers to male students. These statistics indicate that the abuse is widespread and that female perpetrators represent a larger percentage than ever imagined.

One would think if the problem were so widespread, our legal system would provide stricter penalties, sentences that are on par with their male counterparts. Yet time and time again female perpetrators are given little if any jail time, instead typically being sentenced to probation or sometimes house arrest like my former wife Debbie.

We live in a world where there are many double standards; this area is clearly one of them. In few countries can one commit a sexual crime and be rewarded for it. Mary Kay got paid got a $200,000 advance on her book deal, had a TV movie made about her life, and received a reported $750,000 for the video footage of her wedding. Additionally, she's recently appeared on TV with Vili updating all of us on their love story.

My brain started to form questions after my first interview on the *Larry King Live* show. I haven't stopped wondering. I think about:

...Why do female offenders receive more lenient sentences for the same crime?

...When will judges and prosecutors recognize that lenient sentences in these cases sends a bad message to teachers and the society?

...When will female abusers be viewed as a predators?

We only need to take a look inside ourselves to answer these questions.

District Attorney **MICHAEL A. RAMOS** was born in Redlands, California, is the father of two adult children and has been married to his wife Gretchen for 25 years. He obtained his Bachelor's Degree from the University of California at Riverside and his Doctor of Jurisprudence from Citrus Belt Law School in Riverside in 1988. In his private life, he enjoyed coaching youth baseball and soccer and is a former Board member of the Redlands Boys and Girls Club.

He was a Probation Officer for San Bernardino County from 1984 to 1989. He served as a Deputy District Attorney in the Career Criminal Unit for five years and the Major Crimes Unit for four years, prosecuting public corruption, as well as death penalty cases. In 2002, he was elected the District Attorney of San Bernardino County where he continues to serve the people of California. His government service has also included being a member of the Redlands Board of Education; serving as a member of Governor Schwarzenegger's Transition Team in 2003; being appointed to the California Victim Compensation and Government Claims Board to assist the victims of crime; acting as a member of the National Hispanic Steering Committee to reelect President Bush in 2004; and as a Board member of the California District Attorney Association. He was honored with the M.A.D.D. Prosecutor of the Year award in 1998, a Victim Service Award in 2000, and was the recipient of the Inland Empire Hispanic Image Awards Influential Latino of the Year in 2005.

Beyond a Reasonable Doubt

By Michael A. Ramos

As the District Attorney of the 14th largest District Attorney's office in the United States and as a member of California Governor Arnold Schwarzenegger's Victims Compensation and Government Claims Board, I believe beyond a reasonable doubt that protecting victim's rights should be a priority in the criminal justice system.

Prior to being elected District Attorney, I tried over 125 jury trials and spent eight years out of thirteen working in the career criminal prosecution unit and the major crimes unit as a deputy district attorney.

It was during this time period that I developed a passion for victims and their families. I saw firsthand the physical and emotional effect crime had on our community members.

It was also during this time that I realized we needed to do a better job of protecting victim's rights as they proceeded through our legal system.

The following guidelines should be followed to protect victim's rights:

Treat victims fairly and with respect and dignity throughout the criminal justice process. As a prosecutor, I encountered many situations where victims were treated like second-class citizens in our legal system. One example occurred several years ago in a murder case.

The victim was fourteen years old and was lured into the home of the sixteen-year-old defendant. The defendant brutally murdered the victim and then cut the victim's body into pieces. The defendant disposed of the victim's body in the city sewer system. The victim's bones were found several months later. We were able to get a jury conviction with both physical evidence and a confession. At the sentencing, over my objection, the judge allowed the defendant's mother to plead for leniency for the defendant prior to the victim's grandmother's being allowed to make a victim impact statement. This should never happen! We must always protect the victim's rights over the defendant's, especially at sentencing.

Protect victims from the accused. Many times victims are forced to endure contact with the defendant, especially in domestic violence cases. Family Law courts have been known to order the victim to attend counseling with the defendant abuser. This is wrong! Prosecutors should facilitate better communication between family law and criminal courts to ensure this does not happen. Further, the victim should never be in a situation where she is alone in court with the defendant. If victims do not have a support system, prosecutors must have one in place for them.

Communicate with victims. Prosecutors should always inform victims of any pending dispositions before the trial and continuing through sentencing. Prosecutors need to inform victims of their constitutional rights, such as their right to give a victim impact statement. The victim's day of justice comes at the time of sentencing. Victims have a right to let the court and the defendant know the pain and suffering they have endured at the hands of the defendant.

The victim shall have the right to be present at all criminal proceedings where the defendant has the same right. Again, communication is the key. Many family members of murder victims are not notified of court days. There must be a system in place to ensure this does not happen. Moreover, I believe the victim's family should have priority over the press or the general public to sit in the courtroom. It was a travesty of justice in the trial of Scott Peterson that the victim's mother, Sharon Rocha, and other members of Laci Peterson's family had to give up courtroom seats for the press and others. Mrs. Rocha is currently pushing legislation to help secure victim's rights in this area. We should fully support this position.

All victims should have a right to a victim advocate. It is essential in serious felony cases that the victim has an advocate who will help the victim navigate through the criminal justice process. The victim advocate should serve to support and advocate for victims. In the murder trial of a local schoolteacher, the victim advocate assigned to the case not only helped the family through the trial, but formed a bond with the family that endured well after the court process ended.

Continue to represent victims after the conviction. In 2003, I created a "Prison Lifer Hearing Unit" in my office to ensure that victims and their family members were notified of parole hearings and, if requested, that a prosecutor would be present with them at the parole hearing.

There were two cases that brought to light the importance of this and made this a passion of mine. In the first case, a murderer was released unbeknownst to the surviving victim—until he read about it in the newspaper. Terrified, the victim called me and asked if he should sleep with a gun under his pillow. A proper notification system could have prevented this victim's distress.

The second case involved the parole hearing of a murderer who had killed a fourteen-year-old girl on her way home from school. The family was concerned, as they had no representation at the parole hearing. This was the murderer's first parole hearing, after having been in prison for 25 years. The family was distressed and obviously apprehensive about being face to face for the first time since the jury trial 25 years earlier with the man who raped and killed their daughter. In order to calm their fears and lend support, I took it upon myself to prepare for the hearing by reading the defendant's history and the case file, took the day off from work and drove to Corcoran State Prison to be present with the family.

The defendant entered the room and, as the victim's mother and sister choked back tears, the defendant attempted to mitigate the facts of the murder while feigning remorse for his actions.

Fortunately, parole was denied for five years. I will never forget the emotions of the family and how thankful they were. We must always remember that a victim's pain may subside, but it never goes away.

Restitution. We must hold *all* convicted defendants financially responsible for their crimes. If there is not direct restitution, then the court should impose a restitution order that will be placed into a general state restitution fund that helps victims throughout the state recover from both the physical and emotional trauma they have suffered.

It is the duty of all those involved in the criminal justice system to ensure that victim's rights are a priority—beyond a reasonable doubt.[1]

---

[1] Some of the language and concepts for this essay come from the proposed California Victim's Bill of Rights being supported by Governor Arnold Schwarzenegger and California Assemblyman Parra.

PUNISHMENT in AMERICA

Anthony Pellicano
Dr. Kevorkian
Susan Atkins
Bruce Davis
Charles Watson
Daniel Kelly
Kamala D. Harris
John Walsh
Peter J. Nickles
Abbe D. Lowell

*"The degree of civilization in a society
can be judged by entering its prisons."*
—Fyodor Dostoevsky

ANTHONY PELLICANO is a former high-profile Los Angeles private investigator. Pellicano was known in the mass media as the "PI to the stars" because of his work for many prominent Hollywood celebrities. He has been accused of taping conversations between Tom Cruise and Nicole Kidman during their separation; wire tapping Sylvester Stallone; and digging up information about Gennifer Flowers and Monica Lewinsky for Bill Clinton, in order to discredit them. Billionaire Kirk Kerkorian, film director John McTiernan and high-profile attorneys Bertram Fields and Terry Christensen, are among those accused of hiring Pellicano to investigate for them.

As a result of an investigation involving one of his former clients, actor Steven Seagal, FBI agents raided Pellicano's offices on November 21, 2002, searching for evidence. During the search, agents found two practice grenades modified to function as homemade bombs as well as military-grade C-4 plastic explosives sufficient to take down a passenger jet.

After his arrest in 2002, Pellicano pleaded guilty to illegal possession of dangerous materials and was sentenced to thirty months in federal prison. On February 3 2006, the day before his due release, he was transferred to a Los Angeles County jail, pending new charges. On February 6, Pellicano was indicted on 110 counts in federal court in Los Angeles, alleging crimes of racketeering and conspiracy, wiretapping, witness tampering, identity theft and destruction of evidence. To date 13 other associates have also been charged. Pellicano has been denied bail and is only accessible to immediate family members and attorneys.

From the Joint

By Anthony Pellicano

The concept of reasonable doubt s simply nothing more than the concept of hope.

An enterprising and imaginative defense attorney would endeavor to instill hope in his client's mind, and then try to work out a plan to enable himself to attempt to persuade a jury with this elusive concept.

Defendants are usually desperate enough to embrace this concept; because it equates to hope, and hope is what many defendants so desperately seek. Their desire is that at least one jurist may accept this concept and give himself "that reason" when deciding.

The enormity of this task sometimes overwhelming, especially if the evidence is also overwhelming. This becomes so very evident when you look at the number of plea agreements that exist. It has been stated that approximately 97% of all criminal cases are resolved as a result of the defendant pleading guilty. So we are only talking about the 3% or so of the remaining cases that actually would apply.

Let's talk about that 97% again. Most of the overwhelming evidence comes as a result of those defendants, informants, snitches, stool pigeons and the like, who have ratted out or otherwise told their co-defendants (those who have not agreed to testify or give evidence against others). Where do you attempt to find reasonable doubt when your client's partners in crime are telling on him, or otherwise supplying information to the prosecution?

You can attempt to discredit these witnesses, try to persuade the jury the reasons for testifying are self-serving, or any other creative idea you can muster, but wherein lies the reasonable doubt?

So in that 3%, how many cases that actually go to trial, does the defense have the slightest hope that his defense embodies reasonable doubt?

Many people, especially defense lawyers, like to embrace this concept because it gives the impression that there will be fairness applied. In my opinion, it simply does not exist. What does occur, rarely, is that you get lucky or very creative and find an argument that some jurist can use, if he is already looking, to give you that not guilty vote.

When asked how I was able to get information from those I sought it from, I stated that you have to give the person you're seeking the information from *a reason* for telling you what you want to know.

The same holds true in a criminal case wherein the defense attorney, while trying the case, and in final argument, tries to fortify that reason, attempting to convince, or otherwise persuade, those who would listen, that his theory is possible. Not always true, but possible, and thus striving for that reasonable doubt.

Most of the time, he is unsuccessful, and while he may get that virtually impossible hung jury or verdict, it is often due to the jurist's finding his own, or their own, *reason*.

I am sure that there are many defense attorneys that would not agree with me, but all one needs to do is research the verdicts and they will find my opinion to be close to the truth, if not a fact.

How many reasonable doubt *related* verdicts are there? They are almost non-existent in Federal cases, a few occur in State cases, usually those that involve murder, and certainly not those cases that involve theft, or drugs or non-violent crimes.

The deck is so stacked against anyone who is charged, and even more so in those cases where one is indicted by a Grand Jury.

The jurists are reminded that another jury has already decided that there was probable cause for this case to go to trial. Now, *that* defendant is presumed guilty, not presumed innocent, as we would like to think.

Is there any reality in the concept of reasonable doubt? In my opinion, probably not. When you go further and state "beyond" reasonable doubt, you are really stretching it. Does that mean that you should stop trying? Of course not. But, to totally buy into that concept may lead you down an unfortunate path, one that may lead to a dead end.

The defense attorneys that I have worked with over the years, those that I thought of as intelligent and creative, have always sought to uncover every scrap of evidence that they could to attempt to prove their clients innocence. My theory has always been that if I do my very best to try to prove my client guilty, and cannot, then I may accept the premise that he may not be found guilty at trial, but it so often depends on so many variables.

Most people are not stupid, and if you try to force them to swallow a concept that they know is seemingly impossible or implausible, then they may resent you, and by doing so, vote against the concept itself.

The people that are most subjected to rejections, even more so than actors, are defense attorneys. Jurists sometimes look for a reason to reject the defense and by doing so, reject the defendant.

I have found when polling the jurists, the media and the like, that the defense attorneys they most respected and believed, were those who did not try to con or otherwise float doubtful defense theories, but simply tried to defend their clients with the best *reasonable contraposition*.

All in all, the best persons to ask if they believe in the concept of reasonable doubt are those that are about to be tried, or those who are incarcerated.

We know.

DR. JACK KEVORKIAN—physician, social activist, author, artist and amateur musician—was born in Pontiac, Michigan on May 26, 1928. A 1952 graduate at the University of Michigan Medical School, he served as a medical officer in Korea. His broad interests in controversial subjects sparked his medical research and writing on a wide variety of topics, the most important of which was his belief in the fundamental right of an individual to make end-of-life decisions. Although acquitted many times through the 1990s for helping end the pain and suffering of patients, in 1999 Dr. Kevorkian was convicted for assisting a man with ALS. He was sentenced to 10-25 years and is currently in his eighth year of incarceration in a Michigan prison. Since his imprisonment Dr. Kevorkian has written numerous articles and published an anthology of his works, *GlimmerIQs*, and, in 2005, a booklet entitled *Amendment IX: Our Cornucopia of Rights*. For more information on his work, go to www.glimmerIQs.com.

Guilty
Beyond All Doubt

By Dr. Kevorkian

As far back as the time of Hippocrates in ancient Greece, that extraordinary prototype of genuine democracy, euthanasia was practiced by physicians openly, ethically, and honorably. Because it was then and still is a valid and at times necessary medical service, I decided to coin an apt Greek term for it: "patholysis," meaning "elimination of suffering." In addition to being more accurately indicative of intent, the neologism does away with the negative and demeaning connotation of an aim simply to cause death.

Despite the overwhelming acceptance of the practice in that society, it was vehemently opposed by only one small, strange, and very secretive sect of Pythagoreans. Several centuries later some of their weird tenets happened to coincide with and were absorbed by the dogma of early Christianity. Later still, the convenient amalgamation of rudimentary medical practice with the early Catholic hospices during the Dark and Middle Ages inevitably resulted in theologically tainted medical ethics that has persisted to the present time. It was cleverly embedded in a code erroneously ascribed to Hippocrates, but is really a Pythagorean document which has subverted the ethical basis of an entirely secular calling.

Catholic control of both ecclesiastical and secular legislation during the same period led to the criminalization of euthanasia that prevails to our time. Recently, and by chance, I discovered the well

343

obscured fact that for over two centuries we have had a little known way to unshackle the practice. One could easily suspect that its obscurity is due to some sort of sinister collusion of powerful religious and medical authorities and/or their cabals, together with the legislatures they influence or control. Apparently they are determined to maintain a persistent Pythagorean aura favorable for their self-serving agenda of enhancing power and profit irrespective of the harm inflicted on modern medical practice. The highly technological nature of the latter has produced marvelous medical innovations that can lengthen life and at the same time can also intensify and prolong excruciating agony. The increasing prevalence of such unnecessary suffering has spawned an almost universal public demand for decriminalization of patholysis as the only means of permanent relief for such unfortunate patients who plead for it in vain. This critical situation mandates that we identify and make use of the obscure fact mentioned above. What is this obscure fact?

In our society the essence of a right has always been misunderstood and perverted through having been defined by man-made laws under the delusion that words alone can create rights. It was not like that at the beginning when the founders of our Constitution wisely deemed its enshrined rights to have emanated from the universal law of nature as natural rights inextricably incorporated in the physiology of our psycho-physical structure. These enigmatic natural rights are instilled in that structure by a creator some call God and others call nature. These are powerful innate impulses, urges, even instincts for absolute personal freedom and self-determination to do and/or say anything so long as no verifiable threat or harm or involuntary obligation is inflicted without consent on other persons and/or their property. Like all human beings every living animal has these instincts, and in a state of nature will relentlessly struggle to escape when caged. Natural rights are like all instincts—lifelong, unalterable, and completely independent of mere words.

Unfortunately it is the "cages" called laws that prevent the exercise of a person's natural rights through the constraint of invincible physical force exerted by a government that arbitrarily determines what the words of a given law will or will not permit. This tragic situation has doomed us to an oppressed existence fraught with chimerical pseudo-rights created by the fiat of despotic manipulation and control.

We Americans are extremely lucky to have a Constitution that contains the enigmatic fact alluded to, which is the Ninth Amendment. Its unassailable authority will protect our natural rights. That long neglected amendment states simply, clearly, and emphatically: The enumeration in the Constitution, of certain rights, shall not be construed to deny or disparage others retained by the people. These unenumerated or unlisted other rights are with us since birth. Words cannot affect them in any way other than allowing or thwarting their exercise through laws.

Like most Americans I was totally ignorant of this remarkable Ninth Amendment until I discovered its neglected existence several years ago while perusing a small book on the amendments. Its importance was obvious for my own personal life as well as for the practice of patholysis. The amendment must be rescued from undeserved obscurity, because its bounty can defeat the tyrannical designs of obscurantists who withhold vital information from the public. In the final analysis it will save our tottering not so free democracy.

The key words are ". . .shall not be construed to deny or disparage. . ." Among many of the unenumerated rights authorized by the Ninth Amendment is not only the natural right of an intolerably suffering, incurably afflicted patient to choose to request the aid of a physician to end the agony through a humane death accomplished according to stringent guidelines established by medical personnel; but also the natural right of a compassionate physician to choose to honor that request competently in a professional and undeniably ethical manner.

Now we come to the gist of this essay that will explain and justify the allegation of its title. The current legal bans of patholysis throughout the United States are ipso facto illegal if not outright criminal. They obviously more than construe to deny and disparage. They intend to obliterate the above mentioned natural rights of patients and doctors that are eternally validated by Amendment IX.

They have thereby violated the highest law of the land which will always trump enacted laws. Clerical and secular lawmakers who fashion such illegal prohibitions thus commit a high crime that renders relatively ridiculous the gentler stigma of guilt beyond merely reasonable doubt. Such autocratic evildoers should be harshly punished, as they would be in a really civilized and completely free democratic society we have hoped for in vain for well over two centuries. The nagging question is whether or not We the People will ever become virtuous enough to demand the invocation of the power of the Ninth Amendment to neutralize the malevolence of would-be autocrats and to strike their despicable pseudo-crimes from the books; and to demand that our heretofore pusillanimous Supreme Court be infused with the requisite degree of integrity.

In a truly just society the very first unenumerated rights proclaimed and certified by that kind of honorable Court would, without a doubt, be the most worthy aforementioned rights of choice by patients and doctors in cases of medically justified patholysis. After all, the right to choose death with relative dignity is as fundamental as the universally acclaimed rights to choose a dignified life and the pursuit of happiness.

The ruling by the envisioned honorable Court with respect to the stunning magnitude of this high crime committed by state legislators and governors would surely vindicate my verdict of their guilt beyond all doubt.

SUSAN ATKINS-WHITEHOUSE a.k.a Sadie Mae Glutz (born May 7, 1948) is a convicted murderer and former member of the Charles Manson "Family." She swore before a Grand Jury to have stabbed actress Sharon Tate to death, and to have been present at, or an accomplice to, several other murders.

Manson, Krenwinkel, Van Houten and Atkins were sent to trial on June 15, 1970. Watson was later tried separately as he was at this time in Texas attempting to fight extradition. It was established that their motive for murder was to incite a race war which was to be called *Helter Skelter* after a song of the same name by the group The Beatles.

Atkins and the other defendants were found guilty and sentenced to death on March 29, 1971. The death sentence was automatically commuted to life in prison the following year after the California Supreme Court's People v. Anderson decision invalidated all death sentences imposed in California prior to 1972.

The time Atkins spent with Manson and the Family, prison experiences and religious conversion were detailed in her autobiography *Child of Satan, Child of God*, which was published in 1977. Since 1974, Atkins has been a "born-again Christian," studied art and married a lawyer.

In 2003, she petitioned the state against her sentence on the grounds that she has become over the years a political prisoner but her petition was denied. Since receiving their sentences, Atkins, Krenwinkel, and Van Houten have been housed at the California Institution for Women in Corona, California.

On June 1, 2005, Atkins was denied parole for the 11th time. She will not be eligible for parole again until 2009.

Beyond a Reasonable Doubt

By Susan Atkins-Whitehouse

The United States government is composed of three equal branches—the Executive, the Legislative, and the Judicial. Although most Americans understand the Executive and Legislative branches, most do not understand our Justice system at all.

The American justice system is an "adversarial" system. Which means the prosecution and defense are not working together to "find the truth," they are working against each other. The idea is that if the defense lawyer puts forth just the evidence that suggests you are innocent and the prosecuting attorney puts forth just the evidence that suggests you are guilty, and if both are allowed to cross-examine each other's evidence, all relevant information will be made available to the jury, who will then be able to best determine whether you are guilty.

Most Americans do not understand that it is not the defense lawyer's job to "find the truth," and it is not the prosecuting attorney's job to "find the truth." The defense attorney is supposed to put forward the best defense possible, and the prosecuting attorney is supposed to put forward the best prosecution possible. And this is regardless of whether they believe you are guilty or innocent. To some people this seems irresponsible, or even terrible. But in our system it is the jury, not the lawyers, who are supposed to determine whether you are guilty or not.

The obvious problem with this system is that the lawyers might not be equally matched, either intellectually or financially. Or one of those lawyers might not be doing his job.

I was found guilty in a trial where Charles Manson was threatening and coercing my attorney to do what was best for Charles Manson, not me. Even the prosecutor in my case admitted Mr. Manson had four lawyers and my co-defendants and I had none.

Charles Manson believed the only way he could be convicted was if my co-defendants and I testified that he was the one who orchestrated the crimes. So, to keep us from testifying he directed that there was to be no defense put forward during the trial. This was a great tactic for Charles Manson but the obvious problem was that it left me with no defense at all. That is why a third of a century later, whenever I insist my part in the crime was coerced by threats to my life and the life of my son, the District Attorney says, "nothing like this was ever brought out in the trial." And he's right—because *nothing in my defense* was brought out at my trial.

Then, when Charles Manson was convicted along with the rest of us, in order to try to escape the death penalty during the penalty phase of the trial he forced my co-defendants and me to get on the stand and "confess" that we'd committed the crimes and he had nothing to do with it.

With years of hindsight it seems odd to me that we were even allowed to be tried together. Considering the State's allegations were that Charles Manson had the power to force us to kill for him, didn't it occur to anyone in the District Attorney's Office that if that was true Charles Manson could probably also force us to lie about it at the trial? If David Koresh had survived to be brought to trial, would anyone have been convinced if his followers had all "confessed" that he was innocent?

And judges are not there to "find the truth" either. Judges serve as referees. It's their job to make sure the trial is run according to the rules of law, not to influence the outcome. And this is true even if the judge knows one of the attorneys is out of his league or is presenting his case poorly or incompetently. In my case, when it became obvious Charles Manson was forcing me and my co-defendants to testify against ourselves, our attorneys went to the judge and told him what was happening. The judge told them there was nothing he could do, defendants have a "right" to testify at their trial. Even if we were being coerced into lying against our own interest, there was nothing he could do to stop it. That's not his job.

In the end, although the DA's office knew I was being coerced into testifying against myself, and though the prosecutor even told my jury that I was being forced to lie on the stand to save Charles Manson, the state can nonetheless continue to insist that I "confessed" to the crime.

In the 36 years since my trial I don't know if anyone in the District Attorney's Office ever realized that Mr. Bugliosi (the Prosecutor) and Manson were both giving me the same deal. Mr. Bugliosi was telling me that if I didn't do what he wanted (testify against Manson) he'd have me executed, and Manson was telling me if I didn't do what he wanted (refuse to testify) he'd have me and my son killed. Both made it clear that they didn't care about me in the least except for what I could do for them. And once I'd outlived my usefulness both threw me away to die. In the end I refused to testify against Manson simply because it became obvious that even if I testified I was still going to prison and I'd have to spend the rest of my life labeled a "snitch" and looking over my shoulder, as well as worrying about the life of my son; while if I refused to testify there was still a chance the prosecution wouldn't be able to get a conviction, and my son would be safe no matter what the outcome.

Unfortunately we don't have a "justice system," we have a "social, political, economic system." And society will always have to balance the interest of "justice" with the very real interests of money, politics, and public pressure. Judges and lawyers are not gods, they are fallible human beings, limited by all the same prejudices, biases, and shortcomings the rest of us have. And they are also vulnerable to the same pressures.

Our Founding Fathers set up our Government with the idea that the Judicial branch would compromise a full third of the governing power of this country. These men had seen firsthand how the British Government, dominated by powerful Executive and Legislative branches, had become an oppressive and unjust system. Our founders deliberately devised our system of checks-and-balances, with three equal and inter-dependant braches, to prevent this. Unfortunately when social, political and economic pressures infringe on the pursuit of Justice this balance is compromised. And this is especially frightening because the Judicial Branch is the branch of government directly empowered to protect the poor and the weak in our society—those who do not have the money or resources or numbers to wield political power through the other branches. In times of social unrest the social or political pressure to demonize some minority within society can become so great that it becomes nearly impossible for the Justice System to provide the protections it was made to provide—the protections that our founders felt were so central to a just Government that they set them down in a Constitution and empowered an entire branch of our Government to defend.

This is also true when you end up in a high-profile case. With all the political pressure and public pressure and costs, all the rules go out the window.

I was convicted in a circus of a trial. Which means even though I have now done more than twice the amount of time in prison than even the prosecutor thought I'd do, and even though my prison record is incredible, and even though my last parole board faulted me for nothing I've done over the last third of a century I've been incarcerated, and even though I have been given a right to parole, I'm continually denied parole on the basis of the facts of my crime—which are recorded in the transcripts of a trial where I had no lawyer, was given no defense, and was forced to testify against myself.

BRUCE DAVIS, now 62 years old, is serving a life sentence at the California Men's Colony in San Luis Obispo. He has been before the state parole panel more than 20 times.

In 1965, he started taking LSD. In the spring of 1968, he met Charles Manson. Manson, who was about 10 years older than Davis, treated him well and welcomed him into his commune. Although names like Tex Watson and Susan Atkins are synonymous with the Manson clan, many people don't know who Davis is. However, according to Stephen Kay, who helped prosecute Davis and Manson, he ran the ranch when Manson was away.

In July 1969, Davis was present when Manson chopped off Gary Hinman's left ear. In August 1969, he assisted Manson, Tex Watson and Steve Grogan, in the murder of Spahn's Ranch hand, Donald (Shorty) Shea. Although he did not participate in the murders, his presence at the scenes was enough to convict him and get him a life sentence.

In prison Davis became a born-again Christian and spends his time reading theology books, playing the guitar and working in the prison's Protestant chapel.

Our Future Depends
on Better Role Models

By Bruce Davis

Down the path of least resistance, I was looking just for love, without the benefit of assistance, from the one who is above.

Into a baited trap I wandered, thought that I had found the way, to satisfy my deepest hunger, didn't know the price I'd pay.

It's beyond doubt that I am sorry for those whose lives were shattered because of my criminal behavior. Specifically, I apologize for my evil actions and acknowledge my moral debt to the family and friends of Gary Hinman and Donald Shea for my part in the murder of these innocent men, and more generally, to all those whose lives were impacted by the Manson gang.

It's beyond a doubt that every day of my thirty-five-year incarceration I have felt the consequences of my associations with crimes, whose ripple effect still destroys. For instance, many of the young men who are coming to prison are the grandchildren of the hippy/flower children. Many coming from essentially amoral backgrounds have neither respect for themselves nor civility toward others. The law of the jungle describes much of their lifestyle. The average convict, at least in Folsom where I did most of the seventies, had some sense of morality informed by the Bible. Even if most were not personal believers, at least they had an admitted sense of Orthodox right and wrong. Not so now.

Many prisoners are exceptions to the dead-enders I describe above. Thousands have matured in admirable ways, but have become grist in the political mill of an important growth industry, the prison business. It's beyond reasonable doubt that the majority of prisoners, both safe and dangerous, are potential neighbors in the "Free World." The question for society is what we are going to do; attempt to redirect their heats and minds, continue to pay the price of habitual criminality, lock them away for life, or greatly expand the death penalty and simply eliminate the ongoing cost. It's beyond a doubt that if individuals fail to consider more than personal peace and hope of increasing affluence, then our culture's future is bleak indeed.

I receive many letters from the spiritually adolescent who, after seeing my name on-line, are full of admiration for Manson and his philosophy. What kind of role models do they have that makes Manson look like a good alternative? On the other hand, I hear from level headed inquirers. Thankfully there are those who are spiritually founded and support my commitment to Jesus Christ. We agree that through Christ evil can be overcome. I answer all writers with warnings about the destructive effect of Manson's ideas, and with encouragement in my personal testimony tract.

It's also beyond doubt that my attempts, and those of others, to positively influence our culture are opposed by a corrosive counterforce. Scientific naturalism as the ultimate cause of life has given us a lethal creation myth which justifies moral relativism and ends with nihilism. Beyond doubt the selfism of popular culture resists and denies the uncomfortable idea of an impersonal basis for life, and encourages the acknowledgement of the obvious: biological life is obviously too well designed to have been done by blind and purposeless chance. The willingly blind are the most dangerous models.

It's beyond doubt that those of us who chose Manson, for whatever reason, believed it was in our best interest. We parents are raising children who are going to make future choices about who their authority figures are. If we fail to set an authentic example, they will pick someone more appealing, who they feel is more authentic. Likely, it will not be a rational decision, but an emotional one. When I adopted Charlie Manson as my father, I didn't realize as such; Manson neither asked for it nor was verbally informed of my decision.

Once that relationship began to function, it was much like my relationship with my actual father, in that I'd never learned to vocally express my disagreement with him. So with Manson, it was outside my thinking to say "no." Of course, we differed philosophically but it was emotionally safe for me as long as our arguments remained abstract. But the few times I actually went against him, I was quite conflicted. Most of the young men coming to prison are likewise un-equipped with proper boundaries.

Had I chanced upon someone who treated me like Manson did, with what I felt as respect and value, had that someone been into something legal, with the same basic attractions of romance and adventure, instead of personal control and manipulation like Manson, I would have become as willing in whatever-it-was.

I was simply looking for someone to be, and so are our children. Therefore, we'd better be the ones to model the values that will allow them to be someone of whom we, their parents and God, are proud.

CHARLES "TEX" WATSON was born in 1945, and grew up in a small town outside of Dallas, Texas called Copeville. He had a happy middle-class childhood, was a star football player and a popular student in his high school. In 1967, Watson dropped out of North Texas University, and moved to California, which promised him a life of drugs, sex, and rock n' roll. Upon his arrival in California, he secured a job, and once again enrolled in college. But the "fast life" proved too seductive, and he soon dropped out. In his scene was a man called Charles Manson, who promised utopia and a life of easy sex and blissful communal living. Charles became part of Manson's "Family," fixed cars, coupled with other family members, and submitted to Manson's "teachings" on how to conquer the self. Manson proved to be a supremely manipulative sociopath, instructing Tex to lead the family members—Susan Atkins, Patricia Krenwinkel, and Linda Kasabian—to the Tate-Polanski Bel Air residence and kill everyone inside the home. The next day Manson escorted the family members to the LaBianca residence, leaving them with the orders to again kill its inhabitants.

Watson was brought to trial and convicted of the murders of Steven Parent, Abigail Folger, Wojciech Frykowski, Jay Sebring and Sharon Tate at the Tate residence on August 8 1969, and also of Leno and Rosemary LaBianca at the LaBianca residence the following night. He received the death sentence, which was overturned in 1972, and was reduced to life.

After a spiritual awakening, Watson began ministry training in 1975. In 1978 he co-authored *Will You Die For Me*, a harrowing account of his experience with Manson and his subsequent enlightenment. The story continues to touch the hearts of thousands of prisoners. Watson founded the original Abounding Love Ministries in 1980, and became an ordained minister in 1983. He has since spent decades ministering to prisoners and others around the world.

"Change is Possible..."

By Charles Watson

After thirty-six years of deliberation in prison, my verdict is in on the California penal system. GUILTY!—On all counts of gross mismanagement, beyond a reasonable doubt! If I were their attorney, I'd ask for leniency due to their admission of trying to solve a spiritual problem through punitive means. Most states have better parole systems and are much less punitive. As a result, their penal systems are less expensive and more productive, with less recidivism.

I was originally sentenced to death for my crimes and it was a sentence I deserved. I believe it was the grace and mercy of God which delivered me from it and, in an eternal sense, from much more. I write not to complain about my own circumstances or experience with the parole or corrections departments. I'd just like to see the system work in a more meaningful way. It seems most people have lost hope that prisoners can really change. Could this be because their own hearts need to change before they can perceive life with a confident expectation of good?

President Abraham Lincoln said:

> It is fit and becoming in all people, at all times, to acknowledge and revere the Supreme Government of God; to bow in

humble submission to His chastisement; to confess and deplore their sins and transgressions in the full conviction that the fear of the Lord is the beginning of wisdom, and to pray, with all fervency and contrition, for the pardon of their past offenses, and for a blessing upon their present and prospective action.[1]

Wouldn't it be nice for a person to come to prison, experience a true change of heart and leave a better person? This could happen if the Legislature would catch the vision and establish laws that require a person to demonstrate change before release. This would entail new sentencing guidelines and parole board procedures, but in the long run it could save the taxpayers money and solve some major problems in our society.

The Law given to Moses has worked on our behalf for over thirty-five hundred years. The Lord intended for the law to show men their sinfulness, so they would repent, turn from their sin to God, seeking forgiveness. Our tough laws are in place for punishment, not to promote repentance and award obedience. In California, a felon is usually given a long determined sentence, and put in prison where he becomes lazy, playing cards and watching television, without any incentive for change. Amazingly, both he and the prison staff realize that once released, he will quickly return to a life of crime.

What we need is a sentencing plan, which would not only act as a deterrent, but would work on behalf of the felon, the state and the public. A person should realize that if you commit a felony, it is a life sentence. There should be a minimum eligible parole date on one to twenty-five years, depending on the severity of the crime. For instance, if a petty thief came to prison with a one year to Life sentence, he could be released in a year if he applied himself for change. If he didn't he would remain in prison for life or until he

---

[1] Abraham Lincoln; Declaring a National Day of Prayer and Fasting following the Battle of Bull Run.

demonstrated a change which would be indicative of being able to succeed in society.

The philosophy of the present parole department would not work. Almost all of those who come before them are automatically denied parole. The few who are found suitable for parole are subsequently denied by the Governor upon review. A non-political parole board could be set up at each prison, saving tax-payers money since it would consist mostly of existing staff. One parole board member would oversee the board made up of an Associate Warden, Psychiatrist, Chaplain, the inmates Counselor, a Correctional Officer and possibly an inmate, who would not have a vote. All these people would be able to continually observe the inmate who is seeking parole. They would hopefully be able to provide a fair and objective hearing.

In fairness to corrections, they have recently recognized the value of rehabilitation by forming a threefold plan for job training, education and religion, but there is little positive incentive for inmates to participate in life skills, moral responsibility and accountability programs. Current incentive programs are punitive in nature. If you don't participate, you lose privileges. By implementing a new vision for change, most inmates would be eager to get their education, develop job skills and allow God to deal with their hearts. I believe they would catch the vision of a plan and purpose for their life.

The correctional community should be able to point every inmate towards programs for his betterment. They should provide every opportunity for change through spiritual means, not fearing the separation of church and state. Inmates should be afforded all their religious rights, in accordance with recent court decisions. Training programs would be supervised by free staff, and some classes could be taught by qualified inmates. These classes could be conducted not only in facilities designed for such purposes, but in housing units, at tables where games are usually played. Religious and training programs could also be made available over the institutional television system. Inmates should have every opportunity to prove that they are serious about change through applying themselves to study programs with the purpose of being released one day.

I doubt that these changes for prison reform will be taken seriously. It would take a miracle for the Legislature to turn back the clock by repealing laws that have been firmly established for punishment during the past twenty-five years. Corrections has become big business in California, so there is a lot at stake here.

In recent days, we've seen people go to prison no matter what their social status or how affluent they are. It takes more than job and educational training to stay out of prison. The way to stay out is through one thing—a repentant heart. John the Baptist, Jesus and Peter all preached repentance of sin. They knew that without a repentant heart that we are all doomed to perish in one way or another. Repentance is the only way for a person to truly have a spiritual transformation of heart, where the true problem lies.

In my case, I agree with my prosecuting attorney, who said I needed a new heart. I needed more than the superficial change that self-help programs and groups offer. I was fearful of someone operating on me who was as sick as I was. The Lord began tugging on my heart, while giving those who knew Him the courage to reach out to me. They told me of the great love God had for me, even after committing such a horrible crime. My eyes were opened to God's goodness, which brought repentance to my life. On a Friday night in May 1975, in the prison chapel, Jesus Christ came into my heart. I returned to my cell that night with a glow on my face. Since that time it has been a continuous growing relationship with Jesus Christ that has transformed my life.

Who could ever believe that something good could come out of something so bad. I believe as the Apostle Paul wrote under the inspiration of the Holy Spirits, that all things work together for the good of those who are called according to God's purpose. The Lord is asking that we believe a person can come out of prison changed for the good. It requires we believe beyond a reasonable doubt in the

Supreme God, who has provided the ability for hearts to be changed through the gift of His Son at Calvary. Let us passionately profess that we can do all things through Christ who strengthens us. Let us believe for change beyond a reasonable doubt!

DANIEL KELLY, a Bronx High School of Science student, shot two people at the age of 17. He was charged with two counts of murder, a count of attempted murder, a host of weapons charges, and multiple robbery offenses. Upon conviction, he received a twenty-two years-to-life prison sentence. In 1992 he was admitted to the Eastern New York Correctional Facility and is due for parole in 1912.

92A5149

By Daniel Kelly

My name is Daniel Kelly. The New York State Department of Corrections knows me as inmate # 92A5149. My family knows me as Danny and my peers in state greens call me Fam. I am originally from Brooklyn, New York but I moved to the Bronx with my grandparents after a tumultuous living experience with my parents. My father was constantly absent and my mother battled Multiple Sclerosis.

I did poorly in school and dropped out of the seventh grade. I felt as if I did not belong among all the White and Asian Students. With the faith of my teachers I took an entrance exam and attended the Bronx High School of Science. The only problem was I wanted to replace a quality education with what I could learn on the dark streets of New York City.

This would prove to be my downfall because at the age of seventeen, on a cold November night, my older brother and I walked into a Bodega with the intentions of leaving with money. I didn't know what I was doing or what to say. What, stick-em-up? I wanted to leave right then, but I knew that if I did I would feel like a pussy. I would not be able to look my brother in his face. So, the same hand I would use to fill in an answer key with a number two pencil also pulled the revolver from my pocket. That day a gentleman named Crisprano Dominguez was shot and I claimed the lives of Felix Fernandez and

Stenny Winter. My brother was also shot in the shoulder during our robbery spree and the hospital where he was being treated dutifully reported the shooting to the police.

The officers that came to the house told my mom that they needed to take me to the hospital where my brother was being treated in order to help them identify who did the shooting. Funny, though, we never made it to the hospital. Instead, a detective whose name I can't remember pulled a chair up to me and started relaying his version of what he thinks happened in that store. I couldn't believe how close he was and he wasn't even there! As I sat there I kind of felt that it was over, but I still tried to minimize the enormity of what happened by lying. I thought that if I could convince these detectives that I fired my gun in self-defense, the consequences wouldn't be as harsh.

Needless to say, I never did make it home that night. I remember being interrogated for what seemed like hours by a host of faceless detectives. I wanted to go home so badly but they wouldn't let me. One detective, in particular hinted that I'd be able to go home soon after I answered a few more questions. It was a female and I believed her, oddly enough, because she smelled nice. Instead, I spent the night traveling from precinct to precinct appearing in line-ups. I was arrested and charged with two counts of murder, a count of attempted murder, a host of weapons charges, and multiple robbery offenses.

I guess one of the things that Americans pride themselves is that they will get their day in court. During my court proceedings I was given offers to plead guilty. The first one, which was twenty-five years-to-life, I didn't take. My attorney, during our allotted visits, asked me if I ever heard the phrase, "Dead men tell no tales." When I replied that I did he asked me, "Then why did I?" I was at a loss for words. I thought that it would be too childish to say that I just wanted to go home. I mean, that's what a little white kid would say, right? Nonetheless, when my next court date arrived I was offered twenty-two years-to-life. My lawyer had already filed motions for suppression, which were denied. The murder weapons, the eyewitness accounts, and most important of all, my confession was admitted into the prosecution's big bag of evidence. I was ready to take what was being offered.

At the young age of nineteen, I accepted the offer of twenty-two years-to-life. I've asked myself over and over again, if I'm even qualified to comment on what constitutes reasonable doubt when I'm actually guilty of the crime of murder. I am not your falsely accused hero as in the case of Rueben "Hurricane" Carter. The reasons for my taking the lives of two people were not from some convoluted sense of honor or dignity. This was not self-defense. This was a seventeen-year-old former Bronx High School of Science student who, in his haste to impress his peers with material wealth, found himself under arrest, charged with two counts of second degree murder. At thirty-three years of age, I now look at life through the eyes of a man.

There were no ill-fitting gloves or fishing boats presented as evidence in any of my court proceedings. No cinematic car chases, stand-offs or hostage situations. Only the words of a foolish young man. Words which seemed to serve as a catharsis for my soul.

In December 2003, **KAMALA D. HARRIS** was elected as the first woman District Attorney in San Francisco's history and as the first African American woman in California's history to hold the office. A career Prosecutor, DA Harris is bringing San Franciscans a "smart on crime" approach—prosecuting crime with resolve while remaining committed to rehabilitation and placing a priority on preserving civil liberties. DA Harris has combated violent crime with intensity and focus. She has significantly raised felony conviction rates, doubled the number of domestic violence cases taken to trial and is aggressively targeting child sexual offenders.

DA Harris' achievements and leadership have earned local and national distinction. She was selected for the prestigious Thurgood Marshall Award from the National Black Prosecutors Association in 2005. California's largest legal newspaper, the *Daily Journal*, has recognized DA Harris as one of the top 100 lawyers in the state. She has been featured on the *Oprah Show* and in *Newsweek* magazine as one of "America's 20 Most Powerful Women." Most recently, she was selected as one of *Ebony* magazine's "100 Most Influential Black Americans." In July 2006, DA Harris was elected to the National District Attorneys Association's Board of Directors. She also serves as the Co-Chair of the National District Attorneys Association's Reentry Committee.

Demanding Solutions:
Being Smart on Crime

By Kamala D. Harris

For many years, I stood in front of twelve people I didn't know and asked them to make a finding based on what the evidence in a specific case proved beyond a reasonable doubt. Now, I sit at my desk as the chief law enforcement officer of a great city, and I would like to present you with what I believe the broader evidence proves beyond a reasonable doubt. What I believe is that there is nothing more important than the security and safety of our families in their homes, schools and neighborhoods. What I have grown ever more certain of is that law enforcement, and all of us committed to creating safe communities, can do better than business as usual. It is time for us to move our dialogue about crime and violence beyond rhetoric about who is "tough on crime" or "soft on crime." What has become clear to me, beyond a reasonable doubt, is that we can choose instead to be smart on crime.

Being smart on crime means focusing on lasting solutions and demanding effectiveness. We can aggressively prosecute violent and serious criminals and, at the same time, be smart about crime prevention and how we use our resources. Being smart on crime is a proactive model for modern law enforcement that goes beyond arrests and convictions to address the question, "What will make us safer?" The true security of our communities will be achieved when, in addition to swift consequences in reaction to crime, we invest in preventing crime and in turning around the lives of young offenders.

As a young prosecutor, I began to see the same people back on my caseload, people I had prosecuted a few years before and who had been sent to prison. It struck me that I could face the same people in court again and again in an endless cycle, and I knew that we could do better than that. Working in my own community, I started to examine how we could most effectively ensure the safety of our neighbors. Looking at what was working best in our local law enforcement strategies, I grew curious about what was happening in other parts of California and across the country. I learned that for every five crimes committed, only one results in an arrest. So in four out of five crimes, my fellow prosecutors and I never even have the chance to hold anyone accountable for the offense. I was forced to stop and ask whether we really were taking the smartest approach to planning for our safety. It became clear to me that we needed to invest more effort in preventing crimes from happening in the first place.

Almost all of the felons my fellow prosecutors and I send to prison will return to the community sooner or later. In fact, nationally, the average prisoner is released after less than two years. More than 650,000 prisoners will return to our nation's neighborhoods this year alone. And unless we do something different, more than half of them will be back in prison within two years after they are released. For every new crime they commit, they harm another victim and community, and when they return to prison, they cost taxpayers an average of $30,000 per year. For some of those criminals, the answer is longer prison sentences. But for many others, we can stop the cycle and in so doing, prevent crimes before they happen.

One of the most promising new approaches to keeping our families safe is to focus on what happens to prisoners when they are released and return home. There is a growing number of prosecutors and other law enforcement officials who have come to understand that we can seize the opportunity, while offenders are behind bars and as soon as they are released, to hold them strictly accountable while opening doors to genuine opportunities for them to leave behind them the cycle of crime and incarceration. We can create "reentry" pathways for former offenders to permanently exit the criminal justice system. It is a leading way to keep our communities safe.

In San Francisco, we have pioneered a new initiative called "Back On Track," and it is working to prevent former offenders from committing more crimes and saving the city a lot of money at the same time. Back on Track focuses on young, first-time drug offenders with no history of violence or gang involvement. The participants are youth with one foot in the world of crime and one foot in our world, and we are working to push and pull them back to our side. The program is a tough deal because it is about accountability and public safety, not social work. Every participant must plead guilty but we will delay final sentencing for a year while they complete a rigorous course that combines intensive supervision with concrete opportunities to get a job and education and to reengage with their children and families.

One Back on Track participant, "Richard," grew up in public housing and as a minor, he was in and out of juvenile hall, arrested several times for minor offenses. He never held a job and dropped out of high school in the tenth grade. When he was 17, Richard fathered a daughter. He was a "deadbeat dad," never paying child support. At the age of 19, Richard was arrested for selling drugs to an undercover officer on a San Francisco street corner. We offered him a choice, plead guilty to selling drugs and enter Back on Track, or face prosecution and time behind bars. Now, after 10 months in the program, Richard is working full time in a warehouse, has gotten his G.E.D, and is enrolled in evening classes at Community College. He is in good standing with his child support obligations. His daughter has been immunized, is covered under his health insurance and has quality child care.

The key to turning around lives like Richard's is having real consequences for failing to play by the rules. If our participants miss a deadline or fail to meet expectations, they go directly back to serving their full felony sentence, no arguments. People tell me that's too tough, but they're wrong. Every two weeks, participants must appear before a judge and report on their progress. They must comply with all court-ordered child support obligations and complete classes on parenting, substance abuse and other issues. Every participant must also do 200 hours of community service to give back to the neighborhoods they harmed.

Back On Track is producing phenomenal results. Now nearly three years into this program, less than five percent of our participants have been rearrested. Everyone in the program is either employed full-time, in school full-time or, like Richard, both working and in school. And it pays to be smart on crime. For every dollar we invest in programs like this, we save five dollars in jail costs alone. In 2006, our program will save the City of San Francisco $2 million.

Innovative prosecutors and other law enforcement officials around the country are starting exciting programs that focus on preventing crime and that create pathways for prisoners reentering our communities. The best of these programs are rigorous, with serious consequences for failure. But when the participants prove they are ready to play by the rules, we invest in their success. In our communities, we must be willing to commit real resources for young people who are willing to play by the rules. Second chances can work.

By choosing to embrace innovation and working hand in hand with the communities we are sworn to protect, law enforcement leaders can own the duty to create long-lasting safety for all of our families and neighborhoods. Creative approaches that couple accountability with opportunity work for the participants. At least as importantly, they can work wonders for the children of offenders, helping to stop the intergenerational cycle of crime. Many defendants have young children who have been placed at risk, through no fault of their own, by their parents' bad choices. By turning the lives of their parents around, we can change the odds for those children.

As a prosecutor, I've stood before many juries to ask for a guilty verdict. If you were my jury, I would argue that as a national community, we have been guilty of thinking too narrowly, of losing sight of the vision that we can create lasting security in all of our neighborhoods. I am convinced, beyond a reasonable doubt, that our country and communities have the resources and imagination to be smart on crime, to break the cycle for offenders and ensure safe futures for every one of us.

In the summer of 1981 JOHN WALSH was a partner in a management company in Florida when his son, Adam, was abducted and murdered. The six-year-old boy's severed head was found in a drainage canal more than 100 miles away from home and his body was never recovered.

Since then Walsh and his family have become known for their anti-crime activism, particularly fighting to help missing and exploited children. They were instrumental in the creation of the Missing Children Act of 1982 and the Missing Children's Assistance Act of 1984 and John is presently advocating a Constitutional amendment for victims' rights.

Since 1988 Walsh has hosted *America's Most Wanted*, Fox's reality show designed to track down the country's most notorious and dangerous fugitives by profiling their cases to a national audience. As of August 10th, 2006, 900 fugitives have been captured and 50 missing persons (including children) have been recovered alive as a direct result of viewer tips. From 2002 to 2004 he also hosted *The John Walsh Show*.

John is also the author of three best-selling books including *Tears of Rage* (1997), *No Mercy* (1998), and *Public Enemies* (2001).

A Voice
for the Victims

By John Walsh

Thank God we live in a country where you are presumed innocent until proven guilty.

The advent of DNA, "the fingerprint of the 21st century," has been a boon to the criminal justice system. It not only convicts the guilty, and solves thousands of rapes and child molestations, it also frees the innocent.

People who may not have the resources, the education or the contacts to prove their innocence have often said that the Criminal Justice System should be renamed the Criminal *In*justice System. But, with the constant scrutiny of a free press, there is always hope that the system will improve.

I hope that someday, legislators and society as a whole, takes a long hard look at this system and police, prosecutors, defense attorneys and judges will finally get the resources and training that they so desperately need; and most of all, that victims get better treatment and a voice that they so desperately deserve.

Until that happens, everyone needs to take a much closer look at what the phrase "reasonable doubt" really means.

PETER J. NICKLES is a senior litigation partner in Covington & Burling's Washington, D.C. office. His practice emphasizes major class actions involving securities fraud and toxic torts; jury and non-jury trials, as well as defensive takeover litigation and other high-profile litigation; international arbitrations; antitrust and trade law and federal regulatory practice. He has successfully represented many companies in federal, state agency and tribal government actions.

He was a member of the Lawyer's Committee for Civil Rights Under Law, 1964; Counsel to the Jackson State Task Force and the Kent State Task Force, reporting to the Scranton Commission on Campus Unrest, 1968-70; and Chairman of Neighborhood Legal Services Program (NLSP), Washington, D.C. from 1970-75. He was an adjunct professor at Howard Law School from 1980-92 and taught an antitrust seminar at Virginia Law School for many years. He is listed in the *Guide to the World's Leading Litigation Lawyers, Euromoney Publications PLC* (1997), and is author of the lead article under the United States section of the *Guide*, entitled "Winning The 'Bet Your Company' Case." He has received the District of Columbia Bar Association's Pro Bono Service Award for his unrelenting years of public service in connection with a number of cases impacting the citizens of the District of Columbia.

Help Our
Community

By Peter J. Nickles

Society puts its troublemakers and its troubled citizens in jails, prisons, institutions—behind bars, behind locked doors. We do not want to see them. We pretend to rehabilitate these kids, these men and women—to treat their mental illness—but do we care? They have no voice, no constituency...they are powerless. And when they depart their closed environments, what do most of them do? They return to these institutions. Society and those individuals pay the price.

I've been drawn to their problems for decades of my legal career and pursued their rights in court. In 1974, a class action was brought on behalf of thousands of men and women housed in a mental institution in Washington, D.C. They—most of them—should not have been locked up. They could function, work, raise a family, and live a meaningful life in society. They had not been convicted of any crime, but the easy solution was to put them away—out of sight. The class action and the Court's orders brought them back into society in a manner consistent with protecting the community and the individual. Now, those individuals—thousands of them—live and work in Washington and contribute to the City's economy and culture.

In another case brought in 1979, we initiated a class action on behalf of 300+ D.C. men in a maximum security prison in Lorton, Virginia. In the 1980s, another class action was commenced on behalf of more than a thousand men in the Lorton medium security institution, and, shortly thereafter, we brought a class action on behalf of 700+ men housed in the Lorton modular medium security facility. Finally, a class action was instituted on behalf of 800 D.C. women, who were transferred from federal prisons and housed in a number of D.C. prisons. In all these cases, the claim was simple—the punishment provided by law was compounded by unconstitutional cruel and unusual confinement.

What does that phrase "cruel and unusual" punishment mean? In the case of the confined women, it meant sexual abuse and degradation, inadequate medical care, and living conditions that fell far below basic standards of decency. In the case of the men, the phrase meant very much the same, but compounded by repeated and notorious instances of physical beatings and sexual attacks. Not pretty. These individuals deserved to be confined; they had committed crimes. But society—we, all of us—took on the responsibility of treating them in a civilized fashion once they were committed to our care and control. Did we win these class actions? Yes. In each case—by Court order and Consent Decrees—we brought some order out of chaos and restored respect to the City's treatment of the men and women in its prisons. Did we help our clients? Yes. Is the fight over? Are you kidding?

And then more than two years ago, I joined lawyers in a case brought almost 20 years ago on behalf of young D.C. boys and girls in trouble with the law. Their confinement in a falling-apart institution needed attention. We focused the public light of attention on these kids and the sorry conditions of their confinement—the gang warfare behind the walls of the institution, the easy infiltration of drugs, the lack of suicide prevention, medical and mental care—and the bleak environment that told those kids—boys and girls—YOU ARE IN JAIL! The result—a recidivism rate that is outrageous. They leave, they come back. And many who leave don't come back because they die on the streets of the City. Now they are getting some help. A new Detention Center has been built. The City has committed to build a new facility for committed kids to replace the decaying buildings—and most important, the jail environment is being transformed and the

City has committed its resources to rehabilitate kids. But more—much more—is needed.

In all these cases, society needed help—the help of lawyers, the courts...and the public's attention. The glare of this public attention has stripped away the isolation of these confining institutions and the individuals behind their walls and focused our attention on those who have no political constituency. With the glare of public attention came reform. No longer would the sentiment—"out of sight, out of mind"—be tolerated.

I was privileged to be a catalyst. But the path is long and arduous; and it is all too easy for the system to take one step forward and two steps back. To my colleagues—the younger members of the legal community—the challenge is there, the need is great and the opportunity to serve the public interest is compelling. Can there be reasonable doubt that those of us privileged to practice law in the Courts of America should dedicate their time to attack institutions which do not treat their wards in a civilized fashion? Dostoevsky said something to the effect that the mark of a civilized society is the way it treats its prisoners. In my view, there is no reasonable doubt. We must not let our fellow citizens be forgotten!

ABBE DAVID LOWELL has been named as one of the top criminal and civil trial lawyers in the country. In addition to the investigation and trial of complex criminal and civil cases across the United States, his practice involves counseling clients with respect to their dealings with legislative and government agencies in enforcement, oversight, investigative, and regulatory matters. He has successfully tried numerous complex criminal and civil jury cases in more than two dozen federal and state courts involving public corruption, securities and bank fraud, racketeering, mail and wire fraud, election law violations, conspiracy and money laundering. He has argued in over a dozen appellate courts, including U.S. Supreme Court. In addition to his private practice, he has served as Special Counsel to the U.S. Congress for ethics cases and the impeachment proceedings of President Clinton and as Special Counselor to the United Nations High Court for Human Rights in Geneva.

Mr. Lowell has been recognized by numerous publications, including: one the nation's 100 Most Influential Attorneys in the 2006 National Law Journal; one of the top 10 white-collar defense lawyers in Washington, D.C. by the 2006 *Legal Times*; one of the country's top 10 most successful trial attorneys in the 2004 *National Law Journal*; one of the top white-collar defense attorneys in the United States by *The Best Lawyers in America*. *Washingtonian* magazine has named him one of its top attorneys in Washington, D.C. every year since 1986 in which a survey has been conducted; Roll Call, a Capitol Hill newspaper, has included him as one of the attorneys whose business card people should keep in their address books. He teaches criminal law at Georgetown Law Center and Columbia Law School.

The Penal
System is Broken

By Abbe D. Lowell

Beyond reasonable doubt, everyone associated with the criminal justice process knows that our system of punishment is broken and has to be started over from scratch. With one of every five African-American males in jail or likely to go to jail and with Congress's and state legislatures' response being to create the appearance of equality by sending more non-violent offenders to jail, enacting more mandatory minimum sentences for all offenders, and taking more discretion away from sentencing judges, we have never had the punishment crisis that faces our country today. America has more jails with more people than any other civilized, democratic country, and we certainly have not created less crime by doing so.

To begin with, there is no longer an agreed-upon goal for punishment. Is it to protect society by taking violent wrongdoers off the street? Is it to exact a form of revenge for the victim? Certainly, no one still believes that we jail people to "rehabilitate" them. Adding to the problem is the fact that more incarceration creates its own set of issues and problems—increased need for jail cells means more money for jails instead of schools, roads and other desperately needed community projects; jails become schools of higher education to teach inmates more crime; we know now that jails produce unintended collateral problems like increased exposure to AIDS and other diseases. It now costs over $25,000 a year to keep a person in prison. With an

American prison population of over 2 million that accumulates to billions for which we could easily find better uses.

Were all of this not bad enough, many states still maintain a form of sentencing and parole that only makes sense to a contortionist. Judges sentence a person to 10 to 20 years but the person serves neither 10 nor 20; instead, the inmate serves some fraction of the 10 years depending on when he is eligible for and gets parole. And parole, which itself can create problems when bias or corruption affects the decisions, is then used to relieve the over-crowded prison population that this system created in the first place. So, someone who the public thinks has been given a 10 to 20 years sentence may actually be out in 3 to 5 years. Talk about a lack of truth in advertising!

Where along the way it became the assumption of our society and the mandate of the criminal justice system to use jail as the punishment of first resort instead of the last resort is hard to tell. Politicians ran for office in eras of increased crime on the platform of getting "tough" on criminals. Then, legislators and governors and even Presidents demanded that we "lock criminals up and throw away the key." So, rather than dealing with the complexities of the most often committed crime—drugs—society copped out by treating all aspects of the nation's narcotics problem as crimes instead of finding a means to break the vicious cycle of despair, using and dealing. Rather than the effort and expense of warehousing thousands and thousands of people involved with drugs in prisons, where they learn how to deal or use drugs under the noses of guards, we should finally admit to and start dealing with the root causes of why people fall into drugs and then provide addicts with the treatment, education, training employment and hope, that would cost less and provide more to society.

Once it became clear that our system had a disproportionate impact on minorities, rather than re-think the incarceration presumption, legislatures' answer was to "spread the misery." So with mandatory minimum sentences and sentence guidelines imposed on judges, the "solution" was to treat white-collar and street criminals similarly. It was easy rhetoric to say: "If a person robs a bank with a gun or if he takes the bank's money through fraud, he should be treated the same way." But should he? If a person uses an automatic weapon in a bank and steals $100,000 and another gets the bank to lend him $100,000 through an inflated appraisal, are they the same threat to society? With what they might offer to pay back their victims and society if required to do so in court-ordered work, are we really well served when the heads of Enron or WorldCom are sent to some prison camp for 20 years just to make the point that we treat criminals equally?

Solutions are not as hard as critics claim—use money for jails and guarding inmates to create opportunities for those who end up criminals from lack of a choice; treat drug addiction as a disease and not a crime; force those who can work for the public good—whether unskilled street criminals for public works or educated white-collar violators for public schools—to do so; and reserve fewer jail cells for those people who cannot be trusted to refrain from violence in their communities.

America is a much different country today than it was 250 years ago. In technology, communications, transportation and industry, so much has changed. Yet, in the midst of our progress and maturation, one lack of change becomes even more glaring. Our system of punishment and use of jails as the main solution is not much different than it was when the Puritans meted out their form of justice before we were even a country. If we are truly a people who hold ourselves out to the rest of the world as models for democracy, then we must find better solutions than simply jailing more and more people. Creative solutions are the only way to improve our security and justice in a society that knows beyond reasonable doubt that the penal system in this country is broken.

A MATTER of LIFE and DEATH

Scott Turow
William Bernhardt
Gerry Spence
Kathleen Behan
Mark Geragos
Gene Wilson
Robert H. Bork

*"To live without killing is a thought which
could electrify the world, if men were only capable of
staying awake long enough to let the idea soak in."*
—Henry Miller

SCOTT TUROW is a writer and attorney. He is the author of seven best-selling novels, including his first, *Presumed Innocent* (1987) and his most recent novel, *Ordinary Heroes* published by Farrar Straus & Giroux in November, 2005. A novella, *Limitations* will be published as a paperback original in November 2006 by Picador following its serialization in the *New York Times' Sunday Magazine*. He has also written two non-fiction books—*One L*, about his experience as a law student, and *Ultimate Punishment*, a reflection on capital punishment. Mr. Turow has been a partner in the Chicago office of Sonnenschein Nath and Rosenthal, a national law firm, since 1986, concentrating on white-collar criminal defense, while also devoting a substantial part of his time to pro bono matters. He has served on a number of public bodies, including the Illinois Commission on Capital Punishment appointed by Governor George Ryan in 2000 to recommend reforms to Illinois' death penalty system. Scott Turow is currently the Chairman of Illinois' Executive Ethics Commission regulating executive branch employees. He is also a past president of the Authors Guild, and is currently a trustee of Amherst College.

Doubting
the Death Penalty

By Scott Turow

I have become convinced beyond any lingering doubt that the death penalty will never work in America. By "work" I mean that we'll never create a capital punishment system that reaches only the "right" cases, without also sweeping in the wrong ones. Because of that, the practice of capital punishment will never give Americans what I think they expect from it, namely a sense of moral proportion, a feeling that acts of ultimate evil have received the ultimate punishment they deserve.

Like many other people, I was in doubt about the death penalty most of my life, even after I went to law school and became a prosecutor and, later, a defense lawyer. Sometimes I tended to favor the death penalty, and sometimes I leaned against it, but I was never completely sure. I often referred to myself as a "death-penalty agnostic." That uncertainty persisted even after I served as one of the defense lawyers for an innocent man who had been sentenced to death and was ultimately released, and even after I represented another young man whose death sentence was far too harsh for the impulsive shooting he'd been involved in, a position the prosecutor in the case ultimately agreed with.

But what made me continue to think capital punishment might be "right" was cases like that of John Wayne Gacy who lured 33 young men to his home, tortured them to death, and then buried many of their bodies under his house. Thinking about the misery of those deaths and of the families who spent years wondering what had become of their sons and brothers, I often felt that executing Gacy was a punishment that equaled the monstrousness of his offense.

In 2000, George Ryan, then the Governor of Illinois, declared a moratorium on executions in our state and appointed a fourteen-person commission to recommend reform of our capital system, in which 13 times young men, including the client of mine I have mentioned, had been sentenced to death and later legally absolved of the crimes. I was one of the fourteen persons appointed by Governor Ryan to tell him how to fix a system he thought was broken.

When I started on the Commission I thought that might be possible. But I realized over time that I, like most Americans, had made a fundamental mistake. I was uncertain about the death penalty because I thought there were cases, like Gacy's, where death was the appropriate sentence. But the proper question to ask was not whether there were cases where death seemed "right." The correct question was whether we'd ever be able to construct a legal system that reached only those right cases, without sweeping in the wrong cases, cases like those of my client who was innocent or my other client whose crime, by any sense of proportion, did not merit death. I realized that we were never going to do that. Here's why.

Capital punishment presents an essential paradox. We think it should be imposed in the cases, like Gacy's, which we regard as the worst of the worst. But those are the crimes that most horrify us, that create the greatest anxiety in the communities in which they occur, and which most challenge our ability to reason, whether as police, prosecutors, judges or juries. In these frightening cases everyone wants an offender arrested and kept off the street, making it hard to apply the beyond-a-reasonable-doubt standard. Who would let someone accused of crimes like Gacy's go free, even if the evidence left room for doubt? Who would take the chance on unleashing a potential monster again? There is an inherent tendency confronting crimes that are the worst of the worst to rush to judgment, which makes those cases especially prone to error.

The other problem comes at the other end of the spectrum. We never can figure out which cases are really "the worst of the worst." Several states have recently extended the death penalty to offenders who sexually abuse children, even if the children survive. These are unspeakable crimes, but in those same states not every murderer is subject to capital punishment. Does it make sense to give life in prison to someone who killed his victim and death to another offender whose victim survived? These kinds of inequities riddle our capital punishment system. In Illinois we found that killers of white persons were three times more likely to get sentenced to death than murderers whose victims were black, and that death was applied five times more often in rural areas as opposed to our state's cities, where the prevalence of crime requires a more measured approach.

Besides ceaseless problems in the equal application of capital punishment, there are also systemic inequities: differences in the time and resources for public defenders as opposed to the best retained counsel; the random variation in attitudes of prosecutors, some of whom relish capital cases and others who avoid them; and widely varied financial abilities in the prosecuting counties that control how often capital punishment is sought, since death prosecutions are very expensive and can't afford to be mounted often.

These constant inequities undermine capital punishment. Americans don't favor capital punishment because they're bloodthirsty. They favor it because they think it sends a clear moral message. Some people may argue that the death penalty deters other people from committing murders, but the statistics don't bear that out. Others may believe that capital punishment gives justice to the victim families, but that argument ignores the fact that in 49 first degree murder cases out of 50, death is not the sentence, meaning that far more often prosecutors set aside the victims' desires, in favor of an outcome that they think is best for the community. That is the ultimate consideration—community values—and those values will forever be undercut by a system so prone to death sentence the innocent—in Illinois by now we've had 18 men exonerated who were once sentenced to death—or to impose capital sentences on persons whose crimes are less morally grave than those sentenced to life.

For all these reasons, I'm convinced that we will never do capital punishment the "right" way, and that we're better off applying the enormous resources consumed toward the solution of many other problems.

WILLIAM BERNHARDT is the author of twenty-two books with more than ten million copies in print worldwide, including his internationally bestselling series of novels featuring attorney Ben Kincaid, which inspired *Library Journal* to name Bernhardt the "master of the courtroom drama." His most recent novel is *Capitol Murder*, which takes attorney Ben Kincaid to Washington, D.C. for a controversial, high-profile case involving a national sex scandal, political skullduggery, and murder. Bernhardt has twice won the Oklahoma Book Award for Best Fiction as well as the Southern Writers Guild's Gold Medal Award. In 2000, he was honored with the H. Louise Cobb Distinguished Author Award, which is given "in recognition of an outstanding body of work that has profoundly influenced the way in which we understand ourselves and American society at large."

Mr. Bernhardt obtained his law degree at the University of Oklahoma, where he was a member of the 1985 National Championship Moot Court team and was personally named Best Speaker at the national finals in New York. He worked as a trial lawyer at a large law firm for ten years and was repeatedly recognized for handling pro bono cases for the underprivileged. The Oklahoma Bar Association presented him with a special award for Outstanding Service to the Public, and he was named one of the top twenty young lawyers in the nation by the *American Bar Association's Barrister* magazine.

Bernhardt's many activities within and beyond the world of literature led OSU to dub him "Oklahoma's Renaissance Man." Other recent Bernhardt projects have include writing the music, lyrics, and script for a musical (he is an accomplished pianist and songwriter), creating a board game, producing two music CDs, constructing crossword puzzles published in the *New York Times*, jumping out of an airplane at 10,000 feet, and kissing a dolphin.

Doubting
the Eyewitness

By William Bernhardt

The first lawsuit I ever tried—the one every lawyer remembers with great clarity—involved the allegedly odd behavior of a young receptionist. Eyewitnesses testified that she had been acting strangely, suspiciously. On occasion, they reported, she seemed flushed, nervous, ill at ease. They concluded that she was behind a scheme to bilk the company, especially after she disappeared from work for a week. On the final day of the trial, the woman in question took the stand. She revealed that she had in fact missed work for a week—to have a baby. None of those brilliant eyewitnesses had even noticed she was pregnant, which might also explain why she had been flushed and behaving oddly.

Eyewitness testimony is the linchpin of most prosecutorial efforts to prove a defendant guilty "beyond a reasonable doubt." In the United States, about two hundred people a day are identified by alleged eyewitnesses. This testimony is highly prized by prosecutors who know that an eyewitness is the surest way to convince a jury that there is no cause for doubt. Defendants have been given the death sentence based upon the testimony of a persuasive eyewitness, even when there was no other corroborating proof. Jurors struggle with cases built upon "circumstantial evidence," which typically means anything other than eyewitness testimony. If they hear from a witness who claims to have seen the defendant commit the crime, however, what basis can there be for doubt? In a study conducted by psychologist Elizabeth Loftus, mock jurors were presented with a felony murder case. When given only circumstantial evidence, eighteen percent of the jurors voted to convict. When presented with the same evidence plus an eyewitness identification, the conviction rate soared to sixty-eight percent—even though the jurors were told the eyewitness had 20/400 vision.

The disturbing truth is that jurors give the greatest weight to the most fallible form of evidence. Some circumstantial proof is keenly incriminating. DNA evidence, for instance, can provide irrefutable confirmation of guilt or innocence, as can blood tests and similar forensic evidence. Eyewitness testimony, however, even when offered by honest, well-meaning people, can not only be wrong, it can be dangerously convincing. Psychologist Gary Wells, an expert in eyewitness identification, has said, "It's not just that they make mistakes. Unfortunately, they can also be highly confident even when they're wrong."

Wells conducted a study at Iowa State University in which 172 students were asked to view an actual surveillance video of a convenience store robbery that culminated in murder. After watching the video, each student was asked to identify the killer from a book of mug shots. The study mirrored typical police procedure; eighty percent of all defendants are identified from photos, not lineups. Every student fingered someone in the photo album—but the true killer's photo was not there.

What happened after the student identifications is even more chilling. In a third of the cases, an interviewer suggested indirectly that the student had made the correct identification. Another third were given indications that they had made the wrong choice, and the last third were told nothing. The students were then interviewed by a third party to test their certainty level. The students who had received negative reinforcement or no reinforcement expressed doubt about their identification, but about half of those who received supportive remarks were absolutely certain they had nailed the killer. Some even said they had gotten a clear view of the murderer's face and had paid close attention to his features. In reality, of course, every student had chosen an innocent man.

Inevitably, real-life eyewitnesses receive the same encouragement from police officers when they identify a suspect. Police are only human, and it would be hard to hide their pleasure in a positive ID, especially since the eyewitness will then become an integral part of the prosecution. The more positive the witness, the stronger the case, even if, as in the study, the identification is dead wrong. A U.S. Department of Justice report identified twenty-eight convicted defendants who were freed after DNA evidence proved they had not committed the crime. Twenty-four of those convictions were based upon eyewitness testimony. A subsequent study by the Center on Wrongful Convictions at Northwestern University revealed that seventy-six percent of all wrongful convictions reversed due to DNA evidence were attributable to flawed eyewitness testimony. Other studies have indicated that eyewitness identifications are wrong about fifty percent of the time. According to Rob Warden, Executive Director of the Center at Northwestern, erroneous eyewitness testimony is by far the largest cause of wrongful convictions in the U.S. criminal justice system.

Researchers have known for some time that human memory is far from perfect. As early as 1908, in a book titled *On the Witness Stand*, Harvard psychologist Hugo Munsterberg advocated altering court procedures to reduce dependence on inherently unreliable eyewitnesses. More recently, Elizabeth Loftus has argued that every witness identification is tainted by imperfect viewing conditions, brevity of exposure, external pressures, police and family expectations, personal biases and stereotypes, or the desire to be of service. In *Eyewitness Testimony*, Loftus demonstrates how memory can be inadvertently altered or intentionally manipulated by police questioning. New memories can be created or implanted during the interrogation process. As a result, the certainty of the witness bears no relationship to the reliability of the memory. Many jurors—many people—assume that our memories store experience with precision and accuracy, but research indicates that our memories are more like video recorders with one battery missing, poor focus, and constant outside interference.

What's the solution to this problem? In their book, *Mistaken Identification: The Eyewitness, Psychology and the Law*, authors Brian L. Cutler and Steven D. Penrod advocate the use of expert psychological testimony in the courtroom to educate the jury on how memory works, how it can be flawed, and how to evaluate the reliability of these witnesses. Recently, in <u>The People v. Lee</u>, the New York Court of Appeals, the highest court in the state, approved the use of such testimony in certain cases. As a former trial lawyer, I question whether such expert testimony will help a jury. In my experience, jurors tend to disregard experts as "hired guns," and following the testimony of an eyewitness with an expert on eyewitnesses could be hopelessly confusing. In one of my novels, *Capitol Murder*, my series character, defense attorney Ben Kincaid, represents a U.S. Senator involved in a sex scandal that leads to a murder charge. Ben is faced with a defense attorney's nightmare—a keenly convincing witness who is not consciously lying, but is nonetheless dead wrong. An expert on eyewitness testimony cannot alter the jury's mind, so Ben adopts a tactic that is more controversial, but entirely consistent with the current research on human memory.

Another alternative to the current judicial dependence on eyewitnesses would be the creation of a universal DNA database. DNA evidence is simply more reliable than eyewitness testimony. Over one hundred wrongly convicted defendants—many of them on death row—have been freed by DNA test results. Many wrongdoers have been convicted by their DNA in cases that lacked any other evidence. More extensive use of this scientific identifier could lead to quicker, more efficient, less expensive trials, and could reduce convictions lost as a result of witness intimidation. My faith in DNA evidence has a long history. I used it in my first novel, *Primary Justice*, well before it had ever been introduced in a real-life courtroom.

To make the most of this powerful evidentiary weapon, however, the police need a DNA photo album, the largest possible record of DNA samples. The government already routinely takes DNA samples from convicted felons, and hospitals often retain blood and tissue samples from patients. If we made DNA recordkeeping universal, we would maximize the value of this evidentiary tool. The creation of a DNA database has been supported by Rudy Guiliani and many law enforcement officials, but has been condemned by the ACLU, which fears it could lead to Aldous Huxley's dystopian "brave new world" of genetic manipulation and discrimination. I am sensitive to civil libertarian concerns, but in truth, DNA samples don't provide much information about the subject. They simply create a means of identification, much like fingerprints, which the government has been collecting for decades. The benefits in terms of increased accuracy in our criminal justice system could be enormous.

In the last lawsuit I ever tried—the other one every lawyer usually recalls—a witness was accused of letting a bad situation get worse all the way from Easter to Mother's Day. The question was, given that Easter moves around the calendar each year, how long was that? The witness recalled it being two weeks, not long at all. I produced a calendar from the year in question and asked the court to take judicial notice of the fact that it had in fact been seven weeks, long enough to make the defendant very liable. Perhaps the witness was intentionally lying, but I really don't think so. He just forgot, or perhaps, his brain rewired reality to be more favorable to him. Fortunately, this was a civil lawsuit, so the memory blip only cost the defendant a lot of money, not his freedom. If we're going to continue to ask juries to convict criminals and incarcerate them or perhaps even condemn them to death, we need to give jurors evidence they can trust beyond a reasonable doubt.

GERRY L. SPENCE is recognized nationwide for his powerful courtroom victories, first gaining national recognition when he received a $10,500,000 verdict against Kerr-McGee in the Karen Silkwood case on behalf of her children. Later he earned such verdicts as $26,535,000 against Penthouse for Miss Wyoming and successfully defended Ed Cantrell in the famous Rock Springs, Wyoming murder case. Spence received a $52,000,000 verdict against McDonald's Corporation, the fast-food chain, on behalf of a small, bankrupt, family-owned ice cream company for McDonald's breach of an oral contract. A Utah medical malpractice verdict of over $4,000,000 established a new standard for nursing care in that state. In 1990 he won acquittal for Imelda Marcos on multiple charges after a three and one-half month trial in New York City. In 1992, he received a record-breaking $15,000,000 verdict for emotional damages incurred by his quadriplegic client because a major insurance company refused to pay the $50,000 policy more than twenty years earlier. Two weeks later he added $18,500,000 in punitive damages to the award. In 1993, Spence successfully defended Randy Weaver on murder, assault, conspiracy, and gun charges in the famous Idaho federal standoff case. He has not lost a jury trial since 1969, and he has never lost a criminal case.

He is the author of fifteen published books and the creator of *The Gerry Spence Show*, which aired in 1995-96, discussing legal and social issues that affected the lives of the people of our country. He the founder and director of the nonprofit Trial Lawyers College, where lawyers learn to try cases on behalf of the people and the College also conducts a yearly death penalty seminar for public defenders and others defending against the death penalty. He has also founded the New Judicial College for judges, an annual retreat for judges at Thunderhead Ranch. He is the founder of Lawyers and Advocates for Wyoming (L.A.W.), a nonprofit public interest law firm. Spence served as legal consultant for NBC television, covering the O.J. Simpson trial, and has hosted and appeared on *Larry King Live*, *Geraldo* and numerous other national television shows repeatedly.

Gerry Spence is the founder of the law firm of The Spence Law Firm, and practices in Jackson Hole, Wyoming with his partners.

We,
the Killers

By Gerry Spence

It is all so easy to agree when someone we do not know kills a person we also do not know. An executioner settles the wretch down in that iron chair in the gas chamber and drops the cyanide pill into the acid. Someone else watches him gasp while his eyes bulge out of their sockets and the bloody drool forms on his lips and for ten minutes he explodes in spasms and still is not dead. It is easy to read about the latest execution on the third page of the morning's paper while we peacefully, with a pure heart, drink our coffee and smear raspberry jam on our toast.

It is quite nice, this safe position we occupy at the breakfast table. We are safe from witnessing the pain of the condemned's family, the terrorized children, the old mother who sits alone with no one to hold her hand while the state murders her child. We are not required to consider the lawyers who fought for the accused until they fell, who lost and who are tortured with guilt for having failed him. A certain righteousness surrounds us like a dark, macabre halo. We have joined the mob of inquisitors from afar, the breakfast club executioners, and we are safe both from the condemned and from ourselves. But we are killers just the same—we, the avowed advocates for the death penalty.

None of the European countries embrace it. Even our neighbor, Canada, rejects it as savagely unworthy of an enlightened culture. Of course, countries like China and Iraq where human life is not valued still impose the sanction, and we blithely, blindly join them. But why? Why does a nation that claims to place great value on human life, so willingly, so hungrily, want to kill its killers? Is there something endemic about being America that urges us to kill, to embrace these executions, yes, to rally behind these endless wars?

We all know that the death penalty does not deter murder. When was the last time that a kid with a gun about to rob a 7-Eleven stopped at the door and said, "Man, I better not go in there and rob the joint. I might kill someone and get the death penalty?" When was it that a husband, bent on murdering his wife, decided to take her to a state where the death penalty has been abolished, so that if caught he won't be executed? We all know the facts: Those states without the death penalty suffer fewer murders per capita than states that kill their killers. So what is the point?

From the standpoint of the victims the yearning for revenge is understandable. But life must go on. How can a useful life stay focused on revenge? The savage need for retribution puts the killer in charge of the victims. A once peaceful mother becomes obsessed with seeing that her son's murderer is murdered. When the execution is accomplished, perhaps ten or twenty years later, what has become of the mother's life? Has it not been transformed into a life of hatred and frustration and the ugliness that always marinates the vindictive soul? Has not yet another life been wasted?

But when the mother of a murdered child comes to terms with the fact that the killing of her child's killer only mars the beauty of her child's memory, when she realizes that another killing ought not be made in the name of the child and she wishes to proceed in her own life with beneficial and creative works—perhaps in aid of other parents who have become victims as she—then a different light is cast upon these tragedies. The once horror of it has been transformed into a living monument to the child.

And how do we distinguish between a legal killing and one that is not? A legal killing is merely the consensus of a certain group of humans that the killing is right. Others in other governments have concluded it is wrong. Consensus does not make killing right. That a majority of Americans support death as a punishment does not make the killing right. It only makes it legal. That citizens depend on government to tell them what is right and what is wrong, that they permit the government to create their own conscience, is a rather bizarre abdication of individual responsibility. We are responsible for what we believe, for what we support. Conscientious objectors refused to fight in Vietnam. Millions marched against our government's invasion of Iraq. As for the death penalty, one need merely ask, if I, alone, were given the duty to deliver justice would I be unable to find a better solution than to kill the killer? Killing is so easy. It is also so mundane and uncreative. It is the act of ultimate, blunt power, the same power that was used by the killer in the first place against his victim.

The killer, although unconscious of his power, renders power over an entire nation. His venal, unspeakable act turns all who support the death penalty into accomplices. We celebrate his execution. We revert to our neo-primal murderous selves—I say neo-primal because most primitive societies know nothing of the death penalty. The American Indian only banished their miscreants. In a way we wonder if the death penalty isn't the product of a dissolute society, one that gives lip service to the sacredness of human life, but out of the same benumbed lips chants its death chants?

Who grows these killers? Mostly they come from the poor, the uneducated, the forgotten, the voiceless and the hated in our society. They are the abused children, those who have been nurtured on violence, who have suffered the twisted, distorted souls of their parents and peers and whose role models are those who believe life is not valuable, theirs or anyone else's. They are members of an underclass who have been punished from the day they were born, innocent children who are hurled from their hospital cribs into the torture chambers of filth and lawlessness and hatred where the innocent child is punished with poverty and prejudice. These are our failures and, like anyone, we do not wish to face our failures. We hide them in our closets, in our locked memories, in the revision of our histories. As a society we dump them into the garbage heap, and if any turn out to be killers we bury them in some pauper's graveyard and continue in our addicted cycle of hatred and killing that is satisfied only with further hatred and killing.

I should hope that someday we could break this sadistic cycle like an addict one day awakens to the possibility of a better life beyond his addiction. An awakening is in order. Already we have suffered our own killing too long.

KATHLEEN BEHAN is an attorney in Washington, D.C. who practices corporate and constitutional law. Ms. Behan was raised in Georgia and now lives in Alexandria, Virginia. She has represented many of the nation's leading corporations and a number of government officials in lawsuits and investigations, and also has represented numerous prisoners and men on death row pro bono. Among her numerous awards, she has been named one of the nation's top fifty women litigators by the National Law Journal and has been featured on the cover of the *American Lawyer* for her work on behalf of indigent defendants.

In Quest of
Equal Justice:
A Lawyer's Dharmic Duty

By Kathleen Behan

*"Better your own dharma, your personal duty—even
if unsuccessful, than the dharma of another done perfectly."*
—Lord Krishna to Anjuna upon fighting kinsmen in world war.

Equal Justice: it is a commodity much espoused, much invoked, often beleaguered and often revoked. It is, to be sure, just a myth, but a noble myth. It is one, beyond a shadow of doubt, in which I deeply believe.

In my many years of practicing law, I have had the good fortune to represent the best of the best, the worst of the worst, the truly innocent and the very guilty. In each of my cases, and for each of my clients, I sought to do my very best job—for them, for the legal system, and for the zealous pursuit of my duty as a lawyer. In short, I sought to provide them with equal justice under law.

It has not been easy. Just getting onto death row to see a client can be a difficult task, and sitting with a client in the moments before he is executed can be harrowing. But in a world of gray, I have found this truth to be black-and-white: a lawyer must first, last, and above all, pursue justice—including equal justice under law.

As a law student, struggling with the role I would take on in service of that myth of justice, I spoke with a professor and mentor. "There are few things," he said, "that are really black and white. I have practiced law for many years, and here is one of them. The death penalty is morally wrong. And if you fight it, you will never face regret."

Since then, I have saved some lives, and lost some others. I have felt like a surgeon, sewing one wound, while opponents open another. When I have thought my clients to be innocent, the pain has been particularly acute.

But I would like to tell you about my client Frankie. Frankie should be alive today. He was found to be guilty—escaping from work duty, he killed two women in a matter of days. He then took some chocolate, and went to sleep beneath the bushes—nearby the closest police station.

But Frankie was also deemed to be severely mentally retarded, a paranoid schizophrenic, and as a child grew up under a house. He missed the boat when his brothers and sisters escaped to foster care—he was living, like a dog, under the house.

I helped Frankie in his last appeal. His rights were definitely violated—the evidence did not support the basis for an execution—and few could challenge the deficiencies in his mental state. But the court called it a case of "harmless error."

I recall visiting Frankie on the row shortly before his death. We were locked together in a room. Seriously facially deformed, Frankie was hard to view. But he was also my client, and I was his lawyer. I tried to explain to him an execution. Frankie listened closely. In the end, I don't think he really understood. But I knew that he knew me to be his lawyer. And I hope that made a difference for Frankie that day. Frankie's case haunts me still. Every life is precious—even his. So that is why I fight for the myth of equal justice. It is what I was meant to do.

There are surely lost causes, and there are also causes that are lost. But my dharma tells me to follow the path of equal justice for all. It is a course I will never regret.

As the Principal with the 14-lawyer firm of Geragos & Geragos, **MARK GERAGOS** has represented some of the most prominent figures in the world. Geragos cemented his national reputation as a trial lawyer with back to back State and Federal Court jury trial acquittals for renowned Whitewater figure Susan MacDougal, the former business partner of former President Bill Clinton. In early 2001, Geragos completed his representation of MacDougal by securing a presidential pardon for Ms. MacDougal for a conviction she sustained prior to his representation of her.

Mark was one of the lead lawyers in a pair of groundbreaking Federal Class Action Lawsuits against New York Life Insurance and AXA Corporation for insurance policies issued in the early 20th century during the time of the Turkish genocide of over 1.5 million Armenians. These two cases have settled for over $ 37.5 million dollars in the last 12 months. Also this year, Mark was awarded the prestigious California Lawyer of the Year award in Civil Litigation for his groundbreaking work involving these lawsuits. Mark has also previously been named "Trial Lawyer of The Year" by the Los Angeles Criminal Courts Bar Association, making him one of only two lawyers ever named Lawyer of the Year in both the Criminal and Civil arenas. (Johnnie Cochran was the other). *California Law Business Magazine* named Mark "one of the 100 Most Influential Attorneys in California" three years in a row and Mark has been repeatedly voted by his peers every year as one of Los Angeles' Super Lawyers.

Geragos' client list has included former Congressman Gary Condit, former first brother Roger Clinton, Academy award-winning actress Winona Ryder, pop star Michael Jackson, hip hop star Nate Dogg, international arms dealer Sarkis Soghanalian and Scott Peterson. This year, Mark won dismissal of prostitution charges against the internationally renowned James Bond movie director Lee Tamahori. In February of this year, Mark successfully won dismissal of all felony charges, including kidnapping and torture, for his client, Hung Bao Zhong, the recognized exiled leader of the shadow government of China, who has an estimated 38 million followers worldwide.

Mark has regularly appeared as both guest and legal commentator on the *Today Show*, *Good Morning America*, *Dateline NBC*, *Larry King Live*, *On the Record with Greta Van Susteren*, *60 Minutes* and *48 Hours*.

I Know Beyond a
Reasonable Doubt That There Was an
Armenian Genocide

By Mark Geragos

Beginning in 1915, one million, five hundred thousand Armenians were slaughtered and hundreds of thousands more left for dead after being forcibly deported from their ancestral homeland to the Syrian desert by a Turkish government hellbent on its maniacal campaign to ethnically cleanse Eastern Anatolia of all Armenians. As a result of this genocidal campaign carried out by the Ottoman Turks, for more than ninety years Armenians have taken refuge in countries around the globe. The largest population of Armenians in the diaspora is right here in California, where an estimated one million Americans of Armenian descent reside. The one thing that almost all of these proud Armenian-Americans have in common is that they themselves, their parents or grandparents left their ancestral homes and eventually made their way to the United States to escape the Genocide.

Despite overwhelming and conclusive evidence to the contrary, successive Turkish governments have steadfastly denied that a genocide against the Armenians ever occurred. While some nations have succumbed to Turkey's political pressure and have balked at officially commemorating this tragedy, Turkey is alone in its untenable position that the Genocide of the Armenians never happened.

At the time the Genocide of the Armenians was being perpetrated, the plight of the Armenians received unprecedented coverage in the world press and was a known fact and cause for great concern in the international community. The United States Ambassador to Turkey, Henry Morgenthau, wrote to the Department of State warning that the Young Turk government had embarked on what he termed "race extermination" against the Armenians.[1]

Fortunately, Ambassador Morganthau was not alone in his concern about the plight of the Armenians. European missionaries working in Eastern Anatolia eyewitnessed the carnage and implored the Turkish authorities to cease its mass murder of innocent civilians. Turkey's attempt to annihilate the Armenians also received extensive press coverage in Europe and the United States. *The New York Times*, like many major newspapers across America, ran front page articles citing firsthand accounts of the atrocities. These articles recounted in graphic detail the horrors visited upon the Armenians living in the Ottoman Empire, including reports of babies being cut from the wombs of their pregnant mothers and the torture, rape and mutilation of teenage girls as their parents were forced to watch in abject horror. These harrowing tales of mass murder prompted the creation of the Near East Relief charity which, with the support of President Woodrow Wilson, raised over one hundred million dollars to rescue the impoverished Armenians from annihilation.

Nine decades later, I personally reviewed internal documents in connection with class action lawsuits that our firm filed here in California against insurance companies and banks that did business in the Ottoman Empire during 1915 to 1923. As expected, these documents closely corroborate contemporary accounts of the Armenian Genocide. In fact, during the course of reviewing these genocide era records in one of the lawsuits we stumbled across a policy that was issued to Boghos Guiragossian, a candy maker from the ancient town of Adana. As it turns out, Boghos was my grandfather's brother for

---

[1] Ambassador Morganthau did not use the term "genocide" to describe the systematic murder of the Armenians since the word was not yet in existence. It was roughly a decade after the Armenian Genocide that Raphael Lemkin, a lawyer of Polish-Jewish descent, coined the word after studying the mass murder of Armenians. Lemkin, later known as the "Father of the Genocide Convention" lobbied relentlessly for the adoption of an international treaty to outlaw genocide and make it an international crime. It was only after World War II and the Holocaust did the United Nations finally implemented the Convention on the Prevention and Punishment of the Crime of Genocide.

whom my father was named after. My great-uncle Boghos understood that the corrupt Ottoman Turkish Government could easily divest him and his family of his savings. To guard against such a calamity, Boghos, like many other middle-class Armenians living in Adana, put his faith in western-based financial institutions and maintained a valid life insurance policy for which he religiously made payments. One day Boghos' insurance policy payments stopped, as did payments on all the other policies in force for the males of Adana. In fact, in reviewing the records an ominous pattern soon emerged. The policy premiums for the various geographical regions would be paid like clockwork and then would suddenly stop at the same time in each particular geographic region. Like some deadly plague expanding outward and ravaging everything in its wake, one could almost chart the eradication of Armenian towns and villages through the insurance records we reviewed some ninety years later.

The Turks' maniacal method was usually the same in each village. They rounded up all the villagers, stole all their personal property of any value, confiscated their land and homes, slaughtered the men and marched the women and children into the desert where they would rape many of them and leave the rest to die of starvation. The story of my grandmother watching gendarmes cutting the babies out of women's wombs and shearing the newborns on their bayonets is indelibly seared in my mind. My grandmother would often tell me the stories of her harrowing escape. She was able to survive the death march as a very clever and enterprising nine-year-old girl and sought refuge in an orphanage until she would later run away and find a cousin who eventually traveled with her to Ellis Island.

Despite the world's outrage at the events of 1915, the Armenian Genocide, which has come to be referred to as the First Genocide of the 20th Century, was largely ignored in the ensuing years. The international community's failure to hold the perpetrators accountable prompted Adolf Hitler, during a briefing of his generals where he detailed his plan to embroil Europe in history's bloodiest war, to observe "after all who remembers the extermination of the Armenians?"

Turks and those they pay handsomely to deny the genocide take various positions, but all of them involve blaming the Armenian victims. They have put forth the outlandish idea that the deaths were the result of the turmoil of World War I and that the Ottoman Empire was fighting against Russia, who backed Armenian volunteer units. These Genocide deniers conveniently neglect the fact that the contemporaneous objective evidence was that they targeted hundreds of thousands of women and children, burned Armenian villages, razed their churches and looted their assets. These same genocide deniers admit that there were forced deportations but claim these deportations by themselves cannot be classified as acts of genocide sanctioned by the state. They brazenly claim that in 1915 there was only one railway that connects west-east and that the path of what it considers relocation was not a conspiracy to exterminate Armenians. They conveniently neglect the irrefutable evidence of forced marches of Armenians into the desert where those who were not slaughtered were left to die of dehydration, starvation or disease. These repulsive arguments vary only as to time and location with those advanced by Holocaust deniers who seek to rationalize the events leading to the mass murder of millions of Jews who were slaughtered during World War II.

Sadly, because the U.S. government has shamelessly succumbed to Turkish pressure and continues to oppose initiatives to officially commemorate the Armenian Genocide, Armenians have shifted their focus to the Courts, the last bastion for hope and justice, to bring light to the Armenian Genocide. Already two class action lawsuits that we have filed against companies that were doing business in Ottoman Turkey during the years leading up to the Genocide have settled for tens of millions of dollars to be paid out to the heirs of the victims as well as to charities and other community based institutions.

Whether it is the irrefutable firsthand documentation and diplomatic eyewitness reports or my grandparents recounting their chilling personal experiences of how their families, homes and churches were brutally wiped out, I know, beyond a reasonable doubt, that the Turkish denials of the Armenian Genocide are absurd and pathetic. I know beyond a reasonable doubt that when modern-day Republic of Turkey enacts penal laws criminalizing the mere mention of the Armenian Genocide that the Armenian Genocide occurred. I know beyond a reasonable doubt that when the modern-day Republic of Turkey spends millions of dollars on lobbyists to block recognition of the Genocide by the United States Congress that the Genocide occurred. I know that when the modern-day Republic of Turkey threatens to shut down American military bases located in Turkey should the Congress pass resolutions commemorating the Armenian Genocide, that the Armenian Genocide occurred. I know beyond a reasonable doubt that whenever the Armenian Genocide is callously referred to as "alleged," that despots everywhere take solace in their own genocidal aspirations and that such ignorance must still be eradicated, that the Armenian Genocide occurred. And I am certain beyond a reasonable doubt that every time those in power attempt to wipe out, ethnically cleanse, relocate, starve, bomb, eradicate or otherwise engage in some abominable act of inhumanity to man, that the Armenian Genocide occurred and genocides will continue to occur until we universally recognize and memorialize our global history and resolve to eradicate this crime against humanity. Perhaps most importantly I know that as long as people of good will band together and struggle against those who commit genocide, this global scourge will fail. As William Saroyan so eloquently observed:

> Go ahead, destroy Armenia. See if you can do it. Send them into the desert without bread or water. Burn their homes and churches. Then see if they will not laugh, sing and pray again. For when two of them meet anywhere in the world, see if they will not create a New Armenia.

DAVID EUGENE ("GENE") WILSON practices law and serves as a mediator and arbitrator in the Seattle firm of McKay Chadwell, a group of former United States Attorneys specializing in complex civil and criminal litigation. Representative clients include the United States District Court, the Washington State Attorney General, and numerous Fortune 500 companies. From 1992 to 2000, he was a United States Magistrate Judge in Seattle. Before becoming a judge, he was a federal prosecutor specializing in racketeering cases and violations of the federal export control statutes. As a prosecutor he was lead counsel in several successful racketeering prosecutions of national significance, including the prosecution of a group of neo-Nazi extremists who engaged in a pattern of racketeering activity consisting of murders, armored car robberies, arsons and counterfeiting, in an effort to overthrow the government of the United States. For nine years he was Chief of the Criminal Division of the United States Attorneys Office in Seattle. Since 2001, he has been lead defense counsel in the case of OTP v. Obrenovic, a war crimes case arising from the execution of 8000 Muslim prisoners by Bosnian Serb forces, prosecuted before the International Criminal Tribunal for the former Yugoslavia, in the Hague, The Netherlands.

He has received personal commendations from the United States Attorney General and the Director of the Federal Bureau of Investigation, and a number of awards from the United States Department of Justice. He has served frequently as a clinical instructor and moot court judge for the National Institute of Trial Advocacy, The United States Department of Justice, and the University of Washington. He served on active duty in the United States Army Judge Advocate Generals Corps, and retired from the Army Reserves as a Colonel (Military Judge). He is a Fellow in the American College of Trial Lawyers. His undergraduate and legal degrees are from the University of South Carolina and he holds a Masters in International Relations from Boston University.

The Case for
Prosecuting War Crimes and Crimes Against Humanity Before International Criminal Tribunals

By Gene Wilson

In May 2001, I was appointed lead defense counsel for Lieutenant Colonel Dragan Obrenovic, a 37-year-old Bosnian Serb Army Officer, accused of war crimes before the International Criminal Tribunal for the former Yugoslavia ("ICTY") in the Hague, The Netherlands. The ICTY was formed by the United Nations ("UN") in 1993 to conduct criminal trials of persons accused of war crimes and crimes against humanity committed during the wars of 1992-95, which accompanied the break-up of Yugoslavia. It was the first international criminal tribune to be established since the era of the Nuremberg trials conducted by the victorious Allies at the end of World War II. It is one of several temporary or "ad hoc" international tribunals established under UN auspices to try such crimes occurring in the world's hotspots at the end of the twentieth century. Those hotspots included in addition to Yugoslavia, Rwanda and Sierra Leone. In 2002, the international community (notably minus the United States, China, and Israel) created a permanent international tribunal for such purposes in the Hague, the International Criminal Court ("ICC"). For the first time in history, the world community has an international court with jurisdiction over all such crimes committed anywhere on the planet. (The United States declined to participate in the ICC or accept its jurisdiction, for the stated concerns that American citizens might not be treated fairly in an international criminal court, and because it was unwilling to cede the necessary degree of its sovereignty to the ICC .)

As an American lawyer with almost forty years experience as a prosecutor, defense counsel, military lawyer, and judge, I agreed to represent Obrenovic out of a professional curiosity about the international tribunal and the approach to the problem of war crimes which it represented. I also took the case because I found my client to be an appealing individual. An unlikely "war criminal," he was a professional soldier who had graduated at the top of the ethnically diverse Yugoslav Military Academy and had no history of displaying the kind of ethnic hatred which infected all sides during the wars. To the contrary, a number of Muslim witnesses agreed to testify that he had personally saved their lives and protected them during the bloody fighting in Bosnia. (These Muslim witnesses eventually testified in the Hague in closed sessions of the court, because of fear of retaliation by those of their own faith.)

Obrenovic is one of 161 Serb, Croat, or Muslim individuals charged in the ICTY. Approximately two-thirds of the indictees are Serbs, who are almost all members of the Orthodox Christian faith, with the remaining one-third divided between Croats (who are almost all Roman Catholics) and Muslims. The conflicts which accompanied the death of Yugoslavia had a distinctively religious cast to them, overlaid with nationalist aspirations held by all three factions, who were determined to grab land as Yugoslavia dissolved.

It is common knowledge throughout the world that the leading Serb politician during the 1992-95 fighting, Slobodan Milosevic, died in 2006 while on trial before the ICTY. Although the Serbs reaped a lion's share of the international condemnation of events surrounding the break up of Yugoslavia (and probably deservedly so), war crimes were committed by all sides and at all levels of all governments in the conflict. The leading Croat politician in 1992-95, Croatian President Franjo Tudjman, was named an unindicted co-conspirator in an indictment filed in the ICTY. He probably would have ended up in the dock himself but for his timely death from natural causes before that could occur. Similarly, when the leading Muslim politician at the time of the wars, Bosnian President Alija Izetbegovic died in 2003, the prosecutor at the ICTY announced that at the time of his death, he, too, was the subject of a war crimes investigation.

My client Obrenovic was charged with involvement in the notorious execution of approximately 8000 Muslim prisoners by Bosnian Serb Army (the "VRS") soldiers following the fall of Srebenica in July 1995. He had not personally participated in the massacres, ordered anyone killed, or been present at any of the executions. Instead, the prosecution's primary theory was that he was guilty under the principle of "command responsibility," i.e., that he "knew or should have known about crimes committed by persons under his command and failed to prevent those crimes, or failed to punish those responsible." In his case, the specifics were that he was the temporary commander of a brigade in the VRS and that a handful of men under his command had guarded some of the Muslim prisoners awaiting execution, and helped bury them after they had been shot by soldiers from other units.

As I began my assignment in the Hague, I wondered whether the international tribunal approach could succeed, and whether it would indeed be the world's solution to such continuing twenty-first century problems as Darfur, the Congo, and various locations in the Middle East and Africa. Could international criminal tribunals establish credibility as forums for dispensing justice, or would they suffer from a perception in the eyes of many that they could never provide more than "victor's justice," punishing those vanquished on the field of battle or otherwise powerless, while ignoring any crimes by the victorious and the powerful? What were the strengths and weaknesses of such tribunals, whether temporary or permanent? Were there better ways of dealing with the wounds of ethnic and/or regional conflicts, such as national courts sitting at the scenes of those conflicts, or such as the South African Truth and Reconciliation Commission?

Any opinions offered on these subjects must begin with an acknowledgement that the subject of international tribunals and the issues which they raise can be complex. Numerous existing books and learned treatises on those issues establish that experts of equally impressive qualifications and rectitude often disagree on one issue or another. But despite those disagreements among the experts on various questions, I believe that the world's experience thus far with the several options available (international tribunals, national courts, and the Truth and Reconciliation Commission) can provide a basis for evaluating each of those options for their effectiveness. And one need not be a legal scholar, a jurist, or a lawyer to understand both the possibilities and the limitations inherent in each of the options on the table, as the world faces a twenty-first century in which war crimes and crimes against humanity show no signs of abatement.

In Obrenovic's case, after two years of intensive investigation and trial preparation on my part, he agreed to plead guilty to a charge of "persecution" and testify for the prosecution. He was sentenced to seventeen years in prison, which he is serving in Norway. Had he continued to contest the charges and been found guilty of "genocide" under the principle of "command responsibility," he could have received a far more severe sentence. I have continued to represent him as he fulfills his obligations to testify under the "plea bargain" he struck. After twenty-five trips to the Hague and/or the former Yugoslavia, and more than five years of participating in proceedings before the ICTY and being forced by my assignment to consider the issues, I have answered beyond my own reasonable doubt some of my initial questions about international tribunals.

I accept that no system of justice is perfect, in part because all were created by mankind which is itself imperfect and not of one mind as to what constitutes "justice." International tribunals bring with them their own special limitations and create their own special issues. These include new systems of laws and procedures, usually cobbled together to satisfy the various constituencies, which have agreed to support the courts and be bound by their rulings. The result of this typical mixture of legal systems is predictably a hybrid system with which no one constituency feels entirely comfortable. The different national backgrounds and cultures of the judges, lawyers, and others working in the courts present both opportunities for crafting new solutions, and obstacles to developing common understandings and universal values. Being human, those participants do not automatically become new "international beings" upon assuming their duties, and some bring with them strong personal or cultural feelings about other groups of people. A majority of the actors overcome those prior attitudes and meet the high expectations of their new international roles; a minority of them do not.

A large and apparently insoluble problem for all international criminal tribunals is the absence of a meaningful enforcement apparatus. The tribunals lack any "in house" enforcement powers. There are no sheriffs, marshals, or police officers for the tribunals, who can arrest alleged culprits or enforce the courts' orders. Instead, the courts must depend upon the enforcement powers of others. If the countries where fugitives are located refuse to give them up, and if the international community is unable to force such compliance by economic or other pressures, the courts will never see those they indict. Examples of this basic problem exists in the ICTY warrants for Ratko Mladic, wartime commander of the Bosnian Serb Army, and his civilian chief Radovan Karadicz, wartime President of the Serbian portion of Bosnia. The two have remained fugitives for more than ten years, reportedly by flitting back and forth across the border between Serbia and Bosnia. They are charged with, among other things, being the architects of the atrocities at Srebenica. While the reformers in Belgrade coughed up Slobodan Milosevic to the Hague, undoubtedly in part to get him out of their own hair, substantial economic and other efforts by the Western nations to pressure local authorities to surrender Mladic and Karadicz have failed as of this writing. As the ICTY has entered the final phases of its temporary existence, its two "most wanted" indictees have only to remain fugitives a short time longer in order to avoid its clutches.

Another major problem for the tribunals is their lack of capacity to deal with large numbers of potential defendants. Given the limited resources of manpower and funding available to all of the international tribunals, they are able to prosecute only a fraction of those against whom they may have evidence. The ICTY, for instance, has issued indictments against only 161 Serbs, Croatians, and Muslims from the former Yugoslavia, whereas the number of Bosnian Serbs culpably involved in Srebenica, alone, is estimated to be several thousand. Add to those several thousands all of the Serbs, Croats, and Muslims believed to have been involved in other chargeable offenses during the period, and the inability of the ICTY to address all of the criminality within its purview is manifest. Other international tribunals face the same issues. The tribunal in Rwanda can not be expected to call to account all of those responsible for the 800,000 deaths there in 1994. And the new permanent ICC candidly bills itself on its Web site as a court of "last resort," which will act only when national courts fail to do so in a meaningful way. After four years in existence, the ICC opened its first investigation in 2006 (in a case arising out of the Congo).

What of the criticism that such tribunals provide "justice" only as defined by the victors and the powerful? Responsible critics of Nuremberg do not deny that the leading Nazi officials there deserved international condemnation and punishment. Rather, among their concerns they argue that the World War II Allies themselves could have been charged as war criminals for such things as the Soviet massacre of 10,000 Polish officers at Katyn, Poland, the British and American firebombing of Dresden, and the American firebombing of Tokyo and atomic bombing of Hiroshima and Nagasaki. The reason why the Russians, the Americans, and the British were not charged with war crimes after World War II, they contend, is solely due to the fact that they won the War. Similarly, some commentators have argued that the NATO bombings of Serbia in 1999, which resulted in collateral damage including a number of civilian deaths and the destruction of a hospital and of the Chinese embassy, could have been charged as war crimes in the ICTY, but were not for the same reason.

If international criminal tribunals are not the answer, or are only part of the answer, what role can national criminal courts play in addressing war crimes and crimes against humanity? Some countries where such crimes have occurred have begun trying alleged perpetrators in national courts, usually courts created especially for the task and often with the active support of the international community. Supporters of such courts point to the positive effects in a community of seeing perpetrators of war crimes in that same community tried and punished within the community, as opposed to their being tried in the distant Hague. This has occurred notably in various countries that formerly constituted Yugoslavia, and in Iraq, with trials against Saddam Hussein and his top Baathist colleagues. Experience points to the fact that national courts can act in the area of war crimes and crimes against humanity only when a degree of stability has returned to those nations and the courts are strong enough to stand up to perpetrators and their supporters, who may still be active players on the nations' political scenes. (The assassinations of several defense attorneys in the trials of Saddam Hussein in Baghdad provide graphic illustrations of the dangers of proceeding via national courts in an unstable area.)

Prosecutions, whether in international or national courts, are not the only possible solutions for addressing such crimes. In an entirely different approach to dealing with ethnically charged criminality, the South African government sought a solution to decades of crimes committed by both sides during the apartheid period by creating a Truth and Reconciliation Commission. The purpose of the Commission was not to punish perpetrators appearing before it, but to foster a healing of the nation's wounds by requiring them to admit their crimes in return for amnesty, in the hope that both sides could get on with the necessity of living next door to each other.

So, given the imperfections and limitations of the international criminal tribunals and the national courts to address war crimes and crimes against humanity, would a wider use of "truth and reconciliation" commissions such as those in South Africa be a better way to provide closure for the victims of those crimes? Only some of the time.

South Africa's innovative use of the Commission has drawn wide praise. But South Africa did not use the Commissions to provide blanket amnesty for all of the crimes committed by both the apartheid forces and the opposing African National Congress. Less than 20% of those applying for amnesty had their applications approved. Applicants for amnesty were required to confess "up front," and those who had committed murders and some other very serious crimes, were not given amnesty, but were dealt with in more traditional forums. (The confessions which they gave in connection with their amnesty applications could not be used against them if their applications were denied and they were criminally prosecuted instead.)

In places like Bosnia, where the crimes against ethnic groups consisted not only of notorious atrocities like Srebenica, but also of thousands of lesser (or less notorious) crimes and injustices committed in the name of ethnic cleansing or simply hatred of people "different" from the perpetrators, truth and reconciliation commissions might enjoy some success in dealing with the lesser categories of crimes. People who must go on living side by side with their victimizers may well benefit from "clearing the air" between them. It is plain, however, that South Africa's novel approach would not address situations such as Srebenica, Rwanda, and Darfur, involving the deaths of hundreds or thousands (or hundreds of thousands) of victims. The survivors of those victims cannot be expected to find closure by sitting down and talking to their relatives' executioners.

Surveying the tools available on the international scene to deal with the continuing problem of war crimes and crimes against humanity, it seems clear beyond a reasonable doubt that international tribunals must continue to play a role in the solutions, no matter what their shortcomings. The fact that they are imperfect and are limited in their effectiveness by their resources and by international political considerations does not mean that they cannot play important parts in addressing the world's worst crimes. I believe beyond a reasonable doubt that in some situations they will be the only possible solution to a problem which would be otherwise ignored. Further, I am convinced that the existence of the international tribunals has provided a strong impetus for individual nations to undertake their own prosecutions of war crimes and crimes against humanity in their national courts. Without the existence of the international tribunals, it is less likely that national prosecutions will be undertaken. The knowledge that the new ICC may assert its jurisdiction if a nation does not undertake meaningful prosecution of war crimes or crimes against humanity over which it has jurisdiction, can be a powerful incentive for the nation to act. For these reasons, because time and experience may lead to solutions to some of their present deficiencies, and because there are no foreseeable substitutes for them on the horizons, I believe that international criminal tribunals should be encouraged and supported.

ROBERT HERON BORK earned bachelor and law degrees from the University of Chicago. He became a partner in a major Chicago law firm, then taught at Yale Law School, eventually becoming the Alexander M. Bickel Professor of Public Law. He served as Solicitor General of the United States from 1973 to 1977, also serving as Acting Attorney General in 1972 and 1974. As Solicitor General, Bork argued a number of high profile cases in the Supreme Court, including the case that reestablished the death penalty. Bork served as a circuit judge on the United States Court of Appeals for the District of Columbia Circuit from 1982 to 1988. President Reagan nominated him for the Supreme Court in 1987 but he was not confirmed by the Senate.

Mr. Bork has written several books, including *The Antitrust Paradox: A Policy at War With Itself*; *The Tempting of America: The Political Seduction of the Law*; and *Slouching Towards Gomorrah: Modern Liberalism and American Decline*. He has written for a number of publications, including in recent years, *The Wall Street Journal*, *National Review*, *The New Criterion*, *First Things*, and *Commentary*.

Mr. Bork is currently Distinguished Fellow at the Hudson Institute.

Death Penalty

By Robert H. Bork

The debate about the death penalty is acrimonious and apparently endless. It need not be. When the arguments advanced against the punishment are sorted out, there remains a compelling case for retaining capital punishment, and indeed for increasing its use.

The constitutional objection to the punishment is empty and worth mentioning only because some opponents and a few judges resort to the argument that the penalty is, or has become, a violation of the Eighth Amendment's prohibition of "cruel and unusual punishments." This argument can hardly be taken seriously. The Constitution several times recognizes that capital punishment is available to governments that care to use it. The sanction is addressed three times in the Fifth Amendment's requirement of a presentment or indictment by a grand jury in capital cases, its prohibition of double jeopardy of life, and its requirement that there be due process of law in deprivation of life. The Fourteenth Amendment, adopted just over three-quarters of a century later, also provides that no state shall deprive any person of life without due process of law. It is impossible that the framers and ratifiers intended to prohibit as cruel and unusual a punishment while simultaneously specifying the procedural safeguards for its infliction. It is similarly impossible to suppose that they thought the procedures of their times inadequate as due process while specifying that due process must be accorded the accused.

A typical response by those who make the constitutional argument is that our moral standards have evolved so that what once was tolerable is no longer so. (I pass by the peculiar notion that the meaning of words in the Constitution can "evolve." That would make the Constitution meaningless because subject to continual revision by judges.) The real difficulty with the argument is that "our" morality has not evolved in the way suggested. The American public continues to support the death penalty. The "we've evolved" argument means no more than that some judges and some "elites" do not like the penalty. That is not enough. The illogic of this position was illustrated in a speech by Justice William J. Brennan, Jr., in which he announced he would vote against capital punishment in every case. He conceded that the Constitution allowed that penalty and that a majority of Americans favored it. Having neither constitutional grounds nor a democratic mandate for his position, the Justice could rely only upon his personal sympathies. That appears to be the case with many of those who make constitutional attacks upon capital punishment.

The argument about capital punishment is best removed from the constitutional level to the prudential. Here those who favor the death penalty are on solid ground. The first—and I think the dispositive—consideration is deterrence. Opponents of capital punishment often assert that there is no deterrent effect but have no grounds for making that counter-intuitive statement. There is incontrovertibly some deterrent effect in capital punishment. If there is not, it would follow that no punishment deters crime. If that were true, it would be the only instance known in which raising the cost of an activity did not reduce its amount.

An obvious but usually overlooked instance of deterrence is that an executed murderer will not murder again. This is not an insignificant benefit. Some killers who were given life sentences have killed prison staff and other prisoners. If there is no threat of capital punishment, such men are free to continue killing in the prison. The only way to stop them would be solitary confinement for life, constant heavy sedation, or some other draconian tactic. Some murderers have escaped and killed again. In a case in which I was involved some years ago, a man was sentenced to a term of imprisonment for two separate murders. He escaped and within two days kidnapped and raped a 16-year-old girl and robbed and murdered a 16-year-old boy. Similar episodes of murders within prisons and by those who have escaped are not infrequent and would themselves justify execution after the first murder without waiting for more.

Those who deny deterrence typically overlook murders of the type just mentioned and argue that capital punishment has no deterrent impact upon potential killers in the population at large. There has been much disagreement on this question, some investigators finding no deterrence, some arriving at quite high numbers, one study claiming fifty killings avoided with each execution. I will rely on the more modest estimate of Professor Gary S. Becker, a Nobel laureate in Economic Sciences. He writes, "I support the use of capital punishment for persons convicted of murder because, and only because, I believe it deters murders." He assumes that one execution deters three murders, though he notes that is a much lower number than some estimates of the deterrent effect. He believes, as do I, that "The deterrent effect of capital punishment would be greater if the delays on its implementation were much shortened, and if this punishment was more certain to be used in the appropriate cases. But capital punishment has an important deterrent effect even with the way the present system actually operates."[1]

Consider what this means. It is commonly objected that the state should not kill. But on this topic, the state cannot avoid killing. It is inevitable. By failing to execute one murderer, the state condemns to death some number—call it three—of presumably innocent people. It is surpassing strange that the execution of a convicted killer provokes protests while the people who will die because there is no execution evoke no sympathy. That probably has to do with the fact that the only visible living person is the murderer. He wants desperately to live and he looks much like other men; evil is not apparent in his face. Meanwhile, the victim who died terrified and in agony is little more to most people than an abstraction. Even more abstract are

[1] *Hoover Digest* (2006), No. 2, Spring, p. 50.

those now unknown persons who will die similarly in terror and agony because an execution did not take place. (In emphasizing the horror of what the victims suffer I am not seeking a rhetorical advantage. The typical case in which the death penalty is given involves one or more murders of almost incredible savagery.)

Professor Becker relies solely upon deterrence because he thinks "revenge should not be a basis for public policy." Whether or not revenge is an appropriate basis for the death penalty, there is reason to support it in addition to deterrence. One is the reinforcement of important social values, the restoration of a moral order that has been breached. Capital punishment may be authorized because society views that crime as especially serious. It is also true, however, that the use of capital punishment has an effect on society's view of the crime. James Fitzjames Stephen said that we do not hang murderers because murder is wrong; we think murder is wrong because we hang men for it. That is at best a half-truth, but an important half-truth. The failure to execute Richard Speck, who murdered eight student nurses execution-style, surely minimizes the importance and the evil of what he did.

In any case, I am not at all sure that revenge is not an appropriate basis for capital punishment. The desire for revenge is a very natural human emotion and it should be satisfied. Since we are dealing with the attempted absolute disqualification of revenge as a justification for the death penalty, it is fair to test it with extreme examples. Suppose, if you will, that the American and British armies at the end of World War II had captured Adolf Hitler and, as they did, his top lieutenants. What could justify their execution or even imprisonment? Deterrence is out of the question. Would-be world conquerors are not to be put off by the fear of capital punishment. There may be something to the idea that social values need to be reinforced, particularly in Germany at the end of the Nazi regime. That might not play a major role for the evil of aggressive war and genocide are generally recognized. Defeat in the war itself may have sufficiently reemphasized the evil that had taken place. But I think the simple desire for revenge would have been an adequate reason for putting Hitler to death, as it was for some other top Nazis.

I once argued for capital punishment in a case with the following facts. A man told his friends that he wanted to have sex with a young girl, any young girl. He drove his pickup truck to a public swimming pool, dragged a pre-teen girl from the pool, threw her into the back of his truck and drove through town as her screams for help went unheeded. He took her to the river, raped her, then drowned her, went back to buy beer and discuss his adventure with his friends. In the face of the facts, and in the face of the savagery of the crime, it seems lifelessly academic to begin sorting out deterrence and moral reinforcement as justifications for putting that man to death. The first emotion many people feel when they learn of so heinous a crime is a desire for revenge, and I do not see why it should not be satisfied as much for that killer as for the hypothetical capture of Hitler and the actual execution of his top lieutenants.

I cannot escape the feeling that much of the desire to do away with the death penalty is related to a drift in European and American culture toward an unwillingness to make hard judgments about good and evil, a trend, if you will, toward moral relativism. That is obviously not true of every individual who opposes capital punishment, but it may be true generally of the elite segments of our culture. Typically, the elites dislike capital punishment, while the rest of us favor it. I think the rest of us have it right.

WHAT I BELIEVE

David Baldacci

Davis Boies

Stephen L. Braga

Elizabeth Espin Stern

Lanny Breuer

Carole Lieberman

Richard North Patterson

"Human progress is neither automatic nor inevitable...
Every step toward the goal of justice requires sacrifice,
suffering, and struggle; the tireless exertions
and passionate concern of dedicated individuals."
—Martin Luther King, Jr.

Internationally-acclaimed best-selling author DAVID BALDACCI has penned 13 novels: *Absolute Power*, *Total Control*, *The Winner*, *The Simple Truth*, *Saving Faith*, *Wish You Well*, *Last Man Standing*, *The Christmas Train*, *Split Second*, *Hour Game*, *The Camel Club* and his latest new venture into novels for young readers: *Freddy and the French Fries: Fries Alive!* and *The Mystery of Silas Finklebean*. Mr. Baldacci's next adult novel, *The Collectors*, will be released on October 17, 2006. He has also written numerous screenplays, short stories, essays, and op-ed pieces for publications around the globe.

Mr. Baldacci has made appearances on all the major network news channels and other media outlets and has been interviewed by major magazines and newspapers both in the United States and overseas.

Born in Virginia where he continues to reside, Mr. Baldacci attended Virginia Commonwealth University and the University of Virginia School of Law. Mr. Baldacci participates in numerous charities and sits on several boards including the Virginia Foundation for the Humanities and Virginia Commonwealth University. He and his wife Michelle are co-founders of the Wish You Well Foundation, dedicated to eradicating illiteracy in the United States. Mr. Baldacci's works have been translated into 41 languages and sold in more than 85 countries, with over 50 million copies in print worldwide.

"Our Kingdom for a Book"

By David Baldacci

I am certain, beyond a reasonable doubt, that unless illiteracy is seriously addressed in this country that America, sooner rather than later, will no longer exist in its current state. Nearly every statistic you examine is glaring in its revelation about what is to come. According to the latest literacy survey nearly 100 million adults, half the adult population in this country, read at the two lowest levels of literacy. Ten, twenty, thirty percent of entire state populations are illiterate. In some states, a quarter of the entire population doesn't even *own* a single book.

Each year Americans pay nearly 80 billion extra dollars because of health care costs related to illiteracy. That's enough money to fund every new school this country needs, hire every teacher required to teach at those schools, and pay for countless worthy programs, with enough left over to give billions back to the Treasury. It really all starts with being able to read. If you can't, the results are devastating. Sixty percent of inmates, ninety percent of juvenile offenders and half the people on welfare are illiterate.

If those people could read and had followed different life paths, the pay-off to this country would be in the trillions, enough to satisfy the national debt. Yet there is no comprehensive plan or initiative to tackle this problem. There are many heartfelt efforts going on, both public and private, but nothing that can meet the challenge head-on with the resources it will take to eradicate illiteracy in the lifetime of anyone reading these words.

But if the crime, poverty and wasted life factors fail to stir you, there are other reasons to board the literacy bandwagon.

We are a nation founded not on action really, but on words. Our greatest rights as Americans are grounded in three basic concepts of liberty: the freedom of speech, the freedom of the press and the exercise of religious freedom. Take away one and we are no longer a democracy. Take away two and we are a dictatorship. More to the point, these rights presuppose a citizenry that is well-read, thoughtful and reflective.

Many may look at the history of this country and believe that when it was founded we were a nation of non-readers, ill-educated, uninformed. Nothing could be further from the truth. The intellectual abilities and educational backgrounds of leaders then would easily match those of our leaders today. For the everyday citizen books were not as plentiful then as they are now, but at least people read the ones they had, read and understood them fully, and hungered to find more to devour. They knew the issues of the day, everyone from the humble farmer to his equally humble cousin in the city. During the time of Lincoln, a hundred thousand people from all walks of life would travel miles to hear political speeches that stretched on for hours. The listeners knew the platforms and politics of the speakers intimately because they read newspapers and printed copies of the speeches as though they were manna from Heaven. They also vigorously debated those same issues amongst themselves. Today, to get a hundred thousand people to do anything together you either need people driving dangerously fast on an oval track or have enormously large men trying to tackle their equally sturdy brethren because they happen to be carrying an oddly-shaped ball.

Again, so what, people might say.

Well, the "so what" has already come into play, I would say back.

Perhaps now more than ever we need to be a country of thinkers. Yet it's also true that we think in language, so how deep can our thoughts be if our language is not up to the task? It's gotten so that the very issues people don't want to think about are the ones that will define their lives and the lives of their progeny for generations to come. Lives today are so hectic, the argument goes, that people need downtime, they can't be expected to wade into issues of substance. They need to coast, take a breath, live life light. Okay, but there is, of course, a huge price to be paid for what amounts to a dereliction of duty.

Ignorance and intolerance are history's evil twin superstars. For obvious reasons, you never see one without the other. They are at the epicenter of every manmade catastrophe in history. They love people who blindly follow the vision of others: from Adolf Hitler to folks who fly planes into buildings. The basic argument is easy to follow: If you don't read and you don't think things through for yourself, where do you get your ideas and opinions from? You get them, prepackaged with a bright shiny bow on top, from other people. And it seems that today more than ever people are opting for this all-in-one service as the source of their fundamental ideas. Why wade into deep water when you can be spoon-fed a message and be onto something else in five minutes? The notion is tempting in theory and always fatal in practice.

The greatest foe of ignorance and thus intolerance is knowledge. The greatest tool we have in acquiring knowledge is reading. There's the rub. We don't. We read emails of course, and the sports page and magazines that tell us which star wears what and which lipstick and handbag are perfect for a first date. But we don't read.

Much like global warming sends out early warning signals such as beetle-infested forests where those beetles have never been before, green grass where trillions of tons of ice used to lay, and bird-hatching cycles that are completely out of kilter, the impact of a proliferation of nonreaders also sends out its cues. Libraries that have, in effect, become computer centers where people seek Internet access but bypass all the books on the shelves. We have legions of college graduates who can't write a cohesive sentence, prompting companies to either spend billions to teach them to do so or else dumb down the jobs to make up for the lack of reading and comprehension ability.

Movies, TV, newspapers, magazines and even books have been stripped down to basic language and ideas that won't tax us too much. On the personal side, we hide behind anonymity on the Internet, creating elaborate fictions of ourselves on personal space platforms. Not only do these venues prevent us from interacting face-to-face with others and thus enhancing our verbal and body cue skills, it's a boon for Web-based predators.

Other people will say this talk is, at the very least, overly dramatic, and will point to various "facts" to back it up. We are the freest, most open and tolerant society in the world, they will say. Look at our policies on race, gay rights, crime and punishment. And on top of that we're a melting pot, the most successful melting pot in history, in fact. Well, our policies on race and gay rights are decades behind other nations, and we're the only major civilized country that still puts prisoners to death. And as far as the melting pot goes, it is often more of a meltdown than melting pot. Simply because we have more diversity in the bodies walking the streets here doesn't mean that we are more *diverse* in our thinking. Never mistake people's apathy to change for agreement *with* that change. Many folks do not contest diversity until it adversely affects them personally. Then you may suddenly see a lot less embracing of people who look and talk differently. See the current immigration debate for details as to this phenomenon.

People say they are proud to be an American. I am too, incredibly proud. Yet if every credible statistic in the various fields is to be believed, most Americans have little familiarity about their country's origins or history. They can't name a single Founding Father, can't place the Revolutionary War within even the correct century, and often confuse it with the Industrial Revolution, of which they also know nothing. The Declaration of Independence, the Constitution, the Bill of Rights? Uh, they'll have to get back to you. They can tell you little if anything about the Civil War, the bloodiest confrontation in our nation's history, including the reasons why it was fought. Indeed, if people are going to remember anything, you'd think it would be the unforgettable aspects of battle and yet World War I conjures nothing to mind for them and World War II little more, except for those who lived it and fought it. Mention Vietnam and they are more apt to recite scenes from movies about the war than the war itself, and have no clue as to the issues and politics involved. Rosa who? Martin Luther King what? Theodore Roosevelt? Sounds a little familiar. Mark Twain, nope, nothing, must be an author.

So what exactly are Americans proud of?

They can tell you the batting, scoring and rushing averages of every player on their home teams, enlighten you as to the personal histories of every "American Idol" finalist, and gush about the best places on the Internet to illegally download songs or movies, and every detail of the next generation blue tooth technology that will allow them to talk to twelve different people at once while they should instead be paying attention to driving their car, or while writing emails without actually using words, misspelling the ones they inadvertently do use.

Nearly three-quarters of Americans haven't cracked a book since they left school and appear unduly proud of that fact, as though an exercise—reading and learning—that enabled this country to come into existence is somehow shameful and worthy of nothing except disdain.

The result is we can't learn from the mistakes of history, because we don't know any of our collective past. We certainly know nothing about any other country, which was one reason that after we invaded Iraq the media helpfully provided us with a cheat sheet on that particular nation. (You've got your Sunnis, Shiites and Kurds, who don't seem to get along too well for reasons too complex to go into here, not that you'd care anyway. The country we're going to blow off the map has a desert climate, some oil, and a really evil man running it, and that's about all you need to know, so it's bombs away.)

The pace of our lives today dictates that we think only for the short-term and that is how all information is fed to us. When's the last time you listened to anything that dealt with a subject for longer than sixty seconds? Our attention span has been dumbed-down to match the ADD pace of the information technology universe. It doesn't matter anymore which came first: the individual's need for fast information or the world's need that the individual get it fast, that's just the way it is now. The result is we do not think about anything for longer than a few minutes before racing on to the next thing. Society has become a never-ending kindergarten, yet the consequences are not cute or innocuous.

And all this because we don't read? Well, yes. We don't read, we don't think, we don't reflect, we don't debate, we don't discuss, we don't challenge. In sum, we don't use the greatest tool we will ever have: A powerful, well-informed mind that contemplates important matters for longer than our allotted few minutes. The path we are taking now equals one thing and one thing only: We simply don't care, whether we wish that to be true or not.

So the state of the country today is that we are less literate, less well-informed, and our priorities are never based on long-term goals or policies because we are no longer wired to do that. We have never been more divided as a people, never more apathetic about issues that really matter, and never more manipulated by small pockets of people who have come up with pithy lines or rallying cries they believe will entice you, *not* to think for yourselves, but accept what they tell you without debate or hesitation.

Can anyone say ignorance and intolerance?

Eradicate illiteracy. Open the books. Read with and to our children. Start thinking for ourselves. Or I am certain, beyond a reasonable doubt, that the greatest nation on earth, conceived in liberty by and for the people, is doomed.

DAVID BOIES is Chairman of the law firm Boies, Schiller and Flexner LLP. The firm has offices in New York, Washington D.C., California, Florida, Nevada, New Hampshire and New Jersey. Mr. Boies served as Chief Counsel and Staff Director of the United States Senate Antitrust Subcommittee in 1978 and Chief Counsel and Staff Director of the United States Senate Judiciary Committee in 1979. In 1991-1993 Mr. Boies was counsel to the Federal Deposit Insurance Corporation in its litigation to recover losses for failed savings and loan associations, and in 1998-2000 Mr. Boies served as Special Trial Counsel for the United States Department of Justice in its antitrust suit against Microsoft. Mr. Boies also served as the lead counsel for former Vice-President Al Gore in connection with litigation relating to the 2000 election Florida vote count.

Mr. Boies is the author of numerous publications including *Courting Justice*, published by Miramax in 2004 and *Public Control of Business*, published by Little Brown in 1977. Mr. Boies has taught courses at New York University Law School and Cardozo Law School. Mr. Boies is the recipient of an LL.D. from the University of Redlands, the Milton Gould Award for Outstanding Oral Advocacy, the Lifetime Achievement Award from the LD Access Foundation, the Outstanding Learning Disabled Achievers Award from the Lab School of Washington, and the William Brennan Award from the University of Virginia. When Mr. Boies received the Milton Gould Award in 1996 the citation said in part, "No lawyer in America has tried and argued on appeal as many landmark cases in as many different areas as Mr. Boies."

Reasonable Doubt

By David Boies

A house divided against itself cannot stand. In Lincoln's time America was divided by slavery. Today America is increasingly divided by wealth and its consequences. America has, of course, always had its rich and its poor as book-ends to its vaunted middle class. But we have taken comfort and pride in two principles. Anyone, we have believed, could through hard work and talent become successful. And each generation, we have believed, would be better off than the last, the middle class would continue to expand, and the gap between rich and poor would diminish.

For most of our history as a nation these principles were both myth and, to a large extent, reality. Today, however, the gap between rich and poor is greater than it was a quarter century ago—and it is getting greater. In the name of global competitiveness many workers' wages and benefits have lagged behind inflation, even as the incomes of their bosses have increased a thousand percent or more. The pets of the wealthiest fifth of our nation enjoy better food, and better medical care, than the children of the poorest fifth among us. There is no question that we must compete globally, but it strains the cohesiveness of our society when the burden of doing so is borne only by those already at a disadvantage. And it is not necessary to argue that pets should be treated less well to believe that children should be treated better.

Even more troubling, we are developing a durable under-class from which it is harder and hard to escape; and millions of middle-class families are finding it more and more difficult to give their children the opportunity to compete successfully with the sons and daughters of their more well-to-do neighbors, or to maintain, let alone improve, their parents' standard of living.

Attending schools with limited budgets, only the exceptional achieve the education needed for success. The gap in conventional test scores between students in private schools or public schools in wealthy districts and students in poorer public schools is wide and widening. The gap in computer literacy is even more striking; two-thirds of all public high school students lack the computer skills necessary to navigate the digital divide. The escalating costs of a college or professional education, combined with the reduced availability of student loans and grants, act as a further brake on the American Dream. It is not surprising that the single best predictor of the likelihood of a child's graduation from a four-year college is the economic circumstances of the child's parents.

It is beyond any reasonable doubt that this waste of our nation's human capital is an even greater threat to our long-term global competitiveness than living wages for our workers. It is beyond any doubt at all that it is also wrong—and inconsistent with the social compact upon which our entrepreneurial culture is based. We tolerate, and even celebrate, people who strike it rich because we know that their success fuels our economy to the benefit of all of us—and because we believe that we, or at least our children, have a chance to do the same. But if the disparity between rich and poor becomes too great, or if it becomes self-perpetuating, that tolerance is frayed and ultimately broken. Americans are willing to make the most of the hands they are dealt because they believe that their children will get a new deal.

We can, and must, do better. The same technology that threatens to divide us further if only the privileged are educated to take full advantage of it can, if it is shared, become a great equalizer. If we can spend hundreds of billions of dollars trying to reform a dysfunctional nation of 25 million people half a world away, we can increase our spending by that amount and more at home to ensure that all of our 75 million children have the opportunity for a decent education, and the more equal opportunity that such an education promises. Beyond any reasonable doubt it is the sensible thing to do. Beyond any doubt at all it is the right thing to do for our children, and for the society that their grandchildren will inherit.

STEPHEN L. BRAGA is a 1981 graduate of the Georgetown University Law Center, where he was a member of the *Law Journal*. After graduation, Mr. Braga clerked for one year for The Honorable Thomas A. Flannery of the United States District Court for the District of Columbia. He then joined the D.C. litigation boutique Miller, Cassidy, Larroca & Lewin, where he practiced law until 2001 when Miller Cassidy merged into Baker Botts LLP. Mr. Braga is presently a partner in the Litigation Department of Baker Botts' Washington office.

Over the years, Mr. Braga's practice has focused on white-collar criminal defense and complex civil litigation. In white-collar defense matters, he has represented former White House Chief of Staff Michael Deaver, former Congressman George Hansen, former California Coastal Commissioner Mark Nathanson, and he is presently representing Public Relations Executive Michael Scanlon in the Jack Abramoff lobbying scandal. In complex civil matters, Mr. Braga is best known for his successful trial defense of ABC News Anchor Chris Wallace in a defamation action arising from an undercover investigation reported by ABC's *Primetime Live* news show.

Mr. Braga also teaches law as an adjunct professor at the Georgetown University Law Center, and since 1995 has devoted a significant portion of his practice to the pro bono representation of Martin Tankleff in a long-running and notorious New York state murder case recently profiled by *48 Hours*, *The New York Times* and *People* magazine.

The views expressed in this essay are Mr. Braga's personal views and do not reflect the views of either Baker Botts LLP or the Georgetown University Law Center.

Bye-Bye Blu

By Stephen L. Braga

Reasonable doubt is traditionally defined as "the kind of doubt that would cause a reasonable person, after careful thought and reflection, to hesitate to act in the graver or more important matters in life." The hallmark of "reasonable doubt"—as the name implies—is that it is a doubt *"based on reason."* It is not an imaginary doubt, nor a doubt based on speculation or guesswork. It is a rational doubt based on the evidence being considered.

One of the most high-profile topics of our time is global warming. The evidence is continually mounting that it is a real—and deadly—phenomenon. Al Gore's documentary *An Inconvenient Truth* may be a blockbuster report of that evidence, but it is hardly the only one. Gore's indisputable "before" and "after" photographs of massive glaciers melting around the world present as compelling an evidentiary picture as any courtroom has ever seen, especially when combined with his mirror-image graphs of increasing carbon dioxide levels and increasing temperatures. But that is not all the "evidence" that any rational jury would have to confront on this issue. Over the course of the past four months alone, the news media has also reported the following:

In May, Bill McKibben, a scholar-in-residence at Middlebury College and the author of a book about global warming titled *The End Of Nature*, wrote that:

> Newly emerging science . . . shows
> that we have underestimated the scale and
> urgency of the crisis. Everything frozen on
> earth is melting fast, for instance, threatening
> to produce an inhospitable planet *in the decades
> ahead* and an unbearable one in the lifetime of
> those being born. Political rhetoric needs to
> reflect the stark fact that this is an emergency.[1]

Such opinion testimony by an expert in the field is undoubtedly relevant and material evidence to the case for global warming.

In June, MSNBC posted an online article reporting that the National Research Council had advised Congress "that Earth is the hottest it has been in at least 400 years." This "panel of top climate scientists told lawmakers that the Earth is running a fever and that 'human activities are responsible for much of the recent warming.'" As the Research Council indicated, "[m]any scientists tie warming temperatures to rising emissions of certain gases like carbon dioxide," which has "spike[d] as fossil fuels are burned by cars and factories, leading to concerns that it and other gases are exacerbating the greenhouse effect."

Over the Independence Day holiday, the *Washington Post* printed a front-page article reporting that:

> The escalating level of carbon dioxide
> in the atmosphere is making the world's
> oceans more acidic, government and independent scientists say. They warn that, *by the
> end of the century*, the trend could decimate
> coral reefs and creatures that underpin the
> sea's food web. . . .[T]hey describe it as one of
> the most pressing environmental threats facing earth.[2]

[1]McKibben, "Welcome To The Climate Crisis," P. A25, *Washington Post* (May 27, 2006) (emphasis added).
[2]"Growing Acidity Of Oceans May Kill Corals," *Washington Post*, A1(July 5, 2006)(emphasis added).

The solid research data by top climatologists, including government and independent scientists, referenced in this paragraph and the preceding one is classic expert empirical evidence for the jury's consideration.

In July as well, Inupiat Eskimos from the Arctic Circle's North Slope Borough were interviewed on National Public Radio complaining about the devastating effects that warming temperatures are having on their way of life and the whale hunting that supports it. There is scientific consensus that the Inupiats' Arctic is dissipating at an alarming rate; arctic sea ice is now 40 percent thinner than it was in the 1970s. It is no wonder, therefore, that these poor Eskimos can quite literally see their way of life melting away beneath them. They are front-line observers of the effects of global warming. Such anecdotal testimony by these Eskimos, from one of the areas most directly affected by global warming to date, puts a human face to the scientific evidence that no dispassionate jury could ignore.

Finally, in early August, the *Washington Post* again reported on current studies showing dire consequences from global warming.

> Two new scientific studies measuring Greenland's rapidly melting ice sheet and the pace of Arctic snowfall suggest that the sea level may be rising faster than researchers previously assumed.[3]

How much more evidence is required? Following on the heels of the compelling case for global warming made in Gore's movie, the monthly build-up of these additional reports from May through August (and continuing) should clinch the conclusion—beyond a reasonable doubt—that global warming is quite real indeed.

The reasonable doubt standard does not require the government to prove its case to a mathematical or scientific certainty. Yet on this issue, if the peer-reviewed scientific articles referenced in Gore's movie are accurate, there may well be such scientific certainty. Of

---

[3] "Greenland's Melting Ice Sheet May Speed Rise in Sea Level," *Washington Post*, p. A3 (August 11, 2006).

course, there are some global warming doubters out there—like hurricane expert Bill Gray, who relies on natural cycles to explain the current warming trend—but their doubts tend to be tied to global generalities rather than scientific specifics. More often, those taking a position against action to remedy global warming do so on economic grounds. For example, the current Administration has maintained that not enough is known about the global warming threat to warrant new emission controls that it says would have cost 5 million Americans their jobs. Of course, everyone worldwide will lose their jobs if we kill the planet.

With regard to the "cost" of fixing this problem, in May of this year, Professor Cass Sunstein of the University of Chicago Law School authored an op-ed piece in the *Washington Post* noting that the costs of the war in Iraq would dwarf the purportedly prohibitive costs associated with the United States' joining the Kyoto global warming treaty. In that piece, Professor Sunstein wondered why we could not pay for the latter global need if we could pay for the former more limited need.[4] Polar bears drowning because of melting ice floes at the North Pole may not be as troubling to some as the prospect of fighting Al Qaeda. But what will have been gained by freeing Iraqis from terror in the Middle East, if they merely become free to participate in the death of the planet with the rest of us? The best rewards of freedom are in the long run. Will there be a long run to come for Planet Earth?

This is not someone else's problem to fix, as we so "conveniently" like to conclude with many wide-ranging issues. It is all of our problem. We can think about it globally, but we need to act locally. As Professor McKibben puts it, even government-mandated "technological change alone cannot achieve the 70 percent reductions in fossil fuel use needed to stabilize climate. We'll also need real shifts in attitude, behavior and habit. These changes are possible (the average Western European uses half as much energy as the average American while leading a quality life), but they will take real political leadership on issues ranging from mass transit to sprawl to the size of cars." McKibben concludes that "[p]recisely because we've wasted the past

[4] *Washington Post*, P. A25 (May 10, 2006).

two decades, we need real, not token, action now." The "moral imperative" for action now, which the proselytizing Al Gore also makes the closing argument for so eloquently in his movie, simply cannot be ignored.

I have become convinced beyond a reasonable doubt that we must begin to take action now to save our planet from the consequences of our environmental negligence. Global warming is real, and those who do not accept the demonstrable scientific and anecdotal proof of its existence would condemn the planet to a meltdown with speculative and fanciful doubts about its reality that would never pass muster in a court of law. There is no "reasonable" doubt to the contrary.

On the macro level, I believe that the United States absolutely must sign onto the Kyoto treaty and accept its protocols for the reduction of CO2 emissions. We are one of only two developed nations in the world who have not signed this treaty, which largely guts its effectiveness since we are by far the world's largest producer of these problematic greenhouse gases. It is time for our country to become more of a leader in helping to solve the problem of global warming rather than in creating it. Such a sea change in our national attitude toward global warming would be up to the politicians to implement, of course, but it can—and must—be done. It is embarrassing to me that other lesser developed countries, like Brazil for example, are so much ahead of the United States in trying to contribute to the solution to such a potentially catastrophic problem. We need to make our politicians feel the "heat" until they bring the mighty resources of the United States to bear on this problem.

On the micro level, I also believe beyond a reasonable doubt that there are individual actions that all of us can take to help this problem incrementally. (See generally www.climatecrisis.org.) Like many "hotshot" litigators, I drive a sports car. It is a beautiful deep blue Porsche 911 Carrera, with the license plate "GU BLU" representing my law school alma mater (Georgetown University) and its team color (blue). I love to drive this car. However, I have become convinced beyond a reasonable doubt that I need to act locally to help impact the problem of warming globally. So it's Bye Bye Blu! I am going to trade in the Porsche and find a more environmentally friendly car to commute in each day. A car that uses hybrid technology or operates on ethanol is the way to go for me.

I do not want the world I leave behind for my children and grandchildren to be devastated by rising sea levels and ravaging storms, like Katrina. We need to take better, and proactive, stewardship of our planet for them right now. This is what I believe beyond a reasonable doubt, and I truly hope—for all of our sakes—that you will agree.

ELIZABETH ESPIN STERN, a partner with Baker & McKenzie, LLP, has established one of the leading business immigration practices in the country, representing major commercial entities in a variety of industry sectors, including financial services, information technology and telecommunications, multimedia and manufacturing. Ms. Stern's practice offers the full breadth of business immigration solutions, focusing on issues that are unique to dynamic commercial entities with a global work force.

Ms. Stern has testified before Congress on U.S. immigration reforms affecting the global business community. She works closely with the federal agencies and the Members and Committees of Congress involved in the development of immigration laws. Similarly, Ms. Stern has a network of contacts with the international embassies and immigration and labor ministries that govern the immigration laws of the European Union, the Pacific Rim, Latin America, Canada, Russia and Eastern Europe.

The daughter of an Ecuadorian diplomat, Ms. Stern is fluent in Spanish. She was ranked as one of Washington's top 30 lawyers by *Washingtonian* magazine.

Migration Is,
As It Always Has Been, Integral to America's Societal and Economic Evolution

By Elizabeth Espin Stern

Migration of people—students, workers, executives, and investors—is pivotal to the development of the economy and culture of America. Migration addresses gaps in the labor market, diversification of skills, and the expansion of opportunities at all levels of society. In the business arena, migration is a key tool for the launch of new and expansion of current business operations. At a more fundamental level, our society is based on the achievements of people from all regions of the world—despite our isolationist tendencies, we are unquestionably a mixture of cultures.

Beyond a doubt, national policies need to respond to the realities of our globalized society. Yet there is an inherent tension between a nation's need to control and to facilitate migration, one made more potent by an incalculable fear about new, foreign cultures overtaking and displacing those of us who have been here longer. In the United States, that tension has been exacerbated since September 11, 2001. The realization that systems in place to date may not be effective in securing our borders—a lack of control that seems to allow underground access to our country—has led to severe hesitation in some political circles about any type of migration.

The challenge lies in transcending the tension between these two drivers—control and facilitation of migration. We need to recognize the paradox that security and service are in fact interdependent elements of the same organism; neither can function unless the other is working properly. Absent a system that is facilitative, millions of foreign nationals will continue to enter underground, without any type of screening. Similarly, if the border admissions system is not administered effectively, one cannot expect our highly-burdened administrative agencies to ferret out security threats.

As we contemplate comprehensive immigration reform, at a minimum, the synergistic relationship between migration and economic growth must be taken into account. Free trade agreements and ongoing attempts by the United States to achieve an increasingly free flow of capital, goods and services are laudable, but the impediments to the movement of people stifle the benefits of the former. Recognition of the impact of migration liberalization is plainly overdue.

In this regard, recent global migration studies have projected that even a modest liberalization of the temporary movement of persons for provision of services under Mode 4 of the General Agreement of Trade in Services (GATS) would produce global welfare gains of between USD 150 billion and USD 200 billion per year, on an analysis of total economic impact.[1] These statistics, which exceed expected gains from liberalization of trade in goods, do not address the day-to-day contributions made by foreign students, visitors, and workers who contribute billions of dollars each year to countries of destination. Nor do they take into account the prototypical need of business today—to have an international pool of workers available to work anywhere, anytime.

To develop a viable liberalization of migration policy, some dissection of the global worker pool must be made. On one level, the problems posed by an increasingly large pool of "undocumented" aliens—those who cross the border illegally, typically to take on jobs requiring limited skills—cannot be ignored. That pool has grown to an estimated 12 million, and the method to resolve the situation requires a clean, pragmatic analysis of the true economic value of these "guest" workers. To what extent do businesses in manufacturing,

---

[1] See *Theme: Towards Policy Coherence on Migration*, International Dialogue on Migration, 2005; World Commission on the Social Dimension of Globalization: *Creating Opportunities for All*, 2004; WTO, World Trade Report 2004.

agriculture, hospitality, and other mass production/delivery industries depend on these workers? And as our policy-makers evaluate this conundrum, they need to be conscious of the risk in an artificial system that attempts to close the door too rigidly when in fact millions of aliens are bypassing any admission and screening.

On another level, the migration of the highly-skilled and executive corps needs to be incentivized. Ours is a nation that has grown rich by attracting premier global talent to our shores. Today, international student admissions are lagging,[2] including in scientific and technical specializations in which American enrollment is limited. Multinational companies face repeated obstacles to mobility of their global workers, at a time when the dynamism of business mandates fluid cross-border movement. If we refuse to recognize that commercial organizations require access to global talent, we will undermine our position as the world's leading economic power.

Secretary of State Condoleeza Rice and Secretary of Homeland Security Michael Chertoff recently unveiled a new vision to help attract foreign visitors of the United States. While the initiative is still in the formative stages—and currently focuses primarily on fluidity for travelers en route to the United States—it alludes to the need to restore a welcoming message to foreign talent, students and travelers.

The Rice-Chertoff initiative is a positive but incomplete step. True reform must surmount current barriers and create meaningful incentives for professionals and executives from abroad. Australia, the United Kingdom, and Canada have passed targeted immigration reform legislation to attract such highly-skilled global professionals. Western European leaders are focusing on global "brain circulation" as a means to address a shrinking work force.[3] Not only have such reforms made the process more fluid, they have incorporated value-based systems that allow the candidates (and their employer-sponsors) to qualify for entry based on their expected contribution. At the same

---

[2] See *White Paper, In America's Interest: Welcoming International Students-The Role of Higher Education*, NAFSA Association of International Educators Symposium, April 2005 (citing recent declines in the U.S. share of the worldwide flow of international students and attributing, among other factors, migration barriers in U.S. visa policy).

[3] See "EU's New Tack on Immigration," *Wall Street Journal*, February 10, 2006, A8.

time, these types of reforms have addressed the pragmatic relocation needs of today's international professionals—for example, in view of the increasing volume of dual-career couples, broad authorization for employment of the spouse or partner of each principal worker is included in many new laws.

The United States has not kept pace. At a time when competition for global talent is at its most intense, we remain wedded to a system that the country has outgrown. Visa quotas are set at levels that were plentiful based on migration patterns in 1990, when the nation's last comprehensive immigration reform was launched. Fifteen years later, those amounts are absurdly constrained, creating a disincentive for top candidates who are considering competing options in various countries. Significantly, corporate behavior reflects a similar pattern—U.S. businesses are increasingly opting to expand operations offshore.

The American dream has attracted human capital from every corner of the globe. Our schools, our businesses, and our communities are enriched by the diversity of ideas and the financial and societal contributions of immigrants. The unparalleled prosperity of this country is inextricably linked to the entrepreneurial endeavors of our multicultural populace. It is time to face the reality of our heritage and embrace it. Beyond a reasonable doubt, migration is, as it always has been, the future of our country.

LANNY A. BREUER is a Partner at Covington & Burling. He specializes in white-collar criminal and complex civil litigation, internal corporate investigations, congressional investigations and trial work. Mr. Breuer is a fellow of the American College of Trial Lawyers. In January 2003, Mr. Breuer was selected by American Lawyer magazine as one of the top 45 private practice lawyers under the age of 45 in the United States. In the January cover story, the magazine stated "from defending the President of the United States on the floor of the Senate to defending alleged murderers in the D.C. courts, Breuer has built a reputation as a man to see when trouble is close by." Mr. Breuer is also featured in the Chambers USA publication as one of America's leading lawyers for litigation and was honored by his peers as both a top white-collar criminal defense attorney as well as top commercial and product liability litigator in The Best Lawyers in America.

From 1997 to 1999, Mr. Breuer served as Special Counsel to President Clinton. During his tenure, Mr. Breuer represented President Clinton and the White House staff in the presidential impeachment hearings and trial, various independent counsel and Justice Department investigations, and numerous congressional investigations. From 1985 to 1989, Mr. Breuer served as an Assistant District Attorney in Manhattan. Mr. Breuer has served as a presidential appointee to the United States Holocaust Memorial Council and as a member of the Council's Committee on Conscience. Mr. Breuer is the son of Holocaust survivors. He lives in Washington, D.C. with his wife and their two sons.

I Believe,
Beyond a Reasonable Doubt, That We Should All Have One Set of Manners

By Lanny A. Breuer

Growing up in a two-bedroom apartment in Elmhurst, Queens, my mother always insisted that I have only one set of manners. This mattered. Whether we were going out, visiting or simply eating dinner at home alone, I was always to be polite and mindful of how I acted. No elbow should be on the table and no napkin off my lap, nothing should be passed without a please and thank you. And when someone spoke you listened intently and then you responded respectfully. As a kid, living in Apartment 2A, my friends would tease me about the "fancy" way my mom would treat them. She had baked for them the way she baked for her own friends. When I told her that a bag of potato chips would be good enough, she explained that in our home everyone was to be treated the same. This was our code: "You have only one set of manners—universal respect."

My mother's moral authority derived from her experiences as a Holocaust survivor. Her code of ethics permeated her perspective on something arguably as mundane as table manners because it was rooted in personal knowledge of the catastrophic consequences of a society not governed by the rule of law. As the child of Holocaust survivors, I learned that to fail to challenge what is wrong is to be a coward and to abdicate your responsibility to yourself and to those in your community. But you must challenge with reason, humility and respect; never with insults or vulgarity. The latter can lead to feelings of humiliation and then violence and ultimately to a break in the social fabric.

My mother's principles guided me in my chosen career as an attorney. Civility is an effective strategy for anyone advocating on behalf of a position and for a lawyer representing a client's interests. A system of respect will not obviate the need for a criminal or civil justice system, but clients and lawyers achieve better results in an environment of civility. Whether I am dealing with a senior Department of Justice prosecutor in a high-profile criminal case, making a closing argument to a jury, or speaking with the most junior lawyer in a small civil case, I act respectfully and promote real and open dialogue. Such an approach has helped me time and again achieve great results for my clients in and out of the courtroom.

Respect and restraint are inextricably linked in our legal system. My first job was as a prosecutor with Bob Morgenthau, the iconic Manhattan District Attorney. Prosecutors have extraordinary power; one of the most important exercises of that power is to stay one's hand and refrain from prosecuting a case not substantiated by the facts, no matter how powerful the public pressure to bring someone—anyone—to justice. Morgenthau taught me to bring or not bring a case based on the facts and a belief in fairness. Understand what happened and do right, based on the evidence, don't do easy and popular. The importance of this lesson and the effects of ignoring it came to light time and again in the late 1990s during the era of the independent counsel investigations. Independent counsels investigated for many years and spent tens of millions of taxpayer dollars only to announce that they were bringing relatively insignificant charges or charges with relatively little factual support. The years since have shown the terrible personal and societal cost of such decisions. On the other hand, the independent counsel who investigated allegations of perjury against then-Secretary of the Interior Bruce Babbitt conducted an efficient, fair and impartial investigation. She ultimately decided that no charges should be brought. The independent counsel received great praise for her willingness to show restraint and did not feel obliged to bring charges (where none should be brought) simply to legitimize her investigation.

As Special Counsel to President Clinton, handling campaign finance investigations and the impeachment proceedings, I saw how government officials of all political persuasions were affected by the culture of litigation in which we live. I recall receiving subpoenas based on no more than allegations made on television the night before. This dynamic can exist irrespective of which political party is in power. There is too much finger-pointing and shouting in both directions. Civility cuts through the "noise" and restores the ability of reasonable people to use the legal and political system effectively and efficiently.

All too often in Washington, we do not have one set of manners. We say and act as we want and as we think will get attention; and we do not act based on what is fair and right. Fair and right can be boring. Insults and dire proclamations can be exciting and momentarily newsworthy. The TV networks are filled daily with self-proclaimed pundits willing to say almost anything if it guarantees them another invitation on the tube. The more damning and sensational the charges, the more likely you will be heard (though probably not listened to) in the media. By permitting insults to trump respect and reason, we foster demagoguery and laziness. You do not really have to support your position; you just have to attack your adversary. Just hurl a charge and repeat it over and again. Indeed, you do not have to be right. You just make a claim long enough to try to hurt your opponent and if the charge doesn't pan out, just make a new charge and start over again. Although such conduct might get you a gig in front of a TV camera and an audience that might find what you say fun to hear and easy to understand, it degrades our society. Time and again, those so damningly accused and insulted become bitter and develop a deep-seated sense of being wronged. Those who accuse in such a manner get a flash of celebrity but a hollow one at best. In the back of their minds they know that their turn as accused may come with a change in the political winds.

As a society we have grown accustomed to going to court. But our legal system is not the solution to every problem. We are fascinated by lawyers and what we think they do. Many TV shows are focused on law and lawyers, and we reflect what we view on our screens. Although too many of us have little understanding of our Constitution and its rights and obligations, most of us know that if we don't get what we want, we can always sue. We live in one of the most litigious nations in the world. As a result, we threaten to sue too often, and many of us have replaced reason, accommodation, and plain speaking with litigation. Suing someone instead of resolving a dispute without lawyers, or at least without going to court, is time consuming, expensive, and emotionally exhausting. The average person does not feel like a winner after going through such an experience.

As we in our society have become more contentious and less respectful, it has naturally followed that too many lawyers today lack a sense of civility as they fight on behalf of their clients. All too often, we see lawyers accusing each other of wrongdoing. Lawyers throw around threats all the time. Threats often replace reason and dialogue. Respect goes out the window. Having one set of manners is nothing more than a cute anachronism to be seen on PBS Specials depicting 19th Century life. But our current litigation climate all too often does not result in anything constructive. It certainly does not result in the merits of a case getting resolved any quicker or increase the chances that justice will be achieved.

So why do so many of our lawyers yell too much and why do we as a society sue too often? I believe that too many of us have forgotten that having one set of manners really matters. As a people, we are far too ready to honk our horn or hurl an epithet. We are also too ready to express our anger in the face of daily frustrations. That feels good momentarily, the way junk food feels good going down. Yet it does not bring about any meaningfully positive changes. Yelling at the driver next to you takes no effort and really accomplishes nothing (though it might reveal a death wish)—the light remains red and the gridlock continues—but so many of us act this way on a regular basis. Conversely, most of us are loathe to engage in serious and respectful debate on the issues of the day. We are unwilling to express our thoughts cogently and to listen intently to those with whom we disagree. We do not want to tackle the hard issues that confront our lives. That takes real effort, some real study, and real commitment.

Universal respect (one set of manners) not only breeds respect from others but exposes the fallacy of doctrines founded on hate and discrimination. Doctor Martin Luther King taught us that words spoken eloquently and respectfully—in the face of bigotry and ignorance—can move a nation. His words and actions forced a nation to listen and ultimately to embrace the undeniable truth of his ideas. Had he acted otherwise, his message could have been clouded by those who did not want to accept Dr. King's message of equality and dignity. But acting as King did takes great effort, patience, and restraint. Former Supreme Court Justice Thurgood Marshall, and current Supreme Court Justice Ruth Bader Ginsburg, while still lawyers, fought in court for racial and gender equality. No matter how deep the indignities they and their clients suffered, and how many threats were hurled against them as a result of their legal positions, Marshall and Ginsburg always advocated with dignity, reason, and respect. Consequently, the power of their arguments against discrimination could never be distorted. Respect (and one set of manners) is the most effective tool to promote justice, but sadly it is often at odds with the fast-food, entertain-me-now culture in which we live.

We all recognize that for our legal system to succeed, it must strive to guarantee equality, fairness and justice. Such a legal system is essential to the fundamental fabric of our society. Whether you are sitting at the kitchen table, the boardroom table, or walking the halls of Congress, we should behave with manners and grace because those around us benefit from such demonstrations of respect. We live in remarkable and dangerous times. As a nation and a world, we face security threats unknown to our predecessors. Now more than ever we need to listen before we talk. I believe beyond a reasonable doubt that only if we all have one set of manners will we be one step closer to coexisting peacefully as citizens of the world.

CAROLE LIEBERMAN, M.D., M.P.H. is a Media Psychiatrist, based in Beverly Hills, and an Assistant Clinical Professor of Psychiatry at U.C.L.A.'s Neuropsychiatric Institute. Dr. Lieberman was the Chair of the National Coalition on TV Violence. Her anti-media violence activism includes: initiating the ratings scale for television, stopping a NASA rocket from being launched with an ad for *Last Action Hero* on its exterior, and ending the run of some violent media.

Dr. Lieberman is the author of *Coping with Terrorism* and *Bad Boys: Why We Love Them, How to Live with Them, and When to Leave Them*. She serves as a Psychiatric Expert Witness for many high-profile trials and covers trials as an Analyst for numerous media outlets. A multiple Emmy award winner, she hosts *Dr. Carole's Couch* and is a regular guest on top TV and radio shows, as well as being regularly quoted in print.

Countdown to
Copycat Violence

By Carole Lieberman

"I know not with what weapons World War III will be fought, but World War IV will be fought with sticks and stones," said 20th century physicist and Nobel Prize winner, Albert Einstein, as he campaigned for peace and the abolition of nuclear weapons. Were he alive today, Einstein would know with what weapons an insidious war is already raging throughout the world: the game controllers of violent videogames and the ideas and inspirations implanted in our minds by all violent media. Modern weapons of mass destruction: from violent movies to magazines, television to toys, rap lyrics to literature, cartoons to computer games, and videocassettes to videogames, are causing us to destroy each other—on playgrounds and battlegrounds.

These conclusions are based not only upon years of my own psychiatric clinical research and forensic examinations, but upon myriad experiments on the impact of media violence conducted for decades by other researchers, as well. All categories of media, using various types of subjects, in most parts of the world have been analyzed. And the conclusions (except from researchers funded by the media) have been essentially the same: real life violence begets real life violence. The more media violence we consume, the more aggressive or violent we become, and the more desensitized to violence. We develop psychological symptoms such as anxiety, nightmares, depression, phobias, and so on. We come to believe that the world is a meaner place, and, ironically, since violent media incites violent impulses and actions, this becomes a self-fulfilling prophecy.

We keep close watch on the countdown to encroaching bird flu and bio-terrorism. "When will it infect my family?" we wonder. Yet we turn a blind eye to the billion-dollar shipments of virulent media that spread "germs" even more swiftly around the globe. Research has revealed that, as countries introduced television and other modern media, their rates of violence increased proportionally. It is no wonder that headlines blare ever louder with staggering news of savage eruptions everywhere. Why? Because violent media has managed to infect even the most remote corners of our world.

Many of us still refuse to take this danger seriously, just as tobacco companies and smokers originally refused to take research seriously when it concluded that cigarettes cause cancer. We have no trouble believing that 30-second commercials sell soap, since why else would companies spend so many advertising dollars? But we don't want to believe that hours of high-tech images of murder and mayhem sell such malevolent messages. Even some criminals, whose legal fate might be softened by their admitting to being under the influence of a violent movie or videogame, deny such mitigating factors. They would rather be convicted of homicide than be seen as a gullible consumer of media that incited them to commit a copycat crime. Regrettably, the list of documented copycat crimes keeps growing. But, the one benefit of these clear and convincing acts of mimicry is to awaken even the most devout non-believers to the fact that we are what we watch, listen to and play.

The most vulnerable consumers of cruelty are children who have trouble distinguishing make-believe from reality; people alienated from society whose obsession with violent media makes them lose touch with reality; and victims of abuse or neglect, whose wrath is given expression by the dialogue and action of the vengeful scripts. Though not all of us become killers, we all unconsciously copy aggression, and express it in our mean words, cold-hearted deeds, and stockpiles of weapons.

One of the first instances that awakened parents and teachers to the nefarious influence of violent media was *Teenage Mutant Ninja*

Turtles, which led tiny tots to make martial arts moves on their play-mates. After watching Glenn Close boil Michael Douglas' pet rabbit in *Fatal Attraction*, an epidemic of scorned women and men cooked their former lover's pet as punishment. *Natural Born Killers* sparked an international plague of Mickey and Mallory wannabes, leaving trails of dead bodies in their wake. Prisoners have been spotted taking notes while watching crime shows on TV. Rap stars teach generations of teens that misogyny is the coolest path to romance. Toy guns result in true deaths. The list is endless.

The two Columbine High School students, who shocked the world with their shooting spree, were aficionados of violent media, including the movie *The Basketball Diaries*, and the videogame *Doom*. The teenage boy who perpetrated the school massacre in Red Lake, Minnesota trained on *Grand Theft Auto* and *Manhunt*. Despite these, and other school shooting tragedies, an insatiably greedy videogame manufacturer is threatening to release *Bully*, a sadistic orgy of violence in which players receive points for being the most vicious student in a reform school.

Media violence is addictive—especially in videogames—where you not only watch, but get to push the button to rape, pillage, plun-der, annihilate and behead your opponents. No wonder the Department of Defense funds the development of videogames that train new and future recruits to hit their target and develop a taste for gore. Now people are playing such games on the Internet, torturing and slaughtering their opponents: players in all parts of the world, in the most gruesome ways possible. From the privacy of their own rooms, virtual "wars" between people of all nationalities, religions, and beliefs are being waged 24/7.

The more powerless and out of control we feel in our increas-ingly bloodthirsty chaotic world, the more we want to pretend to feel powerful and in control by identifying with fantasy super-heroes and evildoers. But this only perpetuates the downward spiral to barbarism. Beyond a reasonable doubt, I believe that if we don't stop the prolif-eration of violent media, society will soon self-destruct. Indeed, it will be *"GAME OVER"* for us all!

RICHARD NORTH PATTERSON is the author of thirteen internationally bestselling novels, most recently *Balance of Power* (2003*)*, which confronted one of America's most emotional and divisive political and social issues—gun violence; and *Conviction* (2005), which dealt with the law and politics of capital punishment. *Exile*, which will be released in January, 2007, is set against the backdrop of the Israeli-Palestinian struggles and the lethal politics of the Middle East. He has won an Edgar Allen Poe Award (1979); the French Grand Prix de Litterateur Policiere (1995); and his novels *Degree of Guilt* (1993) and *Eyes of A Child* (1995) were combined into a mini-series by NBC TV.

Mr. Patterson has served as: Assistant Attorney General in Ohio; a trial attorney for the Securities and Exchange Commission (SEC) in Washington, D.C. and San Francisco; and a partner in the San Francisco office of Bingham-McCutchen. In 1993, he retired from the practice of law to devote himself to writing. He is the Chairman of Common Cause, and has served on the boards of his undergraduate and law schools (Ohio Wesleyan University and Case Western Reserve), as well as those of the National Partnership for Women and Families, the Family Violence Prevention Fund, PEN Center West, and the Brady Campaign to Prevent Gun Violence. Mr. Patterson lives San Francisco, CA and on Martha's Vineyard, MA.

What I Believe

By Richard North Patterson

To my sorrow, I believe beyond a reasonable doubt that our society is afflicted—and divided—by too little doubt, and too much certainty.

At a time when Americans face historic challenges at home and abroad, many of our political leaders, and much of our media, seek competitive advantage by confirming our prejudices, narrowing our points of view, and casting our fellow citizens as our political and cultural enemies. Our politics is a prime example. Historically, our president and other elected officials won elections by seeking consensus, and enlisting the support of those in the political center. But our modern political strategists follow a very different model: turn out supporters with a fixed point of view, demonize those fellow citizens who support the other side, and persuade those in the middle through negative campaigning that our electoral system is too toxic to care about. This has created a politics of bitterness—where political discourse is meant to perpetuate prejudice, not enlightenment, and where political leaders do not engage opposing ideas, but villainize those who voice them.

In this new politics of disparagement, division, and distrust, the political exploitation of cultural and religious division has become a surrogate for addressing the very real problems Americans face in common. Never mind that much of this divide is based on a parody of one side or the other, and that truth and fairness is not the exclusive property of either. In the echo chamber of modern politics, the political strategists of our time have figured out that if they can appeal to our fears by repeating the same lies and exaggerations until they become accepted truth, they will never have to address the wealth gap, the health gap, the loss of jobs, the failure of our schools, the decline of opportunity and the dawn of a new Gilded Age where a wealthy few increasingly enjoy privileges reminiscent of the late nineteenth century. In this grotesque over-simplification of American society, millions of Americans have been a political lab experiment, and discussion of a coherent public policy which addresses the common good has been replaced by a nation filled with people who—increasingly—see the other as the enemy of the America they imagine.

A glance at our mass media reveals how corporate interests seek to profit from this phenomenon. Increasingly, our purveyors of news occupy niches, in which the written and spoken word is meant to confirm our settled biases, persuading us that media outlets with a different editorial point of view are peopled by charlatans and liars. The result is sad: for a society which is bombarded with so much news—albeit that much of it comes from the same five or six corporate sources—too little of it encourages empathy for people and problems outside our own direct experience. A look at the *New York Times* best-seller lists confirms this: on any given week, the books about our politics are the literary equivalent of a food fight, waged by profiteers and propagandists spattering their targets with calumny instead of presenting reasoned argument intended to promote thought, not foreclose it.

In this environment, very little is out of bounds—including the private lives of our public officials. Ideally, of course, all our public officials would be exemplary all the time, in every aspect of their lives . But they, like we, are flawed. So perhaps it is fair of us to ask ourselves whether *private* perfection is a little *too* much to ask.

The current Hobbesian state of nature—the use of personal scandal by the media and politicians to destroy other politicians—threatens to drive the higher decencies from public life. It has, and will, cost us the services of men and women of good public character. And it contributes, like the slow dripping of water on a stone, to the erosion of our *own* sense of decency and compassion. Martin Luther King was an adulterer, and he showed us all how to be far better than we were. And yet one must wonder whether, in the modern era, Reverend King would become a sad footnote, a man whose private flaws prevent him from ennobling our public life.

We cannot afford this. We face a time of national peril unique in our history, confronted by external and internal challenges—including a gradual erosion of security for ordinary Americans, which could, over time, spell the end of the expanding opportunity, which was the hallmark of America in the century which has just ended. We have done better before, and can again. But to do so, we must rise above this cacophony of bitterness, and reach out for each other with compassion, good will, and the humility to know that all of us have much more to know about each other.